Pulling Up the Ladder

RICHARD R. BROCKHAUS

Pulling Up the Ladder

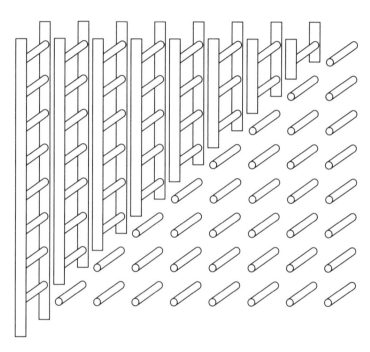

The Metaphysical Roots of Wittgenstein's
Tractatus Logico-Philosophicus

Open **※** Court

La Salle, Illinois

First printing 1991

Printed and bound in the United States of America.

Library of Congress Cataloging-in-Publication Data

Brockhaus, Richard R., 1946-
    Pulling up the ladder :   the metaphysical roots of Wittgenstein's
    Tractatus logico-philosophicus /   Richard R. Brockhaus.
        p.   cm.
    Includes bibliographical references and index.
    ISBN 0-8126-9125-3. — ISBN 0-8126-9126-1 (pbk.)
    1. Wittgenstein, Ludwig. 1889-1951. Tractatus logico
-philosophicus. 2. Logic, Symbolic and mathematical.   3. Languages-
-Philosophy.   4. Metaphysics.   I. Title.
    B3376.W563T73223   1990
    192—dc20   90-19192
                                                                       CIP

To Tracy Brockhaus and Mike Brockhaus

"... for every living being ... the most natural act is the production of another like itself, ... in order that, as far as its nature allows, it may partake in the eternal and divine."

ARISTOTLE, *DE ANIMA*

And God said: "Go—take the mother's soul, and learn three truths: Learn *What dwells in men, What is not given to men,* and *What men live by.* When thou has learned these things, thou shalt return to heaven."

T<small>OLSTOY</small>

Contents

Preface

This book has been a long time in the making; my book and I are, as Nietzsche puts it, "friends of Lento." The first time I can remember thinking seriously about Wittgenstein's *Tractatus* was in 1970. A. J. Ayer (not yet Sir Alfred) gave a series of lectures at Brown, after one of which I, apparently the handiest graduate student, drove him to the Providence train station in my disreputable old VW Beetle. I had with me a copy of the *Philosophical Investigations* (then largely a source of anecdote), and we fell to talking about Wittgenstein. He told me that he held the *Tractatus* in much higher regard than the *Investigations,* and I was chagrined by my total ignorance of Wittgenstein's early work.

I finished my dissertation at Brown (on the relational theory of space) and began teaching at Bucknell University in 1971. Called upon the following year to offer a seminar for seniors, I chose as my subject "Wittgenstein and Austin" (perhaps better entitled "The Blind Lead the Blind Through Early Contemporary Philosophy") and was thus confronted with the task of finding something to say about those philosophers. Both charmed and baffled by Wittgenstein's terse, cryptic, and often strangely beautiful remarks, I spent the summer poring over the standard commentaries: Anscombe, Stenius, and in particular Max Black's *Companion.* Although my references to those works may be sparse and sometimes negative, I wish here to acknowledge my great debt to them. Summer grants from Bucknell enabled me to spend two summers reading the vast (and unfortunately often less than rewarding) secondary literature. When I offered a seminar on Schopenhauer in the fall of 1977, much more of Wittgenstein's philosophical program suddenly made sense to me. A sabbatical grant in the fall of 1978 allowed further study of Schopenhauer, Hertz, and Mach, and gave rise to a distant ancestor of chapter VII. I spent the summer of 1980 in Amherst attending an NIH Summer Seminar, where I did a good deal of work on chapters IV through VI, and where the intelligence, erudition, and kindness of Gareth Matthews renewed my flagging faith that academics in general and philosophers in particular could be respectable people.

Unfortunately, the fall of 1978 also brought about a protracted and demeaning tenure review. I was ultimately recommended for tenure by the Philosophy Department but rejected by Dennis O'Brien, then President of Bucknell. I then spent one rather unsatisfactory year teaching at Colby College in Waterville, Maine. The time I spent that year reading Frege, Husserl, Mill, Sigwart, and Boole made me aware of the crucial logical issues surrounding the historical debate between Realism and Psychologism. For the next two years I hung drywall, ran wiring, did plumbing, substitute-taught Geometry, Algebra, Physics, and Industrial Arts, and completed drafts of all the present chapters of the book. Some of my research was done (surreptitiously) in the Miller Library at Colby, and I belatedly thank the staff of that institution.

Since 1985 I have taught Mathematics and Physics at the Landon School for Boys in Bethesda, Maryland, where the support I enjoy should serve as a model for all academia. The encouragement and cooperation of the Headmaster, Malcolm Coates, the head of the Upper School, Spud Parker, and Bob Long, Chairman of the Department of Mathematics, have been a tremendous help and are deeply appreciated. A generous Schinnerer Grant from Landon enabled me to spend the summer of 1987 editing the manuscript, and I thank the Schinnerer family for their support.

I am philosophically indebted to many people. David Kennicott and John Peaks first stirred my interest in philosophy as an undergraduate. I acknowledge a great debt to my teachers, especially philosophers Spud Hannaford and Robert Tyree, and physicists Dino Zei and Wayne Broshar of Ripon College, and Roderick Chisholm, Philip Quinn, Ernest Sosa, and Robert Swartz, all members of the Department of Philosophy of Brown University during my graduate studies. My fellow graduate students, in particular Tom Lockridge, Richard E. Olsen, Marlene Gerber Fried, Carolyn Korsmeyer, and Jesse Bohl, all shaped my approach to philosophy and teaching it. My friend and former colleague Frank Wilson of Bucknell University showed me more about philosophy than I could have hoped to ever learn from anyone. Professor J. D. Trout of The Stevens Institute of Technology, friend and former student, read early drafts of all of these chapters, and offered encouragement and sage advice. Wendy Pongracz read many of the chapters, and Joanne Werther all of them, and together they helped to smooth stylistic sharp corners and remedy logical and syntactical gaffes. Bob Beard, Professor of Russian, and J. Ernest Keen, Professor of Psychology, both of

Bucknell, and Gary Hochberg, now Associate Dean of the School of Business at Washington University, spoke for me during dark times at Bucknell when the world was, as Wittgenstein would say, waning. My former students—I fear that when I mention David Weinberger, Joe Schillinger, Gary Weaver, Wendy Pongracz, Bill Fisher, Frank Kosempa, Ted Chappen, Meg Block, Mike Schutz, Sharon Gromer, Nancy Kelly, David Pearson, Andy Cheskis, Bob Anderson, Jim Andrews, Richard Burnor, Bruce Hicks, Bill Jackson and Mike Paladini, I will omit many—were with me when I worked through the many issues of Wittgenstein's philosophy, as well as the general development of western philosophy. Their influence is to be found on every page. I profited greatly from the criticisms of the publisher's reviewers, Gershon Weiler and David Pears. Finally, Kerri Mommer of Open Court carried the manuscript through its various stages with deft grace.

But books are things of the spirit as well as the mind, and many people made this book possible. My parents were willing to offer to me the possibility of a college education from their own modest resources, and I can never thank them enough. Avner Eisenberg offered work, support, a timely loan and greatly appreciated friendship during hard times in Maine. Steve and Lucy Stamos, Tom Riddell, Debbie Lawrence Riddell, June and Gary Hochberg, Becky Kronisch, Bob and Faye Beard, Meg Block, Sally Morrison, Jim and Kate Reifsnyder, Amy D'Addetta, Wendy Pongracz, Ann Klusman, and Carol Brockhaus offered support through good times and bad. The help and comfort of Joanne Werther and J. D. Trout sustained me through the bleakest periods. My children, Tracy and Mike Brockhaus, are *sine qua non*. Their love and presence confer meaning to my world.

RICHARD R. BROCKHAUS

Kensington, Maryland
November 21, 1990

I

The Philosophical Problems
of the Tractatus

> I don't think that I have ever *invented* a line of thinking.
> I have always taken one over from someone else. I have simply
> straightaway seized on it with enthusiasm for my work
> of clarification. This is how Boltzmann, Hertz,
> Schopenhauer, Frege, Russell, Weininger, Spengler, Sraffa have
> influenced me . . . —What I invent are new *similes*.
>
> —WITTGENSTEIN, 1931

Ludwig Wittgenstein's *Logisch-Philosophische Abhandlung*—
given the Latin title *Tractatus Logico-Philosophicus*[1] (apparently at
the suggestion of G. E. Moore, who detected in it a Spinozistic flavor)
in its English Translation—was written quite literally on the front
during the First World War. Protracted, Byzantine, and frequently
discouraging efforts on Wittgenstein's part finally secured publication of the rather unconventional manuscript in the 1921 volume of
the German periodical *Annalen der Naturphilosophie*.[2] Although its
effect permeates much of the philosophy of this century, it has been
misunderstood (at least if we accept Wittgenstein's testimony) from
the date of Russell's introduction to the 1922 English translation.[3]

It lends itself well to misinterpretation. Compressed, presented
ex cathedra without argument and in a curious vatic voice,[4] it offers
an accelerating series of remarks on the world, logic, and the essence

---

[1] L. Wittgenstein, *Tractatus Logico-Philosophicus*, trans. D. F. Pears and B. F. McGuinness
(Routledge and Kegan Paul, London, 1960). An earlier translation (by C. K. Ogden) appeared in
1922. All quotations in this book, with rare and usually minor exceptions, are from the
Pears-McGuinness translation.

[2] For a publication history of the book, see G. H. von Wright's "Historical Introduction" to L.
Wittgenstein, *Proto-Tractatus*, trans. Pears and McGuinness (Routledge and Kegan Paul, London,
1971), pp. 11–29.

[3] See the letter from Wittgenstein to Russell dated 6.5.20, in L. Wittgenstein, *Letters to Russell,
Keynes and Moore* (Cornell U. Press, Ithaca, NY, 1974), p. 88.

[4] For example, Carnap writes "Wittgenstein ... tolerated no critical examination by others, once
the insight had been gained by an act of inspiration." Cf. K. T. Fann, *Wittgenstein: The Man and
his Philosophy* (Delta Books, New York, 1967), p. 35.

of language, suddenly and quite mysteriously blossoming into cryptic claims about the will, ethics, "God," and "The Mystical." Even the general philosophical stance of the book is difficult to discern on first reading. On one hand we are told that the lion's share of philosophical problems arise due to failure to understand "The logic of our language" which leads us to "speak nonsense," and that a belief as natural and apparently commonsensical as that in causality is "superstition." Yet we are asked to swallow whole such remarks as "I am my world (The microcosm)" (5.63), "The world and life are one" (5.62), and "It is not *how* the world is that is mystical, but *that* it exists." (6.44) Even more distressing are the closing remarks (6.54–7), which seem to consign the very contents of the book to the category of irrevocable nonsense,[5] yet in almost the same breath represent such remarks as "ladders" which when climbed and then discarded yield valuable insights.

The difficulty of merely *stating* the theses of the book—never mind ascertaining their truth or falsity—has produced some rather astounding claims about its contents. For instance (to offer but two examples) one commentator writes, "It is clear that the *Tractatus* is a kind of commentary on Whitehead's and Russell's *Principia Mathematica*," while another construes Wittgenstein's prefatory remark that perhaps the book will be understood only by someone who has had the same thoughts to imply that:

> Only a mystical communion of souls (that is, a communion not demonstrable empirically or rationally) guarantees that the meaning of a phrase be understood by someone other than the person uttering it.[6]

With considerable justification could Judith Thompson write in 1961 that "The literature on the *Tractatus* is starting to resemble the literature on the real meaning of the White Whale."[7]

---

[5] Hume's writings seem to suffer from the same apparent suicidal self-reference. Since they contain neither experimental reasoning about matters of fact nor formal reasoning about connections among ideas, the *Treatise* and the *Enquiry* ought to be "committed to flames." We shall later see a deeper version of this same problem, regarding why philosophical books ever need to be written at all.

[6] The first quote is from J. K. Feibleman, "A Commentary on Wittgenstein's *Tractatus*," in his *Inside the Great Mirror* (Martinus Nijoff, The Hague, 1973), p. 51, the second from Tullio de Maura, *Ludwig Wittgenstein: His Place in the Development of Semantics* (Reidel, Dordrect, Holland, 1967). The former represents a view perhaps more prevalent twenty-five years ago than today, the latter but a sample of similar mystifying claims.

[7] J. J. Thompson, "Professor Stenius on the *Tractatus*," in Copi and Beard, eds., *Essays on Wittgenstein's "Tractatus"* (Hafner, New York, 1973), p. 217.

The advancement of Tractarian scholarship has reduced the frequency of such blatant errors, and they ought not arise today for the philosophically sophisticated and attentive reader who appreciates the historical context of Wittgenstein's writings. Unfortunately, a close and sympathetic reading of the text uncovers a whole new level of problems which seem to threaten with incoherency the very foundations of Wittgenstein's early philosophical program. I will offer in this section a preliminary sketch of the two most general difficulties; their full exposition will occupy much of the succeeding examination.

In the opening passages of the *Tractatus* Wittgenstein sketches an uncompromising atomistic ontology as the metaphysical underpinning for most of the central Tractarian theses: the picture theory of propositions, the analysis of the status of scientific laws, his views on causation and his analysis of the relation between the ego and the world representing a few. The world is "All that is the case" (1)—that is, everything which has (contingent) existence—and the world is composed of *Sachverhalte*, "atomic facts" which have no other facts as proper parts. *Sachverhalte* are in turn articulated, being composed of Objects standing in immediate relation to one another (2.01, 2.03–2.031). Objects—the "substance of the world" (2.021, 2.024)—are not themselves contingent existents, but are, to echo Meinong, "beyond being and non-being." Being the world's substance, they represent the common elements of *any* possible world (2.022–2.023). But for atomic facts the case is quite different; the existence of each *Sachverhalt* is wholly contingent, and no reasons can be offered for why *this* fact but not *that* one obtains. Likewise, the existence of each is independent of the existence of any other (1.21), so that from the existence of any *Sachverhalt* we can draw no conclusions concerning the rest of the world (2.062). The world is thus a *contingent aggregate* (as opposed to an organic whole), and no reasons can be given for the existence of either the world as a whole or any particular item it contains. The world is, in the existentialist's pregnant phrase, "absurd." Specifically, the mutual independence of *Sachverhalte* entails that there can be no real connections, no causal links, between happenings in the world, at least on Wittgenstein's rather Draconian interpretation of what would count as a philosophically significant connection. "The only necessity is *logical* necessity," Wittgenstein writes, and as we shall see in chapter VI, even logical necessity appears in strange garb.

On the other hand—and I hasten to add that the following claim is obscure prior to certain discussions later in this book—Wittgenstein is certain that value can enter the world, and thus that the world can have a moral dimension, only through a relation to the *willing subject*. Further, the possibility of such significance demands that the moral consequences of any act of the will (the "reward or punishment") must not merely contingently follow from the action, but must be *necessary consequences* of that action. Yet the aforementioned absurdity of the world seems to insure that the will could not be connected with the world in the requisite necessary manner, that value therefore cannot enter the world and thus that morality can find no foothold, as it were, in human life. As we shall see in chapters III and X, Wittgenstein finds repugnant any attempt to ground ethical significance in human psychology. But he does not for that reason avail himself of the easy escape by denying any non-anthropomorphic status to value. As we shall see in a moment, Wittgenstein on occasion emphasized that the whole point of the *Tractatus* was *ethical*. Yet how can a contingent aggregate of *Sachverhalte*, each valueless in itself, allow of the presence of value? Where in the world does morality find a foothold? Wittgenstein's analysis of the self (chapter VIII) seems to exclude the possibility of the ego affecting even some limited portion of the world. This option, which would appear to make some portion of the world seem "closer to the ego or self" (as Wittgenstein puts it), is unacceptable to him, although pursuing the consequences of this argument leads us to the central notion of the *metaphysical* ego. But this impartiality of the metaphysical ego with respect to the world leads to the conclusion—paradoxical given the atomistic background of the opening pages of the book—that the result of any ethically significant action must be that the world "wax and wane as a whole" (6.43).

Wittgenstein's atomistic ontology forces him to reject any real connections between events in the world, rendering it difficult to see how the will could affect the world at all. Yet Wittgenstein demands that this atomistic world, devoid of real connections, not only be affected by the will but "wax and wane *as a whole*." We are presented, then, with a dilemma: how can we reconcile the ethical "monism", as it were, of the closing passages of the book with the ontological pluralism of the opening four-fifths? This tension in Wittgenstein's early philosophy (often reinforced by a certain philosophical predisposition) leads some philosophers to simply reject the closing passages, with their elusive references to ethics, God, and so forth, as mere *obiter dicta.*[8] As we shall see, the easy and attractive route of ignoring these passages cannot withstand examination; at the very least it runs counter to Wittgenstein's intentions. We must also, however, examine the equally misleading assumption that there must be for Wittgenstein two different "worlds," one a scientific world of "facts," the other an ethical world of "values."[9] There is no hint of "otherworldliness" in Wittgenstein's early philosophy, with respect to either ethics or logic.

The second dilemma we face in attempting a consistent interpretation of Wittgenstein's early work is methodological. The sole ability of propositions, Wittgenstein contends, is to represent certain possible facts and claim that those facts are actual. The existence of a given fact is for Wittgenstein a contingent and thus "scientific"—not philosophical—matter; philosophical claims cannot be mere contingent claims about the existence of this or that. (It cannot, for example, be a *philosophical* truth that there are thirty-seven different sorts of apples.) But if propositions can only represent just such contingent facts, no proposition could possibly be a philosophical proposition. Philosophy, Wittgenstein tells us, is composed of "logic and metaphysics," the former being "the basis" of the latter.[10] But logical propositions (as we shall see in chapter V) say nothing—represent no facts in the world—although in Wittgenstein's technical sense of the word they do "show" something about the logical form of all propositions and thus the logical structure of the world. They are not, as Russell and Frege held, representatives of a realm of very general and perhaps necessary facts; they are not "about" anything at all. What, then, becomes of the very statements of which the *Tractatus* is composed? Are they too to be condemned as either senseless tautologies or amateur scientific claims?

---

[8] I have in mind primarily but not solely the "scientific philosophers" of the Vienna Circle, and their British and Polish counterparts. In the course of this investigation it will become evident that Wittgenstein's differences with such philosophers run very deep indeed, deeper than just their tendency to treat ethics as a branch of social psychology. Wittgenstein's views on science, for instance, are extremely important for understanding these differences. This we shall see in chapter VII and X below.

[9] Cf. for instance Gershon Weiler, "The 'World' of Actions and the 'World' of Events," *Revue Internationale de Philosophie*, vol. 70 (1964), pp. 439–57.

[10] "Notes on Logic," (henceforth abbreviated *NoL*) in L. Wittgenstein, *Notebooks 1914–16*, ed. G. E. M. Anscombe (Blackwell, Oxford, 1969) (henceforth abbreviated *NB*), p. 93.

Such difficulties are compounded by Wittgenstein's distinction between two sorts of senselessness. Logical propositions are *"sinnlos"*—they have no senses, meaning that they picture no possible facts. But other sentences which purport to embody propositions (e.g. "Truth is identical with beauty") are *"unsinnig."* Violating the conditions for sense in general, they are reduced to mere noises or written signs. Philosophical propositions (for reasons that we have yet to examine) appear to fall *en toto* into this category. Wittgenstein is not unaware of these consequences; at 6.64 he writes in apparent self-condemnation:

> My propositions serve as elucidations in the following way: anyone who understands me eventually recognizes them as nonsensical [*unsinnig*], after he has used them—as steps—to climb beyond them. (He must, so to speak, throw away the ladder after he has climbed it.)[11]

But how can nonsensical pseudo-propositions serve even *temporarily* as ladders? The *Tractatus* closes with the notorious remark "What we cannot speak about we must pass over in silence." (7) Is not all that precedes in the text either a violation of or a counterexample to this precept? Might not the ladder—and thus the "climb" up it—be mere illusion?

The effects of this difficulty are magnified when we examine more closely Wittgenstein's distinction (explored in chapter VI) between what a proposition *says* and what it *shows*. This distinction, which Wittgenstein claims constitutes a large portion of the most important lesson of the *Tractatus*, seems to relegate the propositions of the work to the futile attempt to say what can only be shown. But what we can't say we can't say, and, as Frank Ramsey whimsically adds, we can't whistle it either. Thus even in the context of Wittgenstein's technical semantics, his work seems to be placed in the uneasy position of being nonsense if it is correct and correct if it is nonsense. We shall later see an even deeper version of this puzzle: if the logical form of every propositions shows itself, if where there is sense there is perfect sense, what role could philosophical investigation play even if the *Tractatus* did have sense? Later we shall see the difficult role of Socratic midwife in which Wittgenstein

---

[11] Note the unexpected phrase 'understand *me*' rather than 'understand *them.*' Part of this is no doubt the awkwardness of speaking of *understanding* a pseudo-proposition, but there are also deeper reasons, which will surface in due course.

has placed himself, a role best explored (perhaps to Wittgenstein's satisfaction) in Kierkegaard's *Philosophical Fragments.*

Let me say immediately that these difficulties are real, serious, and absolutely central to Wittgenstein's philosophical project, and a good deal of this volume is given over to developing and sharpening these difficulties. But serious does not mean *fatal:* I do not think that the project of the *Tractatus* is ultimately self-defeating. (If the *Tractatus* is wrong, it is wrong on *other* grounds.) I think that Wittgenstein's early philosophy can be treated in a manner which makes it at the very least consistent. To such a treatment of these difficulties we should now turn.

Two remarks of Wittgenstein's will serve to introduce the rationale for the method which I will utilize. The first is drawn from comments he drew up on Frazer's *The Golden Bough.* There he writes, with respect to drawing connections between cases:

> But an hypothetical connecting link should in this case do nothing but direct the attention to the similarity, the relatedness, between the *facts.* As one might illustrate an internal relation of a circle to an ellipse by gradually converting an ellipse into a circle; *not in order to assert that a given ellipse actually, historically, had originated from a circle* (evolutionary hypothesis), but only in order to sharpen our eyes for a formal connection.[12]

The second passage, which was written about 1931, heads this chapter:

> I don't believe that I have ever *invented* a line of thinking. I have always taken one over from someone else, I have simply straightaway seized on it with enthusiasm for my work of clarification. This is how Boltzmann, Hertz, Schopenhauer, Frege, Russell, Weininger, Spengler, Sraffa have influenced me. . . . —What I invent are new *similes.*[13]

Let us see if we can utilize these hints to gain a foothold in Wittgenstein's early philosophy. As able a commentator as Erik Stenius; despairingly recognizes four classes of Tractarian remarks, the last two of which comprise:

---

[12] Luckhardt, ed., *Wittgenstein: Sources and Perspectives* (Cornell U. Press, Ithaca, NY, 1981), p. 69.

[13] L. Wittgenstein, *Culture and Value,* ed. G. H. von Wright (University of Chicago Press, Chicago, IL, 1980) (henceforth abbreviated *CV*), p. 19. Compare: "Often, when I have had a picture well framed, or have hung it in the right surroundings, I have caught myself feeling as proud as if I had painted the picture myself." (*Ibid.*)

Those [remarks] which I do not understand and the value of which I am
therefore unable to estimate . . . and . . . a number of which seem on one hand
to be understandable, but on the other to be so in such a way as to give an
indeterminate and obscure impression, hence they become impossible to
either accept or reject.[14]

We have hinted at the difficulties in making sense out of even some
large Tractarian themes, but James Griffin is correct, I think, when he
observes that "sometimes finding out what point in Frege or Russell
Wittgenstein is reacting to is half the battle won."[15] But this remark
is also misleading, since so very often the real issues lie *much*
deeper. The relation of Wittgenstein's thought to Frege and Russell
has already been admirably explored by Black, Anscombe, Dummett,
Griffin, and others. (I will however contend in chapter III that one
extremely important influence of Frege on Wittgenstein—namely his
extreme reaction to the psychologism of nineteenth-century logical
theory—has been given very short shrift.) But the logico-mathemat-
ical input of Frege and Russell does not begin to exhaust the sources
of problems which Wittgenstein takes on in the *Tractatus;* certainly
Janik and Toulmin have persuasively argued for this in their
fascinating tour of the pre-war Viennese intellectual landscape.[16]
Illuminating as such general historical work is, however, it remains at
once too broad and too narrow—the latter in its neglect of purely
logical issues—to show the unity of the various strands of the
Tractatus. Where then can a unifying elucidation be found?

I offer the suggestion, worked out in detail in what follows, that
the *Tractatus* is best seen as an extremely purified version of
Schopenhauer's voluntaristic monism, cleansed of objectionable
elements through interaction with Frege's robust logical realism and
through a modification of Hertz's views on the nature of scientific
laws.[17] Wittgenstein's monomaniacal zeal for expunging every

---

[14] Erik Stenius, *Wittgenstein's 'Tractatus'* (Cornell U. Press, Ithaca, NY, 1964), p. ix. Stenius's
evaluation of this last class as being a source for clearly false remarks might stand as a metaphor
for the gulf that divides his cast of mind and his view of philosophy from Wittgenstein's.

[15] J. Griffin, *Wittgenstein's Logical Atomism* (Oxford U. Press, Oxford 1964), p. 4.

[16] A. Janik and S. Toulmin, *Wittgenstein's Vienna* (Simon and Schuster, New York, 1973). This
admirable work—*sine qua non* for understanding Wittgenstein's early thought—is most helpful
when read in conjunction with Carl Schorske's *Fin-de-Siecle Vienna* (Knopf, New York, 1980).

[17] Although the connections between Schopenhauer and Wittgenstein do, I think, exist, the
arguments of this book need not turn on the truth of that claim. I am not doing intellectual history
but philosophical elucidation, and thus no *historical* claim is absolutely central to that project.

remnant of psychology from philosophy serves as the motive for as well as the method of this purification. But an examination of the results of this project on Schopenhauer's neo-Kantianism will shed new light on the problems to which Wittgenstein sets himself.

Why pursue this course? Anscombe tells us that as a boy Wittgenstein read Schopenhauer and thought him generally correct, needing only a few adjustments.[18] The scope of these adjustments might well have been somewhat wider than Wittgenstein envisioned in his youth, and what is discarded is often as crucially important as what has been retained, but at the core of Wittgenstein's philosophical problem-set remains Schopenhauer's neo-Kantian concerns. Under the influence of Frege's realism, Wittgenstein rejects any appeal to transcendental principles in logic, construing such appeals (perhaps unfairly) as a regression to psychologism. The "world as representation" accordingly disappears, although traces of the doctrine of representations remain in the picture theory of propositions. The "world as will" suffers serious setbacks from both Wittgenstein's conventionalistic rewrite of Hertz's philosophy of science (chapter VII) and from the Tractarian analysis of the place of the self in the world (chapters VIII–IX). Although the major *theses* of Schopenhauer's philosophy—the transcendental ideality of appearances, the underlying reality of the will as thing-in-itself—are conspicuously absent, very fundamental Schopenhauerian *attitudes* concerning the relation of the willing subject to ethics, the rejection of "otherworldliness" in ethics and art, and a certain pessimistic attitude towards science, form the bedrock upon which the edifice of Wittgenstein's early philosophy is constructed. Part of

---

Compare: in the *Investigations* Wittgenstein is not interested in *specific* facts of nature. Thus, the *imaginary* history of a concept is often as helpful as the real one. Cf. L. Wittgenstein, *Philosophical Investigations*, 3rd ed., trans. G. E. M. Anscombe (Macmillan, New York, 1958) (henceforth abbreviated *PI*), section xii, p. 230.

[18] "As a boy of sixteen Wittgenstein had read Schopenhauer and had been greatly impressed by Schopenhauer's theory of the 'world as idea', (though not of the 'world as will'): Schopenhauer then struck him as fundamentally right, if only a few adjustments and clarifications were made." G. E. M. Anscombe, *An Introduction to Wittgenstein's 'Tractatus'* (Hutchinson University Library, London, 1959), pp. 11–12. Compare with the quotation which heads this chapter. In a later conversation Wittgenstein told M. O'C. Drury that "My fundamental ideas came to me very early in life." [Drury asks] "Schopenhauer?" "No: I think I see quite clearly what Schopenhauer got out of his philosophy—but when I read Schopenhauer, I seem to see the bottom quite easily." Drury, "Some Notes on Conversations with Wittgenstein," in R. Rhees, ed., *Ludwig Wittgenstein: Personal Recollections* (Rowman and Littlefield, Totowa, NJ, 1981), p. 172. I think the last reference is probably to Hertz (cf. ch. VII below). It is worth noting that Wittgenstein sometimes appears as a rather revisionistic autobiographer.

the puzzlement which English-speaking readers of the *Tractatus* incur stems from failure to understand Wittgenstein's intimacy with a number of Schopenhauerian preoccupations, as well as what Wittgenstein perceived as inconsistencies in Schopenhauer's philosophy.

The extent of any putative neo-Kantian influences on Wittgenstein has been a topic of sporadic scholarly debate, and a brief examination of some of that debate will illustrate a misunderstanding of Kant which parallels the positivist's misreading of Wittgenstein, as well as point the way to certain considerations to be raised in the present work. Let me juxtapose two recent comments from the secondary literature on the *Tractatus*. One scholar writes:

> It is *more* accurate, if also a bit misleading, to argue that the movement from the early Wittgenstein to the work of the later Wittgenstein is a movement from a precritical, pre-Kantian position to a post-Kantian, Hegelian-style position *without benefit of Kant.*[19]

Another scholar, producing in parallel columns resonant quotations from Wittgenstein and from Kant's *Logic*, writes:

> I believe that it is impossible to read these various passages from Kant's introduction to the *Logic* ... without ... becoming intensely aware of the curious impact which they seemed to have had on Wittgenstein. ... All these references and parallels make clear that Wittgenstein had obviously read much more of Kant than has been supposed and read him much more closely.[20]

Father Hallett argues that there are no good grounds for the claim of direct causal influence of Kant on Wittgenstein,[21] and I concur that there is no evidence of more than casual reading of Kant on Wittgenstein's part. Further, considerations raised in chapter III below make it very dubious that the young Wittgenstein would have had much patience with the epistemological program of the Critical

---

[19] W. W. Bartley, *Wittgenstein* (Lippincott and Co., Philadelphia, 1973), p. 75. Bartley correctly points out the total absence of epistemological preoccupation in the *Tractatus*, but to construe Wittgenstein's early work as accepting a non-critical epistemology is wrong-headed.

[20] S. Morris Engel, *Wittgenstein's Doctrine of the Tyranny of Language* (Martinus Nijoff, The Hague, 1971), p. 57. The list of parallels runs from pages 54–57. In fairness I must point out that Engel is interested mainly in Wittgenstein's middle period, and in particular the *Blue Book*. But even there his causal, historical claims lack validity. L. Wittgenstein, *The Blue and Brown Books* (Blackwell, Oxford, 1969), henceforth abbreviated *BB*.

[21] Garth Hallett, *A Companion to Wittgenstein's 'Philosophical Investigations'* (Cornell U. Press, Ithaca, NY, 1977), p. 768.

Philosophy. But let us not lose sight of a central consideration which renders any claims of direct historical connection between Wittgenstein and Kant secondary. If Janik and Toulmin are correct, then the very air of Vienna at the turn of the century was charged with neo-Kantianism. The old saw that one can argue with or against Kant, but not without him, is particularly apt in the case of a turn of the century Viennese intellectual. Claims of a *direct* influence on Wittgenstein by the Kantian corpus seem beside the point.

But a more significant point emerges from the question of a direct Kantian influence on Wittgenstein, a point which transcends in importance any mere historical assessment. I have claimed above, and will defend at length, that Wittgenstein's early philosophical preoccupations are best seen as an extremely purified Schopenhauerian neo-Kantianism. W. W. Bartley, the author of the first quotation considered above, offers the following objection to such a claim.

> [It has been suggested] that the *Tractatus* sets out to answer a Kantian-style question, to wit: "How is language possible?" Yet not every question of the form: "How is x possible?" is Kantian in character. For a question of this sort to be Kantian, it would have to be set in the context of some theory or presupposition which made the existence of language impossible—or at least doubtful. (*Op. cit.*, p. 53)

On this view, "How is synthetic a priori knowledge possible?" (*Critique of Pure Reason*, p. 55)[22] would be "Kantian" only in the context of some prior challenge to the possibility of such knowledge. But from whence was Kant supposed to have felt such a challenge? Certainly not from Hume, insofar as the *Treatise* begins with the *hypothesis* that all simple ideas—and by implication all knowledge and belief—come from experience (I/i/1), and consists in significant part of a defense of that hypothesis against such putative counterexamples as the idea of necessary connection (I/iii/3). At best Hume shows that we need not commit ourselves to the existence of a priori knowledge. The *Critique* examines the problem of knowledge not as an answer to some supposed Humean challenge, but rather with the twin goals of showing the sceptic that a priori knowledge is necessary, and then, contra the dogmatist, showing how it is possible.

---

[22] I. Kant, *Critique of Pure Reason*, trans. N. Kemp Smith (Macmillan, New York, 1929), hereafter abbreviated *CPR*.

Now there is certainly an element of reaction to difficulties in the *Tractatus*. As we shall see in chapter IV, a realistic theory of language, when combined with the Russellian puzzles surrounding any attempt to map ordinary language directly onto the world, presents tensions which for Wittgenstein will ultimately require resolution through analysis. This difficulty might be expressed in the question, "How is a thorough-going realism compatible with the obvious failure of certain ordinary language terms to refer?" Importantly, it is for Wittgenstein largely a question that he sets for *himself* rather than a response to a prior sceptical prod.

(There is a rather different sense in which Wittgenstein's work is construable as reaction to a prior challenge. Husserl saw in European thought a "crisis," analogous to the crisis in Greek thought (which was embodied in the Sophists and to which Plato saw himself in opposition) and became convinced that the European crisis was brought on by the rise of various forms of scientific relativism and ethnocentricism. He maintained that only a "general investigation of sense" would resolve the scientific/cultural crisis. Certainly Wittgenstein's work was inspired by premonitions of cultural decay, and his fondness for Weininger, for instance, is perhaps traceable to these fears. But Husserl's end result [the "presuppositionless science" of phenomenology] is, if not opposite to Wittgenstein's, very different in both inspiration and structure.)

Secondly, if a question could be "Kantian" only by virtue of a historically prior challenge, then I think Wittgenstein would hold that no real *philosophical* problem could ever be Kantian. The anti-psychologism and anti-historicism of the *Tractatus*, which we will explore in chapters III and XI, demand that philosophical questions, claims, and concepts be abstracted from their historical context. If in fact Wittgenstein was brought to the position he held by other philosophers, which he obviously was, this fact is for him philosophically uninteresting.[23]

---

[23] This is, incidentally, why Wittgenstein rarely refers to other philosophers when criticizing their views, both in the early and later works. Thus he writes in the Preface "I do not wish to judge how far my efforts coincide with those of other philosophers. Indeed, what I have written here makes no claim to novelty in detail, and the reason why I give no sources is that it is a matter of indifference to me whether the thoughts that I have had have been anticipated by someone else." (Preface, p. 3)

This anti-historicist claim is, in my view, of first-water importance, and represents an extremely important and pretty much neglected point of contact between Wittgenstein and Kierkegaard, for whom he frequently expressed admiration.

But there remains a third point, the weight of which far exceeds that of the first two; in a sense it can be seen as the key to the *Tractatus*. Kant does not set as the philosophical problem of the Critical Philosophy "How is synthetic a priori knowledge possible?" It is misleading even to set this question as *the* primary problem to be addressed in the first *Critique*. I would not be so presumptuous as to attempt here to give even an outline of an answer to the question, What did Kant take to be the fundamental problem of philosophy?, but I can isolate one very important—perhaps overriding—concern. In a famous passage in the second edition introduction to the first *Critique*, Kant writes, "I have therefore found it necessary to deny *knowledge*, in order to make room for *faith.*"(*CPR*, p. 29) This passage reflects Kant's rock-bottom concern, shared by almost every classical western philosopher since Descartes, to wit: How is morality compatible with the rapidly emerging picture of the world—materialistic and deterministic—offered by the New Science? The tension appears in many forms, perhaps most clearly in passages like the third Antinomy (*CPR*, pp. 409–415). The antithesis claims that the world can be understood in terms of causal laws; there is no "freedom," if by that we mean an event not subsumable under causal laws. The thesis retorts that there is another "causality," namely *freedom*, or the will, or volition. Kant's question is therefore, How can freedom and thus morality exist in a world subject to the strict causal laws of the New Physics? Transcendental Idealism provides an escape from this dilemma.

Wittgenstein's concerns are parallel, although cast in a rather different philosophical vocabulary, and thus he might put the question in this way: "How is value possible in a world of pure contingency?"[24] The twist which Wittgenstein puts on Kant's question perhaps masks the common elements. Each view is based upon a particular tenet in the logic of morals, as it were, which holds that there must be lawlike relations between any morally culpable action and the intention which brings it about, and further that any genuine reward or punishment must be directly and necessarily

---

[24] Wittgenstein's emphasis on the tension between value and the contingent or "absurd" character of the world reflects an affinity with the twentieth-century existentialists. Compare: "Written fifteen years ago, in 1940, amid the French and European disaster, this book declares that even within the limits of nihilism, it is possible to find the means to proceed beyond nihilism." Albert Camus, in the introduction to the American edition of *The Myth of Sisyphus* (Vintage Books, New York, 1975), p. v.

connected with that action. This view of the logic of morality is thoroughly Kantian; we will develop it in greater detail in chapter X.

A Positive Conception of the *Tractatus*

The claims which I have presented so far may strike the philosophically sophisticated as rather mundane. So Wittgenstein's fundamental problems (or some of them, at any rate) can be best understood as Kantian, and so they can be understood best by comparing them with the Schopenhauerian doctrines from which they were perhaps derived. Although this may rule out certain very limited conceptions of the *Tractatus*—as, for instance, primarily a commentary on *Principia*—such limited conceptions are in any case not currently influential. Can the comparisons I suggest help us arrive at a clearer positive conception of "the whole sense of the book," as the preface styles it?

I want to move towards such a positive conception, taking as a starting-point Anscombe's remark about Schopenhauer's early influence on Wittgenstein and presenting the major theses of the Tractatus against the background of Schopenhauer's grand vision of the world. As it develops the "two sides" of the world— will and representation—will reappear in Wittgenstein's work in subtle, altered, and highly purified form. My fundamental thesis is that Wittgenstein holds in an extremely rarified version the Schopenhauerian view that there is an irreducibly *human* world, although we must carefully limit the meaning of 'human' to exclude the psychological or biological. There are many such "human worlds," each composed of two indivisibly linked although wholly disparate components, one of the greatest possible generality (a generality so great that its assertion is impossible), the other of the greatest possible uniqueness (so unique that it too escapes language). The first is so general that it represents the bare *possibility* of a world, the latter so particular that its duplication is inconceivable. These two elements—respectively Logic and the Metaphysical Ego—are the elements of what Wittgenstein terms "My World."

Importantly, these elements transcend the bounds of language insofar as they serve as necessary conditions for any symbolic representation. The ensuing ineffability complicates the exposition of the major themes of the *Tractatus*, since so much of what is central cannot be said. But it also leads straight to Wittgenstein's fundamental concern, namely the extent to which linguistic representation—thought—and with it reason are connected with what I shall loosely call *value*. This question represents the nexus between Wittgenstein's concerns about logic and language on one hand, and morality and value generally on the other. Certainly Wittgenstein's investigations into logic were attractive to him precisely because of their neat coincidence with positions concerning art and morality he had previously reached.

The philosophical centrality of logic and the metaphysical ego drastically restricts the range of problems which allow of scientific exploration, which chapter III portrays as flying in the face of late nineteenth-century trends. One important consequence is a rejection of historicism and of the importance of *discovery*. Language must be based on something more secure than conventions, or mental pictures, but that something cannot be anything obscure, esoteric, or distant—if it were, how could ordinary people speak and think at all? Thus meaning must be based on something *immediately present*, and cannot and need not be clarified by scientific investigation. There is nothing to be discovered, and nothing that need be. Similarly, ethics cannot be based on any event or discovery either. If it were, then it would be mere luck that some are saved, and some not. If salvation has any *moral* weight, it must be based on some decision *I* make.

An immediate justification of these claims is of course impossible; even concrete hints must wait until the investigation of Schopenhauer's philosophy in chapter II. But I can speak here in very general terms of the *forces* of purification; the isolation and development of such forces will be a major undertaking of this volume.

The first such issue is difficult for contemporary readers to appreciate due to its distance from current philosophical concerns, although the central issues behind it are fundamental to western philosophy. A powerful force in the theory of logic in the nineteenth century was *psychologism*, the thesis that the principles of logic are very general empirical hypotheses about the operations of the human mind. Psychologism is today unfamiliar, at least in the form in which it was then current,[25] but coming to grips with pychologism and the realistic reaction against it is absolutely necessary for understanding the *Tractatus*. Wittgenstein accepts wholeheartedly Frege's devastating attacks on psychologism and his program to remove psychological influences from logic and mathematics, but he characteristically makes two further moves. The first is to extend the Fregean attacks on psychologism from logic to philosophy in general, for instance by rejecting any theory of value which would make the good and the beautiful definable in terms of mental states. The second move defines rather severe criteria for the non-psychological, so strict that, for instance, the theory of knowledge—usually considered a philosophical discipline—is classified as a branch of psychology (cf. 4.1121). The latter will have very far-reaching consequences with respect to Wittgenstein's treatment of morality. The anti-psychologism of the *Tractatus* runs very deep and is absolutely central to an appreciation of the unity of Wittgenstein's thinking. Yet the historical center of the great battles between psychologistic and realistic logicians is so far removed from the realm of the familiar, that we must regenerate the philosophical weight of such debates.[26]

Chapters II and III thus survey the philosophical landscape across which the battles that Wittgenstein holds to be decisively won are fought. Chapter II examines Schopenhauer's neo-Kantian vision of the world as will and representation, with emphasis on his "universal voluntarism" and on his views of the nature of science, art, and morality. All of these have, if I am correct, profound impact on Wittgenstein's early views. In chapter II we examine in general

---

[25] For instance, the term 'psychologism' does not appear in the index of Kneale and Kneale's monumental *The Development of Logic* (Clarendon Press, Oxford, 1962), nor in Quine's *The Philosophy of Logic* (Harvard U. Press, Cambridge, MA, 1986). Its omission in the former work is particularly striking, since the Kneales give over so much space to that arch-antipsychologist Frege. In contrast, Robert Adamson's *A Short History of Logic* (Blackwell and Sons, Edinburgh and London, 1911), a reprint of articles from the ninth (1882) edition of the *Encyclopedia Britannica*, is filled with discussions of both the historical roots and then-current manifestations of psychologism.

[26] The oddness brought on by this lack of context is not unique to our situation; the queerness of some of Moore's writings—the apparent triteness of "A Defense of Common Sense," for instance—comes to mind. P. M. S. Hacker and G. P. Baker, in the introduction to their fine *Wittgenstein: Understanding and Meaning*, vol. I (U. of Chicago Press, Chicago, 1980), write of their project that if it "were delayed for another half-century or more, the intellectual milieu and philosophical atmosphere of Wittgenstein's work (in particular Frege, Russell, and the Vienna Circle), already increasingly remote to our generation, will be irremediably alien (cf. the fate of Kant's *Critique*)." I would add the name of William James to their list, but the moral they make—and its applicability to the matter at hand—is clear.

terms the development of psychologism in logic, concentrating largely on the views of Mill and Boole, and then develop a realistic critique of that position, drawing from Frege, Russell, Moore, and Husserl.

Acceptance of realism carries with it some far-reaching consequences. Since logic seems to represent the *pure core*, as it were, of all representation, we are inexorably drawn towards a realistic analysis of all language and thought. (This view is itself very Kantian; compare with *CPR*, pp. 92ff.) The object of language or thought cannot then be a mental picture or image, but must be seen as something objective, mind-independent. Such a broader realism solves a number of problems concerning meaning and truth, but generates its share of new difficulties. Chapters IV through VI trace the development of Wittgenstein's realistic theory of linguistic representation and then contrast it with Schopenhauer's transcendental idealism.

Chapter IV examines some historically important considerations which stem from a realistic theory of language, concerning existence and its ethereal cousin, Being. Our major stalking horse will be the extravagant realism of Russell's *The Principles of Mathematics*, and we shall see the problems which Russell himself discovered in that naive realism. Russell's solution to these difficulties is found in the Theory of Descriptions and the more general Theory of Incomplete Symbols, which we will examine in some detail. The upshot of the Theory of Descriptions is that the real referents of ordinary propositions are often quite different from what one would expect, and that correlatively, the real logical form of a proposition is often quite different from its apparent or superficial form. The route from superficial to real form is *analysis*, utilizing the logical resources newly developed by Frege and Russell. Included among the implications of the new techniques is a commitment to the thesis of extensionality, the seemingly innocuous claim that every proposition is analyzable as a truth-function of elementary propositions. The real importance of this logical wolf in sheep's clothing will become increasingly important in what follows.

The realist thesis implies that the real logical form of propositions ought to be mirrored in the general structure of the world, so that logical claims about the analysis of propositions will entail certain ontological theses about the fundamental structure of the world. Just as analysis ends when we reach elementary propositions—propositions which have no other propositions as constituents—likewise the world "falls apart," as 1.2 has it, into atomic facts. These *Sachverhalte* have no other facts as constituents and are thus the fundamental constituents of the world. The linguistic thesis of extensionality is mirrored in a lack of logical connections between *Sachverhalte*, producing the consequent contingency of the world. This will be central to our discussion of the relation between value and the world.

Still uninvestigated is the relation between a given elementary proposition and the (possible) *Sachverhalt* which is its sense. How is it possible for a proposition to represent the world? How is it possible that a proposition has a relation to a possible fragment of the world such that the proposition *means* that fragment? How, for that matter, is it possible for a proposition to be true or false?[27] The centerpiece of Wittgenstein's answer is the "picture theory of propositions," which construes propositions as *logical pictures* of possible facts. Chapter V examines the picture theory, with special emphasis on *intention* as the fundamental link between symbol and symbolized. This will lead us to a preliminary investigation of the presuppositions which, since they underlie *any* system of linguistic representation, cannot themselves be linguistically represented.

Chapter VI begins with an examination of an issue which, although it does not immediately seem to be centrally relevant, leads us to absolutely crucial concerns on Wittgenstein's part. Russell's Theory of Logical Types, introduced to deal with certain mathematical paradoxes, constructs a hierarchy of languages, each of which talks about the syntax and semantics of the language at the next lowest level. Examination of the Theory of Types introduces Wittgenstein's fundamental distinction between what a proposition can *say* and what can only be *shown* by a proposition. This distinction allows us to introduce Wittgenstein's theory of logic, contrasting as it does with the classical view of logic as a theory of deductive hierarchies. Wittgenstein advances the then-startling claim that logical propositions say nothing, make no claims about the world. Thus in a sense both the realistic and psychologistic logicians are mistaken, since they differ only on the issue of what *facts*

---

[27] These questions illustrate what Anscombe means, I think, when she says that in order to understand Wittgenstein (or Frege), one needs to be capable of being "naively struck" by certain innocent-sounding questions. Anscombe adds "The investigations prompted by these questions are more akin to ancient, than to more modern, philosophy." *Op. cit.,* p. 13.

correlate with logical propositions. But although logical propositions say nothing, as "tautologies" they show the structure of the world. Insofar as Wittgenstein will practically identify the sphere of the logical with the sphere of the philosophical, the tautological nature of logical propositions will have extremely important consequences with respect to the nature and function of philosophy.

The end of chapter VI marks an apparent break in the argument of the preceding three chapters, which represent a realistic reaction to the reigning Idealistic picture of the "world as representation." Our interest will be turned more and more towards what we might think of as the "world as will." Anscombe, in the remark quoted previously, claims that Wittgenstein never thought much of Schopenhauer's world as will, but on closer inspection this turns out to be misleading. It is certainly the case that Wittgenstein rejects two fundamental claims upon which Schopenhauer bases his universal voluntarism, namely the nature of scientific laws and the nature of the self as based on the immediate data of introspection. The significance of Wittgenstein's treatment of these issues is extremely easy to obscure, since it is possible to view each in a narrowly linguistic manner. The principles of mechanics, for instance, are irreducibly general, yet they are not tautologies. This seems to violate the conditions of the thesis of extensionality presented in chapter IV. Similarly, statements about the apparent relation of the self to facts, such as "Othello thinks that Desdemona loves Cassio," appear to be compound, yet not truth-functionally so, again in apparent violation of the thesis of extensionality. But further, they appear to bestow a special status to what might be called the empirical ego, and this too Wittgenstein finds intolerable. We will examine in detail each of these issues, insofar as they are immensely important with respect to understanding Wittgenstein's rock-bottom beliefs about value and its relation to science.

Chapter VII addresses the first of these by examining the influence of Hertz's *The Principles of Mechanics* upon Wittgenstein, contrasting Hertz's views with the influential (but for Wittgenstein intolerable) views of Ernst Mach. Hertz's neo-Kantian analysis will highlight what I believe Wittgenstein took as fundamental problems with Schopenhauer's philosophy of science. We will then examine the Tractarian theory of science as a de-psychologization of Hertz's theory. The upshot is that although Wittgenstein rejects the Schopenhauerian argument from the existence of scientific regularities to the thesis of universal voluntarism, he comes down solidly on the side of Schopenhauer's conception of the relative poverty of science.

Chapter VIII examines the relation between the ego and the world, functioning as a further critique of idealism. Central to Schopenhauer's monistic voluntarism is the claim that under certain circumstances we have intuitive access to things in themselves, undetermined—or at least determined less than normal representations—by the transcendental conditions of the world. Our actions, he argues, are Janus-faced. From the outside, they appear as phenomena, as events among other events in the world. But from the inside, as it were, their deeper nature emerges. In introspection I become aware of myself as willing subject, as the will in a relatively undetermined form, and the kernel of Schopenhauer's insight is that the willing self disclosed in introspection can function as a model for the inner reality of *all* phenomena. But since the will is fundamental to any Kantian conception of morality (as we shall see in chapter X), this willing subject becomes the bearer of value.

These Schopenhauerian theses are closely connected with the search for a proper analysis of propositional attitudes, propositions like "Richard thinks that Fenway is picturesque." Such contexts are doubly interesting from the point of view of Wittgenstein's early philosophy; they (a) seem to be about selves and their relation to the world, and (b) appear to be compound but not truth-functionally so. The chapter turns on an examination of certain Russellian ventures into these thorny contexts. As we shall see, each of the three Russellian attempts to make such apparently intentional contexts compatible with the thesis of extensionality have fatal shortcomings from the Wittgensteinian point of view. The upshot: any ego which might serve as the subject matter of psychology thereby fails to be of any possible philosophical interest. But parallel to the waning importance of the empirical ego is an increased awareness of the metaphysical ego,[28] which will emerge as one (with logic) of the twin "conditions on the world," the "Two Godheads" of the *Notebooks*.

---

[28] Much of the transition from the *Tractatus* through the middle period to the *Philosophical Investigations* is marked by Wittgenstein's increasing reluctance to give in to our tendency to think in terms of the metaphysical ego (although he never ceases to take such tendencies seriously.) We shall examine this point in some detail below. It is interesting to note that the popular Wittgensteinian expression "Bumping one's head against the limits of language" has a quite different meaning in the context of the *Tractatus* than it does in the later philosophy; to play on the title of Hacker's work, in one case it yields insight, in the other illusion.

This metaphysical ego, its possible position as a bearer of value and its relation to that world sketched out in chapters IV–VI will serve as the focus for much of chapters IX and X.

Examination of the logic of propositional attitudes also emphasizes another crucial role of the metaphysical subject, the nature of which is further investigated in chapter IX. At 5.62 Wittgenstein cryptically remarks that what the solipsist *means* is quite correct, although he (vainly, of course) attempts to *say* what can only be *shown*. Chief among such pseudo-claims is "The world is *my* world," which similarly attempts to say what can only be shown. But in doing so it directs our attention, in a manner to be examined, towards matters of extreme significance.

The emergence of the metaphysical subject as a possible bearer of value and the complementary notion of "my world" leads to Wittgenstein's theory of value. In a sense the "world as will" reappears, but in highly purified and frustratingly ineffable form. The pseudo-distinction between "the world" and "my world"—which since it can only be made through an attempt to represent in language the existence of the metaphysical subject is ineffable—will allow Wittgenstein to make value consistent with both the atomistic ontology he has sketched in the earlier parts of the *Tractatus* and with his naturalistic analysis of the (psychological) subject. The solution represents a sort of crystallization of a neo-Kantian conception of ethics and the world, and will, if I am not mistaken, allow us to understand in greater depth the relations between Wittgenstein and such diverse fellow travelers as Kraus, Kierkegaard, and Tolstoy.

In the final chapter emerge certain very fundamental Schopenhauerian theses, although in a form much altered both by Wittgenstein's realistic bias and the doctrine of showing and saying. Consider several examples. For Schopenhauer language, and thus discursive thought in general, can deal only with *concepts*. Since concepts are necessarily general they can deal only with plurality and thus with the phenomenal world. They differ from empirical intuitions only insofar as they are more abstract, and thus are less "full." But value resides in the Platonic Ideas, which cannot be adequately subsumed under concepts and thus cannot be (adequately) represented in language. However, they are not theoretical or hypothetical; our experience of the Platonic Ideas is real, immediate, and intuitive. Likewise, for Wittgenstein there is real "experience," in an odd sense, of value, even though value cannot be represented in language, since it involves the metaphysical ego. Neither Wittgenstein nor Schopenhauer exhibits any hint of "other-worldliness"; in each case value is *right in front of us*, although perhaps obscured by certain contingent factors. For each philosopher the "knowing subject" is secondary and of little or no philosophical interest, the latter being concentrated wholly on the "willing subject," the metaphysical ego. These resonances, when set side by side with the significant differences, will offer insight into Wittgenstein's treatment of value.

Problems and Methods

> Abbot Terrasson has remarked that if the size of a volume
> be measured not by the number of pages but by the time
> required for mastering it, it can be said of many a book,
> *that it would be much shorter if it were not so short.*
>
> —KANT, *CPR*, PREFACE, AXIX

At the outset it is important to talk a little bit about the roots of the extreme difficulty of Tractarian exposition, partly because I have muttered about the views of other scholars, but also because such a discussion will go a long way towards explicating the methodology of this book. Clarification and evaluation of epochal philosophical texts is rarely easy,[29] but the *Tractatus* presents special problems.

I have already alluded to the first of these problems: a tendency to read back into Wittgenstein the views of the philosophers whom the *Tractatus* influenced, especially Russell and the members of the Vienna Circle. But these philosophers were motivated by an empiricist epistemology quite foreign to Wittgenstein's thought, as we shall see in chapter III. On one hand, British students of

---

[29] Obscurity is of course a disease to which philosophers often fall prey. But there seem to me to be two classes of obscure philosophers. In one case obscurity is due to indifference to clear exposition or sloppy habits of thought—Mill, Sartre, Whitehead, Husserl after the *Logical Investigations* all spring to mind. But in other cases—Plato, Heidegger, Hegel—a revisionistic metaphysics requires that normal words, even normal syntax, be twisted, tortured, forced, in order to make possible the expression of a radical philosophical position. Cf. P. K. Feyerabend, *Against Method* (Verso, London, 1975), esp. pp. 27–28. Contrast with Austin, "A Plea for Excuses" in his *Philosophical Papers* (Oxford U. Press, Oxford, 1979) and Lazerowitz and Ambrose, *Essays in the Unknown Wittgenstein* (Prometheus Books, Buffalo, NY, 1984), p. 9.

Wittgenstein saw him as a latter-day Hume, endowed perhaps with a superior technical vocabulary but concerned with more or less the same set of neo-Cartesian puzzles about knowledge and justification.[30] Likewise many readers of the book had no natural appreciation for Wittgenstein's views on the nature of science and its role (equivocal at best) in human affairs; thus the members of the Vienna Circle emphasized the negative thrust of Wittgenstein's critique of the sayable, while ignoring the notion of showing and its radical implications for ethics.[31] In the last twenty years the worst of such devastating distortions have been eliminated, but the extent of Wittgenstein's anti-psychologism and the very wide range of things he classifies as "merely psychological" has still not been fully appreciated. This is why the discussion of realism and psychologism in chapter III is so central to understanding the *Tractatus*.

The second difficulty is apparent even to the casual reader of the *Tractatus*. The book is painfully compressed to an extent which cannot be wholly explained away by reference to Wittgenstein's admiration for such aphorists as Nestroy and Lichtenberg.[32] In the compass of perhaps 20,000 often very cryptic words, Wittgenstein addresses an impressive range of philosophical topics, and sheer terseness, other considerations aside, is bound to provide plenty of opportunity for misunderstanding. Unpacking the most important

---

[30] Toulmin writes that he and his contemporaries viewed Wittgenstein as "a uniquely original technical genius, who just happened to adhere personally to an extreme moral individualism and egalitarianism," which produced "a clash between a Viennese thinker whose intellectual problems and personal attitudes alike had been formed in the neo-Kantian environment of pre-1918, in which logic and ethics were essentially bound up with each other and with the critique of language, and an audience of students whose philosophical questions had been shaped by the neo-Humean (and so pre-Kantian) empiricism of Moore, Russell and their colleagues." Janik and Toulmin, *op. cit.*, p. 22.

[31] This is not wholly the fault of those who interpreted Wittgenstein in this manner. Keep in mind that he had little contact with philosophers of any ilk during the twenties, and by the thirties his views had changed, producing, for instance, the *Blue Book* with its strong if cryptic positivistic overtones.

In a similar vein, A. J. Ayer writes "... I took for granted that the 'atomic propositions' ... were propositions which referred to observable states of affairs... [This] is now thought by some of [Wittgenstein's] disciples not to have been what he intended, but it was an assumption generally made at the time by those who had latched onto the *Tractatus*, including some philosophers with whom Wittgenstein was personally in contact. If he did not accept it, one wonders why he allowed them to think that he did." A. J. Ayer, *Part of my Life* (Oxford U. Press, Oxford, 1978), p. 116.

[32] Considerably later Wittgenstein said, in response to a charge by Broad that the Tractatus was "syncopated," "Every sentence in the *Tractatus* should be seen as the heading of a chapter, needing further exposition." John King, "Recollections of Wittgenstein" in Rhees, ed., *op. cit.*, p. 173.

claims is thus part of the role of the commentator and there the commentator, and his work must, as Nietzsche has it, make "a friend of Lento."

But on the other hand, it is unfair to simply accuse Wittgenstein of obscurity for its own sake. The author of a recent book on Wittgenstein prefaces his work with an epigram from Epictetus:

> When a man is proud because he can understand and explain the writings of Chrysippus, say to yourself, if Chrysippus had not written obscurely, this man would have nothing to be proud of.[33]

Allowing for what is presumably facetious self-deprecation, the implication is that Wittgenstein *could* have written more clearly had he wanted to, and thus the expository part of scholarly examination of the *Tractatus* involves trying to figure out what Wittgenstein would have said had he written more clearly. To some extent this is true: there are, as we shall see, a surprising number of passages which must count as loose talk. But when we take seriously the centrality of the say-show distinction, then the textual difficulties seem to have a deeper cause than faulty prose. Wittgenstein's central philosophical doctrines are such that they disallow precisely what seems to be needed, namely the ability to talk about them. What we can't say we can't say, and Wittgenstein recognizes the dangers in trying to do so. (He certainly wants to avoid the predicament of Russell's Mrs. Ladd Franklin, who proclaimed herself a solipsist and couldn't imagine why everyone else wasn't too.) But for Wittgenstein, the dangers of trying to say what can only be shown are not only philosophical puzzlement, but real moral dangers—Tolstoy's "moral" works, for instance, seem to him inferior to "How much land does a man need?" or *Hadji Murat.* We shall examine these reflexive difficulties at various points in the following chapters.

A third difficulty is historical. Wittgenstein's characteristic mode of composition was to record his thoughts, in the form of short remarks, in notebooks, which were then rearranged,

---

[33] Robert Fogelin, *Wittgenstein* (Routledge and Kegan Paul, London, 1976). Compare: ". . . It is not perverse to say that [Hegel] could have written with the elegance of a Schopenhauer only if he had shared that thinker's superficiality. . ." Emil Fackenheim, *The Religious Element in Hegel's Thought* (Indiana U. Press, Bloomington, IN, 1967), p. 5.

juxtaposed, altered, and so forth to create manuscripts. A very large number of these notebooks, including many from the period immediately preceding the publication of the *Tractatus*, were destroyed on Wittgenstein's orders in 1950. A few survived by chance. Published (with additional materials) as *Notebooks 1914–16*, they shed much light on difficult passages in the *Tractatus*. Frequently, for instance, the appearance of a Tractarian remark in an unusual context points to connections which might not otherwise be apparent. In particular, the appearance of a particular remark in a given context often shows (or at least makes probable) that he saw certain difficulties as connected, or that his remarks are directed towards a particular view of Schopenhauer, Frege, or Russell, or that a given technical development meets a certain need. But the very fruitfulness of the existing notebooks raises the disturbing possibility that the now lost notebooks, of which the existent ones are, I repeat, only a tiny fraction, might paint a radically different picture of Wittgenstein's intentions. I suppose that these sorts of worries have to be ignored in the same way that we ignore bad dreams; what is lost is lost, and no scholarly scruples can restore the destroyed materials.

But in addition to these difficulties, there is a deeper and philosophically more interesting problem. One popular opinion holds that the order of exposition in the *Tractatus* does not reflect the order of argument.[34] The book begins with some very general pronouncements about the world, offered without supporting arguments even though they are far from self-evident.[35] It is tempting to invoke the distinction, familiar in the history of philosophy, between synthetic and analytic exposition. The synthetic method of exposition (Descartes' *Meditations*, Kant's *Foundations of the Metaphysics of Morals*) starts from the familiar—if vague and unanalyzed—material of common experience and critically offers a path to the less familiar yet more fundamental, while the analytic method (Descartes' *Principles of Philosophy*, Kant's three *Critiques*) advances from the logically although not epistemologically fundamental principles to

---

[34] For instance, Anscombe writes, "The *Tractatus* is not presented in an order of demonstration from premises; if we want to find the grounds for its contentions, then we must start in the middle and not at the beginning." *Op. cit.*, p. 18.

[35] Even if we accept self-evidence as a sign of truth; cf. 6.1271, but contrast with 5.42.

deduce less distant claims. It is crucial for Wittgenstein that the distinction is, from a philosophical point of view, essentially wrong-headed.

Central to Wittgenstein's anti-psychologism is a systematic rejection of epistemology; at 4.1121 he tells us that the theory of knowledge is merely "the philosophy of psychology." Just as, for instance, Mach's historical account of the development of the concepts of physics is irrelevant to both the truth and the sense of such claims, any description of the progression from better-known to lesser-known is merely a philosophically irrelevant commentary on the psychological development of the individual in question.[36] Thus, although the cause of my belief in the Pythagorean Theorem may be the authority of my third-grade teacher Miss Bredehorst, such evidential genealogy provides no philosophically respectable basis for believing that proposition. For Wittgenstein any philosophical "proposition" would have to be a proposition of logic, and propositions of logic are tautologies, which make their truth manifest on their own, not depending on deducibility from some other proposition. Thus any philosophical proposition should show that it has no sense, either because it is a tautology or because it is *unsinnig*. (As we shall see, the fact that certain philosophical propositions turn out to be senseless in this second sense often shows or points the way to something of great importance. This we shall investigate in chapters IX and X.) It follows that there is no inherent order in the comments of the *Tractatus* or of any philosophical book (and that Wittgenstein's own numbering system, which purports to show, e.g., that 5.01 is a subsidiary comment on 5, has no philosophical justification); in philosophy, the distinction between analytic and synthetic exposition fails. Thus, the order of argument in the book cannot differ from the order of exposition, since there is no order of argument.

---

[36] We must be careful to sharply distinguish this claim, which will be developed in later chapters, from Descartes' superficially parallel claim that his reasonings in the *Meditations* offer no grounds for others to believe his conclusions, but merely map out a schema for a philosophical pilgrimage which every reflective person must take once in his life. Descartes' claim is based on the *personal* nature of the data involved; "Now this knowledge is not the work of your reasoning nor information passed on to you by your teachers; it is something your mind sees, feels and handles ..." *Descartes' Philosophical Letters*, ed. A. Kenny (Oxford U. Press, Oxford, 1970), p. 230. For Wittgenstein, the important point is not that the path is personal but that there is no philosophically significant path.

The impossibility of any necessary order presents the commentator with both a problem and an unusual degree of freedom. On one hand, the remark-numbers cannot be taken, without further ado, to show the relative importance which Wittgenstein attached to those remarks—for instance, the "fundamental idea" that logical constants do not stand for objects appears in a remark numbered 4.0312. On the other hand, the commentator is left more or less free to present material in any order he sees fit. Of this freedom I have availed myself.

One final set of difficulties—historical rather than philosophical in nature—arises from the relation to the *Tractatus* of both Wittgenstein's later writings and the mountains of materials written about him by people who knew him at one time or another. In the preface to the *Philosophical Investigations* Wittgenstein says that he wished his earlier work published with that book, so he clearly saw strong connections between the two. Yet the sections in the *Investigations* which are often taken to be directed towards the earlier views (especially sections 89–108, which one commentator labels "confessions of a logical atomist") present views on analysis, complexity, simplicity, and so forth which seem to differ significantly from Tractarian views. On the other hand, it was from the *Investigations* that I first began to understand the importance of the metaphysical subject and its activities of "meaning" and "understanding" in Wittgenstein's early philosophy.

Enormous amounts of material have been written about Wittgenstein, his life and character, his small doings and cryptic remarks. Although such materials are sometimes interesting and relevant, they are not always consistent. To cite a trivial example, Malcolm tells us that Wittgenstein made a practice of sitting in the very front row of his beloved cowboy movies, so as to "fill his visual field" with the action on the screen. But Fania Pascal tells us that Wittgenstein chose these seats because he was nearsighted and too vain to wear glasses![37] Further, most of this material is written by people who have strong opinions about Wittgenstein, and thus often seems filtered through their prior conceptions of him and his views. I have generally treated most of this sort of secondary material with a healthy dose of scepticism.

---

[37] Cf. Malcolm, *op. cit.*, and Fania Pascal, "Wittgenstein: a Personal Memoir" in R. Rhees, ed., *op. cit.*

Finally, the *Tractatus* is complex and difficult because it was written by a complex and difficult man.[38] Russell draws a distinction, parallel to William James's distinction between "toughminded" and "tenderminded" philosophers, between those philosophers whose motives are derived largely from "religion and ethics" and those whose primary motive is scientific.[39] But he writes of Heraclitus:

> ... the facts of science, as they appeared to him, fed the flames in his soul, and in its light he saw into the depths of the world by the reflection of his own dancing swiftly penetrating fire. In such a nature we see the true union of the mystic and the man of science—the highest eminence, as I think, that it is possible to achieve in the world of thought.[40]

Russell's words are equally appropriate for Wittgenstein, although we shall see below that his views on the relation between science and "the depths of the world" are somewhat different than those Russell depicts. But the description highlights Wittgenstein's dedication to the world of logic and the world of value, and at bottom the most difficult part of his early philosophy is the uneasy relation between the pluralistic and valueless world of contingent facts, and what he calls "my world"—monistic, waxing and waning in symphony. But the very uneasiness of this tension reflects both the depth and the purity of his thought.

---

[38] Wittgenstein's realism brought him to attempt to exclude from the book any vestiges of the *personal* journey from which it resulted; perhaps this is why he mentions that the book might make sense only to someone who had himself had the thoughts it contains, who himself had been confronted with its problems. Thus there is no psycho-history in the *Tractatus*, not even psycho-history disguised as epistemology. Whether Wittgenstein's personality intrudes in a deeper manner is open to debate. Compare with Schorske on Freud's *Interpretation of Dreams:* "Its surface organization is governed by its function as a scientific treatise, with each chapter and section systematically expounding an aspect of dreams and their interpretation... Yet a closer look reveals a second, deep-structure of the work which, running from one isolated dream of the author to the next, constitutes an incomplete but autonomous subplot of personal history. Imagine St. Augustine weaving his *Confessions* into *The City of God*, or Rousseau integrating his *Confessions* as a subliminal plot into *The Origins of Inequality:* such is the procedure of Freud in *The Interpretation of Dreams.*" *Op. cit.*, p. 183.

[39] "On Scientific Method in Philosophy," in *Mysticism and Logic* (W. W. Norton, New York, 1929) (henceforth abbreviated *M&L*), pp. 97–98.

[40] "Mysticism and Logic," in *M&L*, pp. 3–4.

II

Schopenhauer's System of the World

Arthur Schopenhauer was born in 1788, the son of a wealthy merchant in the Hanseatic Free City of Danzig. His father, Heinrich Floris, a cultured cosmopolitan who wrote popular novels in his spare time, introduced Arthur to the world of ideas at an early age.[1] If the influence of Heinrich Floris was not sufficient, the salon of Schopenhauer's sister Adele in Weimar—the "Athens of Germany"—brought Arthur in contact with Goethe, Schlegel, the Grimms, and other German cultural lions.[2] Schopenhauer took the bait, and in 1813 was awarded the degree of Doctor of Philosophy by the University of Berlin, his dissertation appearing in print under the title *On the Fourfold Root of the Principle of Sufficient Reason.*[3] Although primarily neo-Kantian, Schopenhauer's philosophical stance was also deeply influenced by Oriental thought, to which he had been introduced in Weimar by the German Orientalist F. Mayer. In a more general way, Goethe's wide-ranging brilliance captivated the young Schopenhauer. The Master's views of him are less clear; Goethe's evasive response to Schopenhauer's *On Vision and Color,* modeled on his own *Farben-lehre,* seems to indicate that he saw Schopenhauer's work as over-subjective. Schopenhauer drew additional inspiration from Plato, whose works he studied intensively at Göttingen from 1809 to

---

[1] Heinrich Floris's death at an early age, perhaps by his own hand, may well have sparked Schopenhauer's philosophical interest in suicide, just as his worsening relations with his mother and sister were the source of his misogyny. Heinrich Floris's suicide, if actual, marks a parallel with the life of Wittgenstein, marred by the suicides of Boltzmann, his brother, uncle, and others. Cf. B. Russell, *Autobiography* (Little, Brown and Co., Boston, 1968), vol. II, pp. 136–37, and B. McGuinness, *Wittgenstein; a Life* (U. of Cal., Berkeley, 1988), *passim.*

[2] For a more complete biographical sketch of Schopenhauer's life, see F. Copleston, *Arthur Schopenhauer, Philosopher of Pessimism* (Search Press, London, 1946), ch. II, or Patrick Gardiner, *Schopenhauer* (Penguin, London, 1967), ch. I.

[3] A. Schopenhauer, *On the Fourfold Root of the Principle of Sufficient Reason,* trans. E. F. J. Payne (Open Court, La Salle, IL, 1974), henceforth abbreviated 'FRSR'.

1811, as well as David Hume, whose writings on natural religion he greatly admired.

Schopenhauer's *opus magnum*, *The World as Will and Representation*, first appeared in 1818; a second edition, incorporating many changes as well as a second volume containing fifty new essays, was published in 1844.[4] The book comprises a detailed working-out of the implications of the doctoral dissertation, although the characteristic voluntarism—the claim that the world is at bottom *will*—is much more pronounced in the later work.

With the publication of his chief work, Schopenhauer offered a course of lectures in Berlin in an attempt to carve out for himself a niche in academic philosophy. With characteristic hubris and combativeness, he scheduled his lectures to coincide with those of Hegel, and when they were almost universally ignored his reaction again was characteristic—vilification and rage. This episode, combined with the general indifference with which *WWR* was received by the educated public and the philosophical community, increased the bitterness which was to characterize his social and professional relations for the sum of his life, and which found reflection in the pessimism of his philosophical stance. But only with the demise of liberalism following the tumult of 1848 did that pessimism become fashionable. By the time of Schopenhauer's death in 1860 at his home in Frankfurt-am-Main, where he had resided for thirty years, courses of lectures on his philosophy began to appear at German universities, and the fame he had sought vainly most of his life finally was realized. A whole generation of young philosophers emerged as his followers, including von Hartmann, author of the influential *The Philosophy of the Unconscious*. In the literary field his influence, derived perhaps as much from the elegance of his prose style as its content, is seen in the works of Thomas Mann and Thomas Hardy.[5] In the wider cultural realm, Richard Wagner in 1854 sent to Schopenhauer a copy of his *Ring der Nibelungen*, inscribed "in admiration and appreciation." Through the early works of Nietzsche, Schopenhauer gained perhaps his widest influence on contemporary

[4] A. Schopenhauer, *The World as Will and Representation*, vols. I and II, trans. E. F. J. Payne (Dover, New York, 1969). I shall hereafter refer to the two volumes as *WWR* I and *WWR* II.

[5] Mann speaks of Schopenhauer's "extraordinary native eloquence, his genius as a writer." Cf. Mann's introduction to *The Living Thoughts of Schopenhauer* (McKay, Philadelphia, 1939). But compare with Fackenheim's appraisal in ch. I, note 32 above.

German cultural and political thought.[6] Finally, he influenced deeply and fundamentally the young Ludwig Wittgenstein, whose early work—and thus, if Wittgenstein's own claims are taken at face value, his later work too—profits greatly from being understood as a radical transformation, wrought largely by the influence of Frege, on Schopenhauer's vision of the world as representation underlaid by will.

Transcendental Idealism and the Problem of Knowledge

In order to understand the essence of Schopenhauer's philosophical work, let us briefly review the general project and outline of Kant's Critical Philosophy, and isolate those problems to which Schopenhauer addresses himself. In the forthcoming discussion of Schopenhauer's philosophy, I will draw not only from *WWR* I and II, and *FRSR*, but from the prize essays of 1839–40, *On the Freedom of the Will* and *On the Basis of Morality*, and the 1835 essay *On the Will in Nature*.[7]

The "subjective turn" brought to early modern philosophy by Descartes is marked by a distinction, latent in the new scientific view of the world, between the contents of our minds and the non-mental objects which these contents are normally taken to represent. Descartes takes the "dreaming argument" of the *First Meditation*[8] to show that those things of which we are immediately aware are not the familiar material objects of the everyday world, but entities of a rather different sort. These entities are *ideas*, which for him were modes of the essential attribute—thought—of the newly discovered mental substance *Res Cogitans*. The Cartesian epistemological project (as well as one major preoccupation of philosophers for the next several centuries) becomes this: how do we get from knowledge

---

[6] For Nietzsche's own estimation of Schopenhauer's influence, see his *Schopenhauer as Educator*, trans. K. Hillessheim (Regnery-Gateway, South Bend, IN, 1965). For an appreciation of Nietzsche's widespread influence, see W. McGrath, *Dionysian Art and Populist Politics in Austria* (Yale U. Press, New Haven, CT, 1974) esp. chs. 1–2. Compare with Schorske *op. cit.*, esp. chs. 1, 3, 5–6, and Janik and Toulmin, *op. cit.*, chs. 1–3.

[7] *On the Freedom of the Will*, trans. K. Kolenda (Bobbs-Merrill, Indianapolis, IN, 1960), and *On the Basis of Morality*, trans. E. F. J. Payne (Bobbs-Merrill, Indianapolis, IN, 1965), to be abbreviated *FW* and *OBM*, and *On the Will in Nature*, trans. K. Hillebrand (G. Bell, London, 1897), hereafter *WN*.

[8] Cf. E. S. Haldane and G. R. Ross, eds., *The Philosophical Works of Descartes*, vols. I and II, (Cambridge U. Press, Cambridge, 1969), pp. 147–48. These volumes will be hereafter referred to as *HR* I and II.

of ideas, of which we are directly aware, to knowledge of the things which the ideas purport to represent? Descartes' solution turns on claiming that a certain class of ideas—those which are "clear and distinct"—carry with them their own guarantee, as it were. Descartes thus echoes the Platonic vision of a *resonance* between the order and connections of our ideas and the order and connection of things in the world. Such harmony is for Descartes a sign of God's benevolence, and in turn it is our knowledge of God's existence and attributes which allows us to advance justifiable knowledge-claims about the external world.

But Hume points out a curious lacuna in the Cartesian justification of belief.[9] While agreeing that we are aware directly only of the contents of our minds (he calls them "perceptions"), he contends that we cannot by reason alone advance from judgments about perceptions to judgments about material objects, at least as Descartes envisions the latter. Hume's argument (much compressed) proceeds as follows: All reasoning is merely the comparison of perceptions to see if certain very general relations hold between them. The generally accepted relations (Hume calls them "philosophical" relations) can be grouped into seven general categories (I/i/3), of which only one—the relation of cause and effect—allows us to move from a present perception to one not present. That is, only cause and effect allow any *synthetic* reasoning. If there is a way out of the circle of our ideas, Hume continues, it must therefore be through causal inferences. So far, there is no serious disagreement between Descartes and Hume, but Hume then sets forth an analysis of causation which casts serious doubt on its ability to support such reasoning. Particular causal relations are not literally *observable*, and thus particular cases of causal reasoning can only be justified by reference to the general causal principle that every event must have some preceding cause. But what grounds have we for accepting this principle? Descartes holds it to be "manifest by the natural light," or in Hume's words:

> 'Tis supposed to be founded on intuition, and to be one of those maxims, which tho' they may be deny'd with the lips, 'tis impossible for men in their hearts really to doubt of. (*Ibid.*, p. 79)

---

[9] All references will be to the Nidditch/Selby-Bigge edition of *A Treatise of Human Nature* (Oxford U. Press, Oxford, 1978). *Treatise* references will be given by volume, book, and chapter; e.g. I/iv/7.

But is this so, Hume asks? To achieve such certainty, the causal principle must be either "intuitive" or "demonstrative" — self-evident or following from premises which have such self-evidence. But certainly we can at least *conceive* of the principle being false, that is, conceive of some event which has no prior cause. So the causal principle, if it is justifiable, must be based on experience. But what finite series of experiences would ever justify us in asserting the principle with the requisite degree of certainty? Clearly there is none. Thus as based on a *philosophical* relation, causal inference is unjustifiable and thus impotent. There are, however, besides the *philosophical* relations of I/i/4, what Hume calls *natural* relations, tendencies of the mind to move from one perception to another which is associated with the first. I smell bacon cooking, and the idea of fried eggs occurs to me. (In chapter III, these natural relations will assume additional importance for us as the ground of *psychologism* in logic.) Natural relations resolve into three general types: association due to contiguity, resemblance of cause, and effect. This latter category is obviously what interests us. Qua natural relation, causation produces movement from one perception to another, which usually are related by temporal precedence and spatial contiguity. Although causation qua philosophical relation is impotent, this *natural* relation of causation Hume sees as a primitive, ubiquitous, and irresistible force of the human mind. But it *is* a natural relation, that is, not based on "scientific" grounds but on the nature of the human mind. The sudden centrality of causation qua natural relation carries with it some surprising and radical consequences:

> [A]ll probable reasoning is thus nothing but a species of sensation. 'Tis not solely in music and poetry we must follow our taste and sentiment, but likewise in philosophy ... (*Ibid.*, p. 103)

and

> *[T]hat all our reasonings concerning causes and effects are derived from nothing but custom; and that belief is more properly an act of the sensitive, than of the cognitive part of our natures.* (*Ibid.*, p. 183; the emphasis is Hume's)

Hume's analysis places us in a curious position. We are slaves to a certain sort of inference, which alone allows us access to an external world, and which cannot be rationally justified, yet from which we cannot refrain.[10] If justification for our causal inferences and their results can be offered, it can be only a *psychological* justification. An analysis of human nature shows us that nothing more is possible.

Kant finds this situation intolerable. In order to see his solution to the dilemma presented to him by his predecessors, let us recast the preceding in Kantian terminology. Judgments or propositions which are true solely by virtue of the concepts they contain Kant calls analytic, while those whose truth depends on some extralinguistic element are synthetic. Judgments which are justified by appeal to experience are a posteriori, those which are not a priori. Normally one would expect the two distinctions to coincide, and in the vast majority of cases synthetic judgments are a posteriori, and analytic judgments a priori. However, certain important and fundamental claims, such as the causal principle, seem to be simultaneously synthetic and a priori. In a sense this is what Hume has shown; the causal principle is not true merely by virtue of the words it contains (as "every *effect* has a cause" is), yet causal judgments are so constitutive of the human mind that we cannot refrain from reasoning causally, and thus the principle *appears* a priori.

With respect to their attitudes towards such synthetic a priori principles Kant categorizes all previous philosophers as *sceptics* or *dogmatists*. Dogmatists (Descartes, Leibniz, Wolff) claim that we are in possession of synthetic a priori knowledge, but fail to show *how* this is possible, while sceptics (the British empiricists) deny such principles the status of knowledge, even while acknowledging that we must necessarily think in terms of them. In this context appears the opening question of the Critical Philosophy: How is synthetic a priori knowledge possible? A skeleton answer—sufficient for our purposes—is set forth in the preface to the first *Critique*, where Kant likens his problems to those confronting Copernicus. Faced

---

[10] I would add that Hume's eliminates much of the paradox associated with this view by offering revised views of the nature of rationality within the confines of the preceding argument. It is also interesting that Hume embraces precisely what Descartes fears in his Evil Genius argument, namely that we were created (in his case by the Evil Genius) with a faulty faculty of knowledge and no way in which to correct for that faulty faculty, so that we constantly and compulsively make unjustifiable claims. This Descartes thought would curse us to *necessary* and *unavoidable* ignorance, which Hume foregoes only by ignoring knowledge in the Cartesian sense and speaking instead in terms of satisfactory and unsatisfactory beliefs.

with reconciling the apparent motions of the sun and planets with any rational model of the universe, Copernicus suggests that any irregularity of planetary and stellar motion (as well as the whole of the motion of the sun) is *merely apparent*, due to compounding the motion of the earth (and thus the *observer*) with the natural motions of the planets. Accordingly we must isolate the "subjective" component of the perceived motion from the *actual* motion of the planets themselves. Analogously, Kant argues that synthetic a priori judgments can claim universal and necessary applicability only insofar as they stem from a *necessary contribution on the part of the subject*, and are necessary conditions for *any* human experience.

Of the contributions of the subject to experience we can distinguish three sorts. The first is purely idiosyncratic; a person afflicted with Daltonism cannot tell the red light from the green. Such purely personal cognitive features contrast with others which are species-wide but still contingent; human retinae are not sensitive to infrared radiation, so we cannot "see" heated objects in the dark. Since we can imagine each of these being different than they in fact are, they are of interest to the psychologist or physiologist, but of no particular *philosophical* interest. However, there is a third possible class of contributions of the subject, those which are necessary to the constitution of any rational discursive intelligence. Hume speaks of such tendencies as those without which human nature would "fall into ruin." It is this third class in which Kant finds the key to his Copernican Revolution.

In the necessary contributions to experience of any discursive intelligence Kant distinguishes two classes, corresponding to the faculties of sensibility and understanding. The sensibility contributes the Pure Forms of Sensibility—Space and Time—while the understanding contributes twelve very general a priori concepts, the Pure Concepts of the Understanding or "Categories." Every possible object of human experience must be spatio-temporally locatable, and must be subsumable under the appropriate categories, one of which is Causation. Thus, to the question: How can we say in advance that the causal principle will apply to every experience? Kant answers: It must, insofar as subsumability under a causal law is a necessary condition for entering into the content of a human experience.

Has Kant then come down on the side of the sceptic, or the dogmatist? Neither, actually. We might say that each has been allotted their assigned sphere. The dogmatist is correct when he asserts that a priori principles must apply without exception to every human experience, but he is wrong when he thinks that they therefore represent necessary claims about the world *as it is independently of being experienced.* The sceptic is correct when he emphasizes the ground of such principles in the human mind, but is wrong in asserting that they are therefore merely psychological and cannot be asserted with universality and necessity.

Kant's Copernican Revolution also yields a new categorization of the *objects* of such experiences. Any object of human experience—my typewriter, for instance—results from two sorts of contributions; some wholly independent of my mind (this is what distinguishes perceiving the typewriter from *imagining* one), some due to the transcendental contributions of any human mind. Is the typewriter thereby "subjective" or is it "objective"? If "objective" means "wholly independent of human minds," then it is not objective. On the other hand, since every human perceiver must perceive it using the same Categories, etc., it is not private and subjective either, like my taste in ice cream or my sensation of warmth. For Kant there are thus three points on the objective-subjective scale. On one end, there are *representations,* the subjective, private, personal contents of my mind. On the other are *things-in-themselves,* things as they exist independently of the pure contributions of the subject, that is, Space, Time, and the Categories. But in between fall such things as the typewriter, which Kant calls *Appearances.* They are objective, insofar as their properties do not depend on the idiosyncrasies of the individual mind, and yet are *subjective,* insofar as their form derives from the pure or transcendental contributions of the human mind. They are, in Kant's terminology, *empirically real*—unlike illusions and sensations like tickles—but *transcendentally ideal*—dependent on the contributions of the subject and thus *not* the way things would appear from a "god's-eye view."

We can now summarize Kant's achievements. On the positive side, he has defeated the sceptics, showing how we can justifiably ascribe to such concepts as causation universal and necessary applicability. On the other hand, the claims of, for example, the causal principle must be restricted to Appearances, to possible objects of human knowledge, and the dogmatist is accordingly wrong in asserting their *unconditional* applicability. Kant has thus simultaneously provided human reason a sphere in which it reigns supreme, and restricted that sphere to possible objects of experience. For Kant perhaps the most significant effect of the limitation of the sphere of Pure Reason is negative; the inability of reason to move beyond the bounds of Appearances eliminates any possible friction between reason and religion. In Kant's words, "I have therefore found it necessary to deny *knowledge,* in order to make room for *faith.*" (*CPR*, p. 29) But for our purposes one further conclusion is salient. The concept of an Appearance allows Kant to hold that certain principles can be anthropocentric without thereby being merely *psychological.* We shall see in later chapters a curious parallel with Wittgenstein's thought.

The Four Forms of the Principle of Sufficient Reason

Much of Kant's Critical Philosophy Schopenhauer takes over unchanged, but he differs from Kant in several important respects. Two of these are central to our project. First (and less important), he holds the distinction between sensibility and understanding, and with it the bifurcation of the Categories from Space and Time, to be unnecessary. The whole range of the pure contributions of the subject, Schopenhauer argues, can be reduced to one general principle, the *Principle of Sufficient Reason* (PSR), which appears, however, in a number of forms. The natural way to view the Principle is as a general version of the causal principle; Schopenhauer presents it in simple preliminary form as "Nothing is without a ground or reason for why it is." (*FRSR*, p. 6) The opening sections of *FRSR* trace its development through the history of Western philosophy, pointing out what Schopenhauer regards as its *systematic ambiguity.* Historically he finds a recognized distinction between the principle of causality proper, and the principle of the *ground of reasons.* Consider the following pair of explanations:

(a) Q: Why is that billiard ball moving with velocity such-and-such?
   A: Because it has mass such-and-such, and was hit by another billiard ball traveling with such-and-such velocity . . .

(b) Q: Why is the Washington Monument x feet tall?
   A: Because the designer wanted it to be the tallest structure on the mall.

Obviously these are very different sorts of why-questions: the first requests a narrative of events and a general covering law, the other asks for an evidential connection between one statement and certain others. Generalizing on our intuitions concerning such differences, and offering two additional forms of why-questions, Schopenhauer sets out four fundamental forms of PSR, which he takes as exhaustive. Each provides an answer to a certain sort of why-question and corresponds to a particular sort of necessity:

> *Mathematical necessity:* Why do the interior angles of a triangle sum to 180°?
> *Logical necessity:* Why must every proposition be either true or false?
> *Moral necessity:* Why is it forbidden to do so-and-so?
> *Physical necessity:* Why does a billiard ball act so-and-so under such-and-such circumstances?

The existence of these four forms entails the existence of four corresponding classes of objects-for-a-subject; the "fourfold root" of the doctoral dissertation's title. It is the fourth of these classes which figures in the remaining, and by far most important, divergence of Schopenhauer from the Kantian orthodoxy. This is the thesis that the world as it is independently of the forms of human knowledge is *will.*

Each of the four forms of PSR finds its applicability in a certain class of representations. The first consists of *complete, empirical, intuitive* representations. My present representation of the typewriter is an example; intuitive insofar as it relates immediately to its object (as opposed to a concept, which relates to the object only mediately), complete (given in one act of consciousness, as opposed to a concept, given through instances) and empirical (gained at least in part through present sensation.) This class of representations is governed by the *Principle of Sufficient Reason of Becoming,* the causal principle in its most familiar sense. Every change in any material body is necessitated by some prior state. (*FRSR,* pp. 52ff.) In merely vegetative entities, where effects are always strictly proportional to the causes, this is the only applicable version of PSR, but in higher organisms—perceptive or apperceptive—this is not the case. In man, the highest of entities, we shall see the emergence of *motives,* abstract representations as causes of action.

Representations of the second class—*concepts*—are universal, abstract and non-intuitive. (*FRSR,* pp. 145ff., *OBM,* p. 81) Only humans have concepts, which for Schopenhauer play the important role of providing springs for action other than present perceptions. Since concepts are not intuitive, they must be fixed by means of words or some other concrete symbols; language becomes the bearer of reason, and the muteness of animals is thus sufficient for denying them concepts. The appropriate version of PSR deals with necessary relations among concepts: it is the *Principle of Sufficient Reason of Knowing*—"If a judgment is to express knowledge, there must be some ground for its truth."[11]

Representations of the third class are complete—that is, intuitions and not concepts—but a priori rather than empirical. There exist but two members of this class, the pure intuitions Space and Time.[12] Why-questions directed towards necessary spatial and temporal relations of things—for instance, "Why are the three angles of an equilateral triangle equal? Because the sides are equal."— appeal to the *Principle of Sufficient Reason of Being*. This version of PSR might be loosely rendered as "In every pure (i.e., non-empirical) relation of space or time, there is some reason why the parts stand in the relations which they do." (*FRSR*, p. 194) Kant's example of "incongruent counterparts"—left and right hands, for instance— shows that such relations cannot adequately be analyzed in terms of concepts, and that we must thus have recourse to the pure intuitions of Space and Time.[13] From this form of PSR stem the a priori judgments of arithmetic and geometry.

The fourth class of representations and the fourth form of PSR are by far the most significant for Schopenhauer's metaphysics. Like concepts restricted to humans, the fourth class is yet special insofar as for each human it is constituted of exactly one unique element. Besides concepts and intuitions, pure and empirical, Schopenhauer

---

[11] *FRSR*, p. 156. Note that although the class of representations encompasses concepts, the principle deals with *judgments*. This is because all we can *do* with a concept is combine it with others to form a judgment. Thus Kant derives the Categories from a table of the Forms of Judgments; *CPR*, pp. 104–19.

If the contemporary reader finds odd the existence of a form of PSR which deals with *knowledge*, compare with Plato's discussion of the difference between knowledge and mere true opinion in terms of the "tie of the cause."—*Meno*, 96d–99a.

[12] For a demonstration that Space and Time *are* a priori intuitions, see *CPR*, pp. 67–70, 74–75. This and *many* other Kantian arguments Schopenhauer takes for granted.

[13] I. Kant, "On the First Ground of the Distinction of Regions in Space" in Handyside, ed., *Kant's Inaugural Dissertation and Early Writings on Space and Time*, (Open Court, Chicago, 1929).

argues that each of us is aware of himself as *willing subject*, and "Insofar as man is a part of nature, this *human will* also has a law ..." (*OBM*, p. 53) That law is the *Principle of Sufficient Reason of Acting*, the Law of Motivation. (*FRSR*, pp. 207ff.) The pivotal position of this fourth class of representations demands a closer look.

Every act of consciousness, Kantians hold, demands both subject and object, and thus no act of apperception or self-reflection can be simple. We cannot be wholly and directly aware of ourselves as knower, insofar as every act of self-reflection generates a "higher-level knower," so to speak. The Lockian metaphor of "reflexion" is thus misleading; if some act of consciousness is to be the object of introspection, it must be made object and thus requires a distinct subject. (*FRSR*, sects. 41–42) The knowing subject accordingly can never be *en toto* object for itself. However, since the human consciousness is not only passive observer but *active agent*, we must be aware of ourselves not only as knowing but as *willing* subject, and this willing subject can, in its entirety, become object for the knowing subject. For each of us, ourselves as willing subject is the sole member of the fourth class of representations. This willing subject cannot be adequately represented through concepts; it is a *primitive phenomenon*, one which is not hypothetical or inferential in any manner, but immediately known to each person through introspection.

Schopenhauer does not fully explore the immense importance of this discovery until *WWR*, but let us roughly sketch some of those implications. Imagine watching a sleeping man who suddenly leaps from his bed, grabs his shotgun and blasts away at the mirror beside his bed. Consider two sorts of explanations of this scene.[14] On one level, the man's retinae recorded images, certain muscles were activated, and so on and so forth. Every event in the list will be an empirical intuition, subsumable under the First Form of PSR. (Compare with a physiologist's explanation of why a certain man *cannot* fire a shotgun.) Yet this is not nearly what we ordinarily would have in mind when we ask "Why did he shoot the mirror?" We are not inquiring into the physiology of the trigger-finger; if so, lawyers would be anatomists. Rather we are asking for

---

[14] For this and similar examples, see Richard Taylor, "Comments on a Mechanistic Conception of Purposefulness," *Philosophy of Science*, vol. 17 (1950) pp. 310–17.

his *intentions*. We want to know what *motivated* him to shoot the mirror?

Notice right off that a clever casual observer could offer quite an array of hypotheses, all different and incompatible, and likewise all fitting the facts. Our man was tired of his mirror and sought to destroy it. He took his reflection in it to be a burglar. He wanted to make a loud noise to scare his dog. From the "outside," then, our actions present a peculiarly ambiguous face. But psychoanalytic difficulties aside, the man in question knew *exactly* what he intended to do. He has direct access to his motives—these motives being states of himself as willing subject—while we can only (fallibly) infer them from their outward guise. Events that are ambiguous, puzzling, or even meaningless to the outside observer accordingly become filled with a special sort of inner meaning for the agent himself.

It is crucial to correctly understand the relation between an act of will and the concurrent physical motion. Every *real* act of will, Schopenhauer argues, is identical with some physical action, and thus the act of will and the motion are not two events but one, seen from different viewpoints. This Schopenhauer contrasts with the "usual view," which takes acts of will as the *causes* of physical motions, and posits two fundamentally different principles of motion—causes from the outside, motives from the inside.

> My doctrine maintains that there are *not* two origins of movement, differing fundamentally from one another . . . [motion from the inside and the outside] are inseparable and take place simultaneously with every movement made by a body. (*WN*, p. 311)

This eliminates immediately the notorious problem that the physical antecedents themselves seem perfectly adequate to bring about the event in question, thus leaving no room for efficacy on the part of the motive. But we also see that the noumenal realm is not some other-worldly place, parallel to but wholly separate from the phenomenal, but is as it were the kernel of reality within every phenomenal event. This we shall see has profound implications for Wittgenstein.

FRSR thus presents two fundamental claims. The first is that the phenomenal world is constituted by certain a priori principles, namely the four forms of PSR. The spatio-temporal world of causally connected events is thus merely phenomenal; Space, Time, and Causality have no applicability beyond the scope of possible human experience. No investigations into the spatio-temporal, causal world can yield any insight into the world as it really is, independent of being an object of human experience. However, each of us has a peculiar access to ourselves as willing subject. In *FRSR* Schopenhauer treats this access rather equivocally, positing for its object (the willing subject) a special form of PSR. But Schopenhauer quickly realizes that this immediate access to the willing self is in fact a radical break with the Kantian camp, a direct, intuitive toehold in the noumenal realm of things in themselves.

The World as Will and Representation

> On the whole, I can confidently assert that there has never
> yet been a philosophical system so entirely cut of one
> piece, so completely without any joins or patches, as mine
> ... It is the unfolding of a single thought.
>
> —SCHOPENHAUER

FRSR presents every person's actions as Janus-faced. Each can be seen from two distinct points of view; from the outside, as mere phenomena, and from the inside, as acts of the willing subject. In *WWR* Schopenhauer sets out to exploit this insight through a daring hypothesis; let us take the dual nature of human action as a *paradigm for the world as a whole.* Every element of the world, then, can be seen either phenomenally, as *representation,* or as it is in itself, as *will.* Let us call this identification of will with the thing-in-itself the *Thesis of Universal Voluntarism.*

The Thesis as stated baldly seems to represent quite a leap, and certain difficulties spring to mind. A natural first objection is that Schopenhauer has fallen prey to a very crude sort of anthropomorphism. But he is quick to point out that he does not mean that something exactly like the human will forms the noumenal reality of, say, a stone, but rather that we "define the genus in terms of the species," seeing the human will as a special case of a much more general element of nature. Certainly no deductive proof can be given for the hypothesis, but Schopenhauer retorts that no deductive proof is forthcoming for *most* philosophical theses, and demanding such proof would be tantamount to abandoning philosophy. On the other hand, there is one solid argument in favor of tentatively accepting the hypothesis. The acceptance of universal voluntarism is based on grounds very similar to those for believing that other human beings have inner lives like ourselves. If we reject the former out of hand, we ought then reject the latter too, falling prey to "theoretical egoism," that is, solipsism. Although solipsism, like other forms of scepticism, is irrefutable—no evidence can be brought *against* it—it is impotent insofar as it can challenge claims only negatively, and counterproductive as it closes any possible avenue of philosophical investigation.

The objections above are perhaps due to Schopenhauer's questionable choice of the term 'will' to represent the inner reality of the world; why does he not instead opt for the more neutral-sounding 'force' or 'energy'? Because the extension of the word 'will' follows the established practice of subsuming the *lesser-known*—energy, force—under the better-known, in this case the will as immediately present in introspection. This points out an interesting argument in favor of Schopenhauer's Voluntarism, to wit, that we are positing no *new sorts of entities;* we are already committed to recognizing will in ourselves, where it is immediately intuited and *not* posited as a theoretical entity whose existence is open to debate. Finally, some of the squeamishness in accepting Schopenhauer's suggestion stems from a tendency to conflate will with *consciousness,*[15] degrading Schopenhauer's Universal Voluntarism to panpsychism. But far from being a manifestation of consciousness, we shall see that the will in reality acts as its *source.*

There are accordingly no *general* philosophical grounds for rejecting Schopenhauer's hypothesis; it must stand or fall on its own merits. Those putative merits are that it offers unified explanations for certain phenomena. The evidence for Universal Voluntarism must therefore be found in its conformity with and illumination of ordinary and scientific knowledge. Verification in terms of the sciences Schopenhauer presents in *WN*, in terms of our moral intuitions in *OBM*, and in terms of our aesthetic experiences,

---

[15] Cf. *WN*, pp. 217, 290. Contrast: "Self-consciousness is the state of desire in general." G. W. F. Hegel, *Phenomenology of Mind* (Harper and Row, New York, 1967), p. 509.

WWR I, book III. That scientific support is abundant Schopenhauer harbors no doubts:

> ... Indeed the two bodies of investigators [scientists and metaphysicians] must feel like two mining engineers driving a gallery, who, having started from two points far apart and worked for some time in subterranean darkness, trusting exclusively to compass and spirit-level, suddenly to their great joy catch the sound of each other's hammers. (*WN*, p. 219)

Let us now look in closer focus at the thesis of Universal Voluntarism and its consequences as presented in the first volume of *WWR*.

WWR I divides into four books, each dealing with a particular aspect of human experience. Book I treats of the world as representation—as phenomenon—insofar as it is seen as governed by PSR. The second book deals with the world in its other aspect, as *will*, but again only as this is manifest through PSR; in this book we see the grounds for natural laws. The third book returns to the world as representation, but considered, as far as possible, *apart* from PSR—here we encounter Schopenhauer's metaphysics of art. The final book concerns the world as will, but again to the extent to which we can free ourselves from PSR; it contains Schopenhauer's metaphysics of morals. I will briefly outline the salient points of the final three books, the first being largely a rather haphazard and unsatisfactory rehash of the central themes of *FRSR*.

Space and Time

> Question: Do you take your starting point 'That there
>   are many things' as a postulate to be carried along all
>   through, or is it to be proved afterward?
>
> Mr Russell: No, neither one nor the other. I should not take
>   it as a postulate that 'There are many things.' I should
>   take it that, insofar as it can be proved, the proof is
>   empirical and that the disproofs that have been offered
>   are *a priori*.
>
>   —RUSSELL, "LECTURES ON LOGICAL ATOMISM"

FRSR has shown the basis of our a priori confidence that every representation can be linked with others in a rational sequence via subsumption under some causal law. The content of these laws cannot be predicted in advance, of course, and must be discovered empirically, but their *existence* is not debatable. This general principle of Transcendental Idealism yields important results with respect to scientific investigation.

Science is Morphology and Etiology. The former catalogues the kinds or sorts of things that populate the phenomenal world, while the latter discovers and articulates functional relations between successive states of such entities. If the world were *merely* phenomenal, *merely* representation, our interest, and in fact our powers, would end there. (In Chapter VII we shall see this as the source of Mach's "disillusionment" with the powers of science.) But:

> ... these pictures or images do not march by us strange and meaningless, as they would otherwise inevitably do, but speak to us directly, are understood, and acquire an interest that engrosses our whole nature. (*WWR* I, p. 95)

Schopenhauer's generalization upon the immediately intuited dual nature of the self entails that the world is *not* mere representation, and accordingly the Voluntaristic Thesis ought to serve as a ground for the etiological regularities of science. Such a ground will render these regularities—irreducible from the *scientific* point of view —comprehensible manifestations of the deeper nature of the world, but still as viewed through PSR.

The central argument of Book II involves a metaphysical analysis of the role of Space and Time as principles of individuation, abetting the move from empirical pluralism to transcendental monism. We might start with the question, To what do we owe the multiplicity or plurality of the homogeneous? Why are there many things of any given type or species? Here we must carefully distinguish the diversity of the homogeneous—the multitude of dogs or cabbages— from the logical plurality of qualitatively different things. Thus if there are many angels, for instance, I am brought to understand that they must all differ logically. We can represent to ourselves the concept of *many*, Schopenhauer argues, only via juxtaposition or succession—that is, only in Space and/or Time. Space and Time are accordingly the phenomenal *principia individuationis*, and only insofar as we think (as we must, of course) spatio-temporally can we conceive of a plurality of things of the same logical sort.[16] But as Space and Time represent determinations of things only insofar as they are possible objects of human experience—phenomena— plurality of the homogeneous must likewise be purely phenomenal. The world as *will*, therefore, must be wholly without plurality of that sort, although we shall see another sort of non-homogeneous plurality arise.

But the primordial stuff of the world can enter into human experience only insofar as it becomes *objectified*, that is, meets the minimum conditions for being an object of human experience. This process of objectification is partly due to the nature of the will, and partly due to the demands of human consciousness. On the side of nature can be distinguished different *grades* of objectification. The lowest grade at which the will becomes objectified is *matter*. Since the will is by definition active, each level of objectification will manifest a certain characteristic form of activity. At the level of matter, this activity is force, and the most basic force manifested by matter is *gravitation*. What precisely *is* gravitation? From the point of view of science, of the world as representation, we can only answer with Newton, "Hypotheses non fingo." Unless it can be reduced to another primitive force (which would then inherit the same status), gravity stands as *qualitas occulta*. The gravitational effects manifested by all material bodies are thus the irreducible characteristic property of one grade of objectified will. (Note that nothing has *as of yet* been explained; we have merely been asked to view a familiar phenomenon in a different light.) Each higher grade of objectification—vegetative, animal, finally human—will be char- acterized by properties irreducible to those at the lower levels; Schopenhauer's hierarchy of sciences is thus, in a non-temporal sense, *emergent*.

Since plurality at one level of objectification is merely phenom- enal, if we abstract from the transcendental conditions (Space and Time) only a single exemplar of each level of objectification remains. This archetype, freed from the conditions on human consciousness

---

[16] *WWR* I, pp. 112–13, and *OBM*, pp. 206–7. Compare to an extent with *CPR*, pp. 180–88. Since Schopenhauer rejects Kant's "method of abstraction," he cannot deal with the pure conditions of all discursive intelligences—the Categories—but only with their schematized forms.

(PSR) *and thus a thing in itself,* Schopenhauer identifies with the Platonic Idea.[17] Viewed apart from the demands of spatio-temporality, the Platonic Idea is necessarily singular. But seen phenomenally, in Space and Time, the result is a *species,* a group of entities with a common characteristic property. The characteristic natural laws which govern the members of this species, which hitherto appeared as mysterious occult connections between otherwise diverse events, turn out to be rather obvious consequences of the phenomenal nature of plurality. Schopenhauer writes:

> If we have grasped this, we shall see that this astonishment at the conformity to law and the accuracy of operation of a natural force, the complete sameness of all its millions of phenomena, and the infallibility of its appearance, is in fact like the astonishment of a child or a savage, who, looking for the first time at some flower through a multifaceted glass, marvels at the complete similarity of the innumerable flowers that he sees, and counts the leaves of each separately.[18]

It is crucial to notice that the relation of a given dog to the Platonic Idea of Doghood is not one of part to whole. The will, Schopenhauer insists, is fully and wholly present (at a given grade of objectification, of course) in every phenomenon of that grade.[19] This point will have crucial consequences for Schopenhauer's theory of art, and serve as an important nexus with Wittgenstein's thought.

Book II of *WWR* supplies a metaphysical explanation of natural laws, by examining the effects of the transcendental conditions, PSR, and therefore Space and Time, on the noumenal unity of the Platonic Idea. Schopenhauer now wants to examine the extent to which the world can be considered *apart* from PSR.

---

[17] Schopenhauer points out that the two greatest insights in the history of western metaphysics—Plato's Ideas and Kant's Things-in-themselves—turn out at bottom to be very nearly identical. "Now if for us the will is the *thing-in-itself* and the Idea is the immediate objectivity of that will at a given grade, then we find Kant's thing-in-itself and Plato's Idea . . .—those two great and obscure paradoxes of the two greatest philosophers of the west—to be, not exactly identical, yet very closely related . . ." *WWR* I, p. 170.

[18] *WWR* I, p. 134. What needs to be explained now becomes not the sameness of phenomena of a certain type but any *divergence* from the norm. We shall see this divergence increase as we move up through the hierarchy of levels of objectification, reaching its zenith with Man.

[19] Note the holistic, Platonic echo in Schopenhauer's claim: "All nature is akin, so that when a man has recalled a single piece of knowledge . . . there is no reason why he should not find out all the rest . . . " *Meno,* 81d.

The Platonic Idea and the Theory of Art

Book III of *WWR* I deals with the world as an object of experience, but viewed as much as possible in abstraction from the PSR. If Book II shows the phenomenal effects of the underlying reality, the will, then Book II sets out to move towards that reality, but *from the side of the object.* Book IV examines the subjective correlate of such a move.

An appreciation of the role of the Platonic Idea in Schopenhauer's theory of art turns on noticing his increasing divergence from Kant's usage of such central terms as 'phenomenon' and 'appearance'. By the end of Book II, these terms are more likely than not to be prefaced with the modifier 'mere', taking on very much the connotation of 'illusion'. *OBM* is quite explicit about this degradation of appearances. In characterizing plurality as transcendentally ideal, Schopenhauer writes:

> Accordingly if plurality and separateness belong only to *phenomenon*, and if it is one and the same essence which manifests itself in all living beings, then that conception that abolishes the difference between ego and non-ego is not erroneous, but on the contrary, the opposite conception [i.e. plurality] must be. We find also that this latter conception is described by the Hindus as *Maya*, i.e. *illusion, deception, phantasm, mirage.* (*OBM*, p. 209, my emphasis)

Such a strikingly un-Kantian identification of the phenomenal with the illusory will underlie a good number of the more dubious claims of Schopenhauer's moral philosophy, as well as the increasing ascendancy of art over science in his philosophy.

The Platonic Idea is a manifestation of the will, even an *immediate* manifestation, but it is not the will in itself. The Idea, being non-spatio-temporal, has a perfect unity. This unity differentiates an Idea from a *concept.* Schopenhauer, like Locke or Berkeley, sees concepts as representations arising from abstraction of experience. Since they arise through ignoring differences among members of a species and concentrating on similarities, the concept always contains *less* than any of the representations from which it arose. *Concepts are always poorer than intuitions.* But the Idea, since it is the archetype from which each of its exemplars arises, contains every property of each of them, and is *more complete* than any one of them.[20] Thus, *the Idea is richer than either intuition or concept.*

Although the Idea is free from determination by PSR, it is not totally free of the most general condition on experience, being object-for-a-subject.[21] Experience of the Platonic Idea (if it is possible) would be as close as possible to being simultaneously (a) an experience and (b) experience of the will in itself. Such an experience would thus be the closest we can come to the experience of reality. Is such experience of the Idea possible? Since the Idea is free from all plurality, Schopenhauer argues, awareness of such an object *is possible only through a corresponding change in the subject.* Only if we become, as it were, "pure subject" can we relate directly to the "pure object," the Platonic Idea. Schopenhauer's explanation of how such an experience is possible bears a close relation to Wittgenstein's theory of value, and examining it in some depth will repay the effort involved.

Knowledge for Schopenhauer is always the servant of the individual will. The human body (including the brain) is, like every other phenomenon, the will objectified at a certain level and is thus conditioned or determined by PSR. Human sense-organs, the brain, our limbs, and so forth mirror the importance of these parts in the functioning of the organism as objectified will. The essential activity of the will is mirrored in the urge towards self-preservation in any sentient organism. Knowledge can serve this goal only as *particular;* only when applied to *this* fire in front of me is the general belief that fire burns useful. Further, only as causally related to me are particular objects of pragmatic interest. The existence of a peach in India or Indiana helps my hunger not one bit, and this particular

---

[20] At first glance this seems paradoxical. Some dogs are black, some red, and we have a concept of Doghood only insofar as we ignore color. Thus our *concept* of doghood ignores color, and is less adequate than any of its instances. But if the Idea of Doghood is to be more adequate than any of its exemplars, it would seem to "contain" both blackness and redness.

Part of the air of paradox can be dispelled by remembering that the Idea of Doghood is not *itself* red, black, brown, etc. But at a deeper level, remember that logical principles like the Principle of Excluded Middle, being corollaries of the Second Form of PSR, apply only to phonomena. Cf. *FRSR*, pp. 161–62. Willingness to accept arguments like the above might well serve as a litmus test for one's metaphysical appetite.

[21] For Kant, the Pure Forms of Experience do not represent requirements on phenomena *in addition to* the general conditions of being object-for-a-subject. Rather, they are determinations or specifications of that more general condition. Thus, Schopenhauer's talk of a condition of being object-for-a-subject apart from such more specific conditions seems wrongheaded. Cf. *WWR* I, pp. 174–75.

snake is of interest to me only as *here*, within striking distance of me. Since such causal relations are necessarily spatio-temporal, my interest in particular objects can be maintained only if I view myself as individual and thus as spatio-temporal. The Idea, since it is *not* particular and bears no causal relations to me, conversely lacks pragmatic interest.

The possibility thus arises of overriding or bracketing the power of particular objects by eliminating one's own individuality, by rendering oneself as it were *self-less*. As Schopenhauer puts it, "Knowledge tears itself free of the service of the will precisely by the subjects ceasing to be merely individual." (*WWR* I, p. 178) Since a change on the side of the subject and on the side of the object are complementary, such a state of selflessness is produced by the very thing it is supposed to bring about, namely bracketing of the individuality of objects. "Thus we no longer consider the where, the why and the whither of things, but simply and solely the what." (*Ibid.*) The relation, which appears circular, is in reality reciprocal. If I see in my dog Heimer not a particular dog but a phenomenal representation of Doghood, then I have simultaneously ceased to see myself as a particular being in spatio-temporal, causal relations to other things. By ignoring Heimer's relation to my will, I have begun to approach the relation of pure subject to pure object.[22]

This state of pure-subject-confronting-pure-object, which Schopenhauer most intimately associates with the artistic experience, is characterized by the *immediate* and *intuitive* nature of the relation to the Idea. In this respect it is to be compared to (e.g.) *seeing* a typewriter rather than merely *thinking* about it through concepts. This is significant since concepts are always poorer than their associated intuitions, and conceptual knowledge hence always less adequate than intuitive knowledge. Now science gains its predictive power by dealing with the world solely through concepts and at the expense of thereby distancing itself from reality, dealing with the real only through representations of representations. Thus he holds that art is superior to science in the immediacy of its relation to its object. But in the artistic experience not only is the relation to the object *immediate*, but the object—the Platonic

---

[22] Schopenhauer attributes this idea to Spinoza: "The mind is eternal in so far as it conceives things from the standpoint of eternity *(sub aeternitis specie)*." (*Ibid.*, p. 179) The quote is from *Ethics*, Bk. V, Prop. 31, Scholium.

Idea—is of a higher grade of reality than either concept or phenomenal intuition. Consider: I have before me an apple. Viewed as an individual apple, my knowledge of it—that it can be eaten, baked into pies, etc.—is at the service of my individual and thus phenomenal will. But abstracted from its relation to my individual will, the apple appears not as individual but as a representation of the Platonic Idea of applehood. The individual apple has become, in Paul Tillich's fortunate phrase, "transparent." With its individuality disappears mine, leaving the relation between the self-less subject and the Platonic Idea. Schopenhauer can now offer the following definition of art: *"The way of considering things independently of the Principle of Sufficient Reason."* (*Ibid.*, p. 184)

The consequences of Schopenhauer's view that under certain circumstances we can have direct intuitive access to the noumenal now begin to surface. For an orthodox Kantian, any attempt to denigrate normal experience as "mere illusion" would meet with the questions, "Mere illusion as opposed to what? With what are you *contrasting* this alleged illusion?" Schopenhauer's contrast is with one's experience of oneself as a willing subject, and with the immediate relation to the Platonic Idea in the artistic experience. Such a possibility of experiencing directly—*not* merely knowing through inference—objects of a superior reality to those of ordinary experience accounts for the air of otherworldliness which permeates much of Schopenhauer's philosophy, giving it a flavor so different from Kant's.

There remains to be introduced one more central theme of Book III,[23] one which will not be fully developed until the final book. This theme is the relationship between the will and "suffering," a foreshadowing of the pessimism of the closing sections of *WWR* I. All willing, Schopenhauer argues, is teleological, end-directed, and implies a *deficiency*, or "suffering." Fulfillment of human desires in life may be rare and transient, but such a mere empirical claim is of

---

[23] This is not to say that Book III contains nothing else of interest to scholars of Wittgenstein. The discussion of light in section 38, reminiscent of Goethe's *Farbenlehre*, compares interestingly with Wittgenstein's own *Remarks on Color*, trans. McAlister and Schattle (University of California Press, Berkeley and LA, nd.). Further, Schopenhauer's architectural theories, in particular his distain for ornamentation, anticipating as they did the Bauhaus movement, probably had lasting influence on Wittgenstein and on the house which he and Paul Engelmann built for Wittgenstein's sister Mining on the Kundmanngasse in Vienna. See B. Leitner, *Wittgenstein's Architecture* (Nova Scotia College of Art and Design, Halifax, NS, 1973) and his "Wittgenstein's Architecture," *Art Forum*, 1970. The former contains many pictures of the house, subsequently destroyed.

no great philosophical significance. However, the essential active nature of the will necessitates that achievement of any goal must necessarily be succeeded by the positing of another. The will is by its very nature therefore damned to *perpetual* striving; this is *not* an empirical claim but the result of a metaphysical analysis of the will. The will's constant striving is a theme which arises in conjunction with the theory of art insofar as the will-less, disinterested nature of the state of pure perception offers temporary respite from the constant demands of the will. For Schopenhauer this respite is the root of the pleasure which we feel in aesthetic contemplation.

Morality and the Intelligible Subject

> On our reasoning then, whatever has virtue gets it by
> divine dispensation.
>
> —PLATO, *MENO* 100B
>
> Virtue is as little taught as genius. . . .
>
> —SCHOPENHAUER

Book III introduces the pure object, and as the reflexivity of subject and object would suggest, Book IV offers a treatment of the world as will from the point of view of the *subject*. Thus it treats of "practical philosophy," that is, ethics, although we shall find very little "practical" about Schopenhauer's moral theory. The problem he addresses is familiar in the Western philosophical tradition. The total determination of all phenomena by PSR entails that every phenomenal event follows with necessity from preceding events. Where then is there room in the world for any moral action? How does morality gain a foothold in a world of rigid causal determination?

Kant's solution to the Third Antinomy points out the consistency of phenomenal determinism and noumenal freedom, showing that the universal phenomenal validity of PSR does not therefore *entail* the impossibility of morality. (*CPR*, pp. 409–14) Although Schopenhauer's criticism of Kant's ethics is often scathing (and, I might add, misguided) he admits Kant's distinction between phenomena and noumena as the key to the problem of freedom and determinism.[24] On the other hand, he rejects the central Kantian claim that moral

---

[24] ". . . Kant's greatest and most brilliant merit in the service of ethics . . . consists in the doctrine of the coexistence of freedom and necessity." (*OBM*, p. 107) "I regard Kant's doctrine of the coexistence of freedom and necessity as the greatest of all achievements of the human mind." (*Ibid.*, p. 111)

worth is ascribable to actions only insofar as their motive is duty. But any ethical principle demands, Schopenhauer claims, metaphysical support: "Metaphysics must come first, and without it there can be no moral philosophy at all." (*OBM*, p. 40) Further the metaphysics of nature, the good, and the beautiful presuppose and mutually support one another. (*Ibid.*, p. 41) Let us begin, then, with an examination of the metaphysical foundations of Schopenhauer's moral philosophy (presented most clearly in *OBM*) in order to fully appreciate the central themes of Book IV.

Schopenhauer's method in *OBM* is analytic; beginning with a class of actions of generally agreed moral worth, he isolates their characteristic shared property.[25] The foundations of morality (as opposed to the philosophical ground of that foundation) cannot be some abstract principle, since even the "coarsest person" often acts in a morally praiseworthy manner. In any case, an abstract principle could never immediately act as a *motive*, moving men to action. Schopenhauer then suggests a radical break with the western philosophical tradition. "I shall probably be told," he writes, "that ethics is not concerned with how people actually behave, but that it is the science which states how they *ought* to behave." (*Ibid.*, p. 130) This he rejects. The concept "ought" has applicability only in the context of *theological* morality; the imperative form, so central in orthodox Kantian ethical theory, has no place in morality at all:

> A commanding voice, whether it comes from within or from without, cannot possibly be imagined except as threatening or promising. (*Ibid.*, p. 55)

Since an act whose motive is a threat or promise—the possibility of reward or punishment—is done through self-interest, no action issuing from such an "ought" can have moral import. Thus *obligation* cannot serve as the basis of ethics.

What then is the mark of an ethical action? Let us approach this question by asking the characteristic property of *non-moral* or *antimoral* actions. In these cases the ground is always *egoism;* they are actions designed to advance my well-being without regard for the

---

[25] That there *is* such a class of generally recognized moral actions Schopenhauer does not debate; in general he has little sympathy and less patience with scepticism. Like Plato, he would see Thrasymachus as simultaneously unanswerable and not worthy of an answer. Cf. *OBM*, #13.

well-being of others.[26] Such egoism has strong psychological roots, evidenced by the philosophical attractiveness of the Hobbesian state of nature—"the war of all against all"—as a picture of man's natural state. But egoism, with its emphasis on the individual, is possible only on the phenomenal level. Is there another motive? Egoism can be construed as the attempt to assert my will over others.[27] Is there some other motive which can counter the deeply ingrained tendency towards egoism?

If there is, its characteristic would be its direction towards the "weal and woe" of others, rather than towards myself. Now my weal and woe can move me to action insofar as they are present to me as representations. But since I am not him, another's weal and woe can be present to me only abstractly, as a concept.[28] This further motive must be something found immediately in *my* consciousness, and if it is to overcome the effects of egoism, it must be powerful indeed. Schopenhauer finds such a motive in *compassion*, that phenomenon wherein the sufferings of others are made painful to *me*. An action is accordingly moral to the extent that it springs from compassion; presumably Schopenhauer would agree with Kant that there has probably never in the history of the world been a *purely* moral action, one whose *sole* motive was compassion, with no admixture of self-interest.

The existence of this phenomenon of compassion is curious. A *natural* phenomenon, not socially inculcated,

> ... [compassion is] an undeniable fact of human consciousness, is essential to it and thus does not depend upon presuppositions, concepts, religions, dogmas, myths, training and education ... it is original and immediate ... (*OBM*, p. 148)

Further, it cannot be analyzed psychologically as derivative on some other psychological state. In particular, it is *not* a perversion of

---

[26] Schopenhauer thus has little sympathy for Eudaemonism, with its emphasis on self-improvement aimed at happiness through a life of reason. One positive effect of Kant's moral philosophy, he claims, is to purge philosophy of this mistaken view. Cf. *OBM*, #13.

[27] I will for the moment ignore another, more extreme source of immoral actions, namely *malice*. Worse than ignoring the consequences of my actions, malice consists of taking positive pleasure in another's suffering, whether my well-being is advanced or not. Compare: a *genuine* Red Sox fan is one who would rather see the Yankees lose than the Sox win.

[28] Note Schopenhauer's tacit Humean assumption that perceptions differ from concepts in their "strength and vivacity," their ability to bring about action. Thus he presents a problem for any abstract theory of ethics; concepts cannot act as motives to move the will.

egoism, where I confuse the sufferer with *myself.* "We suffer *with* him and *through* him; we feel his pain as *his,* and do not confound it with our own." (*OBM,* pp. 147–48) How is such a phenomenon possible?

Like explanation of the existence of etiological regularities, we must seek a ground for compassion in the realm of meta-physics. But a preliminary exposition of Schopenhauer's notion of *character* must precede that metaphysical explanation. Consider this puzzle: if compassion is an "original and immediate" facet of human consciousness, how does it come about that there are ego-istic actions at all? If compassion is an "undeniable fact" of human consciousness, how does it happen that people act in reprehensible ways? For Schopenhauer, human behavior is due to a conflux of two different sorts of factors. The first is the presence or absence of motives. But two people, in externally identical situa-tions and confronted with the same motives, often act in different ways. The motives themselves, then, do not completely determine one's action, but only in combination with *what sort of thing one is.* Just as natural causation involves both an etiological and a morphological factor (magnetic fields influence steel balls but not watermelons), there is in human causation an analogous morphological factor. This facet of the agent, which Schopenhauer calls *character,* is the propensity to be affected by motives in a given way.

We can distinguish *empirical* from *intelligible* character. The empirical character is defined behaviorally in terms of exhibited patterns of behavior: John is vain if he pouts when Mary wins the hammer-throw, blows his own horn frequently, etc. But we have seen that people often act in different ways under the same circum-stances, and so this empirical character must be the phenomenal manifestation of some deeper reality. For Schopenhauer, the propen-sity of some people to perform bad acts and others good acts under the same circumstances is precisely parallel to the propensity of lodestones to attract iron filings but not lambs or cabbages. But a certain person will have a propensity towards goodness, and act in morally laudable ways, under a very wide variety of circumstances. We thus must answer two questions: from whence comes the *consistency* in the actions of any given person, and from whence comes the consistent *difference* between individuals? In answering either, we must leave the realm of ethics proper and enter metaphysics.[29]

"People exhibit empirical characters" means only that human behavior is lawlike, and the explanation of the lawlike nature of human behavior will be parallel to that of the behavior of lower entities. Since the constancy is phenomenal, it is explainable as the pluralizing of some non-phenomenal form of the will, objectified at a certain level. That noumenal entity Schopenhauer calls the *intelligible character*.[30]

> Just as everything in nature has its forces and qualities that definitely react to a definite impression and constitute its character, so man has his *character*, from which motives call forth his actions with necessity. In this way of acting his empirical character reveals itself, [as a disposition is revealed by its occurrences], but in this again is revealed his intelligible character, i.e. the will itself, of which he is determined phenomenon. (*WWR* I, p. 287)

Since it resides outside space and time, this intelligible character must be unalterable and unchangeable, indivisible and permanent.

> If, under the same conditions, a man could now act in one way, now in another, then in the meantime his will would have to have changed, and thus would have to reside in time, for only in time is change possible. But then either the will would have to be mere phenomenon, or time would have to be a determination of the thing in itself. (*Ibid.*, pp. 291–92)

The conclusion of this enthymeme is obvious:

> .. the intelligible character of every man is to be regarded as an act of the will outside time, and thus as indivisible and unalterable.[31]

---

[29] But keep in mind that just as the metaphysics of science do not invalidate or make redundant scientific investigation, so the metaphysics of morals does not supercede morality proper, but complements it. Our investigations into the ground of moral judgment can no more invalidate ordinary judgments of good and bad as the philosopher of science can invalidate the principles of physics.

[30] The term is Kant's; Cf. *Critique of Judgment*, #46–47.

[31] *WWR* I, p. 289. For a striking contrasting discussion of this claim by a philosopher of quite different proclivities, cf. Copleston *op. cit.*, pp. 155 ff. Note the underlying premise, so central to Wittgenstein's atomism: Change is rearrangement of parts. Parts are possible only in Space and Time, so the non-temporal, non-spatial can have no parts. Thus, the non-spatio-temporal must be unchangeable and sempeternal. For a classic exposition of this theme, see the opening passages of Leibniz's *Monadology*, as well as the Cartesian passages cited in Chapter III section 1.

The intelligible character as noumenal correlate of the empirical character explains the lawlikeness of human behavior, but it does not yet fully explain the difference in behavior of different people under the same circumstances. Why do some people consistently act in immoral ways, others in moral? Since Schopenhauer is committed to the view that behavior is wholly determined by the interaction of character and motive—indeed in order for man to be part of the world this *must* be the case—only one avenue is open to him; *some intelligible characters must be good, others bad.*[32] We have accordingly found a deeper ground for an inclination towards compassion or malice. Schopenhauer is quick to grasp the radical implications of this move, which he sees foreshadowed in the work of his predecessors, in particular in a vague way in the Calvinistic doctrine of predestination. (Cf. *WWR* I, pp. 292ff.) Chief among these is that since every human action is necessitated by the combination of externally dictated motive and unalterable intelligible character, moral exhortation, as normally construed, is pointless, and in the most favored sense to say of a man that "He could have done otherwise" is always false.[33]

Yet moral judgment is not wholly excluded from the totally determined world of human phenomenon. We can still justifiably classify actions as good or bad.

> Where are guilt and merit to be found? . . . In accordance with [the Kantian doctrine of the coexistence of freedom and necessity], the *operari* (what we do) is absolutely necessary when the motives make their appearance; and therefore *freedom*, which proclaims itself alone through *responsibility*, can be found only in the *esse* (what we are). It is true that the reproaches of conscience primarily and ostensibly concern what we *have done*, but really and ultimately what we are . . . . (*OBM*, p. 195)

---

[32] While solving the problem of differing reactions to the same stimuli, the division of intelligible characters into good and bad raises a serious difficulty for Schopenhauer. The Platonic Idea represents a prototype of a certain morphological type. Acids and Alkalis, for instance, must have different Ideas since they act in significantly different ways. But what of the good man and the bad man? Do they represent instances of two *different* Ideas? (Are good and bad men different *species?*) If so, why do we call them both *men*? Or does each of us have our *own* Platonic Idea, and if so, is there then some "super-Idea" which subsumes all of *those* Ideas? Such difficulties may be what Copleston has in mind when he writes "Impersonal monism cannot possibly account for individual personality and all attempts to do so must necessarily fail." (*Op. cit.*, p. 212)

[33] It does not follow that we cannot alter people's behavior. The state can do so by providing counter-motives—threats and rewards. But an action issuing from such motives is clearly not *moral*, and although the state can alter what we *do* it cannot alter what we *will*. Political considerations are therefore irrelevant to morality. Cf. *OBM*, p. 194, and compare with the discussion of "eternal justice" below in ch. X.

Note that the object of our moral judgment is not transient and temporary, but something necessary and permanent. Our moral intuitions may still balk at blaming someone for something that could not have been otherwise (unless, as Schopenhauer rather evasively points out, we consider the sense in which he could have been a *different man*[34]) but once the role of morality qua exhorter to virtue is rejected, this is less puzzling. But in any case, Schopenhauer has achieved his major objective, namely to show how it is possible to assign blame and praise in the phenomenal realm.

All that remains is to show the metaphysical root for the phenomena of compassion. Since all good men, at the very least, share a species-unity in the Platonic Idea of the Good Man, compassion arises precisely insofar as I see the suffering of others to be, on the transphenomenal level, *my* suffering. As Schopenhauer puts it, "the veil of Maya has become transparent for the person who performs works of love ..." (*WWR* I, p. 373)

> ... [H]e shows by his way of acting that he *again recognizes* his inner being, namely the will-to-live as thing-in-itself, in the phenomenon of another given to him merely as representation ... To this extent he treats the inner being outside himself [i.e. in another] like himself; he does not injure it. (*Ibid.*, p. 370)

Note that this is emphatically *not the same as mistaking his phenomenal suffering for mine.* As we shall see in chapter X, there is both a striking parallel and a vast gulf between these notions and Wittgenstein's moral thinking.

Denial of the Will-to-Live

Having now discovered the metaphysical ground for the notion of compassion in the good intelligible character, let us graft this moral insight to the larger theme of the Janus-faced nature of the world. By examining what might be called Schopenhauer's "Tran-

---

[34] "Freedom appertains not to the empirical character but only to the intelligible ... everything that [a man] does is necessarily determined from without by motives and from within by character. In *esse* (what he is), however, the freedom lies. He could have been a different man, and guilt and merit lie in what he *is*." *OBM*, p. 112. Compare with the long quote from Porphyry which Schopenhauer approvingly quotes on pp. 113–15.

scendental Deduction of the Concept of Misery," some consequences of knowledge of the nature of the world as will become evident.

Every phenomenon is at bottom will, objectified at a certain level and pluralized by PSR. But as will, each of these phenomena is essentially active or dynamic. In man, the highest of the phenomena, this activity takes the guise of what Schopenhauer calls the "will-to-live," and involves a kind of striving he terms *affirmation*. For example, if I want an apple, I take steps towards acquiring one; those actions represent the will affirming itself with respect to that modest goal. The most general form of human affirmation is the instinct drive for self-preservation. The deeply ingrained status of this drive gives egoism its *prima facie* credibility, making the existence of compassion seem so remarkable. But this human self-affirmation is expectably only a specific example of a much more general phenomenon, exemplified by the falling of stones, reaction of acids with bases and so forth. In humans the range of possible actions is much wider than even the highest sentient entities, since *abstract* motives bring to human life the dimension of *time*. Only humans, for instance, can fear some *non-present* event.[35] The direction of affirmation of the will-to-live in humans is thus affected by *knowledge*.

These considerations serve as preface to the best-known (and most exaggerated) feature of Schopenhauer's philosophy. Although he revels in supplying seemingly endless examples of human misery (cf. *WWR* I, sect. 59), his pessimism in fact is not empirical but rather follows as a consequence from the nature of the will and from its identification with noumenal reality.[36] Let's examine this argument, which appears in section 58 of *WWR* I.

All willing is goal-directed or teleological, and clearly many goals are reached or reachable. But the very *nature* of the will is to strive; "It always strives, since striving is its sole nature, to which no

---

[35] On this ground Schopenhauer criticizes the Buddhist's failure to take into account the vastly different capacity for suffering in humans and animals, most of which is due to our capacity for abstract representations. Cf. *WWR* I, p. 298. "One can imagine an animal angry, frightened, happy, unhappy, startled. But hopeful? And why not? A dog believes that his master is at the door. But can he also believe that his master will come the day after tomorrow ... ?" (*PI*, p. 174)

[36] Copleston quotes Pirandello: "I think that life is a very sad piece of buffoonery," adding "... these words might have been uttered by a disciple of Schopenhauer, not simply because his own observation has taught him to consider them true, but on a priori and metaphysical grounds." (*Op. cit.*, p. 75)

attained goal can put an end." (*WWR* I, p. 308) The final clause is crucial; no meaning can be attached to the notion of a *final* goal, a Teilhardtian Omega. This can be seen in the simple case of moving bodies, where the constant gravitational attraction does not cease even when the bodies are in contact. Schopenhauer's world-view is thus Newtonian; motion is not, as it was for Aristotle, something forced and unnatural, but motion and rest share a Galilean natural equality. But while the Newtonian universe is not *necessarily* dynamic, Schopenhauer's is. His world is a restless, striving, roiling mass, governed by the appropriate forms of PSR.

Man as part of the natural world shares in this constant striving. In fact, there is a sense in which he is *less free* than dogs or cabbages, since he is bound by more forms of PSR.

> What gives force to this command [of the will] is just that the body is nothing but the objectified will-to-live itself. Man, as the most complete objectification of this will, is accordingly the most necessitous of beings. He is concrete willing through and through; he is a concretion of a thousand wants and needs. (*WWR* I, p. 312)

All willing being end-directed, every action allows of two possible outcomes; either the goal is reached or it is not. The former case represents a *satisfaction*, Schopenhauer's usage of this term being broadened in a manner analogous to 'will'. Every striving is motivated by some lack or dearth—I do not seek an apple, for instance, unless I see a certain incompleteness in my present state. But in that case, a satisfaction becomes a *merely negative achievement*, the "end to an evil."[37] The goal is reached, the satisfaction shows itself as merely negative, and the will, expressing its nature, pushes onwards without even temporary respite from having achieved this goal. Thus, *satisfaction is logically self-negating*.

On the other hand, I may encounter some obstacle placed between me and my goal, thus experiencing what Schopenhauer calls *suffering*. The major theme of Book IV is that life involves suffering, not accidentally or intermittently, but *necessarily*. Further, knowledge of the phenomenal world—including scientific knowledge—can do no more than accelerate the rate at which meaning-

---

[37] *WWR* I, p. 375. Schopenhauer's argument here and elsewhere turns on the phenomenologically dubious claim that pain is positive and direct, while happiness is negative, the *absence* of suffering. Cf. *OBM*, pp. 147–48.

less, temporary goals are reached. Fortunately, for Schopenhauer there is another sort of knowledge which is *not* in the will's service, and which can thus serve as "quieter of the will." We have already seen the aesthetic state of pure perception mentioned in this context, and examination of the sort of knowledge appropriate to that state provides the nexus between ethics and aesthetics.

Our discussion of art disclosed two rather different modes through which knowledge can affect the will. In its most determinate objectification, the phenomenal human being, the will uses knowledge as its servant. Knowledge in service of the will is always knowledge of *particular, spatio-temporal,* and thus *causal* relations; even scientific knowledge is of interest to the will only through specific applications to the particular. There is, however, another mode of knowledge, neither confined to the particular like empirical knowledge nor exiled to the abstract like scientific knowledge. The subjective side of this knowledge is the artistic experience, the object of which is the Platonic Idea, and through such knowledge the will is freed from its bondage to the particular. Paradoxical as it seems, the artistic experience, the state of pure perception, *thus represents a conscious denial of the will as individual by the will itself.* Through such a state of pure perception we deliberately place ourselves outside the scope of PSR, conceiving of ourselves as members of the intelligible world and accordingly as *free,* as members of a Kantian realm of ends.

Schopenhauer believes that such respite from the demands of the will must be more or less temporary, although I see no *logical* ground why this must be the case. But we can envision a more permanent denial of the will-to-live in what might be called an *ethical,* as opposed to *aesthetic,* transcendence of the will-to-live. We might characterize such ethical transcendence by contrasting it with the empirical denial of one motive or another. Suppose I want to go to the movies tonight, but have foresworn movies for Lent. In this case, one (empirical) motive has merely been replaced with another, and the active agent is still the individual will. So any *real,* philosophically significant transcendence of the will cannot take place at the level of the individual, and thus in the world of Space and Time.

Like aesthetic experience, where we "see through" the art object to perceive the Platonic Idea which represents the reality behind it, ethical transcendence must lead us to the selfless state of pure perception. But when this pure perception is turned inwards, it yields *pure self-knowledge*, wholly adequate, immediate knowledge of the intelligible character. Since man represents the highest objectification of the will, pure self-knowledge represents the highest possible form of knowledge, *immediate* (intuitive) yet of an object of the highest reality. One manifestation of this state of pure perception is that the barriers between individuals will disappear, and we shall see the true roots for the phenomenon of compassion.

Denial of the will-to-live is thus the closest that humans can come to an ethical life. A first prerequisite of the ethical life is knowledge of the Ideas:

> If the will in itself exists, it cannot, as that which alone is metaphysical or the thing-in-itself, be broken by any force, but that force can destroy only its phenomenon in such a place and such a time. The will itself cannot be broken by anything except *knowledge*. (*WWR* I, p. 400)

However, knowledge of the Ideas is necessary but not sufficient for seeing through the "veil of Maya." Since every real act of the will is also some bodily change, knowledge can only be effective insofar as it too brings about such concrete changes:

> As the knowledge from which results denial of the will is intuitive and not abstract, it finds its complete expression not in abstract concepts, but only in deed and conduct.[38]

Thus, rejection of the will-to-live must begin with rejection of the body, including most importantly the rejection of sexual pleasures, since these represent the most immediate and strongest demands of the will-to-live. This is followed by a thorough-going asceticism, including voluntary poverty and perhaps even worldly suffering. But one who has seen through the Veil of Maya will see such suffering as inconsequential, compensated by the tranquility brought on by the quieting of the will. Likewise, death will not be feared, since the individual life which is lost represents nothing but illusion, and the intelligible character, which is outside space and time, is not affected. (E.g. *WWR* I, pp. 378–83.)

---

[38] *Op. cit.*, p. 384.

Such recommendations Schopenhauer does not see as radical or even unusual; they are manifest in Christianity and to the highest degree in Sanskrit writings (*ibid.*, pp. 384–98), although those sources suffer insofar as these views are advanced dogmatically or with mythical reasons. However,

> Different as were the dogmas that were impressed on their faculty of reason, the inner, direct, and intuitive knowledge from which all virtue and holiness can come is nevertheless expressed in precisely the same way in the conduct of life.[39]

We can thus bring about nothing through concepts that the ordinary man does not know through intuition, and the philosopher can explain but not alter our moral intuitions. (*Ibid.*, p. 383, *OBM*, p. 76)

Two points must be emphasized. First, the unity of the ethical with the aesthetic must to be stressed. Each focuses on the two sides—pure subject and pure object—of the state of pure perception. If the ethical is superior to the aesthetic, it is only because pure self-consciousness emphasizes the characteristic apperceptive feature of the highest level of the objectification of the will. Second, Schopenhauer's analysis renders suicide pointless, since it represents a rejection not of the will in general but *this particular will.* Suicide glorifies individual life by dramatizing in an ultimate way one's distain for *that individual life which one has,* and accordingly represents the ultimate affirmation of the individual. In that sense it is indeed the "primal sin." Each of these points will find striking parallels in the *Tractatus.*

We now have in outline the program of Schopenhauer's Voluntaristic Transcendental Idealism which was presented to the young Wittgenstein, and which he found, in Anscombe's words, "fundamentally right, if only a few adjustments and clarifications were made." We have evidence that it was the influence of Frege and Hertz which instigated these "adjustments and clarifications"; the effects run deep into Wittgenstein's philosophy. In the next chapter we will see the first step in the purification of Schopenhauer's system from the

---

[39] *Ibid.*, p. 383. Compare with *OBM*, sect. 19, where Schopenhauer presents as a preliminary puzzle that we all seem to agree more or less on the worth of actions, even though we offer greatly different (philosophical) analyses of *why* they are wrong. Compare with Moore, *Principia Ethica* (Cambridge U. Press, Cambridge, 1960), ch. I.

inconsistencies and confusions which the young Wittgenstein recognized. Thus in chapter III we will examine Frege's logical realism, and its effects on the picture of the world which we have seen. This will be the first step towards eliminating the epistemological version, at least, of "the world as representation."

III

Realism and Psychologism in Nineteenth-Century Logic

> If I remember rightly, Wittgenstein told me that he had read
> Schopenhauer's *Die Welt als Wille und Vorstellung* in his
> youth and that his first philosophy was a Schopenhauerian
> epistemological idealism. Of how this was related to his
> interest in logic and mathematics I know nothing, except that
> I remember him saying that it was Frege's conceptual
> realism which made him abandon his early idealistic views.
>
> —G. H. VON WRIGHT

Grafted onto the beginning of Plato's *Republic* is a short
dialogue, rather different in texture from the rest of the work, in
which Socrates engages in a discussion of the question "What is
justice?" Chief among the other characters is Thrasymachus, who
advances the thesis that justice is that which lies in the interests of
the strongest. Thracymachus's claim is ambiguous, but subsequent
discussion clarifies that he intended to say that whatever the
strongest believe or say is in their interests is just; their believing it
to be so makes it so, much in the manner that the umpire's saying
"You're out" *makes* you out. Thus Thrasymachus represents the
anthropocentric position that justice is relative to the wants or
beliefs of human beings, or some subclass of human beings.

Plato opens with the Thrasymachus dialogue for a number of
reasons, both dramatic and philosophical, but the position which
Thrasymachus defends is not idiosyncratic (indeed, Glaucon presents a parallel if less robust view later in the *Republic*), but
represents a vigorous strain in Hellenistic thought, centered philosophically on the Sophists. These fifth- and early fourth-century B.C.
thinkers—Protagorus, Hippias of Elia, Prodicus, and the real-life
Thrasymachus—taught the art of eristic rhetoric while holding
anthropocentric, relativistic positions concerning knowledge and
reality. In particular, they denied objectivity to the common distinctions between valid as opposed to merely convincing arguments,

knowledge and mere belief, reality and appearance, and the good and what is desired.

A good deal of Plato's philosophical energies go into discrediting the Sophists, he characteristically portraying them in unattractive terms. They possess, he argues, "a sort of reputed and apparent knowledge of all subjects, but not in reality." (*Sophist* 233c) Parallel to Plato's arguments run those of a long line of thinkers, beginning with Aristotle and Aquinas,[1] each of who embrace some form of *realism*. We shall preliminarily define realism as the position that such notions as goodness, validity, reality, and truth have objective meaning which cannot be analyzed in terms of human choices, desires, or beliefs.

The Platonic characterization and subsequent vilification of Sophism is of course not wholly even-handed. It is significant that Sophism embodies a recurring theme in western thought, occurring again and again, articulated in new form to conform with the dominant intellectual strains of a particular time. In this chapter we shall be centrally concerned with a form of relativism which dominated certain influential schools of philosophy in the nineteenth century, and which finds one embodiment in a thesis called *psychologism*,[2] which is roughly the thesis that the meanings of words are mental entities. We shall be here interested in a somewhat narrower application of this general thesis, and for the time being I will restrict the term 'psychologism' to the view that the laws of logic are general psychological principles concerning the workings of the human mind, wholly empirical in character, and thus a posteriori and contingent. (In chapter X below we shall have occasion to investigate psychologism of a rather different sort, namely a sociological or psychological analysis of ethics.) To this I will contrast an analogously narrowed version of realism, holding that logical laws describe objective, necessary connections between abstract entities.

In this chapter I will concentrate mainly on the psychologism of

---

[1] For Plato, cf. for instance *Theatetus*, 170c–171c, for Aristotle, *Metaphysics* IV, ch. 5–8, for Aquinas, *Summa Theologica* I, Q. II Art. I Obj. 3. The following passage by John Wild hints at the vehemence which often heats these criticisms: "[The Sophist] is essentially an idol-maker. Instead of images, directed outward and proportioned to the real paradigm, he fashions idols, directed towards himself, and proportioned to his own perspective and faculties." "Husserl's Critique of Psychologism" in M. Farber, ed., *Philosophical Essays in Memory of Edmund Husserl* (Greenwood Press, New York, 1968), p. 20.

[2] For a brief discussion of a broader sort of psychologism, see Nicola Abbanano's article "Psychologism" in P. Edwards, ed., *The Encyclopedia of Philosophy* (Macmillan, New York, 1967), vol. 6, pp. 520–21.

J. S. Mill and George Boole; I will mention other thinkers—Husserl or Sigwart—only occasionally. I will then present Frege's reaction to psychologism,[3] outline the realistic theory which results from his considerations, and then widen the focus to examine the more comprehensive realism of Russell and Moore which seems a natural consequence of logical realism.

The Historical and Philosophical Grounds of Psychologism

> Of all things, the measure is man: of existing things, that
> they exist; of nonexisting things, that they do not exist.
>
> —PROTAGORAS

The term 'psychologism' first appeared in Germany in the first half of the nineteenth century, applied to the anti-Hegelian positions of Fries and Beneke. The term is ambiguous, allowing of stronger and weaker interpretations; often a single author will equivocate between the importantly different senses. Weak psychologism claims that logical principles are inherent in the laws of mind, and uncoverable by psychological methods, the stronger version that logic is literally a branch of psychology.[4] In what follows I will restrict my comments to strong psychologism. Nearly every psychologistic argument starts in the same manner; philosophy must be based wholly on psychol-

---

[3] Unfortunately, lack of space forces me to only occasionally bring into play Husserl's considerable contributions to the demise of psychologism, and also to examine the vigorous tradition of American Realism.

For Husserl, the reader might begin with his early psychologism, represented by the *Philosophy of Arithmetic* (1891). Tradition has it that he was roused from his dogmatic slumbers by Frege's review of that work—an English translation is reprinted in Elliston and McCormick, eds., *Husserl: Expositions and Appraisals* (Notre Dame Press, Notre Dame, IN, 1982), pp. 314–24. J. N. Mohanty argues with some effect that this influence was minimal; cf. his *Husserl and Frege* (Indiana U. Press, Bloomington, IN, 1982), ch. 1. This volume also contains as an appendix interesting correspondence between Frege and Husserl. Husserl's own comprehensive critique of psychologism is contained in the "Prolegomena to Pure Logic," which constitutes volume I of his *Logical Investigations* (1900), trans. J. N. Findlay (Routledge and Kegan Paul, London, 1970), while shorter pieces of the same temper are collected in McCormick and Elliston, eds., *Husserl: Shorter Works* (U. of Notre Dame Press, Notre Dame, IN, 1981), pp. 83–158. Finally, an interesting non-technical exposition of Husserl's critique of psychologism is found in the Kolakowski lectures cited in footnote 9 below.

For a brief introduction to the American Realists, see E. B. Holt et al., "Introduction to the New Realism," in R. M. Chisholm, ed., *Realism and the Background to Phenomenology* (Ridgeview Publishing, Atascadero, CA, 1960), pp. 151–85.

[4] Cf. Mohanty, *op. cit.*, p. 20. For a look at some weaker and perhaps more defensible forms of psychologism, see S. Haack, *The Philosophy of Logics* (Cambridge U. Press, Cambridge, 1978), pp. 238–42.

ogy, since its only data is that gained through self-examination. But psychologism has much deeper roots in two rather different philosophical movements. On one hand, German psychologism results in part at least from a corruption of the Kantian Critical Philosophy; for instance, Christoph Sigwart's psychologistic *Logic* represents itself as Kantian and Critical.[5] On the other, psychologism found fertile soil in the antipathy towards abstract entities central to British Empiricism. Psychologism thus serves as a sort of nexus between the empiricists and at least one central strain of neo-Kantianism. But the tendency of both schools marks the intellectual undercurrent of the times; the explosion of scientific knowledge in the nineteenth century made the possibility of grounding logic in some kind of scientific psychology very appealing.

Logic, Kant claims, can be characterized as "the science of the rules of the understanding in general" (*CPR*, p. 93). Within logic we can distinguish general from special logic, the former comprising "the absolutely necessary rules of thought without which there can be no employment whatsoever of the understanding" *(ibid.)*, while the latter involves application of logic to particular subjects. General logic can be further subdivided into pure logic and applied logic, and it is in his discussion of pure logic that Kant offers the following evaluation of psychologism:

> General logic is called applied, when it is directed to the rules of the employment of the understanding under the *subjective empirical conditions dealt with by psychology*. Applied logic has therefore empirical principles.... Consequently it is neither a canon of the understanding, nor an organon of the special sciences, but merely a cathartic of the common understanding.
>
> As pure logic, [logic] has nothing to do with empirical principles, and does not, as sometimes has been supposed, borrow anything from psychology ...[6]

Pure general logic thus abstracts from all *contents* of knowledge and is wholly a priori, dealing only with the formal conditions of thought. There is, however, for Kant another sort of pure logic, one which prior to his "Copernican Revolution in Philosophy" had escaped

---

[5] C. Sigwart, *Logic*, trans. H. Dendy, (Swan Sonnenschein, London, 1895), introduction and *passim*.

[6] *Ibid.*, p. 94–95, my emphasis. Compare with Husserl, *Logical Investigations*, trans. J. N. Findlay (Routledge and Kegan Paul, London, 1970), pp. 214–15. (Hereafter abbreviated *LI*.)

notice. Our concept of an object in general has two components, one empirical and a posteriori, the other pure and a priori.[7] Given this a priori element, there emerges the possibility of a logic which is simultaneously a priori, and thus universal and necessary, yet which still (since it deals with objects) retains some content. Kant calls this *Transcendental Logic*: it might be termed the logic of the pure object.

Transcendental Logic, like Transcendental Aesthetic—the a priori study of space and time—represents conditions which, although they apply to every possible object of human experience (although *only* to such objects of human experience) have their ground in the transcendental constitution of any rational being. They are therefore not "subjective" in the sense of being idiosyncratic to this or that human mind. However, if we allow the distinction between appearances and things in themselves to collapse, transcendental logic begins to take on the character of the purely subjective, appearing as a set of very general psychological laws. Post-Kantian psychologism thus arises from a misunderstanding of the role of objectivity in the Critical Philosophy. This slip is particularly easy for a philosopher like Schopenhauer, who adheres to the Lockian view that all concepts arise from experience, and who in general tends to conflate the phenomenal with the *illusory*. Perhaps it is a natural misinterpretation of Kant; Frege writes:

> It is because Kant associated [both subjective and objective] meanings with the word ['idea', *'Vorstellung'*] that his doctrine assumed such a very subjective, idealist complexion, and his true view was made so hard to discover. The distinction here drawn [between concept and idea] stands or falls with that between psychology and logic.[8]

This tendency to conflate subjective and transcendental senses of words like *'Vorstellung'*, and the subsequent psychologization of logic, was reinforced by the "scientism" of the nineteenth century. Kolakowski writes:

> In giving up the tradition of German Idealism, philosophy gives up its independence from the sciences. It started regarding itself either as a

---

[7] Compare with Descartes' "ball of wax experiment" in *HR* I, pp. 154–55, and Hume, *op. cit.*, I/iv/2.

[8] I shall refer to J. L. Austin's elegant translation hereafter; G. Frege, *The Foundations of Arithmetic*, trans. J. L. Austin (Northwestern U. Press, Evanston, IL, 1974).

synthesis of the sciences or as a psychological analysis. Even the new variants of Kantianism shifted to the psychological standpoint, and explained the Kantian *a priori* not as a set of transcendental conditions on knowledge (valid for any rational being) but as specific qualities of the human psyche, and this led fatefully to generic relativism.[9]

The ascendance of philosophical interest in the science of man, pioneered a century earlier by Hume, was reinforced by the rapid progress of the generic sciences—biology, psychology, anthropology—which constantly emphasized the *relativity* of their data. Kolakowski writes of this situation:

> On [the view of the nineteenth-century German empiricists] the questions of Descartes, Locke and Kant turned out to be wrongly formulated. Cognitive activity was supposed to reveal its real, biologically determined sense. Cognition is a certain kind of behavior in the human organism, and its function is restoring the equilibrium that is constantly disturbed by stimuli from the environment. The predicates "True" and "False" are not found in experience . . . They belong to the human interpretation of experience. (*Op. cit.*, p. 156)

Certain much more general social factors made such attitudes seem plausible.[10] But although the prevailing intellectual currents offered a critique of absolutism somewhat equivocal support, even for liberals the ensuing relativity must have been giddy and unnerving. Probing as they did the alleged absolute foundations of society, liberals were led to ask: If the laws of man and society, morality and politics are not grounded in immutable divine law, then where *do* they find such a ground? One terrifying option is that they have *no good grounding at all*, that they are wholly arbitrary. (This specter of relativism is what bothers Glaucon, who in the opening passages of the second part of the *Republic* presents in more popular and less robust form, and with a certain uneasiness, the relativistic arguments of Thrasymachus.) More comforting by far is the view that moral and social principles are based on *certain general principles of human nature.* To offer but one obvious example, Adam Smith promotes laissez-faire capitalism by extolling

---

[9] Leszek Kolakowski, *Husserl and the Search for Certainty* (Yale U. Press, New Haven, CT, 1975), p. 6.

[10] Kuhn details similar global changes which made possible the rise of the new physics several centuries earlier. Cf. T. S. Kuhn, *The Copernican Revolution* (Harvard U. Press, Cambridge, 1957).

its premises as a true estimation of the most general features of human nature. Likewise, the Benthamites tried to present in simple terms a view relating human nature and morality. Urged on by higher biblical criticism, even theology attempted to provide itself with a scientific basis; Paley's *Natural Theology*, for instance, is very much in the temper of the times, with its emphasis on the natural evidence for religious claims.[11] Further impetus was supplied by the physical sciences, where Helmholtz for instance showed that in music, that sacred preserve of the human spirit, such supposedly "subjective" phenomena as timbre, harmonics, etc., could be analyzed in terms of physiological reactions to wave motions. John Passmore summarizes the effect of the overwhelming trend towards grounding the fundamental principles of society and intellectual inquiry not in philosophy but in the special sciences:

> There was some dispute, acrimonious at times, as to whether psychology, or biology, or anthropology should be proclaimed "The Queen of the Sciences"; but any metaphysics which laid claim to the title was at once howled down as the Old Pretender.[12]

In light of the inevitable methodological and societal chaos, it is not insignificant to our examination of Mill's logical theories that prior to *A System of Logic* the greater part of his energies had been expended in attempting to find a *via media* between absolutism and sceptical relativism, perhaps best expressed in his essays on Bentham and Coleridge.[13] Ironically, although psychologism arose as an attempt to provide logic with an objective foundation, in doing so it introduced just that anthropomorphic relativism which Frege, Russell, and Wittgenstein were to hold in contempt.

If the intellectual ground of the nineteenth century proved fertile soil for the seeds of logical psychologism, they also found consider-

---

[11] Cf. Loren Eiseley, *Darwin's Century* (Doubleday, New York, 1958). We shall see in chapter X that such attempts to reduce religion to science are special targets of Wittgenstein's wrath.

[12] John Passmore, *A Hundred Years of Philosophy* (Penguin Books, Harmondsworth, UK, 1968), p. 175. Compare with Husserl's discussion of Mach and Avenarius, *LI* I, pp. 197 ff.

[13] J. S. Mill, *Bentham and Coleridge*, ed. Leavis (Cambridge U. Press, Cambridge, 1978). For a pregnant discussion of the effects on Mill's philosophical stance of his political views in the context of the prevailing currents of his time, see R. P. Anschutz, "The Logic of J. S. Mill" in J. B. Schneewind, ed. *Mill: A Collection of Critical Essays* (Notre Dame Press, Notre Dame, IN, 1969), pp. 46-83. Also helpful is Alan Ryan's introduction to Mill's *An Examination of Sir William Hamilton's Philosophy*, which constitutes vol. 11 of *The Collected Works of J. S. Mill* (U. of Toronto Press, Toronto, 1979).

able nurture in the technical philosophy of the day. The movement to ground logic in the science of human nature was aided and abetted by a concurrent rebellion against the Aristotelianism of the School-men, the immediate influence being a general antipathy towards formal logic. The two tendencies—psychological theories of infer-ence and a neglect of formal logic—had been bedfellows in the British tradition since Locke. Following a discussion in the *Essay* of the forces which bring about varying degrees of assent, Locke observes:

> If we will observe the actings of our own minds, we shall find that we reason the best and clearest, when we only observe the connexion of the proof, without reducing our thoughts to any rule of syllogism. And therefore we may take notice, that there are a great many men who reason exceedingly clear and right, who know not how to make a syllogism ... If syllogisms must be taken for the only proper instrument of reason and means of knowledge, it would follow that, before Aristotle, there was not one man that did or could know anything by reason and that, since the invention of the syllogisms, there is not one of ten thousand that doth.[14]

Locke's message is not difficult to discern; if the syllogism were the vehicle of knowledge, must not men reason syllogistically when they reason well? And since that seems not to be the case, what is that vehicle? Locke's answer is very Protestant; let us observe what each man does in the course of ordinary reasoning. Logic thus becomes an empirical science, where we discover the laws of reason in the same manner that we discover the laws of the planets, viz. observation and hypothesis.

If Locke presents a potpourri of anecdote and ad hominem argument, Hume strikes at the heart of the Aristotelian conception of logic. All sciences, he argues, depend upon the "science of man." Why is this? As we saw in the previous chapter, Hume held that all reasoning consists in comparing two given things to see what

---

[14] Locke, *Essay Concerning Human Understanding* (Dover, New York, 1959), p. 390. Suspicion of the Schoolmen, and in particular of syllogizing, runs all through Locke's works. In a passage following that quoted, Locke grudgingly admits that the syllogism may be of occasional therapeutic value in faulty reasoning, but continues that its handiness in these (few) cases is outweighed by the very grave danger of masking sophistries with its ponderous terminology.

Note that Locke's assumption that if the syllogism represents rules of valid thinking men must actually consciously use those rules in correct reasoning runs precisely parallel to his absurd construal (in Bk. I of the *Essay*) of innate ideas as being those of which even babies must be aware!

relations hold between them. However, in *Treatise* I/iii/3 he argues persuasively that of the seven "philosophical relations," only *cause and effect* allows us to move from a present perception to one not present; only causal reasoning leads beyond the circle of what is immediately present to us, and supports *inference*. But in I/iii, Hume asks, What is the ground of our propensity to make causal judgments? Is the ground logical? The causal principle which underlies such judgments is neither "intuitive" (self-evident) nor "demonstrable" (deducible from self-evident premises). Is it then empirical? No finite series of observations could establish the causal principle. Stuck in his efforts to find a rational ground, Hume suggests in lieu of further search that we look carefully at what happens in the case of a particular causal judgment. But by the middle of I/iii, this examination has effected a sea-change in Hume's thinking. Rather than seeking the grounds for a belief in causes, Hume embarks upon a long and sophisticated analysis of the *causes of belief*. By the end of I/iii Hume believes that he has put to rest as empty the distinction, dear to the Cartesian tradition, between the causes of and grounds for a belief. Thus logic becomes an investigation of the factors that cause beliefs to be formed and reinforced, an empirical investigation into the principles of the mind which bring about association and thus inference.

The consequences of this argument are far-reaching. Take for example the question, so central to the *Meditations*, Does body exist? We may strive to answer this question and others like it, Hume argues, but the fundamental fact is that we have no choice whether to believe in body, or analogously to make causal judgments. We are constituted to think in such a manner. Logic thus loses much of its *normative* element, as the "art" of correct thinking, and becomes rather the end-point of an investigation into the manner and extent in which thought-processes are conditioned.[15] It becomes an investigation of the "laws of thought." Keeping in mind that this expression is ambiguous, a tendency to confuse the normative with the descriptive

---

[15] This is slightly misleading, since Hume retains a vestige of this normative element. Contrast the "philosophical" probabilities of I/iii/12 with the "unphilosophical probabilities" of I/iii/13, which, although "deriv'd from the same principles ... have not had the good fortune to obtain the same sanction" (p. 143). Thus the pragmatic rules of I/iii/15, of which Hume writes "Here is all the Logic I think proper to employ in my reasoning ... " (p. 175), are apparently justified only on pragmatic or historical grounds.

sense of 'law' makes it possible for neo-Kantians to slip from treating logical laws as transcendental into such an empirical construal.[16]

There is a final aspect of psychologism, quite apart from the considerations examined so far, which makes it a comfortable and attractive position. Consider the question, Could there be a logic *different* from ours? Not merely one which was couched in a different formalism, but a logic which did not (for instance) countenance the Law of Excluded Middle, or the Principle of Contradiction? Conventionalism would admit this possibility, since logic results from certain decisions on our part, while the realist, treating logical principles as representatives of the necessary structure of the world, would hold the suggestion to be incoherent. But each is faced with serious difficulties. The conventionalist cannot tell us what criterion of possibility he uses to say that other logics are possible, while the realist must demonstrate the alleged "necessity" of logic. Psychologism presents a convenient way out. It explains why we cannot conceive of different logics, by grounding logic in the nature of the mind, and thus frees us from the task of showing that certain structures in the world are necessary.[17]

Psychologism in Logic and Mathematics

> Logic is not a science, separate from and coordinate to psychology. To the extent that it is a science at all, it is a part or branch of psychology, distinguished from it on one hand as the part is from the whole, and on the other hand as the art is from the science.
>
> —MILL

> Logic is the physics of thinking or it is nothing at all.
>
> —LIPPS

We must now look more closely at the *content* of psychologism. It is important to keep in mind that psychologism is a theory of the

---

[16] Such conflation is given impetus by the Schopenhauerian failure to distinguish representations and appearances, and thus to treat objects as somehow *subjective*. Thus, no distinction is drawn between transcendental principles, which hold for all appearances, and psychological laws which hold for all representations.

[17] For a discussion of this argument, see Mohanty *op. cit.*, pp. 26–27. The attractiveness to a neo-Kantian of such a solution is evident; it offers a weakened version of the Copernican Revolution without the difficulty of distinguishing between appearances and things in themselves.

nature of logic, of its foundations, not a method for judging the validity or invalidity of a given inference. Its realm is not logic proper but the philosophy of logic.

At the beginning of *The Laws of Thought* Boole offers the following characterization of that treatise:

> [This work] is designed, in the first place, to investigate the fundamental laws of those operations of the mind by which reasoning is performed. It is unnecessary here to enter into any argument to prove that the operations of the mind are in a real sense subject to laws, and that a science of mind is possible.[18]

In a parallel passage in *A System of Logic* Mill approvingly quotes Bishop Whately's *Elements of Logic* (1826):

> Logic [is] the science, as well as the art, of reasoning; meaning by the former term, *the analysis of the mental process which takes place whenever we reason,* and the latter, the rules, grounded on that analysis, for conducting the process correctly.... A right understanding of the mental process itself, of the conditions upon which it depends, and the steps of which it consists, is the only basis on which a system of [logical] rules ... can be founded.[19]

What is logic then *about?* What is its subject matter? Mill's answer is simple and direct:

> Existence, so far as Logic is concerned with it, has reference only to phenomena; to actual, or possible, states of external or internal consciousness. Feelings of sensitive beings, or the possibilities of having those feelings, are the only things the existence of which can be a subject of logical induction. (*Ibid.* II, pp. 133–34.)

Since logic deals solely with relations among feelings or sensations or, more broadly, mental states, the science upon which it is grounded will be psychology, which has as its subject matter:

> [T]he uniformities of successions, the laws, whether ultimate or demonstrable, according to which one mental state succeeds another; is caused by, or at least is caused to follow, another. (*Ibid.* II, p. 423).

---

[18] G. Boole, *An Investigation of The Laws of Thought, upon which are founded the Mathematical Theory of Logic and Probability,* (London, 1854), p. 3.

[19] J. S. Mill, *A System of Logic* (John Parker, London, 1851)(henceforth abbreviated *SoL*) vol. I, p. 2 (the emphasis is mine). Compare with Mill's definition of psychology, *SoL* II, p. 420ff.

Husserl quotes a similar passage by the German psychologistic logician Heymans:

> Just as the chemical formula $2H_2 + O_2 = 2\,H_2O$ expresses the general fact that, in suitable circumstances, two volumes of Hydrogen combine with one volume of Oxygen to form two volumes of water, so [Heymans cites a Boolian syllogistic form] merely represents the fact that, in suitable circumstances, two universal affirmative judgments with a common subject produce two new particular judgments in consciousness.... Why in this case two new judgments are produced [but not in other cases] we are at present ignorant.[20]

Kolakowski offers a general characterization of the position inherent in these passages:

> The consequences of thought, then, are not logical consequences of thought but causal relations between the facts of consciousness. To say that the sentence "all dogs are mammals" entails the sentence "some dogs are mammals" does not really mean that anything logically follows anything. It simply displays a causal relation between two acts of acceptance related to those two judgments. Some mysterious natural laws connect these two acts in a causal succession of events. Thus, logical rules are relative, if not to individuals, at least to the human species. Thus nothing prevents us from supposing that they have no universal validity, and they might lose it for another sentient being; perhaps they might lose it for us if evolution changes some mechanism in the nervous system. Perhaps there is a world where rational beings think according to the principle "if p, then not$-$p".[21]

If logic is not "about" abstract objects and their relations, is it then wholly free from metaphysical commitment? Mill argues that the psychologistic characterization of logic both is and isn't a product of any metaphysical presuppositions. On one hand, he is clear that we must avoid commitment to abstract entities as the referents of logical terms. Yet on the other hand, the characterizations of psychology and thus logic are independent, he claims, of any *particular* theory of the nature of mind, including his phenomenalism.

---

[20] Husserl, *LI* I, pp. 131–32.

[21] *Op. cit.*, p. 18. Kolakowski presumably intends the last expression to represent something other than material implication, since " p ⊃ ~p " reduces to " ~p v ~p ", which is not puzzling at all.

> What the Mind is, as well as what Matter is, or any other questions
> respecting things in themselves, ... it would be foreign to the purposes of
> this treatise to consider. (*Ibid.* II, p. 420)

Analogously, Boole believes that far from depending upon some
particular theory of mind, logic provides information which may
allow us to choose among competing theories. (*Ibid.*, p. 24)

Since both Mill and Boole appear to hold the truth of psychologism to be nothing short of obvious, why did logicians ever strike
upon any *other* theory? Mill provides an answer, reminiscent of
Berkeley's attack on abstract ideas. The argument appears in his
discussion of the Aristotelian *dictum de omni et nullo*—whatever
can be truly predicated of a class can be truly predicated of each
member of that class. If those of us not awakened to Mill's
nominalism think of a class intensionally, then the dictum appears to
make a claim about some relation between Man—"Something
inherent in men and vastly superior to them in dignity," as Mill puts
it—and individual men like John Stuart Mill, George Boole, Gregor
Princip and so forth. However, "when it is known that a class, a
universal, a genus, a species, is not an entity per se, but neither more
nor less than the individual substances themselves which are placed
in a class," the proposition loses its aura of startling metaphysical
importance, becoming "identical" or tautologous. Of previous logicians, Mill writes:

> Once accustomed to consider scientific investigation as essentially the study
> of universals, men did not drop this habit of thought when they ceased to
> regard universals as possessing an independent existence....[22]

Thus the dictum strikes us as important insofar as we do not see that
it hides the presupposition that universals have independent existence. Once that presupposition is exposed, we immediately see that
to find the ground of logic we must therefore look not outward but
inward, into the laws of the human mind which lie behind thought
and language. In a similar vein Boole asks:

> What is the *logical* import of the processes [involved in symbolic
> reasoning]? Analogies, Mathematical and otherwise, cast aside, what

---

[22] *Ibid.*, p. 198. Compare with Berkeley, *Principles of Human Knowledge* (Bobbs-Merrill,
Indianapolis, IN, 1957), introduction and *passim.*

doctrines of intellectual activity remain concealed beneath the forms themselves?[23]

His answer likewise emphasizes an inward turn. Chapter II of *The Laws of Thought* is entitled "Derivation of the laws of the symbols of logic from the laws of the operations of the human mind," and elsewhere he writes:

> When mental concepts and mental operations are expressed in signs, the laws of those concepts and operations become the laws of the signs. (*Ibid.*, p. 232)

Thus logic is no more than a synoptic presentation of the rules which govern these mental sign-operations.

If Mill and Boole then hold that logic is grounded in psychological laws, what sort of laws do they have in mind? What are the candidates for the mental reality which lies behind the symbolic operations? Boole withholds judgment, but Mill offers a number of rather simple generalizations about mental activity, not too much more sophisticated than those of Book I of the *Treatise*. For instance, one "law of mind" is:

> Whenever any state of consciousness has once been incited in us ..., an inferior degree of the same state of consciousness ..., resembling the former but inferior in intensity, is capable of being reproduced in us.... (SoL, p. 423)

This is of course no more than the familiar Humean principle that every impression can have a correlative idea, which differs from the impression only in its "strength and vivacity." Another "law of mind" is the principle of association, which Mill attributes to his father's *Analysis of the Phenomena of the Human Mind*. This principle of "mental gravitation" concerns the relations between the ideas created through weakened impressions:

> These ideas, or secondary mental states, are excited by our impressions, or by other ideas, according to certain laws which are called Laws of Association. (*Ibid.*, p. 424)

---

[23] G. Boole, *Studies in Logic and Probability* (Watts and Co., London, 1952), p. 212.

The willingness of Mill (and Boole) to ground the ancient doctrines of logic on such a paltry psychological basis is an indication of how certain they are that *some view like this must be true;* we don't yet know the *exact* mechanisms, but there must be some.[24] We shall soon see a rather similar attitude on Wittgenstein's part.

Mill's antipathy toward abstract objects in logic anticipates a parallel hostility towards the view that the presumptively necessary truths of mathematics represent necessary connections among abstract entities. In lieu of that realistic model Mill presents an empiricist version of mathematical truth which proves an amiable bedfellow for a psychologistic logic. Mill's analysis of mathematics appears in two places in *A System of Logic:* the general nature of mathematics is discussed in Volume II—geometry in II/5, arithmetic in II/6—while an equally important discussion appears in III/26. In these passages, Mill considers and rejects two popular (British) views of the nature of mathematics, one traceable to Locke, the other to Berkeley. Locke held the truths of mathematics to be merely *verbal;* they represent nothing more than certain conventions concerning the usage of words like 'straight line', 'three', and so forth. (Locke, *op. cit.*, I pp. 270–75, II 251–66.) But Mill contends (quite rightly) that such a view cannot account for the synthetic use of mathematics (as when I count my change and discover I have $3.84), as well as being so wildly at variance with common sense that "a person must have made some advances in philosophy to believe it." (*SoL* I, p. 279) We cannot, on the other hand, accept the Berkelian thesis that mathematical truths are merely about *ideas.* (*Op. cit.*, sect. 12–14, 118–34.) Mill offers the counterexample of geometry, where we deal with such notions as lines without width, points, and so forth. But if to have an idea is to have a mental image, we clearly cannot imagine—picture for ourselves—a line without width.[25] Thus geometrical propositions cannot be about ideas, since the required ideas are impossible. An analogous argument can be constructed concerning arithmetic. Thus, mathematical propositions cannot be

---

[24] "If I am inclined to suppose that a mouse has come into being by spontaneous generation out of grey rags and dust, I shall do well to examine those rags very closely to see how a mouse may have hidden in them, how it may have got in there and so on. But if I am convinced that a mouse cannot come into being from these things, then this investigation will perhaps be superfluous." *PI,#*52.

[25] *Op. cit.*, I, pp. 279–80. Compare with *Treatise, I/ii/1–5.*

analyzed either as propositions about the meanings of words, or propositions about our ideas.

What then is the nature of a mathematical truth? Mill sometimes distinguishes and sometimes conflates two different questions, which we will treat separately. The first is, What do mathematical concepts like "point" and "three" stand for? The second, distinctly different, is, What is the ground of mathematical principles such as the law of the transitivity of identity? In answer to the first question, Mill holds that numbers refer to common properties of things, to the second, that mathematical principles are the result of inductions from experience, and thus are neither necessary nor certain at all.

Mill's support for the first claim is based almost wholly on his nominalism. All numbers must be numbers of something:

> There are no such things as numbers in the abstract. Ten must mean ten bodies, or ten sounds, or ten beatings of the pulse. (*Op. cit.*, II, p. 280)

However, through some unspecified mental process, we give numbers the property of *complete generality;* "But though numbers must be numbers of something, they can be numbers of anything." (*Ibid.*) To say that two plus two equals four is to say that two dogs plus two dogs yields four dogs, two pebbles and two pebbles four pebbles, and so forth indifferently.

With respect to the nature of mathematical principles, Mill contends that the acquisition of number-concepts leads to the discovery of certain empirical relations between collections of things. For example, we recognize that the two collections XX and XXX can be rearranged to yield XXXXX, and that the angle opposite the greatest side of a triangle is always the largest angle. Note that since each of these principles is based on induction from a finite string of experiences, they are contingent. We cannot say, then, that what holds for pebbles and dogs *must* hold for guinea pigs. Thus "The character of necessity, ascribed to the truths of mathematics, and even ... the peculiar certainty ascribed to them, is an illusion." (*SoL*, p. 25)

In summary, the principles of logic represent nothing more than very general psychological laws governing the operations of the human mind. They are therefore contingent and empirical, and further, anthropocentric and historical. Their apparent universal validity is based wholly on the ubiquitousness of the principles of psychology which they represent. Mathematics likewise does not represent necessary truths about relations between abstract entities, but rather contingent empirical principles concerning common properties of groups of concrete entities. (A consequence, which Mill announces as one goal of his analysis of logic, of the loss of certainty and necessity in mathematics is that ethical reasoning no longer suffers by comparison.)

One immediate problem with this view, one not lost on Mill and Boole, is this: we generally take logic to be normative rather than descriptive. It represents rules which, rather than describing how people (always) *actually* think, sets up norms or standards for how people *ought* to think if they wish to maximize certain features of thought, namely truth-transferring connections between premises and conclusions. But if logic is general psychology, then what do we mean by *bad* or *illogical* thinking? Compare; if we discover a planet at one focus of whose orbit the sun does not stand, we do not say that the planet has "violated" Kepler's first law, but rather that what we *took* to be a law in fact was *not*. Yet we do not react in a parallel manner when someone commits the fallacy of denying the antecedent. Why this disanalogy between "laws of mind" and, say, physical laws? Boole hedges (*ibid.*, pp. 193–94), writing that the nature of the subject is such that we cannot imagine these laws entailing necessity, or "constraining obedience," as he puts it. He contrasts the laws of mind (upon which he confers ethical as well as logical significance) with the laws of nature proper:

> In Nature, [science] exhibits for us a system of law *enforcing* obedience, in the Mind a system of law *claiming* obedience. Over the one presides necessity, over the other the unforced obligations of Reason and the Moral Law. (*Ibid.*, p. 197)

But the notion of moral laws "claiming" obedience is anthropomorphic at best, incoherent at worst. As we shall see, this difficulty represents the first crack in the plausibility of psychologism, a crack which, along with other shortcomings, Frege will be quick to exploit.[26]

---

[26] I believe, incidentally, that the Millian/Boolian position offers the possibility of a reasonably sophisticated defense, one grounded on Hume's distinction between philosophical and unphilosophical probabilities. The result would be to turn the normative side of psychologistic logic in a more pragmatic direction.

Frege's Critique of Psychologism

> Some logicians ... presuppose in Logic *psychological*
> principles .... If we were to take principles from
> psychology, ... we should merely understand *how* thought
> takes place. ... But in Logic the question is not of
> *contingent,* but of *necessary* laws.
>
> —KANT

> [I]t is important to keep in mind that Husserl and Frege
> belonged to *nearly* the same philosophical world, in which
> a sort of neo-Kantian philosophy prevailed ..., in which
> Hermann Lotze was the towering figure, in which what was
> labeled as "psychologism" in logic and in which
> philosophers were concerned with such concepts as mental
> acts, *Inhalt* or contents of those acts, and made liberal use
> of the concept of *Vorstellung* or presentation.
>
> —J. N. MOHANTY
> *HUSSERL AND FREGE*

In this section I want to examine Frege's critique of psychologism, with an eye towards a discussion of his conceptual realism and the broader realism of the early Russell and Moore. Frege's work represents, in retrospect at least, one major breaking-point in the history of philosophy. Since Descartes' sweeping critique of the foundations of knowledge in the seventeenth century, the major topic of western philosophy has been the justification of knowledge-claims. Frege changed this, or at least initiated the claim which has gained increasing momentum since his death. Michael Dummett, writes:

> Frege was the first [philosopher]—at least since Plato—to make a sharp separation between [the analysis of meanings] and [the task] of establishing what is true and what are our grounds for accepting it ...[27]

> ... [Frege] starts from meaning by taking the theory of meaning as the only part of philosophy whose results do not depend upon those of any other part, but which underlie all the rest. By doing this, he effected a revolution in philosophy as great as the similar revolution effected by Descartes ...[28]

---

[27] Michael Dummett, *Frege: The Philosophy of Language* (Harper and Row, New York, 1973), p. 667.

[28] *Ibid.,* p. 669. Note how 'theory of meaning' for Frege then takes the position occupied for Husserl by his "new science," phenomenology.

These claims, which may seem overblown to those contemporary philosophers who see Frege mostly as a philosopher of mathematics and an innovator in symbolic logic, seem to me both true and very important to understanding Frege's influence on Wittgenstein. But my purpose is not to evaluate Frege's systematic importance. Rather, I will concentrate on two topics: Frege's realistic theory of meaning, and his Platonism in mathematics. Thus this section both looks backwards, as a reaction to psychologism, and forwards to the broader realism of Russell and Moore.

Frege's first major publication was a small volume entitled *Begriffsschrift* (1879)—"concept writing" or "ideography"—subtitled "A formula language, modeled upon that of arithmetic, for pure thought."[29] The immediate purpose of the *Begriffsschrift* is to provide a language free from the misleading oddities and psychological connotations which mar ordinary language, the wider purpose to combat formalism and empiricism in mathematics, and psychologism in logic. Frege considered these two projects as very closely related. Its chief technical novelty lies in the introduction of the quantifier notation, marking the beginnings of modern logic with its dependence on quantified variables. Far from a smashing success, like Hume's *Treatise* it appears to have fallen stillborn from the presses; the murmurs it did excite among the zealots were largely negative. Perhaps discouraged by the minimal response to his work, Frege published in 1884 a non-symbolic presentation of the central arguments of the earlier work, entitled *The Foundations of Arithmetic*,[30] which included a careful estimation of the relation of his thought to that of his predecessors. It is this work, and to a lesser extent the 1893 work *The Basic Laws of Arithmetic*,[31] with which I will be concerned. Later in this chapter, the famous paper "On Sense and Reference" and three chapters of Frege's unfinished book on logic will become important.

---

[29] I shall refer to the English translation by Stefan Bauer-Mengelberg, published in J. van Heijenoort, ed., *Frege and Gödel: Two Fundamental Texts in Mathematical Logic* (Harvard U. Press, Cambridge, MA, 1970). Another translation, with associated shorter papers, is published in G. Frege, *Conceptual Notation*, ed. T. Byrum (Oxford U. Press, Oxford, 1972). Of particular interest among the additional materials is the short paper also entitled "Conceptual Notation," pp. 90–100.

[30] Hereafter to be referred to as *FA*.

[31] Edited and partially translated by M. Furth as G. Frege, *The Basic Laws of Arithmetic* (U. of California Press, Berkeley and LA, 1964), and hereafter abbreviated as *BLA*.

The fundamental purposes of *FA* are three: to argue against psychologism and Millian empiricism in mathematics, to show instead that numbers are real extramental existents, and to promote the "logicist thesis" that the principles of mathematics are reducible to those of pure logic. Of these, Frege sees the last as most fundamental:

> The present work will make clear that even an inference like that from n to n+1, which on the face of it is peculiar to mathematics, is based on the general laws of logic ... (*FA*, p. iv)

Towards this end Frege must entertain other, more pedestrian, projects. The first is the provision of a clear and unambiguous representation of proofs, for which the apparatus of the *Begriffsschrift* is necessary:

> Of course the pronouncement is often made that arithmetic is merely a more highly developed logic; yet it remains disputable so long as transitions occur in proofs that are not made according to acknowledged rules of logic, but seem rather based on intuition. (*BLA*, p. 3)

The rigorous proofs made possible by the quantifier notation offer the methodological tool for such a reduction, and although without the actual reductions the logicist thesis remains an unredeemed promissory note, the plausibility of the project can be established. Thus in *FA* Frege has claimed no more than to have made the logicist thesis "probable." The second project, an adjunct to the first, is the banishment from logic of any psychological element. This is necessitated partly because psychological intrusions tend to mask such crucial distinctions as "the characteristic mark of a concept and a property of an object" (*BLA*, pp. 12–13). But more generally, the failure to distinguish the logical from the psychological promotes conflation of the two, ultimately leading to psychologism, and Frege believes that psychologism entails precisely what Boole, Mill, and others sought to avoid, namely relativism and ultimately scepticism.[32]

---

[32] Here Frege echoes Husserl's worries. Husserl took the search for certainty—that is, avoidance of sceptical relativism—to be a *constituting mark* of western civilization, and held that failure to pursue certainty indicates the decay of such a civilization. Cf. Kolakowski *op. cit.* pp. 7–8. It is

Mill, we will recall, defines number in such a manner that (for instance) three exists just insofar as there are collections of three things. To think that the number three has existence beyond such collections is an illusion, combatable by close adherence to certain nominalistic principles. Arithmetic propositions such as '7 + 5 = 12' represent mere empirical generalizations about the concrete behavior of such collections; if we put seven cookies in a bag, and add five cookies, careful counting shows that there are now twelve cookies in the bag. Frege's attack on Mill's analysis takes the form of a reductio ad absurdum; Mill's position necessitates rejection of certain commonly held mathematical propositions. Note that Frege takes *as a datum* the truth of mathematics; he does not consider, so far as I can tell, the suggestion that since the Millian analysis is true, the nature of mathematics must be rather different from how we normally take it to be. Thus Frege's arguments bear an interesting resemblance to those Moore offers in his notorious defense of common sense; certain philosophical claims can be rejected on the grounds that they conflict with other propositions which we know to be true.[33]

Let us examine a representative Fregean argument. If number concepts have been empirically garnered, and have no reference beyond the empirical, then I have the concept '5' insofar as I once saw (say) five geese or a basketball team. Then the number 5 must have some sensory presentation associated with it, for instance GGGGG. But what then is the sensory presentation associated with (and in fact the reference of) 777864? If there is none, then what (empirical, nominalistic) sense can we make of the claim that a number of smaller numbers, for which we can point to the requisite sensory presentations, are factors of 777864? More generally, from whence comes our certainty that every number has a successor?

It is of course open to Mill to argue that experiences such as the cookie-bag event mentioned above lead to habits, which by projection then move us towards higher numbers. Having empirically verified that 2 + 3 = 5, we then internalize a rule which brings us to

interesting to speculate about the relations between Frege's anti-sceptical realism, his extreme political conservatism, and the accident of his birth in the auspicious year 1848.

[33] At least in the early works, such as "A Proof of an External World" (1903) and *Principia Ethica;* in later works, Moore accepts as fundamental that ultimately analyses must lead to sense-data, and thus exposes a peculiarly British bias towards empiricism.

believe that 777 + 326 is 1103.[34] But if we must fall back on a recursive rule for higher numbers, why not be satisfied with 1 + 1 = 2 as our empirical basis, and leave it at that? Further, if the generation of number-concepts depends on rearranging things such that we achieve a certain sensory presentation, what would happen, Frege sarcastically suggests, in a world where everything was nailed down? If giving sense to a particular number-expression requires that the items in question be physically united, does this mean that we must hold a rally of all the blind people in Germany to give a sense to 'the number of blind Germans'? (Cf. *FA*, p. 30)

The evident ad hominem element in the preceding arguments (and others like them) might bring the empiricist to answer that things in our world are in fact *not* nailed down, and that since it is not incumbent on the philosopher of mathematics to explain how number concepts gain meaning in some possible world a great deal different from ours, such attempts at refutation of Mill's position are simply barking up the wrong tree.[35] Frege's retort, which we will examine soon, is that such objections point to a deeper and more serious problem with Mill's philosophy of arithmetic, namely muddling *how we arrive at the content of a judgment* with *how we justify its assertion.*[36]

But the empiricist analysis of mathematical concept-formation suffers from more serious deficiencies. If I acquire my concept of 5 by observing cookies, how do I then apply it to collections of five which are *logically* different from cookies? Yet we do speak of five commands, five kinds of proof, and so forth, and it would seem miraculous if a property (number) derived from observation of cookies just happened to fit any other sorts of collections we chose. Frege writes:

> It would indeed be remarkable if a property abstracted from external things
> could be transferred without any change of sense to events, to ideas, and to

---

[34] Compare with Hume, *Treatise*, I/iv/2 and I/iv/7.

[35] Compare: Kant argues that the a priori concepts we seek must be binding for any discursive intelligence, or the moral rules for any free rational being. But Hume (or Schopenhauer) would reply; we have no concept of beings significantly different from ourselves, and thus to argue e.g. that a utilitarian analysis of obligation would not hold in a world where pain and pleasure was unknown does not invalidate the utilitarian analysis of moral obligation in *this* world for *people like us.*

[36] Cf. *FA*, section 1, and compare with Husserl, *LI* I, chapter 5.

concepts. The effect would be just like speaking of fusible events, or blue ideas, or salty concepts, or tough judgment. (*FA*, p. 31)

Further, if our number concepts are empirically acquired, from whence come our concepts of zero and unity? Are there sensory presentations associated with *them*? (*FA*, sect. 20) Imagine a green field, Frege invites us, and then picture *one* green field; is there a difference in the presentations? If so, which element of the presentation corresponds to the concept of *one*?[37] Note that such objections deal not with an imaginary world quite different from ours, but with the difficulties of explaining the genesis of certain mathematical concepts in the *actual world*.

Frege's key argument provides an even more devastating blow to empiricism in mathematics. Treating number-concepts as abstractions from collections of things, as representing nothing more than a common property of those collections, pushes all consideration of numerical matters towards an idealistic relativism. Homer's *Illiad* can be considered as one poem, twenty-four books, such and such number of chapters, of lines, of words, and so forth. We can therefore point to the *Illiad* and say, with equal justice, "This is one" or "This is twenty-four."[38] Mill is correct in observing that two books are physically different from one, but seems to overlook two boots being physically the same as one *pair* of boots. If number is some physical property of a collection, then, it would seem to change with our interests or attention. But if whether the *Illiad* exemplifies the number one or the number twenty-four turns on our interests, then number takes on an anthropocentric air seemingly inconsistent with representing an empirical property of collections.

If numbers are thus not a physical property of collections of things, it is tempting to yield to the natural counter-tendency to treat them as *mental*. If numbers are not physical properties of those collections, perhaps (since they seem a function of our interests and attention) they are properties of our *ideas* of those collections. Do considerations like those concerning the *Illiad* then show that

---

[37] Compare with Hume's arguments on the concept of existence: *Treatise* I/ii/vi.

[38] *FA*, sect. 21. An analogous problem concerns "dividing a collection"—we can divide a bundle of straw by untying it, by breaking each straw in half, etc. Cf. *FA*, sect. 23, and compare with *PI*, #48ff.

numbers are *ideas,* and mathematical propositions represent relations between these ideas? Frege quotes Berkeley's support for this position:

> It ought to be considered that number . . . is nothing fixed and settled, really existing in things themselves. It is entirely the creature of the mind, considering either an idea by itself, or any combination of ideas to which it gives one name. Accordingly the mind variously combines its ideas, the unit varies; and as the unit, so the number, which is only a collection of units, doth vary also. We call a window one, a chimney one, and yet a house in which there are many windows, and many chimneys, hath an equal right to be called one, and many houses go into the making of one city.[39]

Does a rejection of Millian empiricism thus lead us to Berkelian idealism? Of course not, Frege responds; neither numbers themselves, nor the principles of their relations and transactions, are mental in any philosophically important sense.

> If number were an idea, then arithmetic would be psychology. But arithmetic is no more psychology than, say, astronomy is. Astronomy is concerned, not with the ideas of the planets, but with the planets themselves, and by the same token the objects of arithmetic are not ideas either. (*FA,* p. 37)

> The botanist gives something just as factual when he gives the Number of the flowers' petals as when he gives their shape. (*Ibid.,* p. 34)

As we shall see, Frege will aggressively press these points far beyond what is needed to refute the psychologistic logician or mathematician.

Do Frege's arguments show that psychologism is *false*? All that has been shown so far is that psychologism is inconsistent with numerous widely held mathematical beliefs. But in addition Frege wants to put forth a stronger claim; at the foundation of the Millian analysis lies a confusion, a natural confusion, perhaps, but a confusion nonetheless. (To this extent Frege's argument is parallel to Moore's "A Refutation of Idealism.") The confusion involved, Frege argues, is that between the act of consciousness—the judgment—and the *object* of that judgment. But underlying this confusion is a

---

[39] Cf. *FA,* p. 33. The quotation is from Berkeley's *A New Theory of Vision* (Dutton, New York, 1910), section 109.

deeply seated belief about the nature of truth. "Surveying the whole question," Frege writes, "it seems to me that the source of the dispute lies in our conception of what is true." (*BLA*, p. 15)

> If we want to emerge from subjectivity at all, we must conceive of knowledge as an activity that does not create what is known but grasps what is already there . . . If I grasp a pencil, many changes take place in my body . . . . But the totality of these changes is neither the pencil nor creates the pencil; the internal changes are not the grasping. In the same way, that which we grasp with the mind exists independently of this activity, independent of the ideas and their alterations that are part of this grasping or accompany it, and it is neither identical with the totality of these events nor created by it. . . . (*BLA*, pp. 23–24.)

> A proposition may be thought, and again, it may be true; let us never confuse these two things. We must remind ourselves, it seems, that a proposition no more ceases to be true when I cease to think about it than the sun ceases to exist when I close my eyes.[40]

Thus an examination of the nature of truth shows that the psychological logician fails to distinguish clearly enough between the idea, the *Vorstellung* (always psychological for Frege) which constitutes the vehicle of the mental act, and the *object* of that act of consciousness.

But what is the ground, we might ask, for Frege's conviction that the alleged confusion *is* a confusion? Just as Mill might complain that the certainty which Frege ascribes to mathematical propositions is specious, isn't the whole thrust of the Idealist's arguments that the very distinction between idea and object upon which Frege puts so much weight is phony?[41] Frege's retort, the weight of which is difficult to assess, is that *if* the objects of our judgments were merely ideas, there could then be no common ground between speakers, and language would be impossible. But without common, objective language, there could be no possibility of *conflicting opinions:*

> If we could not grasp anything but what was within our own selves, then a conflict of opinions would be impossible, because a common ground would

---

[40] *FA*, p. vi. Note the analogy between *thinking a proposition* and *perceiving a physical object;* this analogy will come to the fore in our subsequent discussion of the wider implications of realism. But contrast with *BB*, pp. 35–43.

[41] For instance, Berkeley's arguments in *Three Dialogues Between Hylas and Philonous* (Bobbs-Merrill, Indianapolis, IN, 1954), Dialogue I.

> be lacking, and no idea in the psychological sense can afford us such a
> ground. There would be no logic to be appointed arbiter in the conflict of
> opinions. (*BLA*, p. 17)

Unless we are willing to dismiss putative communication, dispute, and so forth as mere *illusion*, we must accept that at least *some* of our judgments have extramental and thus potentially public objects; Dummett remarks that for Frege the objective sense of a proposition is guaranteed by the publicness of language. (*Op. cit.*, p. 680) Rejection of the publicness argument entails acceptance of an extreme solipsistic scepticism which Frege, like Schopenhauer, would no doubt deem sterile.

Numbers are therefore neither properties of physical collections, nor mental entities, and thus mathematical propositions are not *about* physical objects or ideas. What then is the status of numbers? Frege's answer is that every number is a self-subsistent abstract entity, a real constituent of the world.

> We are driven to the conclusion that number is neither spatial nor physical,
> like Mill's piles of pebbles or gingersnaps, nor yet subjective like ideas, but
> non-sensible and objective. (*FA*, p. 37)

Hostility towards this position, which Frege takes to be a plain consequence of the preceding considerations, stems from several rather different sorts of mistakes or prejudices. Praising Cantor he writes:

> I heartily share [Cantor's] contempt for the view that in principle only finite
> numbers ought to be admitted as actual. Perceptible by the senses [infinite
> numbers] are not, nor are they spatial—any more than fractions are, or
> negative numbers . . .; and if we restrict the actual to what acts on our senses
> or at least produces effects which may cause sense-perceptions as near or
> remote consequences, then naturally no number of any of these kinds is
> actual. (*FA*, p. 97)

More generally, slightly varying his terminology by substituting the word 'actual' for 'perceivable', he writes:

> For me there is a domain of what is objective distinct from what is actual,
> whereas the psychological logicians without ado take what is not actual to
> be subjective. And yet, it is quite impossible to understand why something
> which has a status independent of the judging subject has to be actual, i.e.

has to be capable of acting directly or indirectly on the senses. No such connection is to be found between the concepts [being objective and being actual] and we can even adduce examples pointing in the opposite direction. (*BLA*, pp. 15–16)

One cannot therefore argue that since numbers are not perceptible, they cannot be real.

The second mistake, often accompanying but independent of the first, is the nominalist dogma that concepts are generated only by abstraction from particulars, and thus must be traceable to sensory origins. We have seen the importance which Schopenhauer assigns to this thesis; for him concepts are always paler shadows of perceptions. But concepts are not always abstractions from perception, Frege argues. With respect to their origin, they can be just as readily acquired through their defining characteristics as through experience of an example. But more importantly, the mode of acquisition of a concept ought not be confused with the *nature* of that concept. Thus empiricist arguments concerning the origin of concepts are either unsound or irrelevant.

Finally, Frege holds that acceptance of a realistic theory of numbers is hindered by a failure to understand the importance of a crucial element of his theory of language, namely the *context principle*. This principle can be stated quite simply: only in the context of a proposition does a word have a meaning. If we ignore this principle, we are then tempted to look for some characteristic of an isolated word which makes it a meaningful constituent of a given sentence. But the only likely candidate turns out to be an idea or a sensation or a mental image, which we wrongly identify with the meaning of the word, much as William James identified consciousness with certain feelings in the head and upper chest. As we shall see, the context principle has implications far beyond the opposition of psychologism, but it is important to note its incompatibility with that theory of meaning.

In response to the question, What are mathematical propositions *about?* Frege answers that they are about *numbers*. But an acceptable theory of arithmetic must not only trace the source of mathematical *concepts*, but also show the ground of the truth of mathematical *principles*. We saw that for Mill statements like '1 + 2 = 3' represent generalizations on experience, and for Boole particular consequences of the general laws of psychology. What is Frege's characterization?

Frege's solution is a form of *logicism;* the principles of arithmetic are no more than specific instances of the general principles of logic. The principles of logic themselves are *analytic,* but Frege's usage of that term must be carefully distinguished from the more familiar Kantian sense. For Kant, a proposition is analytic if the concept of the subject "contains" the concept of the predicate, as in "All squares have four sides" or "All bodies are extended." But if mathematical propositions were analytic in this sense—which Kant of course emphatically denies, offering '5 + 7 = 12' as an example of a *synthetic* proposition—it would be astounding that they bear for us the interest that they do. Frege rhetorically asks:

> Can the great tree of the science of number as we know it, towering, spreading, and still continually growing, have its roots in bare identities? And how do the empty forms of logic come to disgorge so rich a content? (*FA*, p. 22)

How can the consequences of the analytic principles of logic extend our knowledge?

> The truth is that [mathematical judgments] are contained in their definitions, but as plants are contained in their seeds, not as beams are contained in a house. (*FA*, p. 101)

What does this mean? Logical principles are analytic insofar as their truth arises from relations between concepts. But insofar as those concepts are objective entities, far from representing conventions about words, such analytic principles represent necessary, objective connections between abstract entities. Analyticity does not therefore imply triviality or conventionality. To play on the relation of the beams to the house, those principles represent the necessary structure, the "logical framework," of the world.

Finally, both formalism and psychologism attempt to provide a ground for logic, to legitimate it. But any such attempt, Frege argues, commits something which is rather like Moore's "naturalistic fallacy," opening the door to the very relativism and scepticism which we seek to avoid. But perhaps more importantly, the entire attempt to provide some ground for logic is misguided:

The question of why and with what right we acknowledge a law of logic to be true, logic can only answer by reducing it to another law of logic. Where this is not possible logic can give no answer. If we step away from logic, we may say; we are compelled to make judgments by our own nature, and if we do so, we cannot reject this law—of identity, for example; we must acknowledge it unless we wish to reduce all our thought to confusion and finally renounce all judgment whatsoever. I shall neither dispute nor support this remark; I shall merely remark that what we have here is not a logical consequence. What is given is not a reason for something's being true, but for us taking it to be true.[42]

In this passage Frege seems to imply that support can be given for the principles of logic, but what form could such support take? If logic cannot provide its own ground, then is there some *further* science, more fundamental than logic, in which logical principles find their ground? And if so, is not *that* science the rightful heir to the title of logic?

Logical Realism and the Nature of Logic

[The laws of logic] do not bear the relation to thought that
the laws of grammar bear to language; they do not make
explicit the nature of our human thinking and change as it
changes.

—FREGE

The psychological logicians characterize logic as the science of the laws of thought; if this is defective, what characterization do we offer in its place? Frege's answer begins, interestingly, with a consideration of the goal of logic, namely *truth*.[43] At first truth does not seem peculiar to logic; after all, every intellectual discipline aims at truth. A biologist, for instance, would not normally make public material that he knew to be false. But logic has a special interest in

---

[42] *BLA*, p. 15. Compare: "Logic cannot have any empirical part; that is, a part in which the universal and necessary laws of thought should rest on grounds taken from experience; otherwise, it would not be logic, i.e., a canon for the understanding or the reason, valid for all thought, and capable of demonstration." Kant, Preface to *Foundations of the Metaphysics of Morals*, p. 1. Also compare the argument of this passage with the opening remark of the *Notebooks*: "Logic must take care of itself." When addressed to a Humean analysis of belief, Frege's argument, with its assumption that a distinction between reasons and causes *can* be drawn, is of course *petitio principii*.

[43] "The Thought," trans. A. and M. Quinton, *Mind* vol. 65 (1956), p. 17, and "Logic," in Frege, *Posthumous Writings*, ed. Hermes et al. (Blackwell, Oxford, 1979), pp. 126–51. The latter, an unfinished piece, is an excellent short introduction to Frege's mature logical theory.

truth; logic is interested in the concept of truth in the same way a physicist is interested in the concept of heaviness or warmth. The logician is not so much interested in whether this or that proposition is true, but in the *nature* of truth and falsity. This may of course involve setting forth propositions which the logician believes to be true, but such is not the end of logic. Frege thus defines logic as "The science of the most general laws of truth." ("Logic," p. 128)

Truth for Frege is primitive, so a definition is obviously not forthcoming. We can, however, delineate the class of entities to which truth or falsity can be legitimately predicated, namely *thoughts*. To explicate this and uncover the proper role of the logician, we must turn to Frege's celebrated distinction between *sense* and *reference*, which makes it's first appearance in the 1892 paper "On Sense and Reference."[44] Consider first identity-statements, propositions where two expressions, simple or complex, flank an identity sign. Identity-statements appear to assert some *relation*. But if this is the case, what are the relata—the objects for which the two expressions stand, or the signs themselves? If we choose the former, a puzzling consequence arises. If 'a=b' is true, then a and b are in fact not *two* objects but *one*, and thus 'a=b' says the same thing as 'a=a'. Yet the latter is necessary and the former not. As Frege points out, 'The Morning Star is identical with the Evening Star' marks a real advance in our astronomical knowledge, while 'The Morning Star is identical with itself' does not.[45] But on the other hand if the putative relation is construed as holding between the *signs*, then every statement of the form 'a=b' is false, since 'a' and 'b' are obviously different signs.

Characteristically resisting the temptation to conclude that identity is thereby *defective*, Frege writes:

---

[44] In Geach and Black, trans., *Translations from the Philosophical Writings of Frege* (Blackwell, Oxford, 1970), pp. 56–78.

[45] In a parallel passage concerning George IV wondering whether Scott was the author of *Waverly*, Russell points out that since Scott *is* the author of *Waverly*, Leibniz's Law ought to allow us to substitute 'Scott' for 'The Author of *Waverly*'. But this yields 'George IV wonders whether Scott is Scott', and as Russell dryly observes, "an interest in the law of identity can hardly be attributed to the first gentleman of Europe." Cf. Russell "On Denoting," in *Essays in Analysis*, ed. D. Lackey (Braziller, New York, 1972), p. 48.

Leonard Linsky, taking the bull by the horns in a wholly admirable fashion, challenges the claim that the identity of the Morning and Evening Stars represents an advance in our astronomical knowledge by denying that it is even *true*. Cf. *Referring* (Routledge and Kegan Paul, London, 1969), pp. 128–31.

It is natural, now, to think of there being connected with a sign . . ., besides
that to which the sign refers, which may be called the reference of the sign,
also what I should like to call the *sense* of the sign. . . . (*Op. cit.*, p. 57)

In 'The Morning Star is identical with the Evening Star', we can
distinguish the reference of the two expressions—in each case
Venus—from the sense, which is in each case different. The sense of
'The Morning Star' is roughly the last star visible to the naked eye
at daybreak, while that of 'The Evening Star' being the first star
visible to the naked eye in the evening. I say "roughly" because to any
given reference there will generally correspond a large number of
different senses; 'Aristotle', 'Plato's greatest student', 'the teacher of
Alexander' and so forth express different senses, but all have the
same reference, namely The Philosopher. The solution to the puzzle
concerning identity thus lies in seeing that statements of the form
'a=b' assert that two expressions with different senses have the
same reference.

In addition to sense and reference, associated with most every
human linguistic expression are certain mental occurrences which
more or less regularly accompany the expression. These might
include feelings, associations, and, in some cases, mental images,
which Frege lumps together as *Vorstellungen*, "ideas." Ideas are
subjective, private, changeable, and "have no fixed boundaries," and
it is crucially important to avoid confusing the sense of an expression
with the associated ideas. It is clear that the reference of an
expression, with the exception of special cases like 'my pain' or
'Hitler's idea of justice', purports to be something objective, while the
associated ideas are subjective. In fact, they differ so much from
person to person that it is probably senseless to speak of "the ideas"
associated with a given expression.

But what of the sense? If senses are subjective, Frege argues,
there could be no common store of knowledge amongst people, and
interpersonal communication would be impossible. There obviously
is a common store of knowledge, so senses must be interpersonal
and objective. With the objectivity of senses, the tripart distinction
between reference, sense, and idea can therefore be likened to an
object seen through a telescope, the real image in the telescope, and
the retinal image of each particular observer. The real image is not
the object itself, but an incomplete or partial representation of it. But
it is not for that reason subjective; it would, for instance, survive the

death of all astronomers. The sense of an expression is an objective constituent of the world, independent of both particular minds and minds in general. The non-spatio-temporal, non-physical, non-subjective nature of senses parallels the status of numbers in Frege's ontology.

We now have the necessary conceptual equipment to answer the question raised above concerning the nature of logic. For Frege logic deals with truth in its most fundamental aspect. Although in ordinary language we attribute truth to beliefs, objects, positions, and so forth, the sort of entity to which it most basically applies is a *thought.* We can combine this insight with the sense-reference distinction to claim that *thoughts are the senses of assertoric sentences,* and since senses are objective, so are thoughts. The role of the logician is to deal with thoughts, their properties and their relations, and since they are objective, *the realm of logic is wholly distinct from that of psychology.* Logic deals with the objective properties of thoughts, and not with the subjective, causal properties of thought-occurrences. Only a failure to distinguish clearly between sense and idea, and a certain prejudice in favor of the perceptible, prevents philosophers from assenting to this claim.[46] Logic so envisioned encompasses a good part of what we now call the *theory of meaning.*[47] This broader sense of logic, as contrasted with the much narrower conception qua theory of inference, will be of fundamental importance for Wittgenstein.

The distinction between sense and idea allows Frege to set another task for the logician, one which also anticipates central Tractarian themes. Since in human beings thought (and speech) is frequently accompanied by images, sensations, and so forth, confusion of these mental occurrences with the thinking itself is tempting.

---

[46] The existence of non-perceptible but real entities entails that there must be some human faculty of knowledge which allows access to them. Frege is thus committed to a non-sensible form of knowledge which might be called a priori in the classical sense. In a letter to Honigswald, written about 1924, Frege distinguishes three sources of knowledge: sense perception, the "logical source," and the "geometrical source." Cf. "Sources of Knowledge in Mathematics and the Mathematical Natural Sciences" in *Posthumous Writings,* pp. 267–77. Frege (like Descartes) believes that sense-perception is unreliable unless buttressed by these non-sensory sources of knowledge, although he holds even them to be fallible.

[47] Cf. Dummett, *op. cit.,* ch. 19. Compare: "Anyone can see from my statements up to this point that for me the pure truths of logic are all the ideal laws which have their foundations in the 'senses,' the 'essence' or the 'content' of the concepts of Truth, Proposition, Object, Property, Combination, Law, Fact, etc." Husserl, *LI* I, p. 144. Mohanty writes "The fundamental concept of logic for Frege is the concept of a truth-value. For Husserl it is the concept of meaning." *Op. cit.,* p. 15. On my analysis the difference between the two on this issue is much less.

If we conflate sense with idea, psychologism ensues, and the role of the logician seems to be to investigate the causal laws which govern this play of images and sensations. An analogous danger arises when we confuse a thought or sense with its *physical* manifestation, as Mill did with Number (or, as we shall see in chapter VIII, the naive behaviorist confuses the spoken sentence with the proposition). Frege's tripart distinction between reference, sense, and idea neatly splits language in two; one part logical and necessary, the other "psychological" (Frege's word; frequently "conventional" is more accurate). It is clear that both elements are operative in ordinary language; if they were not, all languages would for instance have the same *grammar*. Thus the logician is presented with the task of "distinguish[ing] the verbal husk from the logical kernel with which, in any given language, it appears to be organically bound up."[48]

Let's look at an example of the essential and inessential in ordinary language. In most natural languages any sentence can be put in either the passive or active voice, without change of sense.

> The sentences 'M gave the document to N', 'Document A was given to N by M' and 'N received document A from M' express exactly the same thought; we learn not a whit more or less from any one of these than we do from the others. (*Ibid.*, p. 141)

The difference between active and passive voice consequently is without significance *for the logician*, although in order to have survived in language it must of course have some *other* role. In the example Frege mentions:

> We are not in a position to say that it is a matter of complete indifference which of these sentences we use. As a rule stylistic and aesthetic reasons will give preference to one of them. If someone asks "Why has A been arrested?" it would be unnatural to reply "B has been murdered by him," because it would require a needless switch of the attention from A to B. (*Ibid.*)

But frequently such non-logical or conventional elements of ordinary language hinder the discovery of logically important properties,

---

[48] "Logic," p. 142. That there is such a logical kernel present—that is, that our goal is not to *replace* a logically defective system of thought with another—lies beneath the surface of Frege's thought, contrasting his with Russell's and very strongly impressing Wittgenstein. "My method is not to sunder the hard from the soft, but to see the hardness of the soft." *NB*, p. 44. Wittgenstein adopts a characteristically Draconian criterion for being non-psychological.

either by masking those logical properties or by presenting as essential merely conventional elements. For instance, some thoughts are negative, others positive. Is there in ordinary language some reasonably dependable sign of this logical difference? One obvious suggestion is the occurrence of the word 'not', as when we say "The President is not wise." However, the sentence "The Pope is bald" is equivalent to "The Pope is not hirsute," yet the latter alone contains 'not'. Frege observes that there is no workable grammatical sign of negativity in judgments; thus, although we can say with assurance on logical grounds that there must be negative thoughts, we cannot with the same assurance give an example of one. Ordinary language fails to accurately reflect the logical reality of our thoughts both by failing to provide a consistent sign of the negative thought, and by providing a misleading claimant to that title.[49]

The failure of sentences which express negative thoughts to reflect that fact is but one example of the shortcomings of ordinary language. Frege mentions the confusion, so easy in ordinary language, between object-words and concept-words, which leads to many of the puzzles about number investigated in *FA*.[50] But how can we avoid such problems? One way Frege recommends is the study of foreign languages; since each clothes the same thoughts in different garb we often come to recognize what is essential and what not.[51] But this procedure is neither infallible nor general enough, since languages of the same family—Romance languages, for instance— often share general but inessential traits. Thus what is needed is a system of representation which abstracts completely from the psychological-conventional component of language, leaving only the essential or logical element.

In his *Begriffsschrift*, his "concept-writing," Frege believes he has found just such a purified language. Of it he writes:

> If it is the task of philosophy to break the power of the word over the human
> mind, uncovering illusions which through the use of language almost
> unavoidably arise concerning the relations of concepts, freeing thought from

---

[49] The problem of negative thoughts, introduced in *ibid.*, pp. 149–50, is developed more fully in "Negation," Geach and Black *op. cit.*, pp. 117–35.

[50] For the concept/object distinction, cf. "On Concept and Object." *Ibid.*, pp. 42–55. For the puzzles of number, and their relation to the conflation of this distinction, see *FA*, #97.

[51] Wittgenstein sarcastically observes, "A French politician [Elsewhere he adds "I believe M. Briand." Cf. Hallett *op. cit.*, p. 399] once wrote that it was a peculiarity of the French language that in it words occur in the order in which one thinks them." *PI*, #336.

that which only the nature of linguistic means attaches to it, then my "conceptual notation," further developed for these purposes, can become a useful tool for philosophers.[52]

Since the *Begriffsschrift* must meet the minimal demands of human perceptibility and utilize the conventions of writing, it too must contain some inessential components. That human intuition is sensible, for instance, requires that we use perceptible signs for concepts, objects, and functions, and on a more pedestrian level, the pragmatic demands of printing technology require that the array of signs we utilize be two-dimensional. But such discrepancies between pure thought and symbolism, Frege argues, are "unavoidable and harmless," unable to alter the Begriffsschrift's role as the "language of pure thought."

Looking back on the preceding sections, we see that post-Kantian logicians, conflating empirical and transcendental conditions on consciousness, tend to construe the principles of logic as general psychological rules. In addition to this pressure from above, as it were, psychologism is rendered attractive by its affinity for the British empirical tradition, amenable as it is to a nominalistic treatment of logical terms. Frege's critique of psychologism reaches very deep; whether it is sufficient to flatly refute psychologism and the associated Millian empiricism in mathematics is open to debate, but Frege does point out just how much the psychologistic logician or mathematician must surrender. Maintaining any reasonable kind of necessity for mathematical and logical truths thus requires that psychologism be shunned.

The consequence of Frege's argument is that we must demand that both the principles and concepts of logic are mind-independent, that every logical or mathematical judgment has as its object some extramental entity. Although Frege's realistic arguments concentrate on mathematical and logical judgments, the position allows easy and plausible generalization to a wider sort of realism. This broader realism *holds* that every (or almost every) judgment has some extramental object which is independent of the act of judging. But in ordinary judgments like "Nixon resigned in disgrace" or

---

[52] This is from the "Preface"; Bynum *op. cit.*, p. 106.

"Frege wrote well," what *are* those extramental objects? The *Begriffsschrift* has shown that surface grammar can be at best misleading, and as we shall see in the following section, naive acceptance of surface grammar, when coupled with the realist thesis, produces alarming and damaging paradoxes. Thus in the following section we must examine the robust early realism of Russell and Moore, concentrating on these infelicitous consequences of realism, the parallel inadequacy of ordinary language, and the birth of twentieth-century analysis.

The Early Realism of Russell and Moore

When Russell matriculated at Cambridge in 1890, the neo-Hegelian school centered about Bradley, Joachim, and others held, if not total sway, certainly center stage. Under the influence of Moore Russell's youthful enthusiasm for Hegelianism crumbled. He had come to philosophy to find support for the truth of mathematical judgments, and was thus constitutionally unwilling to accept the Hegelian thesis that such judgments were *not* (wholly) true. Together, he and Moore led an attack on Absolute Idealism from which it to date has not recovered, and although the philosophical validity of these attacks is open to debate,[53] the historical influence of the doctrines of Russell and Moore and their almost total dominance of the British intellectual life of the day cannot.[54]

Bradley's opus magnum *Appearance and Reality* (1893) sets forth an Hegelian position which while to some extent decidedly non-orthodox (when compared, e.g., with the writings of his contemporary Bosanquet), argues for and traces for the conse-

---

[53] Cf. for instance A. J. Ayer, *Russell and Moore; the Analytic Heritage* (Harvard U. Press, Cambridge, 1970), ch. 6.

[54] "I went up to Cambridge at Michaelmas of 1902, and Moore's *Principia Ethica* came out at the end of my first year. I have never heard of the present generation reading it, but, of course, its effect on *us*, and the talk which preceded and followed it, dominated, and perhaps still dominates, everything else." J. M. Keynes, "My Early Beliefs," reprinted in his *Essays and Sketches in Biography*, (Meridian Books, New York, 1956), p. 241. "Russell's *Principles of Mathematics* came out the same year as *Principia Ethica;* and the former, by spirit, furnished a method for handling the material presented by the latter." (*Ibid.*, p. 244) Keynes's sketches of the Bloomsbury group provide a vivid portrait of what I can imagine to be those elements in upperclass British society which Wittgenstein found decadent and disgusting.

Keynes's views on the importance of Russell and Moore were apparently not *universally* held: "I think if you inquire you will find that neither your brother nor Russell have in this matter of realism convinced philosophers—at least, I was told so at Oxford with some emphasis." W. B. Yeats in a letter to Sturge Moore, dated January 1926. Cf. *W. B. Yeats and T. Sturge Moore; Their Correspondence 1901–1937*, ed. U. Bridge (Routledge and Kegan Paul, London, 1953), p. 64.

quences of two major Idealist theses. The first is the Berkelian claim that *esse est percipi;* every object of experience is logically dependent on an experiencer, and subject and object are but two aspects analyzed (perhaps illegitimately) from the unity of experience. The other is the *thesis of monism;* reality is in essence unitary and singular, and plurality is the sign of appearance or illusion. We have seen each of these claims in our examination of Schopenhauer, but the neo-Hegelian rejection of the thing-in-itself degrades Appearances to a purely mental level. Bradley's defense of the thesis of monism is logical, based on the so-called *doctrine of internal relations*, although as Russell points out the title is somewhat misleading insofar as the substance of the doctrine is that there are no (real) relations whatsoever, the notion of a relation being logically defective.

Moore assails these twin pillars of neo-Hegelianism in a series of influential papers, the two most important being "A Refutation of Idealism" (1903) and "Internal and External Relations" (1919).[55] Additional impetus for the thrust towards realism and pluralism was provided by the not always critical acceptance of *Principia Ethica;* there Moore puts forth a devastating critique of subjectivism in ethics, arguing in a manner reminiscent of Frege that Goodness is a primitive, objective, non-natural property.[56] Although Russell's realism is slightly later than Moore's, I will choose as my chief stalking horse Russell's *Principles of Mathematics.*[57] This work is almost perfect for our purposes, combining a very vivid and wide-ranging realism with an unusual willingness to accept as significant the surface grammar of ordinary language, perhaps in response to the standard Hegelian tendency to regard ordinary experience as *not* significant. In *PrM* Russell also introduces the important notion of a *primitive*, so central to his work, Moore's and, as we shall see, Wittgenstein's.

In a review of a series of works by Meinong, Russell offers a

---

[55] Both reprinted in Moore's *Philosophical Studies* (Routledge and Kegan Paul, London, 1922), pp. 1–30 and 276–309 respectively. But see Moore's comments on the theses of these early papers in his "Replies" to the critical papers collected in *The Philosophy of G. E. Moore*, ed. P. A. Schilpp (Open Court, La Salle, IL, 1942), pp. 533–688.

[56] *Principia Ethica*, pp. 6–16. Ironically, Moore's realism might well have been influenced by the strong anti-subjectivist spirit of Bradley's monumental *Principles of Logic*, vols. I and II (Oxford U. Press, Oxford, 1883), henceforth abbreviated *PoL*.

[57] B. Russell, *The Principles of Mathematics* (Norton, New York, 1903). I shall hereafter refer to this work as *'PrM'*.

straightforward definition of the sort of realism with which we shall be occupied. He writes:

> [E]very presentation and every belief must have an object other than itself and, except in certain cases where mental existents happen to be concerned, extramental; what is commonly called perception has as its object an existential proposition, into which enters as a constituent that whose existence is concerned, and not the idea of this existent; that truth and falsehood apply not to the beliefs, but to their objects; and that the object of a thought, even when this object does not exist, has a Being which is in no way dependent upon its being an object of thought.[58]

Russell attributes this view to Frege and Meinong, although as we shall see the characterization fits *PrM* perfectly. Perhaps this realism is most easily grasped by way of a simple example. Consider the sentence "The cat is on the mat." What is this sentence *about*? The realist thesis demands that it be something extramental, and we can legitimately ask what the requisite extramental existents *are*. The most natural response is probably that it is about the cat, the mat, and perhaps (the sophisticate will add) the relation of *being on*. This answer rests on the presupposition that surface grammar—grammar in the grade-school sense—is an accurate reflection of what we might call *logical grammar*. The view that ordinary grammar is a reasonably accurate guide to "real" grammar has a great deal of attractiveness, particularly if we keep in mind the historical context in which Russell and Moore wrote; there it comes less from logical naivete than from a firm rejection of the Idealist dogma that appearance must *always* differ radically from reality, and thus can *never* be taken as a guide. But moreover, "The cat is on the mat" is a paradigm example of a straightforward, unproblematic sentence

---

[58] B. Russell, "Meinong's Theory of Complexes and Assumption," *Mind* n.s. XIII (1904), p. 204. The three papers of this series are reprinted in more accessible form in Russell, *Essays in Analysis*, ed. D. Lackey (Braziller, New York, 1972), pp. 17–76. The interested reader would profit from the detailed discussion of this passage in R. M. Chisholm, ed. *op. cit.*, pp. 3–12. Keep in mind that what Russell here calls a proposition is Meinong's "objective" and might best be thought of as a possible fact.

John Wild offers a somewhat looser but perhaps wider characterization of realism; "Plato ... held that there is a fixed and stable world order which is in no way dependent on the opinions and desires of men, that this order can be known by human reason as it really is, and finally that such knowledge is the only reliable guide to human action .... These are the three fundamental theses of realistic thought ..." John Wild, *Introduction to Realistic Philosophy* (Harper and Bros., New York, 1948), p. 12. It is characteristic of the philosophical doldrums of our times, perhaps, that in the chapter entitled "Realistic philosophy and its history," Wild omits any reference to Russell, Moore, Frege, or Meinong.

which is completely clear to all of us, and if there was something fishy about its surface grammar, why should we understand it so well?

A charitable reading of surface grammar seems to fit naturally with a further claim. Russell writes "It must be admitted, I think, that every word in every sentence must have *some* meaning." If this were not the case, he continues, then the occurrence of that word in the sentence would be irrelevant to the meaning of the sentence, and it would not matter whether we included it or not.[59] This observation combines easily with realism to produce the *linguistic correlate* of the realist thesis; the meaning of a word is an (extramental) object which corresponds to the word. Thus every word in a sentence has a meaning insofar as it stands for some object. We might call this the *name theory of language*. Every word is actually a *name* for something; nouns stand for things or concepts, verbs stand for relations, and so forth. The sledding gets a bit tougher when we turn to logical particles such as 'or' and 'not'—we shall have occasion soon to question whether such words name "logical objects".

The charm of such a realistic theory of ordinary language is obvious; it allows us to take surface grammar quite seriously, lending a down-to-earth air to philosophical investigations. It also hints at a sort of egalitarianism: just as Moore argues that we must take the ordinary man's ethical views and his beliefs about what exists seriously, so Russell confers the same status on the ordinary man's utterances.

> The study of grammar, in my opinion, is capable of throwing far more light on philosophical questions than is commonly supposed by philosophers. Although a grammatical distinction cannot be uncritically assumed to correspond to a genuine philosophical difference, yet one is prima facie evidence of the other .... On the whole, grammar seems to me to bring us much nearer to a correct logic than the current opinions of philosophers, and in what follows, grammar, although not our master, will yet be taken as our guide.[60]

---

[59] *PrM*, # 46. One of the reasons Russell offers in defense of this claim contrasts strikingly with Wittgenstein's later position. "A perfectly meaningless sound could not be employed in the more or less fixed way in which language employs words." It does not occur to Russell that, quite to the contrary, the meaning may well be a result of the "more or less fixed way" in which we use the word. This of course is one major theme of *PI*.

[60] *Ibid.*, p. 42. Compare with J. L. Austin, "A Plea for Excuses," *loc. cit.*, esp. pp. 169ff. But also compare with the discussion of Locke above.

The "current opinions of philosophers" might be typified by Bradley's *Principles of Logic*. There Bradley argues that an examination of negative existential propositions ('There are no unicorns'), singular propositions, and others shows us that the apparent grammatical subject is *never* the real logical subject. (*Op.cit.*, pp. 42 ff.) The real logical subject of every proposition is of course the unitary absolute reality, which can never be reached, but only approximated through successive syntheses. Over against such a position, a little school grammar must have looked like a philosophical oasis in a hopeless desert of endless infinite synthesis.

This apparently happy view of the syntax and semantics of ordinary language is not without puzzles, however. Consider the following sentences:

(a) The cat is on the mat.
(b) The Golden Mountain exists.
(c) The Golden Mountain does not exist.
(d) The present Queen of England is married.
(e) The present King of France is bald.
(f) The round square exists.
(g) The round square is round and square.

If (a) is about the cat and the mat, what is (b) about? Since there is no Golden Mountain, our enthusiasm for saying that the sentence must be about it flags somewhat. (c) is even more puzzling because its whole point seems to be asserting that there is *no* Golden Mountain. (d) is true if the Queen has the requisite property, false otherwise. But what of (e)? If there is no present King of France, then common sense would indicate that the proposition in question was false. But is its negation—'The present King of France is not bald'—then true? Or must we reject the Law of Excluded Middle? Finally, even the comforting fall-back position that (b) and (e) are about merely *possible* entities cannot deal with (f) and (g), which appear to be about *impossible* entities. Even worse, (g) seems to be analytic and thus *true*.

Faced with such difficulties, several avenues are open to the logician. In 1903 Russell chooses to swallow hard and preserve both the realist thesis and the name theory of language by admitting that expressions like "the present King of France," which *appear* not to stand for anything, in fact *do* have objects. As a good mathematician, perhaps bearing in mind Frege's warning that we ought not be blinded by a prejudice in favor of the spatio-temporal or "actual," Russell writes:

> Whatever can be the object of thought, or may occur in any true or false proposition, or can be counted as *one*, I call a *term*. This, then, is the widest word in the philosophical vocabulary. I shall use it as synonymous with the words unity, individual, and entity . . . . Every term has being, i.e., *is* in some sense. A man, a moment, a chimera, is sure to be a term; and to deny that such and such is a term must always be false.[61]

Thus anything that we can mention *for that reason* is a term, and the claim that such-and-such is *not* a term must always be nonsensical. There is an obvious difference, however, between the present Queen of England and the (putative) present King of France, which Russell marks by saying that the former exists, while the latter merely subsists or has Being. In a similar vein Meinong writes "The totality of what exists, including what has existed and will exist, is infinitely small in comparison to the totality of objects," and suggests a new science, the "theory of objects."[62]

One consequence of the theory of language here offered is that questions about the objects of thought can generally be reduced to questions about *what we say*. The question, How many sorts of things are there in the world?, for instance, reduces to, How many different sorts of things do we talk about? This move from talking about things to talking about language, so characteristic of much of the philosophy of this century, is often puzzling or infuriating to those who do not understand the development of the theory of meanings; evidence the hostility that such slogans as Quine's "To be

---

[61] *Op. cit.*, p. 43. Moore's realism eschews Russell's individuals in favor of more Platonic entities which he calls *concepts;* cf. his "The Nature of Judgment," *Mind* (1899), pp. 176–93. Contrast Russell's use of 'term' with Frege's claim that a word with no contrary is pointless; *FA*, p. 40.

　　Interestingly, by 1905 Russell attributes this super-realist position to Meinong, when in fact his *PrM* position of 1900 is a much better example than anything that Meinong ever wrote. This is doubly puzzling since Russell wrote the series of very perceptive articles on Meinong's philosophy mentioned above. Russell's widely known characterization provides the basis for the philosophical myth of Meinong as the ultimate ontological spendthrift. For somewhat less biased analysis of Meinong's ontology, see R. Grossman, *Meinong* (Routledge and Kegan Paul, 1974), chs. I–V.

[62] Meinong, "The Theory of Objects," trans. Levi et al. in Chisholm, ed., *op. cit.*, p. 79. Compare with Carnap, *The Logical Structure of the World*, trans. R. George (U. of California, Berkeley, CA, 1967), Part II B.

is to be the value of a bound variable" evince among the unreceptive. Perhaps more reflection ought be directed towards Austin's suggestive term "linguistic phenomenology."

There are problems which stand in the way of this "new science," and to these we shall turn in the following chapter. But it is important to see such robust realism as a natural outgrowth of the turn towards common sense on the part of Russell and Moore; that at one stage it endorses Golden Mountains, contemporary French royalty and round squares represents a great philosophical irony. Likewise ironically, analysis—the reduction therapy Russell prescribes for this bloated universe—brings back to the philosophical spotlight the old idealist insistence on a fundamental distinction between appearance and reality.

IV

Analysis and Denoting

> The question might however also be presented like this:
> it seems that the idea of a SIMPLE is already contained in
> that of a complex and in the idea of analysis, and in such a
> way that we come to this idea quite apart from any
> examples of simple objects, or propositions which mention
> them, and we realized the existence of the simple object—
> *a priori*—as a logical necessity .... The simple object is
> *prejudged* in the complex.
>
> —*NOTEBOOKS* 14.5.15

In the previous chapter, largely given over to a discussion of the realistic reaction to logical psychologism, we saw hints of a broader sort of realism. This realism, founded on the arguments of Husserl and Frege, supports what might be described as *a general theory of consciousness*. In the closing pages of the previous chapter I introduced certain "puzzles," as Russell calls them, which arise from the combination of such a more comprehensive realism with a common-sense theory of the meanings of words and an innocent acceptance of the surface grammar of ordinary language. The core of this chapter will be devoted to an examination of the most important of these puzzles and Russell's procedure for eliminating them. It is flippant to speak of them as "puzzles"; their roots are very deep indeed. Russell's method for dealing with them is best seen in the context of quite older problems.

Existence, Nonexistence, and Being

> The totality of what exists, including what has existed and
> what will exist, is infinitely small in comparison with the
> totality of objects.
>
> —MEINONG

The realist holds that every act of consciousness is directed towards some object, and that save in special cases (thinking about my headache) these objects are extramental. With respect to the first point, Moore invites us to consider that even when we are imaging a centaur we are clearly not imagining *nothing*, since imagining a centaur would then be identical with imagining a griffin, which it is not.[1] Common sense supports the second point; Russell points out that we normally take the objects of our judgment to be external to our minds.[2] For instance, when I judge that elephants are larger than church-mice, I would not normally take myself to be comparing my *ideas* of elephants and church-mice (although of course we sometimes *do* compare our ideas.) Likewise, denying that there are centaurs is not equivalent to denying that I have the *idea* of a centaur—that would indeed be puzzling, since it would entail that I did not know what I am denying .

Yet despite its common-sense roots, realism almost immediately entangles us in paradox. The negative existential propositions I mention in the previous paragraph offer a simple example. For 'Centaurs do not exist' to be meaningful and thus true, each word must be meaningful. On the name theory of language, this is tantamount to saying that there is some object for which each word stands. But 'Centaurs do not exist' cannot be *about centaurs*, one should think, since the whole point of the sentence is to deny that there *are* such things.[3] The problem of negative existentials is but the tip of an iceberg; these logical issues and their treatment are intimately connected with a traditional metaphysical thesis that contingent existents must be based on or supported by a realm of entities which are *not* contingent. This thesis goes to the roots of classical western philosophy, and in it we shall see the genesis of the central Tractarian notion that non-contingent existence cannot be *composite*.

The epistemological critique in Descartes' *Meditations* challenges ordinary beliefs in order to ascertain their foundations. All empirical beliefs fall before the Dreaming Argument. Since there is no "certain sign" that I am not now dreaming, and since if I *were* to be dreaming I could not justifiably make judgment on the basis of my present perceptions, all empirical beliefs must be bracketed. But

---

[1] *Some Main Problems of Philosophy* (Allen and Unwin, London, 1953), pp. 212–14.

[2] "Meinong's Theory of Complexes and Assumptions," *Mind*, vol. 13 (1904), pp. 63–64.

[3] Compare with Plato's formulation of this difficulty at *Theatetus* 189a. Bradley sees the problem of negative existentials as a primary reason for mistrusting surface grammar; cf. *PoL*, p. 13.

though we doubt that "we open our eyes, shake our heads, extend our hand and so forth ..."

> At the same time we must at least confess that the things which are represented to us in sleep are like painted representations which only have been formed as a counterpart of something real and true. (*HR* I, p. 146)

Most artists can vividly represent imaginary things—"sirens and satyrs"—only by composing such images from "a certain medley of members of other animals," in the manner that a griffin is composed of features of lions and eagles. But even if the artist is very clever and imaginative, "it is certain all the same that the colors of which this is composed are necessarily real." (*Ibid.*) (Notice the change in the *kind* of "parts" involved.) Thus if many of the objects of our thought are thus fictitious, "there are at least some other objects yet more simple and universal, which are real and true ..." (*Ibid.*) As examples of such "more simple and universal" entities Descartes offers:

> ... corporeal substance in general and its extension, the figure of extended things, their quantity or magnitude and number ... the place in which they are, the time which measures their duration and so on. (*Ibid.*)

Some sciences, Descartes argues, make existential claims about composite objects, and the dreaming argument has made such claims doubtable. Thus the results of Physics, Astronomy, Medicine, and so forth must be bracketed. But Geometry and Arithmetic and "other sciences of that kind which only treat of things that are very simple and universal" are untouched by the dreaming argument.

> For whether I am awake or asleep, two and three together always form five, and the square can never have more than four sides, and it does not seem possible that truths so clear and apparent can be suspected of any falsity or uncertainty. (*Ibid.*)

This is because these sciences:

> ... treat only of things that are very simple and general, without taking great trouble to ascertain whether they are actually existent or not.[4]

---

[4] *Ibid.* The claim here presented is ambiguous, meaning alternatively (a) we do not care whether mathematical objects exist or not, or (b) they are the sorts of things which necessarily exist or to which existence is not to be predicated. I take Descartes to mean the latter.

The implications of Descartes' argument are apparent:

> ... If we suppose a triangle to be given, the three angles must certainly be equal to two right angles; but for all that I saw no reason to be assured that there was any such triangle in existence ... (*HR* I, p. 104)

Anthony Kenny points out that the antecedent is ambiguous, meaning either:[5]

(a) If a triangle exists, then it has three angles summing to 180°.
(b) Any triangle, existent or not, has three angles summing to 180°.

Claim (a) seems trivial, but (b)—the natural interpretation—implies the paradoxical conclusion that there are truths about triangles even if no triangles exist. On the surface this seems preposterous; Hobbes objects:

> If a triangle exists nowhere, I do not understand how it can have a nature; for what is nowhere, is not, and therefore has not a being or nature ... (*HR* II, p. 76)

Hobbes's prejudice in favor of the spatio-temporal notwithstanding, his point is well taken; must not a thing have *some* sort of being to have properties?

Descartes' solution to this dilemma turns on the "very simple and universal things" mentioned above—the "simple natures" of Rule XII.[6] These simple natures are atoms, as it were, of which complexes, even imaginary complexes, are composed. Their salient characteristic is simplicity or unanalyzability:

> We use the term 'simple' only for realities so clearly and distinctly known that we cannot divide them into realities more distinctly known. (*Ibid.*, p. 41)

---

[5] A. Kenny, *Descartes: A Study of his Philosophy* (Random House, New York, 1968), p. 147. For reasons soon to be evident, it is interesting to note Kenny's observation that the difference between (a) and (b) cannot be brought out in the "Frege-Russell notation," that is, in a purely extensional calculus.

[6] *Rules for the Direction of the Mind*, in *HR* I, pp. 40 ff. Also see *HR* I, pp. 16, 180, 225, and *HR* II, pp. 53, 263–66. Compare with *Treatise* I/i/5 on the "philosophical relations" and Kant's Table of Categories, *CPR*, p. 113.

Note the important corollary; simple things are either completely known or not known at all, since incomplete knowledge entails a part which is known and an unknown part.

Why are sciences which deal with simple natures unconcerned about existence, and how does reference to such simple natures help with the problems concerning the properties of a non-existent triangle? Descartes' answer is that *existence itself* is such a simple nature. Composite existences are combinations of certain simple natures, sometimes including the simple nature existence. One important implication is that existence can be meaningfully predicated only of *composites*. Simple natures stand in certain relations one to another, which may be either necessary or contingent. The relation between a triangle and the sum of its interior angles is a necessary relation between such simple natures. Since mathematics deals only with such relations among simple natures, which are not the sorts of things to which existence or nonexistence can be predicated, the failure to exist of every composite cannot affect the truth of mathematical claims.

Consider the points of interest in Descartes' argument. First, puzzles arise when we try to talk or think about what is *not*. There are apparently true statements which seem to be about non-existent entities, as well as statements whose truth seems quite neutral with respect to the existence of the entities they seem to mention. Second, one way to escape such difficulties is to translate, as it were, the apparent reference to non-existent things into reference to the *components* of those things. Finally, as the problem of non-existence might reappear there, these constituents, or at least the simplest, most ultimate constituents, must be such that existence and non-existence cannot be predicated of them. They have a more fundamental sort of reality, which we will call Being. A study of the nature of existence therefore leads us to a realm of entities which do not themselves exist, but which form the ground of all possible existence.

Variants of the argument above are ubiquitous in the western philosophical tradition. Plato's Ideas, Leibniz's monads, Spinoza's God, Meinong's Objectives, Moore's "concepts," the "terms" of Russell's *PrM*, in a rather different way the Absolute of the British Hegelians and, as we shall see, the Objects of the *Tractatus*, all play the role of providing a non-contingent (and thus non-existent) basis for contingent existence. The technical difficulties which give occasion to such theories crop up in myriad contexts, and the metaphysical urge which gives rise to the postulation of Being runs very deep; at the very least, it infects a large part of the logical/semantic studies of the nineteenth century. But the bloated ontologies that such theories spawn carry with them unattractive aspects, and in the following section we shall examine a method, proposed by Russell, for apparently avoiding commitment to entities which *have Being* (or "subsist") but do not *exist*. Ironically, it will lead straightway back to a new form of the very appearance/reality distinction which, in its Hegelian form, prompted the adoption of a straightforward realism in the first place. It will also lead us back to Being in somewhat new guise.

The Theory of Descriptions and Incomplete Symbols

> The ultimate subject in Judgment is always Reality.
> Of course the logical subject may be quite different from
> the grammatical subject.
>
> —BOSANQUET, *ESSENTIALS OF LOGIC*

> It was Russell who performed the service of showing that
> the apparent form of a proposition need not be its real one.
>
> —4.0031

Russell's "On Denoting" appeared in *Mind* in 1905.[7] Its impact on philosophy in our century is hard to overestimate. Frank Ramsey referred to it as "that paradigm of philosophy," and Russell himself singled it out as "my finest philosophical essay." The thesis which Russell there presents reigned almost unchallenged for nearly fifty years, until the appearance of P. F. Strawson's "On Referring."[8]

The contention of the paper—that the superficial grammar of some propositions is systematically misleading—was not new. Boole recognized that Universal Affirmative propositions ("All men are mortal") must be analyzed as hypothetical or conditional rather than categorical. Bradley—often somewhat hazily portrayed as Russell's philosophical opposite number—frequently stressed the unreliability of surface grammar for reasons quite reminiscent of

---

[7] My references will be to the article as reprinted in B. Russell, *Logic and Knowledge*, ed. R. C. Marsh (Capricorn Books, New York, 1956), pp. 39–56. (This book is hereafter abbreviated as *L&K*.)

[8] *Mind*, vol. 59 (1950), pp. 320–44.

Russell's. Defending the claim that every judgment is directed towards or about reality against the putative counterexample 'The foursided circle is an impossibility,' he writes, "The objection is irrelevant, unless it is maintained that in every case we affirm the reality of the *grammatical subject.*"[9] Bradley likewise maintained that many philosophical mistakes arise through the illusions which the grammar of ordinary language forces upon us.

But credit for the distinction between real and apparent grammar, which the history of philosophy bestows upon Russell, is justifiable for several reasons. Russell consistently maintained that certain technical advances in logic enable us to see through the mistakes of previous generations of philosophers. As early as his work on Leibniz (1900) he argued that Leibniz's monadism arose from the fetters of neo-Aristotelian logic, with its assumption that every proposition can be put in subject-predicate form.[10] Characteristically, Russell adds that all that is needed is a notation which allows of perspicuous treatment of relational terms. This aura of breakthrough, carrying with it the tacit permission to ignore the history of philosophy, no doubt made it attractive to many. No doubt certain social and political factors were operative too; one need only compare Bradley's "My Station and its Duties" with the essays in Russell's *Why I am not a Christian* to sense the chasms present even between British middle-class intellectuals, a chasm which perhaps made rebellion against the philosophical status quo both possible and attractive.[11] But perhaps the most important reason is that Russell surpassed his predecessors in two crucial ways: he showed how logical innovations could pave the way to significant philosophical change, and he provided *concrete analyses* of particular questionable sentences. Without the latter the former is, to use Russell's term, an "unredeemed promissory note."

---

[9] *PoL* I, p. 42, also pp. 13, 154–55, 157 and many other passages. For similar arguments, see B. Bosanquet, *Essentials of Logic* (Kraus Reprint, NY, 1968), pp. 70ff. Significantly, it may have been in reaction to Bradley's neo-Hegelian distrust of common sense and ordinary language that Russell first adopted the rather naive view of ordinary grammar he espouses before 1905. "In my first rebellion against Hegel, I believed that a thing must exist if Hegel's proof that it cannot is invalid." *My Philosophical Development* (Simon and Schuster, NY, 1959), p. 62.

[10] B. Russell, *A Critical Examination of the Philosophy of Leibniz,* (George Allen and Unwin, London, 1900), chs. 1–2.

[11] Bradley's paper is reprinted in his *Ethical Studies* (Oxford U. Press, Oxford, 1876). Russell's collection of essays was published by George Allen and Unwin in 1957, although a good deal of the material was written much earlier.

In 1905 this logical advance takes the form of the Theory of Descriptions, which Russell later generalizes to a more comprehensive theory of "incomplete symbols." Since the Theory of Descriptions is introduced to solve certain logical puzzles, let us first consider those puzzles.

(a) If A and B are identical, then Leibniz's Law tells us that what is true of one ought to be true of the other, and vice versa, since they are in reality not *two* but *one*. Thus, the symbol 'a' ought to be replaceable by the symbol 'b' (and vice versa) without any change in the truth-value of the larger contexts in which they appear. If Cicero is Tully, then we ought to be able to substitute 'Cicero' for 'Tully' in the proposition 'Tully had fun at the party' without change of truth-value.

However, this is frequently not the case. King George IV wanted to know whether *Waverley*, which had been published anonymously, was written by Scott. Thus, 'George IV wondered whether Scott was the author of *Waverley*' is true. Since Scott in fact *did* write *Waverley*, we ought to be able to substitute 'Scott' for 'the author of *Waverley*' *salva veritas*. But such substitution yields the absurd proposition 'George IV wondered whether Scott was Scott.' Russell observes "An interest in the law of identity can hardly be attributed to the first gentleman of Europe."

(b) The Law of Excluded Middle says that either A is B or A is not-B. But consider the pair of sentences, 'The present King of France is bald' and 'The present King of France is not-bald.' If we enumerate all the bald things in the world, and then all the non-bald things, the current French Monarch occurs on neither list. Thus, neither proposition appears to be true, and the Law of Excluded Middle seems to be violated. Russell quips "Hegelians, who love a synthesis, would probably conclude that he wears a wig."

(c) 'A differs from B' can be reworded 'The difference between A and B subsists.' But if A and B are identical, then there is no such difference. But we cannot say 'The difference between A and B does not subsist', since to speak intelligibly of the difference—even to deny it—we must grant it *some* being. Thus, if A=B, it seems that there both is and is not some entity which is the difference between A and B, and the Law of Contradiction seems to be violated.[12]

In examining Russell's solution to these difficulties, it is wise to keep before us the main alternative which Russell seeks to avoid. One solution to (b) (the one which Russell embraces in *PrM*) allows that the putative entity "The present King of France" does not exist but "subsists" or "has Being", and then claims that the Law of Excluded Middle does not hold for merely subsistent entities. (This is of course less plausible with respect to Bradley's "foursided circle") This is Meinong's tack; it has the feature, attractive to some, that logical laws like the Law of Excluded Middle can be treated like natural laws, that is, as having limited applicability. (Note the underlying premise; there is something mysterious about a law which applies to *every* eventuality, a property which *every* object has.) Thus for one class of objects the Law of Excluded Middle holds, but not for another, and so forth for all logical principles. The round square, for instance, is an object for which the Law of Contradiction fails to hold.[13] This solution is particularly repugnant to Wittgenstein, since it implies that there must be some science higher than logic, which indicates when logical principles apply and when they don't. But Russell points out that it also violates a certain "sense of reality" to which logicians must remain sensitive.[14] But perhaps more importantly, the theory of descriptions will provide a *unified* solution to such puzzles, and this unity of treatment must have held a particular attraction for a scientifically minded philosopher like Russell.

Russell's alternative shows that we need not treat such phrases as 'the present King of France' as real (that is, logical) constituents of propositions at all. In simplest form the theory of descriptions offers a correct analysis—one displaying the "real logical form"—of propositions with grammatical subjects having a certain form, and a technical apparatus for translating such sentences into a more

---

[12] This very difficult example (made even more difficult by the use of 'subsists' to denote the mode of existence which relations have) is in reality just the familiar problem of negative existential propositions. How can we intelligibly *deny* the existence of something (here the relation of difference), since to do so we must mention it, thereby making it a term and conferring some sort of reality upon it?

[13] Cf. Grossman, *op. cit.*, pp. 206ff.

[14] B. Russell, *Introduction to Mathematical Philosophy* (George Allen and Unwin, London, 1919), pp. 169–70. (This work is hereafter abbreviated 'IMP'.)

perspicuous form. Russell characterizes *denoting phrases* by offering a list of examples:

> A man, some man, any man, every man, the present King of England, the present King of France, the center of mass of the solar system at the first instant of the twentieth century, the revolution of the earth around the sun, the revolution of the sun around the earth. ("On Denoting," p. 41)

Importantly, a phrase is thus a denoting phrase by virtue of its grammatical structure, its ability to appear in certain places in a sentence. This is not to be confused with the question of whether or not it *actually succeeds in denoting something*. Some phrases, Russell observes, denote just one thing ('the present Queen of England'), others denote ambiguously ('some man'), and curiously, others appear to fail to denote at all ('the present King of France'). Russell terms examples like the second *indefinite descriptions*, and the first and third *definite descriptions*, since if they succeed in referring at all, they refer to exactly *one* thing.

Russell traces the problems with puzzles (a)–(c) above to the occurrence in each of a definite description: 'the present King of France', 'the difference between A and B', and 'the author of *Waverley.*' Russell's technical suggestion is that we eliminate such contexts (as well as indefinite descriptions) in favor of less troublesome expressions. As we shall see, this apparently ad hoc logic-chopping is founded on certain important philosophical insights.

The fundamental logical concept employed is one which Russell inherits from Frege, namely that of a *propositional function:* a function whose values are propositions.[15] 'x is a man' is not itself a proposition, but becomes one (and gains a truth-value) when a name or description is instantiated for x, or when the scope of the variable is indicated via a quantifier. Using quantifiers we can straightaway eliminate indefinite descriptions. Consider the sentences 'I met a man' and 'All men are mortal', which in 1903 Russell construed as being about the *entia suspecta* 'some man' and 'all men'. In terms of quantified propositional functions they become:

---

[15] In "On Denoting" Russell refers to them as "propositional variables", but I shall employ the more standard terminology. I will also present Russell's translations in a form somewhat simpler than his cumbersome (and suspect) metalinguistic versions.

'I met a man' $=_{df} (\exists x)(x$ is a man and I met $x)$

'All men are mortal' $=_{df} (x)(\text{If } x$ is a man, then x is mortal)

The Russellian translations on the right no longer contain phrases which refer to the suspect entities 'a man' and 'all men,' but rather are "about" every value of the variable x in the propositional functions. The first proposition, for instance, is true if there is some entity which is jointly a man and something I met, and is false otherwise. Since 'all men' and 'a man' no longer appear in our translations, we are relieved of the necessity to commit ourselves to entities which correspond to them.[16]

Elimination of definite descriptions is somewhat more difficult, but the logical technique is similar. The proposition 'The present King of France is bald' *appears* to be about the shadowy current French monarch. But Russell offers the following translation:

'The present King of France is bald' $=_{df} (\exists x)(x$ is the present King of France and x is bald and $(y)(\text{if } y$ is the present King of France then $y = x))$

The existentially quantified conjunct claims that there is at least one entity which satisfies both the propositional function 'x is the present King of France' and 'x is bald', while the universally quantified conjunct stipulates that there is at most *one* such entity. Jointly they then claim uniqueness, and the proposition in question is false if any of the conjuncts are false. Let us now see how the logical techniques presented solve the puzzles to which they were addressed. Beforehand note that I have yet to offer any *philosophical justification* for the translation procedure. At this stage it remains little more than a suggested alternative notation.

(a) 'George IV wondered whether Scott was the author of *Waverley*'

is ambiguous, meaning either (i) George IV wondered whether there was exactly one man who wrote *Waverley* and Scott was that man, or (ii) there was exactly one man who wrote *Waverley* and George IV

---

[16] Compare with Bradley's parallel point: "In existential judgments ... the apparent is not the actual subject. Let us take such a denial as 'chimeras are non-existent.' 'Chimeras' is here ostensibly the subject, but it is really the predicate. It is the quality of harboring chimeras which is denied of the nature of things ..." *PoL*, p. 120.

wondered whether Scott was that man. (Compare: "I want a sloop" is ambiguous. Either there is a particular sloop (the *John B.*) that I fancy, or I want, in Quine's charming phrase, "relief from sloopless-ness" — any sloop will do. The former can be true only if the world contains sloops, the latter even in a world without sloops.) The first of these contains a *primary* occurrence of the denoting expression, the latter a secondary occurrence. ("On Denoting," pp. 51–52). The respective Russellian translations become:

(i') George IV wondered whether $(\exists x)(x$ wrote *Waverley* and $x = $ Scott)
(ii') $(\exists x)(x$ wrote *Waverley* and George IV wondered whether $x = $ Scott)

(For simplicity I ignore in each case that part of the translation which stipulates *uniqueness.*) In either case, no occurrence of 'the author of *Waverley*' remains for which to substitute 'Scott', and thus no question of such substitutivity failing arises.

(b) 'The present King of France is bald'

becomes:

(iii') $(\exists x)(x$ is the present King of France and x is bald) and (y)(If y is the present King of France, then $y = x))$

(iii') is clearly false, insofar as the first conjunct is false, and thus the putative counterexample to the Law of Excluded Middle vanishes, since (iii') clearly has a truth-value.[17] Note that the parallel translation of 'The present King of France is *not* bald' is also false for the same reason, and so is not *the* negation (the contrary) of the original proposition. Their joint falsity thus no longer appears to violate the Law of Excluded Middle. Since the words 'the present King of France' no longer appear in a denoting position, we are spared the necessity of providing them a reference. If the occurrence of 'is the present King of France' as the predicate of (iii') is troubling, it can be easily eliminated in favor of a conjunction of properties — being royal, being French, being male, and so forth.

---

[17] Again compare with Bradley: " 'The King of Utopia died on Tuesday' may safely be contradicted. And yet such a denial must remain ambiguous. The ground may be that there is no such place, or it never had a king, or he is still living, or, though he is dead, yet he died on Monday." *PoL*, pp. 124–25. Bradley holds that every negation or "contradiction" of a proposition suffers from such an ambiguity; as we shall see this is not true for elementary propositions, where the distinction between inner and outer negation vanishes.

(c) 'The difference between A and B exists'

becomes:

(iv') $(\exists x)((x = A)$ and $(\exists y)(y = B)$ and $(x \neq y))$

Here too the troubling denoting expression 'the difference between A and B' has disappeared, and with it the temptation to think that some shadowy entity must correspond to it.

Russell has offered a technical device for elimination of both definite and indefinite descriptions in favor of quantification over propositional functions. But what does this technique for manipulating symbols have to do with the *ontological* problem of what there is? Certainly we cannot make, for instance, Jerry Falwell disappear by simply refusing to *talk* about him. Is the Theory of Descriptions then mere logical sleight-of-hand? Not exactly, but a similar question lies deep at the heart of Russell's thought on this matter. Keep in mind that the only positive reason for thinking that there *are* such entities as the present King of France, the Golden Mountain, and so forth is that they appear to be mentioned in meaningful sentences. If we could show that we can say anything we want *without mentioning* such *entia suspecta*, then we shall have not so much proven their nonexistence as eliminated the only really pressing reason to grant them reality.

The Theory of Descriptions holds the additional charm of meshing quite neatly with one major thrust of the new analytic philosophy, namely the search for primitives, indefinables, or "minimum vocabularies." The thrust comes largely from the philosophy of mathematics; Peano thought that he could show that there are only three mathematical primitives, while Russell's (and Frege's) logicism holds that there are really none, since all mathematical terms can be reduced to logical ones. In a parallel move, Moore's *Principia Ethica* attempts to show that a few normative terms— 'good', 'duty', 'beauty'—were indefinable, and that these primitives were sufficient to develop all of ethics and aesthetics. For Russell and Moore, such primitives alone possessed a sort of first-water reality; only the things to which they refer exist in the most fundamental sense, and through these primitives thought "hooks up" to reality. (This will be the topic of the following chapter.) Correlatively, to show that a term was not primitive is to show that its reference does not really exist in the most fundamental sense;

such "logical constructs" enjoy only a sort of secondhand reality.[18] The sign of such secondhand status is definability in terms of the putative primitives. The search for indefinables, and the correlative attempt to construct others from such primitives via definition, is a distinguishing mark of much of the philosophy of the first half of this century.

But the Theory of Descriptions does not offer "definitions" of terms such as 'the present King of France' in the manner that 'four-sided regular polygon' offers a definition of 'square'. To see the rather different sense of 'definition' operative in the Theory of Descriptions, let us examine the more general *Theory of Incomplete Symbols*, which supplies the philosophical underpinnings for the Theory of Descriptions.[19] An incomplete symbol is one "which is not supposed to have any meaning in isolation, but is only defined in certain contexts." (*PM*, p. 66) We always contrast incomplete symbols with complete symbols, which for Russell are always "proper names", a term which is introduced in a quite ordinary sense but rapidly acquires a technical sense. Russell writes:

> "Socrates," for example, stands for a certain man, and therefore has a meaning by itself, without the need of any context. If we supply a context, as in "Socrates is mortal," these words express a fact of which Socrates himself is a constituent ... (*Ibid.*)

Names have meanings by virtue of standing for objects; thus Socrates is the meaning of the name 'Socrates'. 'Socrates' therefore has the same meaning in every context in which it appears, and even by itself, in isolation. Since incomplete symbols have no meaning in isolation, *it therefore follows that they do not stand for objects.* Their connection with the world is wholly parasitic upon the context in which they appear. This is why for Russell showing that a particular

---

[18] Later in his career Russell became somewhat more cautious about making metaphysical inferences from minimum vocabularies. In 1943 he writes "... broadly speaking, minimum vocabularies are more instructive when they show a certain kind of term to be indispensable than when they show the opposite." P. A. Schilpp, ed., *The Philosophy of Bertrand Russell* (Open Court, La Salle, IL, 1944), pp. 15-16.

A particularly ambitious attempt at a reconstruction of the world from primitives is represented by Carnap's *The Logical Structure of the World*.

[19] For a non-technical discussion see Russell and Whitehead, *Principia Mathematica* (Cambridge U. Press, Cambridge, 1910), Introduction, pp. 66–84; for a symbolic rendering, *ibid.*, Part I, section B. (This work is hereafter abbreviated '*PM*'.)

expression is an incomplete symbol is tantamount to showing that it lacks existential import.

Chapter III of *PM* treats incomplete symbols of three sorts: descriptions, symbols for relations, and class-terms. (Russell argues that although we cannot *prove* that class-terms are incomplete symbols, it seems pretty clear that only their members are genuine objects. [*Ibid.*, pp. 71–72]) At present we shall concentrate on descriptions. But before advancing to the consequences—some unforeseen—of the Theory of Incomplete Symbols, let us survey what has transpired. If we subscribe to the "Name Theory of Language," and accept with some innocence the grammar of ordinary language, we appear to be committed to the reality of a myriad of odd objects, such as the present King of France, the Golden Mountain, and the round square cupola on Berkeley College. Common sense tells us that many of these pseudo-objects do not exist, and that some *couldn't* exist. On the grounds of a metaphysical hunch, Russell sets out in 1905 to find a path to a more parsimonious ontology. But importantly, the major linch-pin of the Name Theory of Language that led to the bloated ontology of *PrM* is untouched; *genuine* constituents of propositions still have meaning by standing for objects. All that the Theory of Descriptions shows is that some expressions which *appear* to be constituents of propositions in fact are *not;* they disappear under analysis. One upshot, apparently harmless but potentially radical, is that Russell must abandon his earlier view that surface grammar is a reliable guide to real logical grammar. (*IMP*, p. 168) This admission will have deep implications indeed.

One Consequence of the Theory of Incomplete Symbols

> A statement cannot be concerned with the logical structure
> of the world, for in order for a statement to be possible
> at all, in order for a proposition to be CAPABLE of making
> SENSE, the world must already have just the logical
> structure that it has. The logic of the world is prior to all
> truth and falsehood.
>
> —*Notebooks*, 18.10.14

The Theory of Incomplete Symbols is introduced to solve the puzzles we have just seen, but it plays several central roles in

Russell's philosophy. First, it serves to eliminate ontological commitment both to abstract entities, like those apparently denoted by class-terms, and to *entia suspecta* like the present King of France. But for Russell such parsimony almost always has at least in part an epistemological basis, rather than a Quinean "taste for desert landscapes." Even the ontological extravagance of *Principles of Mathematics* is prefaced with:

> The discussion of indefinables — which forms the chief part of philosophical logic — is the endeavor to see clearly, and to make others see clearly, the entities concerned, *in order that the mind may have that kind of acquaintance with them which it has with redness or the taste of pineapple.*[20]

So the second, and for Russell increasingly important, role of the Theory of Incomplete Symbols is to facilitate the analysis of sentences which appear to be about entities with which we are not acquainted into sentences about objects of our acquaintance. Although the (contingently) non-existent present King of France provides a clear example of an object with which we are certainly *not* acquainted, Russell is far more concerned with sentences about material objects, which on his view are *never* objects of acquaintance. These epistemological concerns, which Russell inherits from the tradition of British Empiricism,[21] increasingly dominate his thinking after 1905. The motivation is antisceptical; on Cartesian grounds Russell became convinced that unless sentences about ordinary objects are translatable into sentences only about immediate experiences, then we can never justifiably make claims like "The cat is on the mat."

   Although in Russell's philosophy they are intimately related, the use of the Theory of Descriptions to explain the meaning- and truth-conditions of ordinary sentences, including 'The present King of France is bald,' is quite different from its use to show how sentences about material objects, which according to Russell *nobody* is ever acquainted with, can be analyzed into sentences which refer

---

[20] *PrM*, p. xv; I have added the emphasis. In addition to the epistemological foundations of Russell's reductionism, his political views led him to view abstract entities — the State, history, etc.— as fraught with danger when treated realistically. Here the early influence of Mill on Russell is evident; cf. Jager, *op.cit.*, ch. 9.

[21] For an excellent discussion of such connections, see David Pears, *Bertrand Russell and the British Tradition in Philosophy* (Random House, New York, 1967), chs. 2–3, 11.

only to sense-data. But the latter epistemological concern is wholly absent from Wittgenstein's early thought, as it is from Frege's; each holds such matters to be purely psychological, and failure to appreciate this leads to many misreadings of the *Tractatus*. But the dominant epistemological concerns of Russell's philosophy lead him, I think, to ignore certain important consequences of "On Denoting."

Let us examine more closely the logical apparatus of the Theory of Descriptions. In *Principia* Russell argues that phrases of the form 'the so-and-so' (symbolized as '$(\iota x)(\phi x)$' $=_{df}$ '*The x which is ϕ*') are always incomplete symbols, yet he strongly implies that they are of philosophical interest only when the corresponding existential proposition 'The so-and-so exists' — '$E!(\iota x)(\phi x)$' — is false.

> As soon as we know $E!(\iota x)(\phi x)$, the fact that $(\iota x)(\phi x)$ is an incomplete symbol becomes irrelevant, so long as we confine ourselves to truth-functions of whatever proposition is its scope.[22]

But consideration of the following pair of propositions displays a certain uncomfortableness in Russell's position:

(a) The present King of France is bald.
(b) The present Queen of England is equestrian.

The position of *PM* seems to be that the status of the denoting expression in (a) as an incomplete symbol is of great logical importance, insofar as it may tempt us to postulate shadowy royalty, yet the occurrence of an incomplete symbol of exactly the same kind in (b) is irrelevant in most contexts. The only difference between the two is that there is some complex which corresponds to the definite description in (b) but not in (a).[23] But if the Theory of Incomplete

---

[22] *Ibid.*, p. 83. '$E!(\iota x)(\phi x)$' means roughly that the propositional function 'ϕx' is satisfied by exactly one thing; cf. *14.02. Note that the incompleteness of the symbol is still relevant in non-extensional contexts such as "George IV wonders if . . .", since there it will limit the possibilities of substitution *salva veritas*.

[23] Leonard Linsky writes "It may be the case that what, for one person, is a proper name is, for others, a disguised description. Since the meaning of a name is the bearer, to know the meaning of the name is to be acquainted with the bearer. Now since we are all not acquainted with the same things, . . . what is a name for one person may be a description for another." *Referring* (Routledge and Kegan Paul, London, 1967), p. 59. Linsky points out that in "Knowledge by Acquaintance and Knowledge by Description" Russell argues that only Bismarck could understand the judgment "Bismarck was an astute diplomatist." As we shall see, part of what follows from Wittgenstein's

Symbols shows that (a) is not "really about" the present King of
France, ought not a parallel point hold for (b)? Certainly logical
matters ought not turn on such wholly empirical matters as the
relative gumption of the French and English bourgeoisie. Or consider
a sentence from Russell's *Problems of Philosophy:* "I have not had
the honor to be acquainted with the Emperor of China, but I truly
judge that he exists." (p. 44) In a note added to the seventeenth
impression (1943) Russell adds that this passage was written "in the
early part of 1912 when China was still an empire." Did subsequent
political developments alter the *logical* significance of that sentence?
Consistency therefore seems to demand that if (a) is not really
"about" the present King of France, then (b) is not really about the
present Queen of England, *irrespective of the existence of the latter
complex.* Russell is willing to distinguish, I think, between the two
cases because in the background lurks an epistemological theory
which holds that no sentence is ultimately "about" anything like the
present King of France or Queen of England at all.[24]

There is a certain analogy between this *semantic* problem and
the Cartesian epistemological enterprise to which I allude at the
beginning of this chapter. Descartes argues that we cannot have good
grounds for believing such things as that the cat is on the mat unless
we have prior good grounds for thinking that certain other, more
fundamental claims are true. Likewise, since for Russell meaning is
at bottom naming, we cannot know that a certain proposition is true
unless we know that its (genuine) referential terms succeed in
referring. But it appears to follow from the Theory of Descriptions

---

technical sense of 'Name' (later adopted by Russell) is that the same entity cannot be both named
and described. Thus 'Name for me' or 'description for you' disappear from the logical vocabulary.

[24] With this insight, realism and common sense begin to part company, but not without paradox.
If I say "He really is a pig," and you have no inkling of whom I speak, then you cannot understand
the claim I make. But the Theory of Incomplete Symbols seems to show that our ordinary
propositions are not about the sorts of things which we take them to be about, and that before 1905
no one really knew what the proposition "The present Queen of England is equestrian" meant. But
if we do not know what such familiar propositions mean, how can we know whether they are true
or false? If this is the case, then what becomes of Moore's work, which Russell takes as his
starting-point?

   Moore's answer to this difficulty is to distinguish between "knowing what a proposition
means" and "knowing the correct analysis of a proposition." (cf. "A Defense of Common Sense"
in *Philosophical Papers* [Allen and Unwin, London, 1959], pp. 53ff.), but in *IMP* Russell commits
himself to the view that to "understand" something entails being able to "give a definition of it" (p.
3). On the other hand, Linsky writes "In expounding his Theory of Descriptions Russell never says
that part of what one is saying when one says S is that S' [The Russellian analysis of S]. What he
says is that the proper *analysis* of S is given by S'." (*Op. cit.*, p. 97, compare with *PI*, #60) Russell's
view of analysis wavers, I think, between these two positions.

that propositions containing definite descriptions are not "about" the apparent denoted complex, but rather about other, *as of yet unspecified*, entities. Thus we cannot even *understand* the proposition in question (much less make a judgment about its truth) unless we know that *other*, as of yet unspecified, existential propositions are true. Yet the realist's starting-point is the claim that such propositions *are* meaningful, *do* make sense, and *certainly are* true.

Wittgenstein's solution to this dilemma can be quickly sketched. The propositions of ordinary language can be analyzed, using Russell's techniques, into truth-functional compound propositions. This process of analysis will (and *must*) end with propositions which cannot be further analyzed, insofar as they have no components which are themselves propositions. These ultimate propositions must have a rather special logical property that *as a matter of logic* their denoting terms cannot fail of reference; they are the logical correlates of the indubitable propositions which Descartes seeks.

Analysis, Extensionality, and Logical Constants

> My fundamental idea is that the 'logical constants' are not representatives; that there can be no representatives of the *logic* of the facts.
>
> —4.0312

The Theory of Incomplete Symbols has eliminated certain troublesome denoting expressions in favor of quantified variables, but such a procedure brings us to a further difficulty. If symbols at bottom have meaning by *naming*, by standing for objects, what are we to make of such logical connectives as 'and', 'or', 'all', 'not' and the symbolic stand-ins for these words in the calculus of *Principia?* Do these, as the realist thesis seems to imply, stand for "logical objects,"[25] or can they be dealt with in another manner? Examining this question will lead us straightway to certain views of Wittgen-

---

[25] "While at Princeton, I came to know Einstein fairly well. I used to go to his house once a week to discuss with him and Gödel and Pauli.... I found that they all had a German bias towards metaphysics.... Gödel turned out to be an unadulterated Platonist, and apparently believed that an eternal 'Not' was laid up in heaven, where virtuous logicians might hope to meet it hereafter." Russell, *Autobiography*, vol. II, p. 341.

stein's on generality, and ultimately to what he characterizes as his "fundamental thought."

The Russellian translation of sentences containing incomplete symbols are couched at least partly in terms of logical constants: '.', 'v', '⊃', '∃x', and so forth. Russell's early views imply that since these are meaningful constituents of sentences, that they must themselves be meaningful and therefore must stand for objects. The Theory of Incomplete Symbols has put some restrictions on the first part of this claim by showing how phrases which contribute to the meaning of a sentence might nevertheless have no meaning in isolation and by providing a method for "translating away" such expressions. However, logical constants clearly appear in the Russellian translations of such sentences, and thus the Theory of Incomplete Symbols as it stands has not shown logical constants to be incomplete symbols.

Do symbols like '⊃' and '∃x' then name *logical objects?* For instance, if 'A' stands for some complex, does 'not-A' name some *other* complex, composed of the objects which constitute the first complex *plus* the "logical object" negation? If so, then in a like manner the conjunctive proposition "Lyndon Johnson was president and Richard Nixon was president" must mention, in addition to all the objects which its conjuncts mention, some additional logical object corresponding to the word 'and'. This is shown, the argument might go, by the obvious difference in sense between that conjunction and the *disjunction* of the same two propositions, a difference in sense achieved wholly by substituting 'or' for 'and'. Analogously, since some sentences contain quantifiers—'all', 'some' and their symbolic stand-ins—it seems to follow that there are *real general facts* in addition to particular facts, and that quantifiers too stand for objects. Further, insofar as there are deductive connections between '$(x)(\phi x)$' and 'ϕa', the realist seems committed to accepting objective connections between particular and general facts. Indeed, since 'ϕa' entails '$(\exists x)(\phi x)$', no fact—even a particular one—could stand quite alone in the world, without logical connections to other facts.

(Note the attractive ease with which the psychologistic logician can deal with the problem of inference from general to particular. Under the proper circumstances the mind, when confronted by 'ϕa', is irresistibly drawn to accept '$(\exists x)(\phi x)$'. Such inference finds its basis not in the nature of the world, that is, in the existence of logical relations between general and particular facts, but rather in the nature of the human mind. Psychologistic logic thus in this manner comes to the rescue of a nominalistic ontology.)

The problem with allowing logical constants to denote objects is the extreme difficulty of making this thesis consistent with an ontology committed to many real, independent things. Such pluralism is tied not only historically but logically to the realism of the preceding chapter. It must be sharply contrasted with the opposite view:

> Reality is one. It must be single, because plurality, taken as real, contradicts itself. Plurality implies relations, and, through relations, it unwillingly always asserts a superior unity. To suppose the universe is plural is therefore to contradict oneself and, after all, to suppose that it is one.[26]

The trick is to find some manner of construing logical relations that allows us to both maintain that there are relations between propositions (and thus facts) and yet that the propositions (and the facts) are not *changed* by those relations. The alternative seems to be monism and the subsequent degradation of the ordinary world of experience to illusion. For this reason Russell finds himself committed to a thesis which he characterizes as "one that came to dominate all my subsequent philosophy." (*My Philosophical Development*, pp. 12ff.) This is the "doctrine of external relations," which asserts that there are relations which do not "penetrate," do not change, the terms which they relate. For Wittgenstein, this is intimately tied up with the *"Grundgedanke"*— the "fundamental thought" — of *Tractatus* 4.0312; that logical constants do not name objects.[27] The intimate relationship between pluralism and analysis will emerge in chapter VI, when we look closely at truth-functions of propositions.

But in order to see the crucial role of this claim in the *Tractatus*, we must examine a more limited (though hotly disputed) thesis, viz. that there are no "general facts," that all generality disappears under analysis. First, Wittgenstein claims that every quantified proposition

---

[26] F. H. Bradley, *Appearance and Reality*, (Oxford U. Press, Oxford, 1897), p. 460. Hereafter this work will be abbreviated as *A&R*.

[27] It is not until he has fully assimilated Wittgenstein's views that Russell rejects denoting status for logical constants. In 1913 he asserts "Besides the forms of atomic complexes, there are many other logical objects which are involved in the formation of non-atomic complexes. Such words as *or*, *not*, *all*, *some*, plainly involve logical notions; and since we can use such words intelligently, we must be acquainted with the logical objects involved." From an unpublished book entitled "Theory of Knowledge," [!] quoted in D. F. Pears, "The Relations between Wittgenstein's Picture Theory of Propositions and Russell's Theories of Judgment" in Luckhardt, ed., *Wittgenstein: Sources and Perspectives* (Cornell U. Press, Ithaca, NY, 1979), p. 192.

can be translated without loss of content into a truth-function of particular propositions. Although the full impact of this assertion will not be clear until the next two chapters, we can here at least see the intuitive plausibility of the claim. The proposition 'Every American League regular hit at least one home run in 1990' seems nothing more than convenient shorthand for 'Dwight Evans hit at least one home run in 1990, and Wade Boggs hit at least one home run in 1990, and . . .', where the ellipses will be replaced with an exhaustive list of propositions asserting of every *particular* AL regular that he hit at least one home run in 1990. Analogously, 'Some American League pitcher won at least 20 games in 1990' becomes 'Roger Clemens won at least twenty games in 1990, or Mike Boddicker won at least twenty games, or . . .'

In general,

$$(x)(\phi x) =_{df} \phi a \cdot \phi b \cdot \phi c \ldots$$

$$(\exists x)(\phi x) =_{df} \phi a \vee \phi b \vee \phi c \vee \ldots^{28}$$

where 'a', 'b' etc. are the possible values of the quantified variable. *Assuming that we assign no ontological weight to the logical connectives*, on this view generality enters language only as a convenient shorthand device for unmanageable strings of particular propositions. We thus have no reason to impute real generality to the world.[29]

---

[28] Avoid confusing these propositional conjunctions and disjunctions with propositions whose subjects are disjunctions or conjunctions—(e.g.) 'ϕ (a v b v c . . .)'. This introduces propositional connectives in an illicit manner, as relating names, and leads to paradox. Cf. Jager, *op. cit.*, pp. 148–53, and Ramsey, *The Foundations of Mathematics* (Littlefield Adams, Paterson, NJ, 1960), p. 124.

[29] Wittgenstein's treatment of generality notoriously allows of alternative interpretations; here I follow Black *op. cit.*, pp. 280ff. But consider one example of a difficulty which arises with my preliminary attribution of this view to Wittgenstein. In a series of extremely opaque remarks following 5.52, Wittgenstein contrasts his view of generality with that of Russell and Frege by saying "I disassociate the concept *all* from truth-functions. Frege and Russell introduced generality in association with logical product or logical sum." (5.521). This sounds as if he doesn't "introduce" generality in this manner. But in "Wittgenstein's Lectures of 1930–33," Moore tells us that Wittgenstein represented his Tractarian views as being that '$(x)(fx)$' was identical with the logical product, implying a view quite like the one he seems to reject at 5.521. Cf. G. E. Moore, *Philosophical Papers* (Routledge and Kegan Paul, London, 1922), p. 297. Further puzzlement arises from Russell's introduction of the quantifiers in *PM* as "two new primitives" (p. 15), and thus *not* in terms of logical products or sums. Part of this confusion will be cleared up in chapter V, when we see how, although a general proposition is equivalent to a logical sum or product, it doesn't have to be *defined* in such a manner.

Attractive as it might seem, there are cogent objections to the reduction of generality to logical sums or products of unquantified propositions. Is it not possible that the string of dots which we use to represent "and so forth" merely replaces the quantifier notation with an equivalent and less perspicuous notation? Suppose each of the exactly four things in a universe—Albert, Beatrice, Corrine, and Dennis—decides to go for a walk. If 'Wx' abbreviates 'x took a walk', then in this case '$(x)(Wx)$' is true, and in this universe, that claim is equivalent to 'Wa · Wb · Wc · Wd'. Now a sceptic might object that the latter formula doesn't *quite* catch all of what is asserted by the former, insofar as we have implicitly smuggled in the information that a, b, c, and d are *all the things that there are* in this particular universe. But to make this added bit of information explicit, we need to resort to one of the following devices:

$$\text{Wa} \cdot \text{Wb} \cdot \text{Wc} \cdot \text{Wd} \cdot \sim (\exists x)(x \neq \text{a} \cdot x \neq \text{b} \cdot x \neq \text{c} \cdot x \neq \text{d})$$
$$\text{Wa} \cdot \text{Wb} \cdot \text{Wc} \cdot \text{Wd} \cdot (x)(x = \text{a} \vee x = \text{b} \vee x = \text{c} \vee x = \text{d})$$
$$\text{Wa} \cdot \text{Wb} \cdot \text{Wc} \cdot \text{Wd} \cdot \sim (\exists x)(\sim Wx)$$

But of course each of these added conjuncts is itself a general proposition, and thus our proposed elimination of generality is circular. This is why, I think, Russell and Whitehead choose to introduce the universal and existential quantifiers as "two new primitive ideas."[30] Wittgenstein's answer to such an objection cannot yet be introduced,[31] insofar as it presupposes the central semantic notion of *showing*, the subject of chapter V. I will thus for the present bracket this objection, proceeding as if generality has been shown to be a logically accidental and thus dispensable feature of logic and language.

Elimination of generality granted, let us return to the Russellian analyses of propositions containing incomplete symbols. We have seen that 'The present King of France is bald' becomes:

---

[30] *PM*, p. 15. It is less clear why they feel a need to introduce both as quantifiers, since Frege defines existential quantification in terms of his concave content-stroke and negation.

[31] That notion will also contain the key to his response to Russell's parallel argument that there must be general *facts*. "Suppose that you have succeeded in chronicling every single particular fact throughout the universe ... you still would not have a complete description of the universe unless you also added: "These that I have chronicled are all the particular facts there are." So you cannot hope to describe the world completely without having general facts as well as particular facts." (*L&K*, pp. 183–84.) This passage is as good a contrast as one could find to Wittgenstein's central contention that the limits of the world must be ineffable.

(i) $(\exists x)((x$ is the present King of France $\cdot x$ is bald) $\cdot (y)(y$ is the present King of France $\supset y = x))$.

or in Principia notation:[32]

(ii) $B((\iota x)(\phi x))$ (That one thing which has the properties of being the present King of France also has the property of being bald.)

The Russellian analysis of (ii) (ignoring again the "uniquing clause" which states that *exactly* one thing satisfies a given propositional functions) yields:

(iii) $(\exists x)(\phi x \cdot Bx)$ (Something is both the present King of France and bald.)

where the denoting expression '$(\iota x)(\phi x)$' has disappeared in favor of predicates and bound variables. Since the questionable phrase 'the present King of France' no longer appears in a denoting position, (iii) is clearly not "about" the present King of France, and since (ii) is equivalent to (iii), the upshot is that (ii) is not about the current French monarch either. But what *is* (ii) about then? The elimination of real generality dictates that it cannot be about some general entity: "some man," "a man," etc. Quantified variables are incomplete symbols and thus replaceable. (iii) must therefore be analyzable into some truth-function of propositions, none of which contain quantifiers—that is, into a truth-function of singular propositions.

Although analysis will probably lead to a rather complex expression, composed of many constituents, let us for simplicity pretend that it yields just one such proposition, namely:

(iv) Wa

What we find to hold for 'Wa' will also hold for the other propositions which would appear in the more complicated analysis. Now (iv) contains only the monadic predicate 'W' and the (apparent) name 'a', but any *ordinary* proper name can be replaced with a definite

---

[32] '$E!(\iota x)(\phi x)$' means that there is exactly one thing which has the sum of properties (ϕ) of being the present King of France. 'Bx' is the propositional function, 'x is bald'. Thus this expression claims that there is exactly one thing satisfying 'ϕx' and that that same thing satisfies 'Bx'. Here as elsewhere I have used the more manageable bracket notation in lieu of the dots of *Principia*.

description.[33] For instance, we can (at least in primary occurrences) replace 'Aristotle' with 'Plato's most famous student' without changing the truth-value or meaning of the proposition in question. Thus (iv) translates to:

(v) W $(\iota x)(\phi x)$ (That one thing which is a ϕ is also a W.)

where 'ϕx' is a complex propositional function embodying the distinctive properties of the entity a. Notice two crucial facts about (v). First, it has the same superficial form as (ii), and thus we can apply Russell's technique anew. Second, it can only be meaningful if its denoting expressions succeed in referring, and thus if '$E!(\exists x)(\phi x)$' *or some other existential proposition about its real, as of yet undiscovered constituents* is true. Thus the move from (ii) to (v) has, from a logical point of view, gotten us nowhere at all.

Two cases seem possible; either the looping procedure of analyzing descriptions, eliminating variables in favor of names, substituting descriptions for names, then analyzing again goes on indefinitely, or it stops somewhere. The first option, although not strictly self-contradictory, entails some distasteful consequences, among them that we can never confidently assert that *any* proposition has a meaning, since we could not know the truth of the infinite series of existential propositions which guarantee the successful reference of its denoting expressions. More generally, it would seem to make the *logical* matter of whether any proposition had a meaning dependent upon the *empirical* question of whether certain propositions of the form '$E!(\exists x)(\phi x)$' were true or not. The second option, on the other hand, is itself not wholly without paradox, implying as it does that analysis must end with certain propositions which, *as a matter of logic*, could not fail of reference. These propositions—the "bedrock," as it were —would then play the same role as the "simple natures" which we discussed in the opening section of this chapter. The remainder of this chapter will be given over to investigation of the nature of such a stopping-place.

---

[33] Russell and Whitehead argue at *PM* *14.15 that we can always find a unique description of any particular, a consequence of Leibniz's Law (no two things differ *solo numero*). Leibniz's Law is deeply imbedded in the fabric of *PM*, insofar as the authors use it at 13.01 as a definition of the identity sign '='.

Elementary Propositions and Extensionality

> There must be simple substances because there are
> composites; for a composite is nothing more than a
> collection or *aggregatum* of simple substances.
>
> —LEIBNIZ

If analysis terminates it must be with unanalyzable propositions. Such propositions obviously must have no (logical) constituents which are themselves propositions. These *elementary propositions*[34] Wittgenstein introduces in the text via their relations to the possible facts which are their senses; this will be the topic of the following chapter. In this chapter we will examine them solely as the termination point of analysis.

But before we descend to the level of the text, we must investigate a preliminary point, one which has engendered a good deal of misunderstanding with respect to Wittgenstein's early semantics. Ordinary propositions must be analyzable, we have seen, into other propositions which are free from the semantic problems which plague surface grammar. (We shall see that their grammar also more closely accords to the structure of the world.) But what then is the relation between *these* propositions and those of ordinary language? To begin to answer this, I want to raise some points about the familiar notion of a *truth-function*, and ultimately examine anew the metaphysical debate between monists and pluralists.

A proposition is compound if it contains as constituents other propositions,[35] and it is truth-functionally compound if substitution of a proposition with the same truth-value for any of its constituents does not change the truth-value of the compound proposition. 'Lyndon Johnson was president and Spiro Agnew vice-president' has this property, while 'Gregor Princip shot Arch-Duke Ferdinand and World War One ensued' does not. The notion of truth-functionality is rooted in Frege's semantics, where it appears as a correlate of

---

[34] Cf. 4.21 ff. Wittgenstein's usage must be distinguished from Russell's rather different but related sense, as a proposition which contains no variables; cf. *PM*, p. xvii.

[35] "Contains" is difficult. There is a sense in which '(y) (If y is the present King of France, then $y = x$)' is *contained* in 'The present King of France is bald,' although it of course does not appear as a surface constituent of that proposition. Likewise, there is a sense in which 'Lincoln was an actor' appears in 'The man who shot Lincoln was an actor.' I will at present pretend that we are confronted with a fully analyzed language, where every component is an explicit component.

Leibniz's Law. That principle tells us that we can substitute equireferential terms *salva veritas*, and since for Frege the reference of a proposition is (normally) a truth-value, substitutivity follows.

The principle that *every* compound proposition is a truth-function of its constituents is called the *thesis of extensionality*,[36] and it is difficult to overestimate the role of that principle in twentieth-century philosophy. In any case it is central to the *Tractatus:* at 5 we read "A proposition is a truth-function of elementary propositions" and much of the rest of the book consists of drawing out the rather striking consequences of this principle, consequences which we shall examine in chapters VII–X.

The Thesis of Extensionality is equivalent to the claim that every proposition can be written as an expression of elementary propositions, using the familiar truth-functional connectives which represent conjunction, disjunction, negation, material implication and material equivalence. The purely formal search for primitives mentioned earlier in this chapter begins to become entwined with metaphysics. It is easy to show that given negation and any one of the other four connectives, all possible truth-functions can be constructed. The apparent special position of negation might be thought to assign to it a special ontological significance, but this special place was eliminated through Sheffer's demonstration that a *single* connective — the "Sheffer Stroke," representing joint negation and symbolized '$x|y$' — is sufficient to generate *all* truth-functions.[37] Wittgenstein introduces what is essentially the same operation at 5.5, where he writes — without much explanation, as usual — the rather daunting formula:

$$(\text{———}T)(\xi,\text{………})^{38}$$

---

[36] In appendix C to the second edition of *PM*, Russell and Whitehead point out that although within *PM* the thesis is true by definition, it is also universally true. Interestingly, Russell had prior doubts. In 1910 he writes that the most problematical connective — the hook ($\supset$) representing material implication — captures only that part of the meaning of 'implies' "which is most convenient to give to 'implies' in symbolic logic . . ." "Some Explanations in Reply to Mr Bradley," *Mind* ns 19 (1910), p. 375. The implication is of course that some of the things which we normally say (or take ourselves to be saying) cannot adequately be represented in symbolic logic.

[37] Cf. *FA*, section 1, and compare with Husserl, *LI* vol. I, chapter 5.

[38] This device, introduced explicitly at 4.442, is shorthand for a truth-table. The contents of the second pair of brackets represent an arbitrary number of elementary propositions, while the first bracket contains the final columns of a truth-table, omitting all the preceding columns to be generated by convention. The convention stipulates that the dashes stand for 'F', so the result is

This is, Wittgenstein tells us, the general form of a proposition; every proposition is a truth-function of its components, and the operation of joint negation is sufficient to generate all possible truth-functions. That is, the Thesis of Extensionality is true. In the following chapter we will see some striking ontological consequences of that claim.

Wittgenstein attaches no particular importance to the operation of joint negation, since the number of primitives necessary in a system is wholly a function of the notation which we choose (5.474). However, the interdefinability of all truth-functional connectives shows something much more important, namely that they are *incomplete symbols*. Having no meaning in isolation, they are contextually defined by truth-tables, which show us, for instance, the results of putting 'v' between two propositions. Remember that being an incomplete symbol is equivalent to not standing for an object, so their lack of independent meaning demonstrates at least part of the *Grundgedanke* of 4.0312—that they are not "representatives" for things in the world. In other words, they are not names for logical objects. This implies a number of crucial corollaries, including that there are no "compound facts" which correspond to compound propositions (chapter V) and also the difficult but absolutely central thesis that the logic of a proposition cannot be represented linguistically but only "shown." (Chapter VI)

But these technical points are indications of a deeper issue. Russell singles out as the foundation of his thought the "Thesis of External Relations", a term which he coins in contrast with the Hegelian's "Thesis of Internal Relations." Let us consider that claim for a moment. Hume distinguishes between *constant* and *inconstant* relations. The former—Hume cites resemblance, contrariety, and so forth—are such that their roots lie in the essential natures of the things so related. If a and b resemble one another, we cannot imagine them *not* standing in that relation unless we imagine their natures being *different* from what they are. The constant relation of resemblance, then, contrasts with the inconstant relation of a and b being six feet apart, which of course can change without a correlative alteration of a or b.

The monist's strategy turns on the thesis that *every* relation is necessarily constant or "internal". Bradley argues that the notion of

---

some operation which is true only when all its arguments are false, in the binary case '~p · ~q' or 'p|q'.

a relation, as well as that of a quality (we might see these as respectively relations between two substances, and between a substance and its attributes), is infected with contradiction. (*A&R*, ch. III) All relations are therefore internal in the sense that we cannot consider the relata *without* the relation. The alleged relata in isolation are not wholly "real," but rather have the status of illegitimate abstractions from a greater whole. Thus Bradley argues that reality must be at bottom singular, and that pluralism can be excluded simply on grounds of the Principle of Contradiction. (*Ibid.*, ch. XIII). But if this is true, then common sense, with its commitment to pluralism, falls by the wayside, mathematics becomes infested with falsehood, and analysis degenerates into a process of increasing falsification. For Russell and Moore, and in a somewhat different manner for Wittgenstein, this is intolerable.

Commitment to the Thesis of Extensionality thus becomes intrinsically tied up with the possibility of pluralism. If logical connectives stood for real objects in the world, then any compound proposition would say more, speak of more things, than the sum of the senses of its constituents. If we reject a realistic interpretation of the connectives, then the results of analysis will be aggregates of propositions which bear only external—thus not logical—relations to one another.

The radical consequences of the above cannot be fully appreciated until we rectify a lacuna in the above exposition. We have seen that normal propositions like 'The present King of France is bald' are *not* about what they appear to be; can we provide a positive characterization of their reference, and thus their connections with the world?

Elementary Propositions, Facts, and Objects

Analysis ends when we reach propositions that allow of no further Russellian decomposition, that is, with explicit truth-functions of elementary propositions. These elementary propositions will be composed wholly of "simple signs" (3.2–3.201). Such "simple signs" ("symbols" would be better) Wittgenstein calls *Names* (3.202).[39] The meaning of such simple signs are the Objects for which

---

[39] Henceforth I will use 'Name' with the uppercase N to indicate Wittgenstein's special technical usage of the term. I will adopt a parallel convention with 'Object'.

they stand (3.203, 3.22), and Names are thus *complete symbols* in Russell's sense—they have meaning by themselves.[40] We have also seen that they must somehow be guaranteed a reference, although the mechanism of this guarantee has yet to be explicated.

It is tempting to think of elementary propositions as composed of Names of different sorts, words which play different logical roles in the proposition. Russell thought that each proposition must contain a verb, whose role it was to provide the "logical framework" for the proposition, as it were, to bind together the other words. Wittgenstein seems unconcerned with whether there are Names of different logical types—in any case, he thinks that the question cannot be settled a priori—but he is quite clear that there is no special class of Names whose work is to bind together propositions. The apparently subsidiary question about the existence of "framework words" will in fact have very important consequences for Wittgenstein's semantics, intrinsically connected with the peculiar *unity* which propositions display. Propositions are complexes of signs, but complexes are of two sorts: mere aggregates and real unities. In a mere aggregate the elements of the complex stand in only accidental relations one to another (as the pieces of stone in a gravel-pile), while a real or organic unity has a special *structure*. Propositions, Wittgenstein maintains, must be organic complexes rather than mere aggregates of Names (we will see why in chapter V).

> A proposition is not a medley of words *(Wörtergemisch)*—(Just as a theme in music is not a medley of notes.)
> A proposition is articulated.[41]

The *determinate* structure of propositions, which will feature prominently in the following chapter, brings to mind fitting together

---

[40] This seems to contradict 3.3— "Only propositions have sense; only in the nexus of a proposition does a name have a meaning." I will dispel the apparent tension between my remarks and Wittgenstein's version of Frege's "Context Principle" in section 5.6.

[41] 3.141. Wittgenstein's correspondence with Ogden concerning the original English translation of the *Tractatus* yields several interesting comments on this remark. Wittgenstein suggests 'mixture' for *'gemisch'* in *'Wörtergemisch'*, suggesting that chemists contrast mixtures with *compounds*, the latter not allowing of physical separation.

With respect to the final word in the passage, most naturally taken as meaning "composed of parts" (as the body of an insect is articulated), Wittgenstein writes that he is using the word "in the sense in which one might say that a man speaks articulately, that is, that he pronounces the words distinctly." Read as such, the remark seems connected with the Fregean principle that where there is sense there is *perfect* sense, with the demand that propositions be complexes as a means towards this end. Both remarks are from *Letters to C. K. Ogden* (Blackwell, Oxford, 1973), p. 24.

tinker-toys, building blocks or the parts of a jigsaw puzzle. But the realist thesis leads us to expect a certain parallel between language and the world, so the determinate structure of propositions (yet to be fully explored) is a reflection of certain properties which *reality* has. Even if this parallel does not hold on the level of ordinary language, at the level of fully analyzed propositions the structure of those elementary propositions will mirror the structure of the world. Let us now examine the mirroring.

Wittgenstein's fundamental ontological insight is that the world is a world of *facts* rather than a world of *things*. (1.1) This apparently straightforward remark, however, is not terribly helpful, insofar as Wittgenstein uses 'world', 'fact', and 'thing' in special technical senses. Bus since we have to start somewhere, I will use these words in their normal senses for a bit. A fact is thus something like the cat being on the mat; the cat, the mat, Socrates, and a cabbage are things, and the world is the totality of actual existents.

What reason is there, then, to assign ontological priority to facts? Max Black constructs a straightforward argument, which runs parallel to Russell's argument for the necessity of general propositions. (*Op. cit.*, pp. 29–30). Wittgenstein will not—in fact, cannot—accept it, but it will serve as a suitable jumping-off point for our examination of the outlines of the Tractarian ontology. Suppose, Black suggests, that we attempt to completely describe the world by setting forth a *universal catalogue*, a complete listing of every *thing* which there is in the world. Would the universal catalogue constitute a complete description of the world, sufficient to distinguish it from every other possible world? Only when combined with a further statement that the things listed are *all* the things that there are. But this statement refers to a fact, in the straightforward sense that it is a fact that there is but one person in the room I currently occupy. On the other hand, a *universal chronicle*, which listed every actual *fact*, has two advantages. First, by mentioning every fact, I thereby also mention all things; if I assert that the cat is on the mat, in doing so I mention the cat and the mat. If a "closure statement" to the effect that these are all the facts that there are is needed, this too refers to a fact, albeit a rather suspect second-level fact. The universal chronicle thus exhibits a sort of ontological economy; in either case we are committed to the existence of facts, but the universal chronicle allows us to treat things merely as constituents of facts.

The reasons why Wittgenstein cannot avail himself of this argument must wait until we examine the show/say distinction in chapter V. But it is worth pointing out several assumptions upon which the above argument rests. First, Russell's realism before 1916 treats facts as mere complexes, which stand at the same "ontological level" as things. The ordinary senses of the terms give credence to this, but Wittgenstein's technical senses will not. Hand in hand with the first is the assumption that things have reality only insofar as they are constituents of some fact, and Wittgenstein will draw some very careful distinctions here. Finally, the argument seems to provide no good reason for its acceptance save ontological parsimony, and we shall have occasion to question whether this methodological basis is sufficient.

On the positive side, the argument stresses *structure*. Even in a purely spatial world, a mere listing of things is not sufficient to differentiate one possible world from another. Consider a simple one-dimensional world, consisting only of a, b, and c standing in spatial relations one to another. Merely listing a, b, and c is clearly not enough to differentiate between the following two worlds:

(i) a b c   (ii) b a c

Any attempt to fully characterize the world by listing things, then, seems to ignore the crucial *structural* element which facts incorporate.[42] This structural element will be central to Wittgenstein's semantics and ontology; only insofar as the world is a world of facts can we represent it in language and thought.

The preceding must now be altered by the introduction of Wittgenstein's technical senses of the central terms. The *Tractatus* opens with the remark, "The world is all that is the case." Why "is the case" and not "has reality" or something similar? Because Wittgenstein deliberately restricts the meaning of 'world' to include only what *contingently exists*, which for him is always *facts*. The necessary elements which underlie and support contingent being,

---

[42] It is possible, I think, to try to build the structural properties into the things. This makes all of the properties of things internal and probably necessary, and is probably the first step on the road to Leibnizian monadism. This is a large part of Russell's claim that Leibniz's metaphysics is forced upon him by his logical inability to deal with relational statements, which in turn is a result of the logical strait-jacket of the subject-predicate form. Cf. *A Critical Examination of the Philosophy of Leibniz*, Preface to the second edition and *passim*.

although they have a sort of reality, are not "the case" and thus are not strictly part of the world. (Cf. e.g. 5.634) Put another way, the world is not composed of necessary and contingent parts in the sense in which gin and tonic is composed of two liquids—one alcoholic and one not. In the *Tractatus*, then, 'world' always means *the sum of contingent existences.*

Wittgenstein's technical use of two terms more or less parallel to 'fact' needs some explication. Facts come in two sorts, *'Tatsachen'* and *'Sachverhalte'*, translated respectively as 'fact' and 'state of affairs' by McGuinness and Pears. *Tatsachen* are facts which have other facts as constituents, while *Sachverhalte*, having a sort of complexity, have no constituents which are *facts*. Russell, in a similar distinction, offers the expressions 'molecular fact' and 'atomic fact'. (*L&K*, pp. 203ff.) *Tatsachen* taken jointly are "all that is the case", and 2 tells us that they are the existence of various *Sachverhalte;* the two claims in conjunction with 1 yield the result that the world—all that is the case—consists of the existence of *Sachverhalte.*[43]

A central property of *Sachverhalte* is that they are mutually independent (2.061); from the existence of one *Sachverhalt*, nothing follows about the existence or non-existence of any other. Thus there are no "real connections" between *Sachverhalte*, a point which will bear extremely important consequences for Wittgenstein. One immediate consequence is that *Tatsachen* have no real unity and are merely aggregates or collections of *Sachverhalte*. This claim functions as the ontological correlate of the *Grundgedanke;* just as no reality corresponds to the logical connectives which bind together compound propositions, so no "glue" holds *Sachverhalte* together to form *Tatsachen.*

Although *Sachverhalte* are not further analyzable into simpler facts, they are complex insofar as they are a combination or connection of Objects, the third of the trio of ontological terms which dominate the opening passages of the book. Wittgenstein introduces the term 'Object' at 2.01 by offering several ordinary German terms—*'Gegenstände'*, *'Sachen'*, *'Dingen'*—indicating indif-

---

[43] Given the ontological priority of *Sachverhalte* to *Tatsachen*, it is curious that Wittgenstein chooses to introduce the latter first. He cryptically writes Russell that "The reason I introduce *Tatsache* before introducing *Sachverhalt* would want a long explanation." L. Wittgenstein, *Letters to Russell, Keynes and Moore*, (Cornell U. Press, Ithaca, 1974) R. 37, pp. 71–73. (This work hereafter abbreviated '*LRKM*'.)

ference to the specific ordinary connotations of these terms. *Sachverhalte* are completely composed of Objects. Lest we be tempted to imagine the Objects which constitute them as externally bound together (like bricks by mortar), Wittgenstein insists on the absence of logical intermediaries, likening the connections to those of "the links of a chain," (2.03) speaks to two concerns. Wittgenstein is eager to reject Frege's notion that there must be some "unsaturated" element in a complex, whose role it is to bind together the rest of the constituents.[44] But on a deeper level he no doubt felt the force of objections frequently raised against traditional forms of atomism. If things are ultimately composed of atoms, what makes the atoms stick together? If we resort to some sort of metaphysical "glue" to produce the bond, we have merely moved the problem back one step; what makes the glue stick to the atoms? Newton ridicules Hooke's explanation of cohesion in terms of tiny hooks or catches:

> The parts of homogeneal Bodies which fully touch each other stick together very strongly. And for explaining how this may be, some have invented hooked atoms, which is begging the question.[45]

The logical parallel is that a proposition cannot be analyzed into function and object, into a complete and an incomplete part, in the Fregean manner. Propositions consist solely of Names in immediate connection with one another.

Wittgenstein incorporates into the notion of an Object several important features which parallel the properties of Names. Objects have no properties in the normal sense, the sense in which Scott has the property of being the author of *Waverley*. Wittgenstein introduces Names as "elements in the propositional sign [which] correspond to the objects of the thought." (3.24) The characteristic of Names is that they resist elimination through Russellian analysis. This entails that they cannot be replaced with descriptions; in Wittgenstein's ontology, describability is the kiss of death. Thus if Objects had properties, they could be described, and thus the signs which stood for them would not be Names, the "simple signs" of

---

[44] "The Thought," trans. A. and M. Quinton, *Mind*, vol. 65 (1956), p. 17, and "Logic," in Frege, *Posthumous Writings*, ed. Hermes et al. (Blackwell, Oxford, 1979), pp. 126–51. The latter, an unfinished piece, is an excellent short introduction to Frege's mature logical theory.

[45] *Opticks* (Dover, New York, 1952), vol. III part 1. Compare with N. R. Hanson, *The Concept of a Positron* (Cambridge U. Press, Cambridge, 1963), chapter III.

3.201. Objects are, in Wittgenstein's picturesque metaphor, "colorless" (2.0232). They do, however, have what Wittgenstein calls "formal" or "internal" properties (4.122, 4.124). Part of the content of this difficult notion can be grasped from 2.012:

> Nothing in logic is accidental: if a thing can occur in a state of affairs, the possibility of the state of affairs must be written into the thing itself.[46]

That a given Object is a constituent of a certain *Sachverhalt* is therefore not accidental, but a function of the sort of Object it is. Objects cannot be randomly thrown together to make a *Sachverhalt* in the manner that children may mix random ingredients from the kitchen shelf in play "cooking." The property of being capable of combining with other Objects in certain ways to form *Sachverhalte* we will call a formal or internal property of that Object; note the close connection with what we might call the *logical type* of the object. But this formal or combinatory property cannot be described, but (to anticipate chapter V somewhat), "shows itself" or "makes itself manifest," presumably by the Object appearing in a certain (possible) *Sachverhalt*. What are these formal properties like? At 2.025 Wittgenstein tells us that Objects have form and content. The forms of Objects, a notion which seems closely related to, if not identical with, the formal properties of Objects, are "Space, Time, and Color." (2.0251) This does not mean that Objects themselves are spatial, colored, or temporal, but rather that they can come together to form spatio-temporal, colored facts. (I also take Wittgenstein to be saying here that Space, Time, and Color are the *kinds of things* which would count as the forms of Objects, rather than representing an *exhaustive* listing.) Since we normally think of contingent existences as being at the very least temporal, this is further evidence for Objects being rather different sorts of things. Wittgenstein plays explicitly on this distinction when he writes:

> My *whole* task consists in explaining the nature of the proposition.
> That is to say, in giving the nature of all facts, whose picture a proposition *is*.
> In giving the nature of all being.

---

[46] Compare with 6.37 and 6.375, and with the converse of the claim at 6.3. Robert Fogelin draws from this passage the rather bizarre conclusion that there are no "eligible bachelors," that every Object which *can* enter into a *Sachverhalte must* do so. (*Op. cit.*, p. 6)

> (And here being does not stand for existence—in that case it would be nonsensical.) (*NB*, p. 39)

The preceding entails a rather striking corollary. The totality of Objects "contain in themselves," as it were, all possible situations, insofar as the possibility of a given *Sachverhalt* depends on the internal or formal properties of the requisite Objects. To "know"—to specify—an Object, therefore, is also to specify every possible occurrence of that Object (2.0123). No *new* possibility can come about at a later date, and thus logic can be given "all at once." Therefore logic leaves no room for new *discovery;* it is given, as it were, "all at once." This surprising claim will be the basis for a good number of the characteristic but difficult claims in the *Tractatus,* some of which will surface in chapters V and XI.

Objects are eternal, or better, *timeless.* Complexes we can picture existing or not existing, and so we can imagine various possible worlds. But Objects are not constituents of the world in the sense that facts are; they are "the substance of the world" (2.021), that which *this* world shares with every other possible world (2.022–2.023). This substance is what "subsists"—has Being—independently of what is the case (2.024) and is thus not part of the world but a presupposition of *any* world. Wittgenstein thus subscribes to the traditional atomist view; the world consists of a configuration of atoms, constantly joining and separating. But he introduces to this atomism a twist parallel to Descartes' introduction of simple natures. The substance, the atoms, which are presupposed by contingent existence cannot themselves be contingent existents, but must stand at a different level.

Since Objects are not subject to the vicissitudes of contingent existence, the Names which represent them cannot fail of reference. So analysis stops with propositions composed wholly of Names, propositions having as their senses (possible) *Sachverhalte,* combinations of eternal, immutable Objects. This is why Wittgenstein writes:

> If the world had no substance, then whether a proposition had sense would depend upon whether another proposition was true. (2.0211)

The second proposition mentioned would be one stating that the referential terms of the first proposition in fact succeed in referring. That ordinary propositions have meaning requires that analysis end with just such propositions, or, put the other way around, the meaningfulness of ordinary propositions is guaranteed by the necessary success of reference of these ultimate propositions. But as we shall see in chapter V, any attempt to say any of this will result in nonsense.

It is important to stress here what Wittgenstein does not build into the concept of an Object. He does not require, as the logical positivists later did, that they be sense-data, nor that elementary propositions be reports on immediate experiences. Making such an assumption melds Wittgenstein's logical atomism with the presuppositions of the empiricist tradition. Russell does so in *Our Knowledge of the External World* and Carnap in the *Aufbau*, but there is no shred of evidence in the *Tractatus* to support this view. A. J. Ayer writes:

> ... I took for granted that the 'atomic propositions' which served in the *Tractatus* to determine the sense of everything that could be said, were propositions which referred to observable states of affairs. This was not made explicit by Wittgenstein himself ... but it was an assumption generally made at the time by all those who latched on to the *Tractatus*, including philosophers with whom Wittgenstein was personally in contact. If he did not accept it, one wonders why he allowed them to think that he did.[47]

It is a bare possibility that Wittgenstein *did* think that elementary propositions referred to sense-experiences, and that Objects must be something like sense-data, although Frege's polemics against "prejudice in favor of the observable" must have influenced him against such an assumption. But the important point is that such a decision could not be made on *logical* grounds. Malcolm writes:

> I asked Wittgenstein whether ... he had ever decided upon anything as an *example* of a simple object. His reply was that at that time his thought had been that he was a *logician,* and that it was not his business, as a logician, to try to decide whether this thing or that was a simple or a complex thing, that being a purely *empirical* matter! (*Op. cit.,* p. 86)

Language and the World

> Logic is not a body of doctrine, but a mirror-image of
> the world.
>
> —6.13

---

[47]*Part of My Life* (Oxford U. Press, Oxford, 1978), p. 116.

We are now in a position to summarize this long and rather polyglot chapter by presenting in graphic form the Tractarian parallels between language and the world. Language is composed of propositions, each of which is analyzable into an explicit truth-function of elementary propositions, whose characteristic mark is that they have no further propositional components. Such elementary propositions are composed wholly of Names—logically simple symbols—standing in immediate relation to one another. The world—that which contingently exists—is composed of *Tatsachen*, facts which have other facts as constituents. Such *Tatsachen* can be resolved into *Sachverhalte*—atomic facts—which have no components which are themselves facts. They are, however, complex, being composed of Objects—logical simples—standing in direct relation to one another. We can represent the parallels between the linguistic and the ontological on the following chart:

Linguistic	*Ontological*
Compound Propositions	*Tatsachen*
Elementary Propositions	*Sachverhalte*
Names	Objects

The horizontal line represents an ontological break. Compound and elementary propositions, for instance, share many features, but are radically different from names. Further, above but not below the line the concepts of truth and existence have applicability. The parallel is not perfect, insofar as although there are certainly molecular propositions, there really are no *Tatsachen*, these being just aggregates of *Sachverhalte*. Finally, as we shall see in the following chapter, what really correspond to elementary propositions are not *Sachverhalte* but possible *Sachverhalte*. Thus a false (elementary) proposition does not correspond to a "false fact," but no fact at all.

We began this chapter with a discussion of certain traditional problems concerning a non-contingent basis for contingent existence, and we saw those difficulties reappear in logico-linguistic guise as semantic puzzles about reference. How can a proposition be meaningful if the denoting expressions it contains fail of reference? Convinced that it cannot, the immediate tendency is to adopt a bloated ontology of Terms, replete with the necessary distinction between Being and existence. But dissatisfaction with this solution led Russell to challenge the superficial grammar of ordinary propositions and provide an analytical technique whereby the troublesome expressions which seem to refer to pseudo-entities disappear in favor of bound variables. But a consistent working out of the program of Russellian analysis shows that it must ultimately terminate with propositions composed of terms whose referential success is guaranteed. This leads us to the notion of an elementary proposition, composed wholly of Names, simple symbols which cannot fail of reference. Oddly, the very distinction between contingent existence and being which the theory of descriptions was in part designed to eliminate appears again in new garb.

V

The Picture Theory
of Propositions

"You mean, 'tis not the truth? I must say, Henry, it sounds
reasonable to me. In sooth, there is a seed of poetry in it; it
hath an elegance."
"Aye, it hath every virtue and but one small defect, which
is, that the universe doth not operate in that wise."

—DISCUSSION OF DESCARTES' THEORY OF VORTICES
IN JOHN BARTH, *THE SOT-WEED FACTOR.*

In the preceding chapter we examined the internal workings of
both language and the world. We must now investigate the linkage,
the connection, between the two. The world resolves into *Sachverhalte*, language into elementary propositions; how are the two
related so that a given elementary proposition *means* a given
Sachverhalt? What is the relationship between Names and Objects?
Is it like or unlike that between propositions and their senses? Are
propositions, as Frege thought, merely complex names? Most
generally, what must be the relationship between one thing and
another so that the first *means* the second?

Wittgenstein's answers are embodied in his "picture theory of
propositions." Probably the most familiar facet of the *Tractatus*,
much can be said about it, but my discussion will center on those
elements which bear either on the nature of Names, which in chapter
IX I will link with the metaphysical subject, or with the crucial
distinction between showing and saying, which will be the topic of
chapter VI.

Some Features of Ordinary Language

The picture theory can perhaps best be grasped against the
background of certain features of ordinary language which, on first
blush, appear unusual or puzzling. Frege takes propositions to be
simply *complex names*. 'The cat is on the mat' thus differs in no

fundamental way from 'Bismarck' or 'the father of modern Germany'. As names, propositions have both a sense and a reference; the former a thought, the latter a truth-value. This treatment of the semantics of propositions has the virtue that primary occurrences of propositions, at least, are treated wholly extensionally. But a little reflection is sufficient to show that propositions are in fact quite different from names, or at least that Wittgenstein cannot consistently treat them as such.

(a) Propositions differ from names insofar as they have *truth-values*. Every proposition is either true or false, while names, although they can denote, denote ambiguously or fail to denote, never have truth-values. This difficulty can be mitigated somewhat by adopting the Fregean method of treating propositions as denoting their truth-values. But if those *entia suspecta*, The True and The False, are both real elements of the world, the superiority of true propositions over false ones becomes wholly mysterious. Likewise the truth of the Law of Excluded Middle becomes problematical: how can we say a priori every proposition will denote exactly *one* of these entities, and that there is no third possibility?

(b) The role of names is to go proxy for the things which they denote. If a name fails to denote anything, it ceases to be a symbol and becomes instead an empty noise or mark.[1] However, there clearly *are* false propositions, and it seems initially acceptable to say that a proposition is false when it corresponds to no fact. If propositions are a sort of name, then false propositions ought to be meaningless. But they clearly are not.

(c) To know what a name means is at bottom to be acquainted with the thing named. We sometimes know things by description ('The winner of the 1918 American League batting crown'), but it seems plausible that our knowledge by description must ultimately be grounded in knowledge by acquaintance. (The meaning of a Wittgensteinian Name *is* the thing that it stands for.) Yet we can clearly know what a proposition is about without being acquainted with the fact it represents or even know if there *is* such a fact. Otherwise, it would be senseless to wonder whether a given proposition was true or not. (Occasionally, as in fiction, or in the antecedent of a hypothetical, we don't even *care* about the truth-value.)

---

[1] Wittgenstein later challenges this thesis, which he holds as fundamental in 1918. Cf. *PI*, #41–42.

(d) Jerrold J. Katz writes:

> The most remarkable fact about human speech communication is that,
> except for clichés and bits of social ritual like "How do you do?", the
> sentences we speak and hear daily bear little or no physical resemblance to
> familiar ones. Yet we understand almost every new sentence we encounter,
> and our understanding is immediate. This is in striking contrast to our
> attempts at understanding new machines or gadgets, which often take
> considerable time and effort, and sometimes never succeed at all.[2]

Conversely, we can *say* new things, create wholly new propositions.[3]
This creative aspect of language strongly implies that propositions
are *essentially* complex, standing in stark contrast with names.[4] For
instance, I cannot understand the name "Michael Paladini" if I know
Michael Brockhaus and Enzo Paladini. In the case of technical
Names, this feature of simplicity is built in.

These points jointly illustrate both differences between propositions and names, and putative features of propositions which stand
in need of explanation. Wittgenstein satisfies these common-sense
demands, along with certain technical demands, by construing a
proposition as a special sort of *picture*, which displays the fact that
would correspond with it were it to be true. The notion of a
proposition-as-picture first emerges in a *Notebooks* entry (p. 7) dated
29.9.14, where it is prefaced with a remark about the "quite general
conception of coordination of proposition and situation." There
Wittgenstein offers as an example the representation of an automo-
bile accident in a court of law via model cars, dolls, and so forth.[5] The
facts of the case—that the red Renault hit the green Mercedes—are
represented in the model by virtue of two different relations. First,
each toy car stands for a real car involved in the accident. Second,

---

[2] *The Underlying Reality of Language and its Philosophical Import* (Harper and Row, New York, 1971), p. 52.

[3] "Generations of linguists have rightly stressed that the distinctive trait of language, not shared by the signal systems of lower animals, is its production of combinations. We learn modes of combination as well as words, and thus are prepared to produce and respond to complex expressions never heard before." W. V. O. Quine, *The Roots of Reference*, (Open Court, La Salle, IL, 1973), p. 59.

[4] Cf. Jay F. Rosenberg, *Linguistic Representations* (Reidel, Dordrecht, 1975), p. 3ff.

[5] Von Wright repeats Wittgenstein's claim that the inspiration for this remark came while reading a magazine story about a law-court in Paris, where just such a model was used. Cf. his "biographical sketch" in Malcolm *op. cit.*, pp. 7–8.

the relations between the toy cars represent (or *claim* to represent—importantly, a model can be inaccurate) the relations between the actual cars in the accident. An immediate analogy between the model and a proposition is seen in the clear sense in which one model can be "true" while another is not. (We sometimes speak in ordinary language of someone "not giving a true picture of how things are.") But more importantly, we can tell *of what a model purports to be a model*, without knowing whether it is a "correct" model, that is, whether it models an actual fact or not. Put another way, the *meaning* of a model is prior to and independent of its *truth*.

Possibly such homely cases of models inspired Wittgenstein's picture theory, reinforced perhaps by resonances with certain facets of Hertz's theory of "dynamical models" and Boltzmann's work, both of which Wittgenstein greatly admired.[6] (In chapter VII below we shall see a rather different Hertzian influence on Wittgenstein's thought.) Such resonance perhaps gave Wittgenstein encouragement towards "defining the genus in terms of the species," moving from straightforward cases of models to the more abstract and powerful picture theory.

Pictures

The development of the picture theory in the *Tractatus* takes place in two stages. The first (roughly 2.1 through 2.174) examines ordinary pictures and their *material* relations to the depicted, extracting the essence of such depiction. But starting at 2.18, Wittgenstein begins to extend and generalize, replacing material relations with *logical* relations and giving the picture theory great power and generality. I will follow Wittgenstein's two-stage process.

Consider a straightforward realistic painting, copied from an actual case, of a man and woman standing on a beach. For simplicity, let us assume the picture to be composed of unitary "elements," such as the man and the woman. (We will later justify this assumption.) Consider some of the properties of such a purely *iconic* representation.

---

[6] For an account of this influence, see Toulmin and Janik, *op. cit.*, ch. 5. In addition, after a rather puzzling sketch in *NB*, p. 30, which deals with "the projection of the picture on to reality," Wittgenstein adds parenthetically "(Maxwell's method of mechanical models)," indicating perhaps a further influence of Wittgenstein's physical studies.

(a) The elements of the painting—the *images* of the man, the woman, and the beach—correspond one-to-one with the elements of the scene pictured, viz., the man, the woman, and the beach. The images in the painting *take the place of* the elements of the scene; in order to do so the images and the elements must be equinumerous.

(b) The relation between picture-element (or "grapheme," to take up Black's felicitous play on the linguist's 'morpheme'), is that of *resemblance*. For example, the (pictured) yellow hair of the woman in the painting resembles the (actual) blond hair of the woman on the beach. Thus the connection between grapheme and element is *iconic*. This iconic relation of course also holds in the case of an accurate, non-doctored colored photograph, but the mechanism of the camera provides straightforward *causal* relations as well. It is also less intuitively meaningful to speak of a "false photograph."

(c) The graphemes alone do not constitute the picture, but rather the graphemes *standing in the actual relations that they do.* Thus if the man-grapheme is to the left of the woman-grapheme, then the man on the beach stood to the left of the woman. Likewise, that they stood *on* the beach rather than above or under it is represented by the spatial relation of the graphemes. Ignoring such devices as perspective, note that the grapheme relations are of the same *logical sort* as the element-relations; in this case spatial relations are represented by other spatial relations. Contrast: on a musical score, the spatial relations between the printed notes represent quite different *relations of relative pitch* between the notes.

(d) Although we have assumed that our beach picture is an accurate representation of an actual fact, a more common sort of (representational) painting depicts purely imaginary scenes. It will be convenient, and even perhaps in accord with ordinary usage, to say of a painting that it *depicts* a scene or fact *even when there is no such scene or fact, and never was.* ("Here we see depicted Romulus and Remus nursing from the wolf.") In a social situation where *actual* depiction was more important than ours, we might naturally term (e.g.) pictures of Republicans romping with nymphs and satyrs as "false pictures."

(e) If we can paint a picture of a scene, it follows that scene is at least logically possible. A painting of Ben Franklin waltzing with Marilyn Chambers is proof that *the world could have been different in such a way* that Ben and Marilyn so did. Picturability guarantees (logical) possibility; there are no "impossible pictures."[7]

(f) Finally, since any painting is a "possible picture," we cannot tell merely from looking at the picture whether it is a "true painting" or a "false painting," whether it depicts reality or only imagination. *There are no a priori pictures.* But our ignorance of the "truth" of a picture detracts not a bit from our appreciation of *that which it pictures.*

In summary: a picture depicts via two relations it bears to the possible scene that it depicts. First, there is a one-to-one correspondence between grapheme and element, in the case examined the relation being resemblance. Second, the arrangement or *structure* of the picture matches the structure of the pictured fact, in our case this structure being largely *spatial.* These are the "semantics," as it were, of a representational painting.

Before moving from purely representational to "logical" pictures, consider two artificial elements in the above discussion. First I chopped the beach up into units, and likewise the picture. But such designation of units was rather arbitrary. Why choose the man as a unity, rather than his arm, or the molecules which constitute his cells? Parallel points hold for the picture. My example thus supposes that the world (or at least this little corner of it) was in some non-arbitrary manner *atomic.* This objection is not trivial; it seems a necessary condition for my picture being a representation of *just this beach scene,* rather than a different one quite like it. (Consider two pictures that are *almost* the same. Both of them purport to picture the beach party. Which is the "true" picture?) The relation of

---

[7] Consider, however, the "impossible pictures" on p. 11 of Coope et al., *A Wittgenstein Workbook,* (University of California Press, Berkeley, 1970), the "space fork" often found depicted on the bulletin boards of university science departments, and the well-known works of Maurice Escher. These apparent counterexamples can be dealt with in terms of psychological expectations engendered by non-standard methods of projection.

resemblance between grapheme and element also allows of considerable vagueness; is this *quite* the right shade of yellow for the woman's hair?

Second, are the things we say as much like pictures as our example might imply? Representational paintings are limited; we can depict only certain sorts of things. I can catch Dennis's silly grin, but can I paint his deviousness? Many of the things which we speak of—dishonesty, transfinite numbers, the Mexican economy—appear incapable of painted representation. In fact, with the dubious exception of hieroglyphics, propositions don't seem very much like pictures at all, and with the equally dubious exception of onomatopoeia, words don't seem to resemble the things for which they stand. On the positive side, however, the hypothesis that propositions are in some sense pictures of possible situations explains some of the linguistic phenomena we have remarked upon in the first section of this chapter. It would show, for instance, how we can know what a proposition *means* without knowing whether or not it is true. Since pictures can be put together from preexisting elements, we can likewise see how it is possible to construct and understand new propositions.

But in order for the picture theory to satisfy Wittgenstein's demands, two conditions must be met. First of all, we must be able to produce a proposition with *any sense that we desire*. Second, for reasons we have not yet seen, every proposition must have a *perfectly determinate sense*, with any hint of vagueness expunged. Wittgenstein accomplishes both these tasks by extending the ordinary notion of a picture to produce the more general and abstract notion of a *logical picture*. His contention is that by so doing nothing of the essence of picturing is lost.

Logical Pictures

If the relation between grapheme and element in a painting is iconic, then the picture is composed of other, smaller pictures. But such a straightforward material connection will obviously not do, not only because of the very wide range of things about which we speak, but also because an explanation of representation ought to be independent of the nature of the signs utilized in that system. It ought to be irrelevant, for instance, that our language involves largely written or spoken signs. (On a more technical level, since the ultimate designata of pictured situations will be propertyless Objects, resemblance—the sharing of certain properties—is not possible.) But further, the notion of a language in which *all* basic signs were iconic borders on absurdity. Consider briefly a language in which pitch-words like 'C-sharp' and 'E-flat' were replaced with the corresponding sounds. In such a language the claim "I cannot sing a double high C" is impossible to make.

The iconic relation between grapheme and element, between word and object, must be weakened to one of *convention*. In a paint-by-number picture the unpainted canvas is a picture of the depicted scene just as surely as is the lithograph on the front of the box; if it were not, we could not go from the canvas to the painting. On the unpainted canvas each color on the palette is represented by a number, and thus we need the number-key—a rule or convention—to map the numbers onto the corresponding colors. But there is certainly no iconic relation between, for instance, the number 2 and vermilion. Compare this with the intermediate case in which every blank spot on the unpainted canvas was keyed with a small spot of the requisite color.[8]

In the paint-by-number example we have a relation between elements which although conventional *could* have been iconic.[9] We contrast this with cases where iconic representation is out of the question. It is certainly clear that we cannot iconically represent with physical signs mental states, states of "that obscure part of me which does not come under the imagination," as Descartes puts it. Thus in a cartoon we display Dagwood's anger not by an iconic representation of that anger (what could *that* be?) but with an angry expression and a cloud of smoke over his head; concentric "sweat-beads" indicate exasperation, a light-bulb inspiration, hearts feelings of love.[10]

---

[8] See the language-game of *PI* #1.

[9] Compare with Swift's "Scheme for abolishing all words" whereby words are replaced by the objects for which they stand. Each "speaker" would be required to carry with him at all times "such Things as were necessary to express the particular Business they are to discourse on." *Gulliver's Travels*, part III, chapter V.

[10] Wittgenstein later emphasizes the degree to which these conventions become assimilated to the point where they appear "natural." Don't the arrows of *PI* #86 have a *natural* sense? Don't they "naturally" know that they tell us to go *this* way? Out of their normal context conventions expose themselves and appear ludicrous. The film critic Stanley Kauffmann points to the droll

A less esoteric example, upon which Wittgenstein himself frequently trades (4.011, 4.014–4.0141) is *musical notation*. Even the simplest elements of a score are sufficient to show the richness of the notation, as well as its lack of iconicity. The shape of a printed note bears no resemblance to the temporal duration which that note represents; only convention dictates that a half-note is twice as long as a quarter-note. Likewise, the symbol 'C^{m7}' bears no resemblance to a chord composed of C, E♭, G, and B♭. The conventionality of this notation is highlighted by comparison with the little guitar chord diagrams which sometimes appear on the sheet music for popular tunes, and which show one *where to put the fingers on the guitar neck*. (And of course here too there is an element of convention.)

Importantly, note that iconic representation is an option only when grapheme and element have some properties in common. The elements of the *Sachverhalte* which propositions will picture, however, are Objects, which have no properties in the normal sense at all. Thus it follows from the nature of Objects that the Name-Object relation cannot contain any degree of iconicity. As we shall see in the next section, the Naming relation is non-iconic in the purest sense possible.

The identity of form between picture and pictured is the other element in the picturing relation. In our beach picture example, this identity of form consists in the graphemes standing in the same spatial relations to one another as did the elements of the pictured scene. The form which the picture and the pictured fact share Wittgenstein calls the *pictorial form* of the picture.[11] Every picture has a structure, insofar as every picture is a fact (2.141), whose characteristic it is to be articulated. At 2.171 Wittgenstein offers spatial pictures, colored pictures, and so forth as examples of different *kinds* of pictures, and presumably pictures with different pictorial forms. A picture can represent *iconically* any reality whose form it shares; I can represent relations between colors in a colored picture, and triangles in a spatial picture. However, there is a looser

---

cinematic convention, usually wholly unnoticed, whereby actors portraying Germans in English-language pictures speak English with a German accent!

[11] 2.15, 2.17. The "pictorial form" of 2.17 is not, I think, the same as the "pictorial relationship" of 2.1213. The emphasis in the latter seems to be the grapheme-element relations (cf. the "feelers" of 2.1515). It is arguable that the distinction is empty if the form of a fact is solely a function of the Objects of which it is constituted. But for expository purposes it seems to me wise to sharply separate the grapheme-element relation from the form-form relation.

relation between forms than identity, one which will ease the preceding restriction without losing what is essential to the form-form relation. Consider a phonograph record, which consists of variegated grooves in a plastic base. When the record is played, the information contained in the grooves is "translated" into pitch, tone, timbre, rhythm, and volume. Obviously it must be possible to store the requisite *kinds* of information on the disc (and also, not incidentally, in the musical score for the same music) since that information can be retrieved, in the form of the music, quite mechanically. And clearly the notes themselves are not present on the disc in the manner medievals saw homunculi as tiny presences inside human beings. Thus the spatial patterns on the record must share a form with the auditory relations of the notes in the tune.

This relation cannot be identity, since the two are of different *types*. Let us call this more abstract *but by no means looser* relation *homology of form*. Two forms are homologous if it is possible to map one onto the other, that is, if there is a method for moving from one to the other, and back again. Thus the song, the score of the song, a digital recording of the song, and an analog recording all share homologous form.[12]

Under what conditions can two systems be considered formally homologous? No doubt Wittgenstein was influenced by Hertz's notion of *mathematical multiplicity*, to which he explicitly refers in a *Notebooks* passage parallel to 4.04. We can create a "dynamical model" for a system, Hertz argues, when certain conditions are met.[13] Of primary interest to us is the demand that the model have as many "coordinates" as the modeled system, where we might see "coordinates" as independent variables or degrees of freedom. For instance, we can display the simple micro-economic relations between supply and price for a particular commodity on a two-dimensional Cartesian chart, since each of the changing quantities—price and demand—can be assigned a coordinate. In a slightly more complex situation, the thermodynamic properties of molecules can be represented in a "phase space" of n dimensions, where n represents the number of

---

[12] This notion of homology of form is central to the work of Alan Turing, and it is possible that he picked it up from his interactions with Wittgenstein, perhaps when he attended Wittgenstein's lectures on the Foundations of Mathematics at Cambridge in 1939; cf. Andrew Hodges, *Alan Turing; The Engima* (Simon and Schuster, NY, 1983), pp. 136, 152–54.

[13] Cf. Hertz, *Principles of Mechanics*, trans. Jones and Walley (Dover, NY, 1956), sect. 418. Henceforth this work to be referred to as *PrMe*.

degrees of freedom of movement of the molecule. Ignoring rotation, for instance, a marble rolling back and forth in a tube has but one degree of freedom, and thus its position at any given time can be represented by a function of a single variable.

Thus a system can have form homologous to another system if they have the same degree of mathematical multiplicity.[14] But mere possession of the requisite degree of multiplicity is not sufficient. There also needs to be a method for assigning values of system A *as representatives of* the requisite values of system B. This assignment Wittgenstein calls the *method of projection* for that particular model. In certain cases—when the model is an iconic one—the method of projection is psychologically obvious. In other cases we must rely on elements of convention. A two-dimensional uncolored spatial picture can represent iconically two-dimensional monochrome facts and through alternative methods of projection any system with two degrees of freedom. A colored, two-dimensional spatial picture can iconically depict colored two-dimensional situations, and through a method of projection (counting two spatial dimensions, hue, intensity, and saturation as independent variables) can be homologous with any system of five degrees of freedom. How rich can a picture be? Wittgenstein answers that the most general sort of form is what he calls *logical form* (2.18), and a picture whose form is logical form is a *logical picture* (2.182).[15] We might think of a logical picture as one with the highest *possible* multiplicity. Logical form is also the "form of reality" (2.19), that is, the form of the world, and thus "Logical pictures can depict the world" (2.19). What we have here is the converse of the "principle of picturability" which we saw above. There we said that *if x* could be pictured, then *x* was possible. Now we see that since depiction is a function of the possibility of homology of form, and since a logical picture shares form with reality, *every possibility can be pictured.* Thus Wittgenstein's

---

[14] For simplicity, I have assumed that if A can picture B, then B can picture A. But that is not strictly true, as is shown by the picturing of a system A with multiplicity n by a system B with multiplicity $n + 1$. In this case, B can picture A (with one "null" or idle degree of multiplicity), but A lacks the richness to model B.

[15] This blanket statement is fraught with some difficulties. 2.182 tells us that "every picture is *at the same time* a logical one." This would seem to imply that the simple two-dimensional picture was at the same time a logical picture, and thus that it had the requisite multiplicity to represent any reality, leaving it wholly puzzling how any picture could *fail* to have sufficient multiplicity to represent *any situation whatsoever.* I will ignore this mystery, saying only that I think an adequate solution lies on distinguishing clearly between the pictorial "sign" and the picture-symbol. The reader might consult Anscombe *op. cit.*, p. 67 for a partial answer.

discovery of the logical picture shows that the picturable and the possible are coextensive, and since "the world" is a subset of the possibles, it follows that the world can be pictured in logical pictures. This is a "completeness-claim," so to speak, for the picture theory.

It is crucial to keep in mind that we move from normal pictures to logical pictures *without losing what is essential and characteristic* to the picturing relation. Janik and Toulmin write:

> Again and again, we understand Wittgenstein's aphorisms better if we think of linguistic *Bilder* as "deliberately constructed verbal representations," instead of misleading ourselves by the use of the much looser English term "pictures." (*Op. cit.*, pp. 182–83)

Leaving aside how 'picture' would be "looser" than 'deliberately constructed linguistic representations', I see no question as to whether Wittgenstein means 'picture' in a quite literal sense.[16] For instance, 4.021 claims that *insofar as* a proposition is a picture, I can understand a proposition without having its sense explained to me, a claim which is mysterious if we insert 'deliberately constructed verbal representation.' Likewise, although it is transparent why there cannot be "illogical pictures" (cf. 3.03–3.031), it is wholly unclear why there cannot be an illogical "verbal representation." Thus, contra Janik and Toulmin, it seems mandatory that we take *'Bilder'* to be quite literally 'pictures'.

Digression: Frege and Wittgenstein on the Determinacy of Sense

> Frege says: Every well-formed sentence must make sense;
> and I say: Every possible sentence is well-formed, and if
> it does not make sense that can only come of our not
> having *given* any meaning to certain of its parts.
>
> —*NB* 2.9.14

Before we examine the consequences of Wittgenstein's identification of propositions (and thoughts) with logical pictures, there

---

[16] It is worth noting that when he intends to discount the normal uses of a term, he characteristically parenthetically inserts ordinary synonyms to show that the *particular word chosen* doesn't make much difference (eg. 'Object' at 2.01). That he does *not* do this with 'picture' is thus evidence that he intended the ordinary connotations to hold. (Much the same sort of argument can be made for 'solipsism'; cf. ch. IX.)

remains to be investigated an interesting and important semantic demand which Wittgenstein inherits from Frege. That claim is that *where there is sense there must be perfect sense*. Frege and Wittgenstein differ with respect to this principle only insofar as Frege saw this as an ideal for a scientific language, while Wittgenstein characteristically extends it to *every* language.[17] The effects of the "determinacy thesis" go very deep into Wittgenstein's system; in particular, we are interested in the effect on his conception of logic. Let us examine Frege's arguments for that thesis, and their influence on Wittgenstein.

Frege offers four arguments in favor of the determinacy thesis.[18] If a concept is not perfectly defined, perfectly definite, then there will be cases where we cannot tell whether or not a particular object falls under that concept. But public communication demands that the sense of any expression be something objective, and if a concept is not precisely defined, then how can we speak of *the* sense or reference of a term? Further, if the logicist program wants to represent mathematical truths as analytic, then (at least given the normal sense of 'analytic') the truth of any mathematical propositions must be decidable by reference to definitions. But if these definitions are vague or imprecise, then mathematics will be infected with uncertainty, which Frege emphatically denies. But moreover, if a concept is vague, then there will be some (objective) doubt as to whether or not a particular object falls under it. But the law of excluded middle demands that every object either have or lack a property: *Tertium non Datur*, Frege insists. Finally, vagueness has the distressing property of being inheritable or contagious. If an expression is vague, the sense of any expression which contains it will also be vague; if 'a' is not precise, neither will 'f(a)' be.[19]

Wittgenstein swallows these arguments whole, agreeing that complete determinacy of sense is a necessary condition for the truth of the Principle of Excluded Middle (4.025), and that the contagious

---

[17] A summary of Frege's arguments appears in section 56 of vol. II of *The Basic Laws of Arithmetic*. This section, not translated in the Furth edition, appears in Geach and Black *op. cit.*, pp. 159ff. as "Frege on definitions".

[18] I have profited here from Baker and Hacker *op. cit.*, pp. 368–372, although some of the claims they there make about Wittgenstein's early views seem to me dubious.

[19] "If ... the relation *greater than* is not completely defined, then it is likewise uncertain whether the quasi-conceptual construction obtained by filling it up, e.g., *greater than zero* or *positive*, is a proper concept." *op. cit.*, p. 165.

ness of vagueness is a serious difficulty (3.318, 4.024 ff.). These are no minor admissions. The demands of determinacy powerfully condition some of Wittgenstein's most fundamental claims: in the *Notebooks* he baldly states that the demand for simple Objects simply *is* the demand for determinacy of sense. (*NB*, p. 63) But perhaps Frege's solution to the problem of vagueness—presented in the form of rules which must hold for definitions—affects his thought the most.

The first of these conditions is directed against "the mathematicians favourite procedure, piecemeal definitions . . ." (*Ibid.*, p. 159) A proper definition *alone* must suffice to determine *all* applications of a concept; we cannot define the concept for some contexts and leave the rest for future investigation, since we cannot say in advance that those later determinations will be consistent with the present one.[20] Likewise, it must be settled *in advance* for *any* object whether or not it falls under the concept. For Frege 'The Moon is greater than zero' must have a determinate sense and a definite truth-value. The definition of the concept "greater than zero," and thus the domain of the function "x is greater than zero," must be determined all at once. If it is not, we cannot *prove* that our definition is consistent.

While Wittgenstein takes seriously indeed the demands for such determinacy, he rejects Frege's solution—the introduction of rules for definitions. If definition is part of logic, then there cannot be some higher set of rules (in this case the rules for definitions) which put restrictions on such definitions. If this were true, then there would be something "higher" than logic, which itself then ought to inherit that title. Since logic must "take care of itself," the problems that Frege sees with certain definitions cannot be real. We can thus say a priori that every concept is absolutely precise, and every proposition has full-blown and absolutely precise sense. Since such precision must be a property of *every* language, the distinction which Frege draws between vague, imprecise ordinary language and scientific languages becomes either empty or merely psychological.

The influence of these Fregean theses concerning definition is

---

[20] Frege's realistic bias demands strict distinction of the "context of discovery" from the "context of justification." That a partial definition, a working thesis, might be necessary for advances in some new area of investigation is therefore not for him a justification for accepting partial definition in logic and mathematics: cf. *op. cit.* #58 and Frege's alternative suggestion in #60.

evident in many places in the *Tractatus*, connected as they are with Wittgenstein's striking claims that logic must take care of itself, that there can be no discoveries in logic, and so forth. But perhaps the most immediate reflection of the demand for determinacy is in the theory of Names. Names—the primitives of language—cannot be defined, and their meanings can only be given by "elucidations," these being propositions or propositional functions which contain the Name in question. Wittgenstein insists that when one such use of a Name is given, *all others must be given at the same time*. From this demand follows Wittgenstein's claims that when an Object is given then *all* Objects are given, that when *one* elementary proposition is given *all* must be, and so forth. Some of the logical consequences of these powerful claims will appear in the following chapter.[21]

Propositions as Logical Pictures

W. W. Bartley tells us that Wittgenstein had originally titled his manuscript *'Der Satz'* ('The Proposition'),[22] but interestingly propositions arise in the expository order of the *Tractatus* only as a sort of adjunct to *thoughts*. At 3, following a discussion of pictures and logical pictures, Wittgenstein tells us "A logical picture of facts is a thought." This is in a way misleading, since we later learn that thoughts—*Gedanken*—are best construed as propositions whose propositional signs consist of mental or psychical constituents rather than physical signs. But this ought not cloud the significance of the order in which Wittgenstein introduces the notions. He wants to investigate the a priori limits of thought and not merely, as the Preface misleadingly puts it, the "expression of thoughts."[23] We shall

---

[21] These claims are also connected intimately with a Tractarian notion which I have avoided, namely "logical space" (1.13, 2.11, 2.202, etc.). Logical space is a metaphor for the web of possibilities represented by the internal combinatory properties of Objects, but it also represents the intimate relations between Objects. I have avoided introducing it insofar as Wittgenstein's development is very murky; the notion itself may be defective. The commentators are not much help; for instance, Stenius (*op. cit.*, ch. IV) seems quite wrong.

[22] *Op. cit.*, p. 52. Oddly, Bartley then writes "... it was not until shortly before publication that the book acquired the Latin title suggested by G. E. Moore." This remark hardly seems applicable to *'Logisch-Philosophische Abhandlung'*. It is tempting to think that Wittgenstein might have called the book *The Proposition: Its Strengths and Limitations*, or something of the like, but the Preface shows why such a title would be unacceptable.

[23] Why does he speak this way in the Preface? First, because it *is* only a preface, and the technical sense of 'thought' has not yet been introduced. But moreover, the say/show distinction allows us to be in some sense aware of that which cannot be said, and in a loose sense of 'thought', it is the expression of thought which is being limited.

have occasion to examine *Gedanken* presently; until then I will deal with propositions alone.

Logical pictures are pictures of reality, and since it is the role of a proposition to represent reality, propositions must be logical pictures of possible facts. Elementary propositions picture *Sachverhalte*. The constituent Names of elementary propositions, with their guaranteed reference, thus correspond to the graphemes of the previous section, while the Objects to which they refer are the elements of the pictured fact. An elementary proposition is true if the Sachverhalt which it pictures—its *sense*—is actual, false otherwise. (With non-elementary propositions the case is slightly more complex but similar—the proposition '~p', for instance, is true when p does *not* exist.) *Note that there are no "false facts" which correspond to false propositions:* the *same* (possible) *Sachverhalt* corresponds to a given elementary proposition whether it is true or false.

Just as pictures can depict what is not the case, propositions have the sense that they do independently of their truth-value. They picture the *Sachverhalt* which would exist were the proposition to be true. However—and this will be exhaustively examined in the following chapter—a proposition stands in a dual semantic relation to its sense. By picturing its sense it *shows*, to use Wittgenstein's central technical term, its sense, and it *says* that this sense is actual. Thus, every (elementary, at least) proposition both *shows* something and *says* something, these two semantic categories being mutually exclusive. This distinction, which although deeply embedded in the picture theory predates it, will quickly assume central importance.

For discursive intelligences at least propositions require a concrete vehicle. In the case of written or spoken propositions, the vehicle (the propositional sign) is mounds of ink on paper or vibrations in the air. Wittgenstein's introduction of thoughts before propositions reinforces the natural tendency to see the former as logically prior to the latter; on this view propositions are thoughts "clothed," as it were, and the thoughts stand behind those propositions like silver used to stand behind paper money.[24] But Wittgenstein deems this view false and dangerously so. Even if it were true

---

[24] "The things of the voice are symbols for the things of the spirit," Aristotle writes (*De Interpretatione*, 16a3). Russell, as we shall see in chapter VII, held this view more or less all of his philosophical career; cf. for instance "On Propositions and How they Mean" (1919) in *L&K*, esp. p. 308.

in some psychological sense (e.g., when I speak little images flutter before my mind and I try to describe them in public speech), from a logical point of view *thoughts are merely propositions with a different sort of vehicle.* In a postscript to a well-known letter to Russell, (dated 19.8.19 and thus written while Wittgenstein was a prisoner of war at Monte Cassino), he responds to a question of Russell's:

> Does a *Gedanke* consist of words? No! But of psychical constituents that have the same sort of relation to reality as words. What these constituents are I don't know. (*LRKM*, pp. 71–73)

A thought is thus just a proposition whose vehicle is signs of a certain obscure sort, but which has no particular logical precedence to ordinary propositions. In particular, *the mental propositional sign is no less in need of interpretation* than spoken or written propositional signs. This point, which will become central in chapters VIII–X below, is the source of much confusion among readers of the *Tractatus.*

Just as it is important not to treat thoughts as the "cash value" behind propositions, it is equally important not to treat the proposition as something wholly other than the propositional sign. In the *Investigations* Wittgenstein writes:

> 'A proposition is a queer thing!' Here we have in germ the subliming of our whole account of logic. The tendency to assume a pure intermediary between the propositional *signs* and the facts. . . .[25]

A proposition is, in a sense, what we *do* with the propositional sign. By this I do *not* mean the doctrine of meaning-as-use of *PI* #43 ff.; rather, there are not *three* things—the propositional sign, the wholly independent proposition and the fact pictured—but rather the propositional sign in its projective relation to the intended fact. The significance of these remarks will emerge as we examine the intending role of the metaphysical subject in the Naming relation.

But on the other hand, the proposition is certainly *more* than mere ink marks, vibrations in the air or clusters of "psychical constituents." "A proposition is a propositional sign *in its projective*

---

[25] *PI* #94; compare with *BB*, p. 32. Wittgenstein is not here alluding to his Tractarian view; Moore (*Phil. Papers*, p. 265) claims that Wittgenstein's target is W. E. Johnson.

relation to the world," Wittgenstein tells us (3.12, my emphasis). The propositional sign is a *fact;* its being so is a necessary condition for its picturing another (possible) fact. But its being such a fact is not also *sufficient;* we also need a "method of projection" to map grapheme on element and form on form. But what precisely is this "method of projection"? We know its purpose; to connect a given Name with an Object, and to map the form of the proposition-fact onto the form of its sense. Wittgenstein is of little immediate help: "The method of projection is to think the sense of the proposition" (3.11). But if "think the sense" means to have a *mental* proposition with the same sense as the physical proposition, this is obviously begging the question. The *Gedanken* is likewise a proposition; how does *it* acquire its sense?[26] Further, the method of projection cannot be contained in the sign itself, as we read "In order to recognize a symbol by its sign we must observe how it is used with a sense" (3.326).

Let us consider this point from a slightly different angle. In the *Blue Book* Wittgenstein writes with respect to a similar discussion:

> "What makes a portrait a portrait of Mr. N?" The answer which might first suggest itself is: "The similarity between the portrait and Mr. N".... It is quite clear, however, that similarity does not constitute our idea of a portrait; for it is in the essence of this idea that it should make sense to talk of a good or a bad portrait....
>
> An obvious, and correct, answer to the question "What makes a portrait the portrait of so-and-so?" is that it is the *intention.*[27]

What then makes a portrait the portrait *of* Mr. so-and-so, and what gives a proposition just *this* sense? The answer to this will take us, I believe, deep into the core of Wittgenstein's thought.

The Tractarian Doctrine of Names

God was God's name, just as his name was Stephen. *Dieu*
was French for God and that was God's name too; and

---

[26] Here we begin to see the attraction of the position to which Russell is frequently driven. When we reach the mental, we reach an arena where signs *no longer need interpretation;* they "interpret themselves," as it were. This is emphatically *not* Wittgenstein's view.

[27] *BB,* p. 32. Compare: "Obviously one would not call a picture true unless there were an intention behind it. A picture must represent something. Furthermore, an idea is not called true in itself, but only with respect to an intention that it should correspond to something." Frege, "The Thought," *Mind* 65 (1956), p. 291.

when anyone prayed to God and said *Dieu* then God
knew at once that it was a French person who was praying.
But though there were different names for God in all the
different languages of the world and God understood
what all the people who prayed said in their different
languages still God remained always the same God and
God's real name was God.
It made him very tired to think that way. It made his head
feel very big.

—JAMES JOYCE
A PORTRAIT OF THE ARTIST
AS A YOUNG MAN

Names by themselves may be empty, but the *act*
of naming. . . .

—THOMAS PYNCHON
GRAVITY'S RAINBOW

In this important section I will argue that in the *Tractatus*
Naming is as it were an act of *"pure intending."* This intending being
a sort of willing, it requires a *willing subject*; the knowing subject, as
we shall see in chapters VIII and IX, cannot possibly perform this
vital act. Thus the Schopenhauerian "world as will" begins to regain
a foothold in the impersonal realistic ontology so far sketched.
However, this reappearance will be significantly tempered and
radically changed by the doctrine of showing, which we shall
investigate in depth in chapter VI. Chapters VII and VIII will examine
Wittgenstein's rejection of two key elements in Schopenhauer's
universal voluntarism—the status of physical laws and the presence
of the subject in experience. In chapter IX we will examine the
metaphysical subject, and in the final chapters the ethical and
aesthetic consequences of Wittgenstein's doctrines, and the correlative view of the nature of philosophy which emerges. But in the
present section, which will serve as a foundation for those arguments, some previously given promissory notes will be redeemed for
hard cash. Here too we will see the first steps of the "ladder" of 6.54,
which must be climbed and then discarded so that we might "see the
world aright."

Names are introduced at 3.202 in the context of a discussion of
fully analyzed propositions. Such propositions are explicit truth-
functions of elementary propositions, the latter allowing of no
further analysis insofar as they are constituted wholly of "simple

signs" (3.201—"simple symbols" seems preferable). 3.202 tells us "The simple signs employed in propositions are called names." If this is intended as a definition of 'Name', it is singularly unhelpful. We can recognize Names insofar as they are constituents of fully analyzed propositions, which we in turn could recognize only by seeing that they were composed completely of Names! In the next chapter we shall see that this predicament is less serious than it appears.[28] Definition aside, however, the logical role of Names is clear, to wit, to go proxy for Objects in logical pictures, to stand in for "the substance of the world." Thus in the *Notebooks* Wittgenstein refers to the "trivial fact" that a fully analyzed proposition contains just as many Names as there are things in the corresponding fact. (*NB*, p. 11)

Frege saw names and propositions as quite similar, but as we have seen, for Wittgenstein they mirror the radical difference between facts and Objects. Propositions picture facts, which requires that they be "articulated," have parts. Names, on the other hand, are "simple signs."[29] They have no logical parts, and cannot be analyzed or dissected in any manner. They cannot picture, but rather assume the role of "going proxy for" the corresponding Object, in the manner that the model cars in the Paris law-court go proxy for the actual cars. (But note the important difference that the model cars resemble the actual ones. Note also that the resemblance is unnecessary.) But their relation is also more abstract; since the whole point of a Name is to go proxy for the requisite Object, *the meaning of the Name is the Object*. Note how in Wittgenstein's semantics the work of Frege's sense-reference distinction is neatly split between Name and proposition. Every proposition has a sense, but not necessarily a reference, while every Name is guaranteed reference, but has no sense, no content. Such a division of labor resolves a certain tension between sense and reference; sense seems to require structure, articulation, while *guaranteed* reference pulls us towards simplicity.

---

[28] In the meantime, mere reflection on the notion of a logical simple ought to exclude the possibility of definition. "I would remark, in the first place, that my explanation is not meant as a definition. One cannot require that everything be defined, any more than one can require that a chemist shall decompose every substance. What is simple cannot be decomposed, and what is logically simple cannot have a proper definition." Frege, "On Concept and Object," pp. 42–43 in Geach and Black *op. cit.*

[29] 3.201. Again, "simple symbols" seems preferable. Note that the Name-*sign* need not and maybe *cannot* be simple; since the Name-sign is the perceptible part of the Name-symbol, it is dubious that it could be simple. Any word in spoken human language, for instance, would be physically composite.

The simplicity of Names is closely connected with their other major property. Since the meaning of a Name is the Object for which it goes proxy, no real Name can fail of reference; this is in sharp contrast with both propositions and incomplete symbols. If 'A' is a Name, 'A exists' is always at best pleonastic, and 'A doesn't exist' at best self-contradictory. We shall see that each is in fact nonsensical, being an attempt to *say* something which is *shown* by the occurrence or nonoccurrence of 'A' in meaningful contexts. From a realistic point of view, such guaranteed reference may at first blush seem puzzling. It is tempting to construe such guaranteed reference in an Idealistic manner; the Object comes into existence through the act of Naming. This is of course heresy to Wittgenstein. Part of the mystery can be dispelled by remembering that Objects, the substance of the world (2.021), are not the sorts of things which enjoy contingent existence.

We shall have to return to this important notion of the guaranteed reference of Names, but as a preliminary we must examine what on the surface may appear an unrelated topic. A Name must refer to a particular Object by (a) picking out the *sort* of Object it is (if there are different "sorts") and (b) distinguishing a particular Object of that sort from the rest (if there are different Objects of the same sort). If there are Names of different logical types, how are these distinguished one from another? Here I use the term 'logical type' not in Russell's technical sense, which will feature in the next chapter, but in the sense in which we commonsensically view adjectives, nouns, and verbs as having different functions or roles in sentences.[30] Although Wittgenstein himself waffles on the issue of whether there are Names of different sorts, let us for the present respect our ordinary intuitions. If there are Names of different logical sorts, mirroring in a logical difference among Objects, knowing the meaning of a Name would involve *at least* knowing what *sort* of Object it went proxy for. Compare: knowing what 'ecru' means involves knowing that it is a color-word, even though we might not be clear *which* color it named.

It is very tempting to think, as Russell and Frege did, that there are some Names whose role is to provide the structure of a proposition. Frege speaks of some expressions as being "unsatur-

---

[30] Compare with *PrM*, chapter IV.

ated," as "proposition-radicals," whose nature it was to be incomplete and to need "filling in" with other terms. We might see these proposition-radicals as having different numbers of openings, different "valences," to continue the chemical metaphor. Analogously, Russell argues that every proposition must contain a verb, whose role it is to express a relation: "The verb, when used as a verb, embodies the unity of the proposition."[31] This view that a proposition consists of other terms hung on a framework provided by a certain sort of term Wittgenstein vehemently rejects. No class of Names assumes the role of providing the unity of the proposition. *Every* Name participates in the unity of the proposition, just as there is no *particular* link whose role is to provide the continuity of a chain.

How do we then discern the logical form of a Name? Wittgenstein suggests a procedure in a series of remarks intended to illuminate 3.3—"Only propositions have sense; only in the context of a proposition does a name have meaning."[32] Every component of a proposition which contributes to its sense Wittgenstein calls an *expression* (3.31). In order for sense to be perfect, if the contribution to the sense of an expression in one context is given, then it must be given in *all* contexts; Wittgenstein rather misleadingly says that one occurrence "presupposes" the others (3.311). If this were *not* the case, then it would be possible for us to discover further logical properties of the Name, and as we shall see in the following chapter, the notions of discovery, surprise, novelty, and so forth have no place in logic. (If they did, logic couldn't take care of itself.)

The context principle thus asserts that we see the logical form of a Name by seeing what role it plays in a proposition. Prominence is given to a particular expression by replacing everything else in a proposition in which it occurs with variables. For example, the logical form of 'Socrates' is displayed by replacing with variables 'taught' and 'Plato' in 'Socrates taught Plato,' yielding 'Socrates R x'. In this case we presumably see that 'Socrates' plays the same role as

---

[31] *PrM*, pp. 49–50. The phrase between the commas refers to a difficulty which we shall see in chapter VIII, when we examine Russell's "Multiple Relation Theory of Judgment."

[32] 3.3 is an echo of course of Frege's "context principle." I do not take Wittgenstein to be claiming that Names are not complete symbols, do not have significance in isolation; the sense in which a Name having meaning is dependent on its appearance in a proposition will be clarified in what follows.

'Plato' but a rather different role than 'taught'. Thus we find the rather misleading passage:

> What signs fail to express, their application shows. What signs slur over, their application says clearly.[33]

The propositional functions which result from highlighting a particular expression in this manner Wittgenstein calls *eluci-dations.*[34] Their efficacy is open to dispute, since immediately after introducing the expression 'elucidation', Wittgenstein writes:

> ... Elucidations are propositions that contain the primitive signs. So they can only be understood if the meanings of these signs are already known. (3.263)

Thus elucidations are supposed to show part of the meaning of primitive signs, yet presuppose that these meanings are already known. We shall later examine a possible exit to this circle.

Pushing this replacement procedure to the limit yields propositional signs where *all* the constituent expressions have been replaced by variables, yielding "the completely general description of the world" of 5.526.[35] Wittgenstein casually remarks that it is possible to "completely describe" the world in this manner. In fact the notion of a wholly general description of the world being *complete* is

---

[33] 3.262. 'Says' is presumably a slip for 'shows'. With respect to this passage, see Anscombe *op. cit.*, p. 91 and Black *op. cit.*, p. 115.

[34] 3.263. Black (*ibid.*) argues that elucidations must be *true* propositions (it is puzzling why he considers them *propositions* at all, since they contain variables), "whose senses are grasped by identifying the facts which they state." From this he draws the extremely dubious conclusion that every Object must be a constituent of at least one (actual) *Sachverhalt.* Both claims seem false. Certainly the logical issue of what a Name means cannot demand settlement of the contingent issue of whether certain propositions are true. Further, Black seems to conflate the logical issue of how a Name means with the psychological issue of how we discover that meaning. It may be true that humans would need to see a given Name used in one true proposition (which they must also recognize as true?), but 4.1121 seems to indicate that this is irrelevant. There is also considerable room for disagreement in his claim that "In this installment . . . Wittgenstein considers the question of how the meaning of names can be communicated." (p. 114) Note that the questions which elucidations are supposed to answer arise *even in the solipsistic case.* Although he may be correct when he concludes "There can be no philosophical question here, because it is logically impossible for there to be any philosophical answer," (*ibid.*) this claim is more likely true because of restrictions on the range of the sayable.

[35] Significantly, this is also the "impersonal representation of the world" of *NB*, p. 20. Black shows (*op. cit.*, pp. 287–88) the claim of complete description is probably false, arguing convincingly that such a procedure fails to distinguish between two worlds, one of which consists merely of fact Fa and the other of Fb, both being consistent with '$(\exists x)(Fx)$'.

puzzling. Wittgenstein contends that we can completely describe the world using variables, that such a description is complete, and that all that is needed to arrive at the "customary mode of expression" is to add after every proposition of the form 'E! $(\iota x)(\phi x)$ (it is puzzling how any fully analyzed proposition could contain the expression 'E! ...') another of the form '$x = a$.'

If this is true, then there are two possible methods of salvaging the completely general representation of the world. First we could argue that Objects are like angels insofar as *there is only one of each logical type*. Thus, there would be only one possible argument for 'x' in the general formulation '$(\exists x)(\phi x)$' Although this strikes me as highly implausible, I see no decisive argument against it. Second, we might argue that there are a large number of Objects of each logical type but that at the same time they are "without number." In that case, we cannot say "There are lots of ..." but we also can't say "There is just *one* ..." In this case, although there is a difference between universe ϕa and universe ϕb, it is not a *logical* difference. (Compare: from a logical point of view, it doesn't matter whether George Bush or Jane Fonda is president, but only that the proposition '$(\exists x)(x$ is president)' has a sense.) Thus the "completely general description of the world" would better be called "the description of the world *from the logical point of view*."

Be this as it may, note several important points about such completely general propositions. First—a positive point—even a general proposition has a *perfectly determinate sense*. Generality is not to be confused with vagueness. Second, even setting aside the question of whether the general description gives us as much information as the particular description, nothing is gained in such a completely general description. Russell (and perhaps Wittgenstein prior to 1914) thought that completely general propositions pictured *logical forms*; thus going from '$(\exists x)(\exists y)(\exists \phi)(\phi xy)$' to 'Socrates loves Plato' would be analogous to loading bullets into the cylinder of a revolver, Russell's major concern being to insure that the "wrong bullets" were not put into the cylinder. Wittgenstein's point is that such a guarantee would entail the existence of something even more general than logic, which is unacceptable. Finally, as we shall see in the following chapter, nothing of interest (including an "elucidation") is forthcoming from replacing all or some of the expressions of a proposition with variables. Wittgenstein writes:

> What is peculiar about the generality sign is first, that it indicates a logical
> prototype, and secondly, that it gives prominence to constants. (5.522)

But the logical prototype is merely what a range of similar
propositions share in common, and this is shown just as well by *any*
proposition of that range as by a wholly general proposition.
Likewise, "giving prominence to constants" means nothing more
than underlining, as it were, the occurrence of 'Russell' in 'Wittgenstein knew Russell', and this cannot be of any logical interest. But
this issue of elucidations and their roles, as well as what virtues
general propositions have, reflects a deeper difficulty concerning the
nature of philosophy and logic, which Wittgenstein never satisfactorily resolves.

It is difficult, then, to see how an elucidation gives us the logical
form of a Name, unless we already *know* the logical forms of a whole
range of primitive symbols. As we shall see in the next chapter, this
difficulty is only apparent. But setting this aside until we investigate
the doctrine of showing, consider the second part of our question:
What makes a given Name the Name for a *particular* Object within
a given logical type? Given that 'red' has the logical form of a
color-word, what makes it a Name for *that particular color*?

Let us approach this question obliquely by considering 3.3411.

> So one could say that the real name of an object was what all symbols that
> signified it had in common. Thus, one by one, all kinds of composition would
> prove inessential to a name.

The second sentence obviously refers to the reduction of composite
expressions via Russellian analysis, but the first expresses a central
attitude of the *Tractatus*. What we seek are the essential properties
of *any* language, and this must be what *all* languages share in
common.[36]

The simplicity of Objects makes isolating the essence of the
Naming relation somewhat more difficult than the essence of a
proposition, where both the ubiquitousness of logical form and the

---

[36] Such a project of seeking the essential in language is a natural extension of the rejection of
psychologism and a direct descendent of the *Begriffsschrift*. It likewise brings to mind Frege's
observation that the acquisition of foreign languages functions as part of the sorting out of the
essential from the inessential, since what occurs in one language but not another cannot be
constitutive of the essence of *all* language. The Fregean assumption that there is such an essence
Wittgenstein of course later rejects; cf. *PI* #65–71.

interdefinability of logical connectives offer a place to start. If a Name somehow resembled its Object (by being a mental image of it, for instance, as Russell thought), then we could see the essence of the Naming relation in such resemblance. But resemblance turns on overlap of properties, and since Objects have no proper properties, resemblance seems out of the question. But even if there were resemblance, the question would arise whether it was *just this Object* that the Name referred to, and thus the demands for complete precision would be violated. (This also entails, we have seen, that Names cannot be pictures of Objects, since picturability requires structure, which obviously vanishes as "all kinds of composition" become inessential.)

Objects seem to be "too smooth," as it were, for Names to grip. This is what Bradley has in mind, I think, when he writes:

> Now a sign cannot possibly be destitute of meaning. Originally imposed as an *arbitrary* mark, the very process, which makes it a sign and associates it firmly with the thing it signifies, must associate with it also some qualities and properties of the thing it stands for. If it did *not* to some extent get to *mean* the thing, it could not possibly *stand* for it at all. And can one say that the proper name, if you are aware of its designation, brings *no* ideas with it, or that these ideas are merely chance conjunctions? What connection, I ask you, would be left between the bare name and the thing it stands for, if every one of these ideas were removed. All would vanish together.[37]

Wittgenstein's answer, I contend, is, Yes, every similarity between Name and Object either disappears or is logically inessential, and No, the connection between Name and Object does not thereby vanish. What is common to every symbol that can be used as a Name for a given Object is that the user of that Name *intends* it to be the name of that Object, where "intending" can be taken as the primitive relation that turns signs into symbols. "Naming is like pointing," Wittgenstein writes (*NB*, p. 100), although I would add pointing *ad intellectum* rather than *ad sensum*.[38]

Names are connected with Objects via a primitive, unanalyzable

---

[37] *PoL*, p. 60. Black finds the Name-Object relation equally mysterious: *op. cit.*, pp. 116–17.

[38] This is probably what led Russell to the view, which Wittgenstein ridicules at *PI* #38, that 'this' and 'that' are the only words in our ordinary speech which approximate logically proper names, since they are verbal accompaniments of or substitutes for acts of pointing. Cf. *L&K*, pp. 168, 200–1, 222.

intentional relation. This relation is what Wittgenstein alludes to later when he writes:

> It seems that there are *certain definite* mental processes bound up with the working of language, processes through which alone language can work. I mean the processes of understanding and meaning. The signs of our language seem dead without these mental processes, and it might seem that the only function of signs is to induce such processes, and that these are the things we ought really be interested in. (*BB*, p. 3)

These "definite mental processes" (we shall see [ch. VIII] that it is misleading to call them "mental") serve the following purpose: every propositional sign is "dead" until it is "interpreted" by being "projected onto reality." This is why a *mental* propositional sign has no logical priority over a physical sign, since it too needs projecting, interpreting. But such interpreting must stop somewhere, and it is tempting to choose (as Russell does) to stop with the *mental image*, treating it as that which needed no interpretation. But for a variety of quite cogent reasons this is wholly unattractive to Wittgenstein.

The meaning of a Name, then, is a function of two things: its logical form—its ability to enter into propositions of certain sorts—and the pure intending of the *particular* Object of that range to which the Name refers. But since there are no external *signs* of the former (that is, since it cannot be grounded in any *property* of the Name) it too must be grounded in the intention. The logical type of a Name manifests itself, then, in the experimental "fitting together" of Names to form a proposition, "experimental" being misleading only insofar as there is no chance of error. Thus, although Names are *complete symbols* insofar as they do not vanish under analysis, it is still true that "only in the context of a proposition does a Name have a meaning." Only there does it display its role or use.[39] This observation should dispel any tendency to think that the context

---

[39] Compare: "... Naming is a preparation for description. Naming is so far not a move in the language game—any more than putting a piece in its place on the board is a move in chess.... This is what Frege meant too, when he said a word had meaning only as part of a sentence." *PI*, #49.

For Frege's statement of the context principle, see *FA*, #62. Interestingly, Frege later rejects the principle, e.g. in "On Sense and Reference," where *all* expressions have both sense and reference, even outside a proposition. Wittgenstein seems equivocally committed to it through his middle period; cf. "Wittgenstein's Lectures of 1930–33" in Moore, *Philosophical Papers*, p. 261.

principle entails that every Object must appear in an actual *Sachverhalt.*

The meaning of 5.4732—"we cannot give a sign the wrong sense"—is now clearer. Since the intentional relation involves no interpretation, no recognition of common properties, there is no risk of mistake, and the intending is thus *foolproof.* If I use 'A' as a Name for A, then it *is* the Name of A.[40] In this case the will, in Russell's apt phrase, "comes right up to the thing." Likewise, either a proposition shares common logical form with a *Sachverhalt* or it doesn't; there is no room for play. We might reinforce this point by approaching it from another angle. The sense of a proposition is a fact. No fact is vague,[41] and since the linkage of proposition to fact is foolproof, there is no room for vagueness. Thus no proposition can be vague either. From this follows Wittgenstein's important claim that sense does not allow of degree. Where there is sense there is *perfect* sense. Importantly, there is no need for special notations, formation rules, etc. to produce "correct" or "well-formed" propositions. This is one way in which "logic takes care of itself"; in the following chapter, when we investigate the notion of showing, we shall see more.

"Where there is sense there is perfect sense" is of primary importance for Wittgenstein's logical theory. At the very least it eliminates as the goal of logic or philosophy the construction of a logically perfect language, since no language could fail to achieve this goal. It has even more striking application in the ethical themes which we shall investigate in chapters X and XI. Attempts at moralizing cannot be seen as *approximations* of something which could conceivably be made clearer through philosophical or scientific investigation. I should at once qualify these claims by pointing out they represent the negative side of an argument, the positive side (involving the notion of showing) of which we shall see in the following chapter.

---

[40] It is no accident that the Private Language Argument of *PI* #243 ff. starts with precisely this claim: "Well, at least *I* know what I mean by ..." Cf. especially #247.

[41] At least if we stick to Wittgenstein's technical sense of 'fact'. Ramsey seems to believe that Russell held there to be vague facts; in a letter to Wittgenstein dated 2.20.24 he writes "[Russell] *indignantly denied ever having said that vagueness* is a characteristic of *the physical world."* *Letters to C. K .Ogden,* p. 84. The odd emphasis is Ramsey's. Russell's indignation was probably well-grounded; a year earlier he wrote "Vagueness and precision alike are characteristics which can only belong to a representation of which language is an example." "Vagueness," *Australasian Journal of Philosophy,* vol. I (1923), p. 85.

Ordinary Language as Essentially Pictorial

This chapter began with a general question—How is language connected with the world?—as well as a list of unesoteric but on reflection striking features of ordinary language. In response to each I have offered an account of Wittgenstein's Picture Theory of Propositions. But the picture theory as so far envisioned seems directly applicable only to elementary propositions. It is these which share form and proxy content with possible *Sachverhalte*. Even a fully analyzed elementary proposition—for instance one with the form 'p $\supset$ (q v r)' contains expressions which go proxy for no element and which cannot be construed as graphemes. It is evident, however, that Wittgenstein intends to be offering a semantic theory valid for *all* language, including ordinary language (cf. 4.011, 4.013). But 'Eisenhower beat Stevenson in 1952' does not appear to be a picture, even given the Russellian arsenal of analytic resources. Wittgenstein is of course not unaware of this difficulty:

> At first sight a proposition—one set out on the printed page—does not seem to be a picture of the reality with which it is concerned. But no more does musical notation at first sight appear to be a picture of music, nor our phonetic speech (the alphabet) to be a picture of our speech.
>
> And yet these sign-languages prove to be pictures, even in the ordinary sense, of what they represent.[42]

In order to complete our survey of the picture theory, we must see how ordinary propositions are mapped onto elementary propositions. Whether a fully satisfactory account can be found is dubious.

The notion of "the general form of a proposition" first appears at 4.5, the culmination of a long discussion of truth-functions.

> It now seems possible to give the most general propositional form: that is, to give a description of the propositions of *any* sign-language *whatsoever* in such a way that every possible sense can be expressed by a symbol satisfying the description, and every symbol satisfying the description can express a sense, provided that the meanings of the names are suitably chosen.

---

[42] 4.011; compare with 4.014–4.0141. It is curious that Wittgenstein characterizes these as pictures in the "ordinary sense," since 4.012 seems to immediately undermine that claim.

It is clear that *only* what is essential to the most general propositional form may be included in its description—for otherwise it would not be the most general form.

The existence of a general propositional form is proved by the fact that there cannot be a proposition whose form could not have been foreseen (i.e., constructed). The general form of a proposition is: this is how things stand.[43]

On the other hand, at 6 he writes:

The general form of a truth-function is (p, ξ, N (ξ)).

This is the general form of a proposition.[44]

These two characterizations hardly seem equivalent. Perhaps seeing why Wittgenstein advances both as "the general form of a proposition" will shed some light on the relationship between elementary propositions and ordinary language.

The first of the characterizations presents the proposition as a picture—presents it from the "inside." An elementary proposition pictures a fact and says: this is the way the world is, this is how *this* fact stands.[45] The second characterization concerns the senses of

---

[43] Compare with *PI*, #114. *"(Tractatus Logico-Philosophicus)* 'The general form of propositions is: This is how things are.'—That is the kind of proposition that one repeats to oneself countless times. One thinks that one is tracing the outline of a thing's nature over and over again, and one is merely tracing round the frame through which we look at it."

[44] At 5.2522 Wittgenstein represents the general term of a "formal series" by '(a, *x*, O'*x*)', where a is the first term in the series, *x* any arbitrary later term, and O'*x* the operation which generates the series. For instance, in the series of positive integers a = 1, *x* = (e.g.) 7, and O'*x* = the operation +1.

The formula of 6 is a special case of the formal series. ξ represents (in informal exposition, at least) the totality of propositions which comprise the values of the propositional variable ξ, and 'N' stands for the operation of joint negation, the Sheffer stroke which serves as a single truth-functional connective. Thus the formula represents the series of truth-functions generated by operating on the class of elementary propositions using the operation of joint negation, its range being all possible truth-functional propositions. The gist of asserting that it is the general form of a proposition is rather simply that every proposition can be represented as a truth-function of elementary propositions. Anscombe points out that the notation is defective: *op. cit.*, pp. 136–37.

[45] It is worth mentioning here that one standard criticism of this view (one which Wittgenstein himself later levels at the *Tractatus*), that it neglects the broad range of linguistic activities, is misguided. At *PI* #23 Wittgenstein lists a whole range of linguistic activities, such as giving and obeying an order, reporting an event, speculating about an event, constructing an object from a description and so forth. Compare with J. L. Austin, *How To Do Things With Words* (Harvard U. Press, Cambridge, MA, 1962), ch. I and *passim*.

But in the *Tractatus* Wittgenstein accepts Frege's view that logic is concerned with symbols only insofar as *truth* is connected with those symbols, and thus, from a logical point of view, the list of linguistic activities Wittgenstein gives is irrelevant. Wittgenstein's later critique of course challenges not only the special position accorded to logic but the nature of logic itself: cf. #108, 242.

non-elementary propositions, asserting that every proposition can be analyzed as a truth-function of elementary propositions (Every elementary proposition is a truth-function of itself). Thus every fully analyzed ordinary proposition will consist solely of elementary propositions and truth-functional connectives. Since the *Grundgedanke* tells us that the logical connectives do not stand for objects, the sense of a non-elementary proposition is wholly a function of the senses of its components. We can generate any possible truth-function, so this is tantamount to asserting a priori that we can construct a proposition with any possible sense, much in the manner that Frege's definition of a cardinal number guarantees that we can assign a number to any collection.

However, the relation between propositions and the world is not wholly clarified. There are now *three* classes of propositions with which to deal: elementary propositions, explicit truth-functions of those elementary propositions, and unanalyzed propositions of ordinary language. Even if we accept that the first two are pictures,[46] we still must explain how human beings recognize the senses of unanalyzed ordinary propositions, which are not obviously pictures at all. Without such an explanation the picture theory cannot provide an adequate explanation of some of the linguistic competences listed at the beginning of this chapter.

The weight of this difficulty is underscored by comparing it with an analogous problem which faces Moore. In his classic "A Defense of Common Sense," Moore lists certain propositions which he claims to know, with certainty, to be true.[47] The list contains claims about having a body, being on the surface of the earth, being awake at the moment, having existed for a number of years, and so forth. Now clearly if Moore asserts that he *knows* these propositions to be *true,* then it follows that he also must know what they *mean;* if he did not, then he could not possibly know whether or not they are true. However, he admits that he is ignorant of the correct *analysis* of these propositions.[48] He must therefore be distinguishing between

---

[46] I recommend to the reader Black's elegant analogy showing how explicit truth-functions of elementary propositions are pictures: *op. cit.*, pp. 221–22.

[47] Reprinted in his *Philosophical Papers*, pp. 32–59.

[48] *Ibid.*, p. 53. He does claim to be relatively certain that such analysis must end with propositions about sense-data. This ought to be compared with the 1905 paper "The Nature and Reality of Objects of Perception" (reprinted in his *Philosophical Studies*), p. 64, where he is willing to accept

knowing the meaning of a proposition, and knowing the *correct analysis* of that proposition—perhaps he has something in mind like knowing what water is without knowing its chemical composition.

But this line of defense does not appear available to Wittgenstein. In the *Tractatus* all meaning is ultimately traced back to elementary propositions; if this were *not* so, then the analytical regress of chapter IV would not be a vicious one. But Wittgenstein not only does not present the analysis of any ordinary propositions into truth-functions of elementary propositions, but he seems pessimistic that this is humanly possible.

> Language disguises thought. So much so, that from the outward form of the clothing it is impossible to infer the form of thought beneath it, because the outward form of the clothing was not designed to reveal the form of the body, but for different purposes. (4.002)

This being true, it is then unclear how the picture theory can show how, for instance, we can recognize propositions we have never heard before, or how we can produce propositions with any possible sense. The only option for Wittgenstein I can see is to claim that there is some organic translation-mechanism in the human constitution which maps ordinary speech onto elementary propositions. He could then claim that the operation of this translation-engine is grist for the mill of the psychologist or physiologist, but not the philosopher. But without even a rough explanation of such an operation, the picture theory loses much of its charm *as a theory for explaining the character of ordinary language*. Its logical virtues of course remain.

---

as possible analyses of "Hens lay hens' eggs" the rather improbable "A certain collection of spirits or monads sometimes has a certain intelligible relation to another collection of spirits or monads ..."

VI

Showing and Saying

The whole sense of the book can be summed up in the
following words: what can be said at all can be said clearly,
and what we cannot talk about we must pass over
in silence.

— FROM THE PREFACE TO THE *TRACTATUS*

Now I'm afraid you haven't really gotten hold of my main
contention, to which the whole business of logical
prop[osition]s is only a corollary. The main point is the
theory of what can be expressed [*gesagt*] by
prop[osition]s—i.e., by thought—(and, which comes out to
the same, what can be *thought*) and what cannot be
expressed by prop[osition]s, but only shown [*gezeigt*]:
which, I believe, is the cardinal problem of philosophy.

— LETTER TO RUSSELL 19.8.19

In chapter V I alluded to an aspect of the *Tractatus* which, if
Wittgenstein's words above are to be taken at face value, he held to
constitute not only the "whole sense" of the work, but the "cardinal
problem of philosophy". This aspect is embodied in the distinction
between what can be *said*, and what can only be *shown*. Although the
distinction is easiest understood in the context of the Picture Theory,
its influence on Wittgenstein's thought quite probably predates that
theory.[1] Although in certain contexts reasonably straightforward, the
notion of showing is also beset with certain difficulties, not the least
being that two apparently quite different sorts of things "show
themselves." On one hand we have the ineffability of the logico-

---

[1] So far as we can tell from the fragmentary remains of the notebooks from which the *Tractatus*
was gleaned, the picture theory emerged about 29.9.14. (Cf. *NB*, p. 7) I agree with Black (*op. cit.*,
pp. 77–79) that this is convincing evidence that many important Tractarian themes in which the
say/show distinction plays a pivotal role were developed independently of the Picture Theory. If
that is the case, the easy applicability of the say/show distinction to the Picture Theory might well
have seemed to Wittgenstein confirmation of its deep philosophical significance. Its obvious
resonance with *fin-de-siecle* Viennese interests in the ineffable (cf. Janik and Toulmin *op. cit.*, chs.
4–5) perhaps also made it easier for Wittgenstein to postulate its centrality in *all* linguistic
representation.

semantic, on the other hand the ethico-aesthetic. In later chapters I will try to demonstrate a clear unity in the diverse contexts in which showing plays a role.

Russell's Theory of Logical Types and Levels of Language

In 1902, stimulated by a period of close study of Frege's *Begriffsschrift*, Russell happened upon a contradiction in the central mathematical notion of a class, which he immediately relayed to Frege.[2] Most classes are not members of themselves—the class of teaspoons, for instance, is not itself a teaspoon—but other classes seem to have this unusual property. The class of classes is itself a class, for example, and the class of abstract entities an abstract entity. Self-membership appears to be a perfectly respectable property of classes, and the realm of classes ought to neatly cleave into those of which self-membership can be predicated, and those of which it cannot. Consider, however, the class of all classes which are *not* members of themselves; is this class a member of itself or not? If it is *not*, then it is a member of the class of all classes which are not members of themselves, and thus *is* a member of itself. On the other hand, if it *is* a member of itself, then for that reason it is *not* a member of itself.[3] Although the concept of the class of all classes not members of themselves does not seem formally self-contradictory, it must contain some element of inconsistency, insofar as from it we can derive the contradiction that a given class both is and is not a member of itself.

Parallel to the paradox of classes is the "Liar Paradox" or the "Epimenides", so-called after Epimenides the Cretan who asserted that all Cretans are liars. The Liar in its simplest form can be represented by any of the following:

---

[2] Russell writes (*IMP*, p. 25) that he believes himself to be the first person to read that work, twenty years after its publication! Although the albeit unsympathetic reviews (cf. Frege, *Conceptual Notation and Related Articles*, ed. T. W. Bynum [Clarendon, Oxford, 1972], pp. 48–49) indicate that Russell's claim is perhaps exaggerated, that Russell could seriously make such a claim indicates the obscurity in which Frege labored during his lifetime. For Frege's reaction, cf. the biographical introduction, #16–17, in Bynum *op. cit.*

[3] For Russell's development of the class paradox, see *L&K*, pp. 259–69, *PM*, Introduction ch. II, and *PrM*, ch. 10.

(a) I am now lying.
(b) This proposition is false.
(c) Every proposition is false.

Each appears significant, but a truth-value cannot be consistently assigned to any of them. Although Frank Ramsey demonstrated that the Liar and the paradox of classes are logically distinct,[4] Russell treats them as identical, offering the same solution to both. That solution is the Theory of Logical Types.

To see the significance of both the paradoxes and the Theory of Types, it is crucial to keep in mind the absolutely fundamental place which classes occupy in Frege's theory of arithmetic. The simplest solution to the paradox of classes is to assume that the notion of a class is logically defective. The apparent contradiction thus brings the whole logicist program under suspicion, and with it of course the yet-to-emerge program of *Principia*. But the available alternatives to logicism all seemed to Frege and Russell unacceptable. Both speak contemptuously of Hilbertian formalism.[5] Even if the formalist's program succeeds in reducing mathematical *propositions* to rules for the manipulation of otherwise meaningless marks, it cannot, as Ramsey points out (*op. cit.*, p. 2) account for the uses of mathematical *concepts* when we say such things as "I have six dollars" or "I've been waiting for you for fifteen minutes." The intuitionism of Brouwer, on the other hand, involves rejection of the Law of Excluded Middle, as well as (through a rejection of anything like Russell's Axiom of Infinity) the Dedekind cut and thus most analysis more complex than elementary arithmetic.[6] Surrendering significant parts of mathematics having always been anathema to Russell (recall that this issue precipitated his split with the Hegelians), following the completion of *Principles* in 1902 he set for himself the task of eliminating the paradoxes which threatened the basis of the class calculus. The task, considerably more arduous than Russell had envisioned, required the

---

[4] F. P. Ramsey,"The Foundations of Mathematics" in his *The Foundations of Mathematics* (Littlefield Adams, Paterson, NJ, 1960), p. 24. (Hereafter this book referred to as *FoM*.)

[5] For Frege, see Geach and Black *op. cit.*, pp. 182–233, for Russell, *PM*, Introduction to the second edition, p. v.

[6] Ramsey *op. cit.*, p. 4.

collaboration of Whitehead and produced not the expected second volume of *Principles of Mathematics* but *Principia Mathematica.*[7] The locus of the logical rehabilitation of classes is the aforementioned Theory of Types.

Russell's paradox of the class of all classes not members of themselves—only one of a set of similar paradoxes (cf. *PM*, pp. 60 ff.)—arises, so its namesake holds, through the violation of the so-called "Vicious Circle Principle," that is, "from supposing that a collection of objects may contain members which can only be defined by means of the collection as a whole". (*Ibid.*, p. 37) Consider the assertion "Every English utterance has preceded this one." This proposition purports to be about the class of English utterances, but being itself an English utterance, it must be included in the class about which it appears to speak. But the class therefore cannot be given in advance of the utterance in question. Likewise, the class of all classes not members of themselves can be defined only in terms of its members, but if it is a member of that class, then the class cannot be given prior to it.[8] We can avoid these difficulties, then, by abiding by the "Vicious Circle Principle"—whatever includes *all* of a collection must not be one of the collection. (*Ibid.*)

Stated so the principle seems rather ad hoc, but it can be given plausibility by considering the correlative ontological thesis that the universe can be treated as a hierarchy of different sorts of entities. On the lowest level are individuals, the next highest classes of individuals, then classes of classes of individuals, and so forth. It is easy to show that puzzles arise when we try to "mix" these levels. Assume for instance that the universe is composed of exactly three things, particulars a, b, and c. How many things are there in this universe? Well, there's the entity composed of a and b, the class whose members are a and c, the class whose members are a and the class of b and c, and so forth. Thus it appears that from the

---

[7] For an historical appreciation of the task of writing *PM*, cf. Jager *op. cit.*, pp. 154–78, Russell's *Autobiography* vol. I, ch. VI, and *My Philosophical Development* (Simon and Schuster, New York, 1959), chs. 6–8.

[8] Note the assumption on Russell's part that classes can be given only extensionally, in terms of their members. This (dubious) claim is part and parcel of both the assertion that class-terms are incomplete symbols, and the theory that possibility, necessity, and impossibility can be treated extensionally.

assumption of three entities in the universe we can prove quite conclusively that there are an indefinitely large number of things. "You have in fact," Russell quips, "a perfectly precise arithmetic proof that there are *fewer* things in heaven and earth than are dreamt of in *our* philosophy," adding "That shows how philosophy advances." (*L&K*, p. 260) Our intuitions of course tell us that something here is fishy, and it doesn't take long to realize that speaking of {a, {a,b} } as being an "entity" or "existing" in the same sense that a is an entity and exists is dangerously misleading. Thus saying of a class that it exists is different from (although derivative of) saying that a member of that class exists. Words like 'exist' and 'entity' are thus *systematically ambiguous*, and the Vicious Circle Principle says that unless we keep straight what level we are talking about, puzzles are bound to arise. In particular, we cannot ask of a class whether it is a member of itself, since we mix talk about classes with talk about classes of classes.

The mysterious multitude of purported "entities" in the previous paragraph parallels the linguistic difficulties which led to the paradoxes. Thus we need to distinguish among an analogous hierarchy of sorts of propositions. The lowest level—the "object language"—consists wholly of propositions about particulars, while the next level—the "first metalanguage"—will contain only propositions about object-language propositions. Thus we generate the following hierarchy:

1. OBJECT LANGUAGE
   The cat is on the mat.
   Eisenhower defeated Stevenson in 1952.
   Leningrad is in the USSR.
2. FIRST METALANGUAGE
   'The cat is on the mat' is a proposition.
   'Dog' is a common noun.
   'Descartes' has nine letters.
3. SECOND METALANGUAGE
   " 'The cat is on the mat' is a proposition" is a proposition.
   "'Descartes' has nine letters" is true.
   etc. . . .

We can see that odd propositions like 'All propositions are false' arise when we try to mix levels indiscriminately. The best that we can do, observing the Vicious Circle Principle, is to say 'All object-language propositions are false,' which is a proposition of the first metalanguage and thus does not fall within its own scope. Although it is false (and perhaps necessarily false), it is not *logically* objectionable.

Such distinction of levels of discourse, and the subsequent application of them, is *roughly* what the Theory of Logical Types is about. The intuition behind it is fairly simple to grasp, but like so much else in philosophy it is difficult to get an axiomatic formulation which says *exactly* what you want. Fortunately, we need not pursue that task.

Unlike the Theory of Descriptions, with its unchallenged fifty year reign, the Theory of Logical Types was met with suspicion by logicians and philosophers. Frank Ramsey, for instance, sets forth as one of the two major goals of his long essay "The Foundations of Mathematics" (along with "extensionalizing" *Principia*) the removal of contradictions like Russell's paradox without recourse to a theory of types. (*Op. cit.*, p. xi) But Wittgenstein, for reasons which will become increasingly central, is convinced that there could never *be* such a thing as a theory of types. Although this may at first seem like a mere crotchet on his part, it is not: the issues reach very deep into his system. They are intimately connected with the topic of this chapter, in particular the claim that certain semantic features cannot be linguistically represented but only shown. Russell writes in his Introduction to the *Tractatus:*

> What causes hesitation is the fact that, after all, Mr Wittgenstein manages to say a good deal about what cannot be said, thus suggesting to the sceptical reader that possibly there may be some loophole through a hierarchy of languages, or by some other exit.[9]

This remark of Russell's, and Wittgenstein's antipathy towards the suggestions that it embodies, will become increasingly central to our investigation. But more immediately, the reasons for Wittgenstein's

---

[9] P. xxi. Russell adds that Wittgenstein's view on the inexpressible "leaves me with a certain sense of intellectual discomfort." This claim marks not only of Russell's increasing hesitancy to accept paradoxical philosophical conclusions (compare with his facetious remarks in *L&K*, p. 193), but also of the great cultural gap between Russell the British liberal and Wittgenstein the wealthy refugee from the ruins of the Hapsburg Empire. Janik and Toulmin (*op.cit.*, chs. 4–5) show convincingly how the multifaceted themes of expressibility and ineffability were ubiquitous in Austrian thought.

rejection of the Theory of Types will allow us to see with more clarity the *semantic* basis at least of the show/say distinction.

Showing, Saying, and the Picture Theory of Propositions

> I should like to say, "These notes say something glorious,
> but I do not know what." These notes are a powerful
> gesture, but I cannot put anything side by side with it that
> will serve as an explanation. A grave nod. James: "Our
> vocabulary is inadequate." Then why don't we introduce a
> new one? What would have to be the case for us to be
> able to?
>
> —Philosophical Investigations, #610

A proposition represents its sense by virtue of being a logical picture of that sense. But a proposition means in two radically different ways. Every picture *shows* what its sense is—that is, pictures or displays that sense—and propositional pictures in addition *say* that that sense is actual. Thus, 4.5 tells us that the most general form of a proposition involves holding up a picture and saying, "This is the way the world is." But the notion of showing is more important to Wittgenstein than being merely one aspect of propositional representation. Let us look carefully at the semantic significance of showing.

Showing makes its first serious appearance at 4.022,[10] from whence it increasingly dominates both the written and "unwritten" parts of the book. It warrants mention that the verb 'say' usually occurs in active constructions, 'show' in passive ones. Thus, we *say* things by means of propositions, but the sense "shows itself," "makes itself manifest." This resonance with the central thesis that "Logic must take care of itself" (*NB*, p. 2) makes it plausible to assume tentatively that *what shows itself is always some logical feature of a symbol.* Such a characterization works quite well for

---

[10] I ignore the dubious occurrence at 3.262, where Wittgenstein tells us that the application of a sign "shows" (*zeigt*) what the sign fails to express. I take this to be a remarkably loose use of a central technical term, especially since Wittgenstein then tells us that the application *says* (*spricht*) what the sign "slurs over."

most of the occurrences of 'show,' and will give us a basis for dealing with the remainder.

Matters showable fall roughly into the following categories:

A.

(i)   The sense of a proposition (4.022)

(ii)   That a Name names a given Object (4.126. 4.1211)

(iii)   That a proposition is about a given Object (4.1211)

(iv)   That the sign '~' corresponds to nothing in reality (4.0621)

(v)   That logical propositions say nothing (4.461)

(vi)   That two propositions contradict one another (6.1201)

B.

(vii)   That there is no soul "as conceived in the superficial psychology of the present day" (5.5421)[11]

(viii)   That "the world is my world" (5.62)

(ix)   "The mystical" (6.522)

All of these, then, are things which Wittgenstein claims show themselves and thus cannot be said, cannot be represented *in* language. Let us call the claim that certain things can only be shown and not said the "thesis of ineffability." Setting aside for a moment the entries in B (which Black labels "doubtful"), let us look for grounds for the ineffability of the entries in A. In a later place I shall argue for the unity of A and B.

We will start with the most plausible case of the thesis of ineffability. Consider the elementary proposition 'p', whose sense is the (possible) *Sachverhalt* p. Thus p is what 'p' *means*. But suppose that we attempt to say this by asserting the putative proposition " 'p' means p." (" 'The cat is on the mat' means that the cat is on the mat.") In order to speak of the nexus between a proposition and its sense, we would need *another* proposition (let's call it 'p*') which represented what 'p' and p had in common. However, the common element between 'p' and p consists of (at the very least) having the same *logical form*. But if 'p*' shares logical form with 'p', then rather than picturing the nexus between proposition and fact, it is rather

---

[11] Significantly, Black (*op. cit.*, pp. 190–91), from whom this list was derived, omits the last clause. We shall see some of the unfortunate consequences of doing so in chapters VIII–X below.

another token of 'p', differing from it only in logically inessential ways. Thus our attempt to *say* what a proposition means, to *say* that it pictures its sense, fails. The best that we can do is generate another token of 'p'. But it is of course no shortcoming that we cannot *say* what 'p' means, because a proposition *shows* its sense by picturing it. If 'p' means p, then mere inspection of the proposition discloses this.

" 'p' means p" is a representative of a whole class of semantic pseudo-propositions, which includes as members the following:

(i)   'A' is a Name.
(ii) 'p' is a proposition.
(iii) 'A' is the Name of (Object) A.
(iv) 'p' is meaningful.

and so forth. Note that each of these tries to say something about the meaning of a symbol, either that it *has* one, or that its meaning is such-and-such, and each attempt will fail in a manner parallel to " 'p' says that p." That 'A' is a Name, and the Name for A, is shown by 'A' "going proxy" for A in fully analyzed propositions. For 'A' to mean A, the requisite intentional connection must be made, and of course this cannot be said.[12] However, this is *shown* by 'A' going proxy for A in the propositional representations of facts in which A occurs. Similar points can be made for the remaining examples.

The upshot is that there can be no first metalanguage, no language which talks about first-level propositions, and thus the hierarchy of languages which Russell envisions cannot get started. If we attempt to construct a proposition which speaks about the semantics of another proposition, then we fail by either creating no more than another token of the original, or we end up with a series of signs to which we cannot assign a meaning at all. Wittgenstein puts this in both a negative and positive manner at 3.332:

> No proposition can make a statement about itself, because a propositional sign cannot be contained in itself.
> (That is the whole of the 'theory of types').

---

[12] As we shall see when we look more deeply into the matter of the metaphysical subject (chapter IX), such an act cannot be represented *in* language, insofar as it (a) lies outside the world and (b) is a prerequisite *for* language.

If we have a propositional function 'F(x)', and attempt to make it its own argument—F(F(x))—the inner and outer 'F' cannot possibly have the same meaning; as we have seen, this would represent a nonperspicuous and redundant way of saying 'F(x)'. On the other hand, if the inner and outer 'F' mean something different in each case, then what we have is not a proposition which is a function of itself, but rather some *other* function of 'F(x)', rendered again in the sort of imperspicuous notation which might arise were I to name each of my children 'John'.[13] Further, since the only allowable functions of propositions are truth-functions, 'F(F(x))' turns out to be rather dull. No proposition can refer to itself.[14] *Note that this is not a restriction that we stipulate, but rather something which flows from the very roots of linguistic representation.*

The impossibility of a theory of types turns out to be harmless, since there is no *need* for such a theory. We cannot say anything about the semantics of propositions because these depend upon the *logic* of the world, not the contingent existence or nonexistence of *Sachverhalte*. There can be no propositions of the sort envisioned because there can be no representatives *in* language for the necessary condition of language, that is, the logic of the world. But on the other hand, "logic takes care of itself": there are no surprises in logic (2.012) simply because there is no *room* in logic for such surprises. For in order for there to be such "room," there would need to be something *outside* logic, and in that case, *that* something would be the real claimant to the title of logic. A corollary of this point is that special notations like that of the *Begriffsschrift* or *Principia* can offer only pragmatic advantages—psychological but not logical protection from confusion.

Another class of pseudo-propositions, parallel to but distinct from attempted semantic claims, are *modal* propositions:

---

[13] "[Detroit Tiger outfielder Willy] Horton, by the way, has seven children, and two of his sons have the same name—Darryl I and Darryl II." Roger Angell, *Late Innings* (Simon and Schuster, New York, 1982), p. 240. Angell is of course wrong in his claim that 'Darryl I' and 'Darryl II' are the *same* name.

[14] John Wisdom writes "To me [the alleged impossibility of self-reference] looks fishy. If I write 'This is written in haste' on a letter, presumably 'this' refers to all the writing on the notepaper." J. L. Wisdom, *Logical Constructions*, (Random House, New York, 1969), p. 209 note, quoted in Black *op. cit.*, p.147. It is tempting to say that Wittgenstein's a priori certainty that there cannot be self-referential contexts leads him to ignore such folksy examples. But at a deeper level, being written in haste is not a *logical* property of a symbol, any more than being Tycho's favorite animal is a logical property of a moose. Thus the alleged counterexample fails.

(i) "A exists" is necessary.

(ii) P is possible.

and so forth. What we can say is restricted to claims about the world, "all that is the case." What is the case is the contingent existence of *Sachverhalte*, and thus all that can be said, on this theory, is that a *Sachverhalt* exists or fails to exist. Thus it is difficult to see how any modal claim could be made. Further, modal claims appear to be non-truth-functional compound propositions. If we replace the imbedded proposition in a context such as "It is necessary that p" with another true proposition, there is no guarantee that the truth-value of the whole will not change. In fact, it is likely that it will. Finally, if there are elementary propositions which contain the words 'possible' or 'necessary', then there would be Objects which corresponded to them, and this seems implausible.

Russell's solution is to extensionalize such claims. Necessity, Possibility, and Impossibility, Russell argues, are not properties of propositions, but rather of *propositional functions*. (*L&K*, p. 231) A propositional function is necessary when *every* instantiation is true; possible when *some* instantiation is true, and impossible if *none* is true. Thus 'x is a man' is a possible propositional function, insofar as there is at least one name which when substituted for x yields a true proposition, while 'x is a unicorn' is impossible for analogous reasons. This has the disadvantage of making modal claims empirical, since we need to know whether the world contains unicorns before we can decide whether or not 'x is a unicorn' is possible or not. But more seriously, it cannot distinguish between the propositional function 'x is a unicorn,' which just *happens* to have no true instantiations, and 'x is a four-sided circle.' It is dubious, then, that Russell has analyzed any philosophically interesting senses of modal terms.

Wittgenstein's treatment of modal claims is a good deal more sophisticated, albeit less straightforward. We saw in chapter IV that Objects are immutable and eternal. Thus, it is tempting to think of 'A exists,' where 'A' is a Name, as not only true but *necessary*. (See, for instance, Russell's answer to an audience question: *L&K*, p. 241.) Likewise, insofar as there are no "impossible pictures," picturing in the *Tractatus* seems to guarantee possibility; thus, " 'p' pictures a possible fact" seems necessary. Let us examine 'A exists' and 'P is possible.'

One obvious reason why Wittgenstein might want to reject the legitimacy of 'A exists' is that 'exist' has been reserved for the contingent being of *Sachverhalte*. But certainly we cannot base our rejection of modal claims on the stipulative definition of a certain *word;* I cannot prove that there are no pigs by restricting the word 'pig' to what we would now call unicorns. But there are deeper problems, problems which point to certain familiar difficulties with the notion of existence.

All elementary propositions picture possible *Sachverhalte*, and 'A exists,' if it were a genuine proposition, would be elementary, since a Name occurs in it. (Although 3.201 leaves open the possibility that there might be a proposition which (a) contained Names but (b) did not meet the criteria of full analysis given at 3.2, I find it implausible that existence can be further analyzed.) The proposition would then consist of two Names, 'A' and 'existence', and its sense (if actual) would consist of the corresponding Objects in combination. The view that existence is an Object, capable of combination with other Objects to form existents, is not absurd. We saw earlier that Descartes held such a view, and it features prominently in Russell's *PrM*, where Russell writes "To exist is to have a specific relation to existence—a relation, by the way, which existence itself does not have." (*PrM*, p. 449) The thesis that existence is a property which some complexes have and others lack has been roundly criticized.[15] It has, however, a *special* shortcoming for Wittgenstein. If there were to be an elementary proposition of the form 'A exists,' then it would contain exactly two Names: 'A' and the Name for the Object existence. What would such a proposition be attempting to say? Either (a) that the Name 'A' has a referent, or (b) that it is possible for the Object A to be an actual constituent of some actual fact. But (a) is already *shown* by the Name 'A' having a meaning, and (b) is likewise shown by the occurrence of 'A' in (meaningful) propositions. Thus, existence-propositions *about Objects* are at best redundant. We saw in the previous chapter that non-analyzed existence claims disappear under analysis.

Thus at the very least we can see that 'A exists' is redundant and useless. But it is also important to note that showing the uselessness

---

[15] For instance, Hume *Treatise*, I/ii/6, Kant *CPR*, pp. 504–6, and Moore, "Is Existence a Predicate?" in *Philosophical Papers*, pp. 115–26.

of such propositions is not quite what the thesis of ineffability aims at; it characterizes such claims as impossible. There often appears in the *Tractatus* what seems to be an easy slide from "doesn't need to be said," "is useless," "is redundant," (because it attempts to say what can only be shown) to "can't be said" (because it attempts to say what can only be shown). What needs to be argued for, then, is that such contexts are not only useless, but fail to meet the minimum conditions for being propositions; that is, that there are no such pictures. This would eliminate the apparent area of overlap between showing and saying, where showing just seems to have gotten the *upper hand*, as it were. The stronger claim is particularly important, I think, when we look at Wittgenstein's concerns about ethics. There he certainly wants to strongly assert that (real moral) preaching is not just ineffective but *impossible*.

It is tempting to model such ineffability on the following case. Assuming that our color-concepts are acquired empirically, a child who asserts "I have seen red" is making a claim which if it is (for him) meaningful must be true. He cannot meaningfully make the claim without knowing what 'red' means, and this implies that he has experienced some instance of redness.[16] But unhelpful as it is, "I have seen red" does not appear to be a pseudo-proposition, even if it represents a case where meaningful assertion (like the cogito and Russell's 'This term exists' in *PrM*) implies truth. Has Wittgenstein thereby overshot his mark in claiming that 'A exists' is not only worthless but *meaningless?*

I cannot yet give a full answer to this challenge. 'A exists' is, I think, significantly different from "I have seen red." Its alleged necessary truth presupposes " 'A' means A," which in a manner we have not yet seen involves the metaphysical ego. For this reason " 'A' means A" is *not* merely redundant, and also is not even possibly in the realm of the sayable. Thus "can't be said" doesn't always mean merely "doesn't need to be said." (Light can be thrown on the preceding remark by considering the question "On Wittgenstein's account of picturing, why isn't the world a picture of language?"[17] The answer is that the picturing relation requires not only the homology of logical form between picture and pictured (which is always symmetrical) but the "method of projection," the intending

---

[16] Cf. W. V. O. Quine, *The Roots of Reference* (Open Court, La Salle, IL, 1974), p. 127.

[17] Cf. Coope et al., *op.cit.*, p. 11.

act which maps sign onto signified. This cannot come from some constituent of the world, but only from the metaphysical subject.)

We can also now see why 'P is possible' is both unnecessary and unsayable. It is unnecessary since the mere existence of the logical picture—the proposition 'p'—guarantees the possibility of the corresponding sense. But it is also unsayable insofar as it presupposes " 'p' means p," which is neither redundant nor even possibly picturable.

Apparent examples of necessary semantic propositions, or, derivatively, putative propositions about necessary or possible features of the world, thus turn out to be *pseudo-propositions*, which are "senseless" or "meaningless." Wittgenstein employs two significantly different terms which can be roughly translated 'nonsensical' in English: *sinnlos* and *unsinnig*. *Unsinnig* is almost always derogatory; Pears and McGuinness translate it as 'nonsense'. Typically, something is *unsinnig* if it tries to say something which can only be shown: e.g., asserting that a situation has a certain formal property (4.124), saying 'There are Objects' (4.1272) and so forth. On the other hand, logical propositions (to which we will turn in the following section) are *sinnlos*—'senseless' in Pears's and McGuinness's translation—insofar as there are no facts which correspond to them. They are *without senses*. (As we shall see, this is why they can be true independently of how the world is.) But this is not a deficiency, since their role is rather different from propositions with senses. For instance, we find such claims as "Tautologies and contradictions lack sense" (4.461) and "Laws of inference . . . have no sense" (5.132). Both *unsinnig* and *sinnlos* depend upon the show-say distinction, the former attempting to say something which can only be shown, the latter, although they say nothing, showing various aspects of language and the world.

There is a third sense in which a sign can be meaningless, which is from a *logical* point of view considerably less important than the preceding. For instance, 'bubububu' is meaningless insofar as it has been assigned no meaning.

Wittgenstein observes that "Most of the sentences and questions found in philosophical works are not false but senseless."(4.003) It was this strain of Wittgenstein's early thought upon which the positivists pounced, taking it to mean that such pseudo-propositions contained terms to which no meaning had been or perhaps could be assigned. Although Wittgenstein probably held that traditional metaphysics was full of such pseudo-propositions, he did not, like the positivists, hold traditional philosophy in disdain; his interest is frequently centered on the attempts of traditional philosophy to say what can only be shown. Thus, the interesting nonsense of traditional philosophy always falls into one of the first two classes, and expresses a tendency to try to penetrate beneath language to speak of the necessary conditions which underlie it. (This we will have opportunity to investigate in chapter IX.) The recommended therapy in both cases is the same: to move from *disguised* nonsense to the patently nonsensical, from confusion to a perspicuous overview. What is unique to Wittgenstein's approach is that it yields positive as well as negative results. In addition to our escape from confusion, seeing *why* certain things cannot be said heightens our appreciation of what for now I will vaguely characterize as "certain facets of reality."[18]

Necessity, Tautology, and Logical Propositions

In chapter II I alluded to Frege's views on the nature and significance of logical propositions. They are, Frege holds, wholly *analytic*, although not in the trivial (and pre-Quinean) sense in which "All cats are felines" is analytic, its truth depending solely upon the meanings of the terms involved. Far from being merely verbal, such principles are based on a priori connections between concepts like 'proposition', 'object', 'truth', and so forth, where these concepts and thus the truths based on them are construed realistically. The truth of logical propositions indeed follows from the senses of these terms, but insofar as these senses are objective and necessary, so are the propositions in question. The senses of such propositions thus represent the logical structure of the world, although their reference, like all other true propositions, is merely the True.

Russell's views in *PrM* are similar to Frege's, but he replaces Frege's emphasis on necessity with a rather different criterion for being a logical proposition. The reason for this, I believe, is that he can construct no adequate analysis of modal terms, but is unwilling to accept them as primitive. Logical propositions, he tells us, differ

---

[18] This is the element of the *Tractatus* which Ramsey (as well as a series of less worthy successors) found difficult to swallow. ". . . the chief proposition of philosophy is that philosophy is nonsense. And again we must take seriously that it is nonsense, and not pretend, as Wittgenstein does, that it is important nonsense." "Philosophy" in *op. cit.*, p. 263.

from such claims as "Pete Rose has more than 4000 hits" by speaking of *the most general aspects of the world.* The sign of a logical proposition will thus be *complete generality*; such propositions will contain only logical terms and variables. But this in itself is not sufficient to delineate the class of propositions (like the Law of Excluded Middle) which we normally take to be logically true. As Ramsey points out, "Any two things differ in at least thirty ways" is wholly general, but certainly also contingent.[19] Russell himself intermittently feels the force of this objection; in *IMP* he distinguishes purely general propositions from those which logic can confidently treat as true. The latter, he says, "all have the property [of being] tautological," adding that, "For the moment, I do not know how to define 'tautological'."[20] The problem of offering some criterion for logical truth which does not admit apparently contingent propositions will plague Russell for a long time. The axiom of reducibility in *Principia*, for instance, which Russell needs to extend the theory of truth-functions to all propositions, appears to be a contingent proposition, and for this reason Wittgenstein, Ramsey, and others query its status as a *logical* principle.[21] Although it may *in fact* be true in every case, it is not *necessarily* true.

The Fregean view (as well as Russell's in *PrM*) is unacceptable to Wittgenstein insofar as it implies that there are logical objects. Perhaps on a deeper level it leaves wholly mysterious why logical truths *are* true, and thus leaves open the door to some discipline more fundamental than logic which would supply that explanation. The *Grundgedanke* not only asserts that logical constants do not stand for objects, but that there can be no representatives for the logic of facts, and thus of the world. Given the wide range of things that Wittgenstein is willing to consider logical,[22] the rejection of such pseudo-propositions as " 'p' is a proposition" and " 'A' is a name"

---

[19] Ramsey *op. cit.*, p. 4. Given *Principia* *13.01, it is not clear whether "Any two things differ in at least one way" is contingent or not.

[20] Pp. 204–5. In a footnote on page 205, Russell attributes the term 'tautological' to Wittgenstein, adding that he did not know at the time whether Wittgenstein was alive or dead. (Compare with *L&K*, p. 177). Since a usable theory of tautologies seems to depend on the picture theory, this lends some credence to the view that the picture theory evolved later in Wittgenstein's thought.

[21] The axiom of reducibility claims that for every "non-elementary" (that is, first-level) function, there is an elementary function which is "equivalent" in the sense of being coextensive. Cf. *PM* *12; Ramsey (*op. cit.*, p. 28) discusses the contingent nature of the axiom.

[22] I again encourage the reader to consult Dummett *op. cit.*, chs. 18-19 for an excellent discussion of Frege's views which applies almost equally to Wittgenstein.

represent steps towards the goal of unseating all pretenders to that crown. Wittgenstein advances the theory that logical propositions are tautologous, and are thus *sinnlos*, having no correlates in the world, the final step towards the realization of the program of the *Grundgedanke*. As we shall see later in this chapter, this step will also have wide-ranging effects on Wittgenstein's conception of the role of philosophy

Wittgenstein's solution to the problem of logical propositions involves not only claiming them tautologous, but also producing a mechanical method for deciding whether or not a given proposition is a tautology. Tautologies themselves are introduced in the general discussion of truth-functions. (4.4 ff.) Truth-functionally compound propositions, so the *Grundgedanke* demands, make claims about the world only through their constituents. Thus they can be identified with their truth-conditions, that is, the truth or falsity of their component elementary propositions. The truth-table for 'p v q' not only provides a contextual definition for the wedge (thus showing it to be an incomplete symbol, by the way), but identifies it with the "states of the world" which are compatible with the truth of 'p v q'. Some truth-functional propositions are compatible with more states of the world than others; there are, for instance, three distinct situations compatible with the truth of 'p v q', but only one compatible with the truth of 'p . q'. Elementary truth-functions can be arranged in a series, according to the relative breadth or narrowness of the circumstances in the world which make them true or false.[23] This sequence will be bounded at either end by two special cases; one where the truth-conditions are so broad that the proposition is compatible with *any* state of affairs, the other where it is compatible with *none*. The former case represents a tautology, the latter a contradiction.

In conformity with mathematical usage, Wittgenstein refers to tautologies and contradictions as "degenerate cases" of truth-functions. The notion of a degenerate case is worth looking at. For instance, a circle is a degenerate case of a polygon: if we increase without limit the number of sides of an n-sided polygon, the resulting series of figures will approach as a limit a circle. We can

---

[23] Cf. 5.101. Wittgenstein rather obscurely links this sequence of truth-functions with probability; see 5.15–5.156. Note that there being three distinct states of the world compatible with the truth of 'p v q' does not mean that it is *vague*.

approach the circle as closely as we wish. However, the circle *lacks* an essential property of polygonhood, namely having *angles*, and thus as a convenient fiction we refer to it as a degenerate case of a polygon. To call a circle a degenerate polygon is to ask us to consider it in a certain way, to see it as the limiting case of a certain series.

Tautologies and contradictions are in a like manner degenerate cases of propositions. They are arrived at by the same route as other compound propositions—connection of elementary propositions with truth-functional connectives—yet they lack what we have seen to be an essential property of propositions: picturing a possible portion of the world. Though composed of constituents each of which has a sense, these constituents are arranged in such a manner as to "cancel out," in one case leaving nothing, in the other everything. Thus they say nothing, pick out no possible world, in one case because no possibility is included, in the other because every possibility is. Thus they are *sinnlos:* without senses. In lectures, Wittgenstein likens a tautology to a cog-wheel connected to nothing, a contradiction with two wheels jammed in opposite directions. In one case, nothing else in the machine can alter the state of the given wheel, in the other, they are immobile. The first case thus represents a wheel compatible with *any* machine, the latter with none.[24] Thus 'p . ~p' is compatible with no world, 'p v ~p' with every world. Neither picks out any particular possible world.[25]

The degenerate status of contradictions and tautologies is for Wittgenstein of extreme significance, particularly since it is often masked by the way we treat them. It is natural to treat tautologies and contradictions like ordinary propositions, insofar as they can appear, for example, as arguments of truth-functions (e.g. 'p v (p v ~p)'). But in such contexts they are idle cogs, and the sense in which they are true or false is much different from that of genuine propositions.[26]

---

[24] I owe this discussion and that of the previous paragraph to Black *op. cit.*, pp. 228–29. Also note the application of Black's ingenious "card-game analogy" mentioned above to this case. Ibid., pp. 229-311.

[25] The case of a tautology thus brings to mind Frege's claim that a word which applies to *everything* is not even a word. (*FA*, p. 40). Compare with Russell, *L&K*, p. 241. "If a sign is not used, it is meaningless. That is the point of Occam's maxim." 3.328

[26] Cf. Ramsey's illuminating discussion: *op. cit.*, p. 11.

The method of truth-tables—invented or perfected by Wittgenstein—provides a mechanical device for deciding whether or not a particular string is a tautology or contradiction. For example, '(p ⊃ q) ⊃ (~q ⊃ ~p)' can be shown to be a tautology using the following truth-table:

(p,q)	(p ⊃ q)	⊃	(~q ⊃ ~p)
TT	T T T	T	F T F
TF	T F F	T	T F F
FT	F T T	T	F T T
FF	F T F	T	F T T

This method, which Wittgenstein took to be effective for all non-quantified compound propositions,[27] answers a number of potentially troubling questions about the nature of logical truth. Let us catalogue these questions and see how the theory of tautologies helps deal with them.

First, *why* are logical truths true? What makes them true and necessary? Consider for instance the Law of Excluded Middle, which dictates that every proposition must be either true or false. Wittgenstein writes:

> ... one might think, for example, that the words 'true' and 'false' signified two properties among other properties, and then it would seem to be a remarkable fact that every proposition possessed one of these properties. On this theory [i.e., that logical propositions have sense] it seems anything but obvious, just as, for instance, the proposition "All roses are either yellow or red" would not sound obvious even if it were true."[28]

But on Wittgenstein's view we see that rather than expressing a remarkable fact about the world, any given logical proposition is true

---

[27] The complete effectiveness of the method with respect to *any* proposition thus involves the thesis of extensionality. Without it the effectiveness of the method is debatable. But cf. G. H. von Wright, "Form and Content in Logic" in his *Logical Studies* (Routledge and Kegan Paul, London, 1957).

[28] 6.111 (partial). In this passage I detect an echo of Schopenhauer on etiological regularities; cf. above sect. 2.2. We might contrast Wittgenstein's view with Meinong's: logical laws are real laws, and *thus there is a class of objects for which they hold, and another for which they do not hold.* Thus the Law of Contradiction holds for Richard Nixon but not for the Round Square Cupola on Berkeley College, the Law of Excluded Middle for Ronald Reagan but not for the Present King of France, and so forth. Cf. R. Grossman, *Meinong* (Routledge and Kegan Paul, London, 1974), pp. 205ff.

precisely because it has been *constructed* so as to be always true. Since it makes no claims about the world, nothing in the world could possibly contradict it. The necessity of the tautology lies not on the side of the world, but on the side of language.

An analogous point concerns the nature of logical *inference*. Consider, for instance, the inference from '$(x)(fx)$' to 'fa', and from 'fa' to '$(\exists x)(fx)$'. On the theory that logical propositions have senses, we seem faced with the necessity of postulating not only general facts, but *necessary connections* between such general facts. God could not, as it were, have created the world populated solely by the particular fact fa, since he would have at the same time been forced to create the general fact $(\exists x)(fa)$. (Cf. 5.123) However, in a series of remarks from 5.1 through 5.135, Wittgenstein offers an analysis of inference which, when combined with a wholly extensional treatment of quantified contexts, eliminates the puzzles which seem to attend a realistic treatment of rules of inference.

Some propositions bear to one another the following relation: the truth-grounds of one proposition—the states of the world which make it true—are a subset of the truth-grounds of the other. For instance, if 'p' is true, then 'p v q' must also be true, insofar as one (among several) of the truth-grounds of 'p v q ' is that p is the case. Since the truth-conditions of any proposition represent the existence or non-existence of the relevant *Sachverhalte*, the truth-conditions can be identified, in a way, with the *sense* of the proposition in question.[29] Thus, if the truth-conditions of 'p v q' are contained in those of 'p', then likewise the sense of the former must be contained in the latter. Since the sense of any proposition shows itself, then we *see* that '(p ⊃ (p v q))' is a tautology. More generally, if 'x' entails 'y', then the sense of 'y' is already contained in the sense of 'x'. All deduction is thus a priori, (5.133), yet there are no necessary connections between facts in the world which support it.

This account of inference entails an important corollary. Since no elementary proposition could contain within it the sense of any other elementary proposition, *no elementary proposition entails any other elementary proposition.* (5.134) Here we find—as Wittgenstein is quick to point out (5.135)—a theory of inference

---

[29] When combined with a thoroughgoing empirical theory of knowledge, this insight yields the notorious Verifiability Theory of Meaning. Cf. A. J. Ayer, *Language, Truth and Logic* (Dover, New York, 1952), chs. I–III. Wittgenstein of course held no such theory of knowledge at the time of the *Tractatus*, and if he had would have found it philosophically irrelevant.

which supports his picture of the world as a contingent aggregate of mutually independent *Sachverhalte*. The upshot, viz. that there are no real connections between states of affairs (5.136), will increasingly dominate our discussion.

As a sidelight, the tautology theory of inference solves a difficulty, repeatedly pointed out by Russell, concerning the representation of fundamental logical principles in a logical notation. The fundamental logical rule of *Principia* is "Anything which is implied by a true proposition is true" (*1.1). But this rule is very difficult to incorporate into the symbolism itself. If 'p ⊃ q' and 'p' are true, then the principle supports assertion of 'q'. But if we attempt to render this as '(p . (p ⊃ q) ⊃ q)', we get, due to the second implication, not the *assertion* that 'p' is true but only the *hypothetical* that *if* the antecedent is true then the consequent is.[30] This difficulty, the discovery of which Russell attributes to Lewis Carroll,[31] is quite easily explained on Wittgenstein's theory. Since entailment relations between propositions are *shown* by the containment of the sense of one proposition in the sense of another, no "principle of inference" is either necessary or possible. The attempt to state one thus involves trying to say what can only be shown, and either falls short of the mark, as in the case Russell suggests, or dissolves into nonsense. In the following sections we shall see the radical consequences for both the theory of logical symbolism and philosophy in general which this position entails.

We can now summarize Wittgenstein's argument up to this point. Logical propositions *say* nothing. They are *sinnlos*, making no claims about the world. This account meshes with our normal intuitions that if, for instance, I know that it is either raining or not raining I know nothing helpful in deciding whether to go to the beach. Logical propositions are tautologies, and can be recognized as such—at least in their fully analyzed form—using truth-tables. But are logical propositions then pointless and uninteresting? Pragmati-

---

[30] "... We cannot express the principle symbolically, partly because any symbolism in which p is a variable only gives the *hypothesis* that p is true, not the *fact* that it is true." *PM*, p. 94. Compare: "At this point, it is necessary to consider a very difficult logical problem, namely, between a proposition actually asserted, and a proposition merely considered as a complex concept. One of our indemonstrable principles ... was that if the hypothesis of an implication is true, it may be dropped, and the consequent asserted. This principle, it was observed, *eludes general statement and points to a certain failure of formalism in general.*" *PrM*, p. 34 (my emphasis). Compare with pp. 14–15.

[31] "What the Tortoise said to Achilles," *Mind* ns IV (1895), pp. 278–80.

cally useful as they are, do they completely lack *philosophical* import?

Wittgenstein's answer is no, and the reasons for his view are both difficult and important. The fundamental claim of his logical theory—that logical propositions are not about the world—is very easy to misconstrue. The analysis of tautological propositions via truth-tables makes it very attractive to treat logical propositions as wholly *conventional*, true due to decisions we make concerning the meanings of symbols. Although conventional choices may dictate *which* propositional signs embody tautologies (and contradictions), that there *are* tautologies is by no means a product of convention. As elsewhere, we find that once we have made *some* choices, logic forces our hand. Thus although the propositions of logic *say* nothing, what they *show* is of great importance.

The first aspect shown by tautologies—immensely important for Wittgenstein's theory of logic—is *that* they are tautologies. (6.127) Every contingent proposition makes some claim—true or false—about the world and thus can be treated as the conclusion of a proof. But since tautologies make no such claims, they constitute, as it were, their own proofs. (6.1264–6.1265) (This is mirrored in the propositional calculus by the familiar method of deriving tautologies from empty premise sets, using *reductio ad absurdum* or other forms of indirect proof.) This "self-validating" status shows itself; the method of truth-tables is only a pragmatic aid in complicated cases. Thus Wittgenstein rejects at 6.125 the "old conception of logic," logic as an axiomatic system in which logical truths are deduced from self-evident axioms. This picture—perhaps as ancient as Euclid's geometry—assigns a special place to the axioms, upon whose certainty the system rests (see 6.127). But such a picture is inaccurate, since every proposition displays its logical form, and the logical form of a tautology shows it to be such. Thus every tautology stands on its own two feet, and *any* tautology could play the role of an axiom. Wittgenstein writes:

> It is clear that the number of 'primitive propositions of logic' is arbitrary, since one could derive logic from a single primitive proposition, e.g., by simply constructing the logical product of Frege's primitive propositions. (Frege would perhaps say that we should then no longer have an immediately self-evident primitive proposition. But it is remarkable that a

thinker as rigorous as Frege appealed to the degree of self-evidence as the criterion of a logical proposition.)[32]

Russell and Frege present as the central question of logical theory, "What are the primitives of logic?" Wittgenstein offers the answer "Take what you like." *Pure* logical systems thus become formal devices for deciding whether or not a given string is a tautology, and has use only when the string is so complex that we cannot take it all at once, or when its logical form is hidden by the notation in which it is expressed. In each case the difficulties are merely psychological.[33]

The sole further use for a logical system can be compared with the parallel use of a mathematical system, namely moving from one contingent statement to another.

> Indeed in life a mathematical proposition is never what we want. Rather, we make use of mathematical propositions *only* in inference from propositions that do not belong to mathematics to others that likewise do not belong to mathematics.[34]

Thus I might use the mathematical formula '2 + 2 = 4' to determine that having started a poker game with two dollars and won two more, I now have four dollars. But the identity which I use as a rule of inference merely displays, in a more perspicuous form, that which

---

[32] Quite a lot is packed into this remark. Russell's logicism springs from a desire to show *why* the truths of mathematics ought to be accepted. On his view, the fewer primitive propositions to which we were committed, the fewer there were for which we had to offer bedrock justifications. But further, the Cartesian notion of self-evidence in the sense of clearness and distinctness had degenerated within the post-Kantian tradition to a sort of psychological attractiveness. The tendency to psychologize self-evidence becomes an important theme in Wittgenstein's later philosophy: cf. Stanley Cavell, "The availability of Wittgenstein's later philosophy" in his *Must We Mean What We Say?* (Cambridge U. Press, Cambridge, 1969), pp. 44–72.

It is not obvious that Frege held this view. "But it is almost certain that in order to avoid contradiction we must assume primitive laws which are far from self-evident." Letter to Russell dated 24.5.03, in *Philosophical and Mathematical Correspondence*, ed. Gabriel et al. (University of Chicago Press, Chicago, 1980), p. 168.

[33] Continuing our parallel with the Cartesian theory of clear and distinct ideas, we might consider propositions like "An evil genius might be constantly deceiving me" or "Possibly there is no God," which on first blush appear to represent real possibilities, but on closer examination turn out self-contradictory.

[34] 6.211. There immediately follows a remark startlingly reminiscent of the opening passages of the *Investigations:* "In philosophy the question 'What do we actually use this word or proposition for?' repeatedly leads to insight."

shows itself in the fact that '1 +1 + 1 +1' can be written as '(1 + 1) + (1 + 1)'.[35]

> If two expressions are combined by means of the sign of equality, that means that they can be substituted for one another. But it must be manifest in the two expressions themselves whether this is the case or not.
>
> When two expressions can be substituted for one another, that characterizes their logical form.[36]

In addition to showing *that* they are tautologies, logical propositions also through this show certain "formal" features of the world. But if I am not mistaken, after giving us this Wittgenstein immediately takes it away, as perhaps he must do to be true to his general notion of a proposition. Let us follow this argument.

> That the propositions of logic are tautologies *shows* the formal—logical—properties of language and the world.
>
> The fact that a tautology is yielded by *this particular way* of connecting its constituents characterizes the logic of its constituents. (6.12)
>
> The propositions of logic demonstrate the logical properties of propositions by combining them so as to form propositions that say nothing. This method could be called a zero-method. In a logical proposition, propositions are brought into equilibrium with one another, and the state of equilibrium indicates what the logical constitution of these propositions must be.[37]

Now the formal properties of Objects, we recall, are the abilities the Object has to combine in certain ways with other Objects; at 4.122

---

[35] But contrast; " 'Now you will admit that five consists of 3 + 2 III II'. I will only admit it, if it is not to admit anything else. Except—that I want to use *this picture.*" Wittgenstein, *Remarks on the Foundations of Mathematics*, trans. G. E. M. Anscombe (Blackwell, Oxford, 1967), p. 18.

[36] 6.23. Note that this continues the line of argumentation of 5.53ff. Identity cannot be a real relation, since the identity sign is an incomplete symbol, this incompleteness being shown by the dispensability of '=' in favor of a suitable convention for sign usage.

[37] 6.121. In a note to Ogden concerning his translation Wittgenstein explains that the "zero-method" or "null-method" is "in German an expression used in physics; when—for instance—you measure an electric resistance by regulating another resistance until the galvanometer points to 0 again ..." *Letters to C. K. Ogden*, p. 34. The device Wittgenstein describes is commonly referred to as a Wheatstone bridge. The point seems to be: you understand what a proposition means by finding another proposition which exactly cancels it out.

Wittgenstein equates the term "formal property" with "*internal*
property." The internal properties of a proposition would presumably then be a function of the Names which constitute that
proposition, their configuration reflecting the internal properties of
the Objects for which they proxy. But precisely how will the fact that
'p v ~p' is a tautology show such internal properties? That such a
formula is a tautology *regardless* of what we substitute for 'p' seems
to indicate nothing about the particular logical structure of a given
elementary proposition uniquely displayed by 'p v ~p' being a
tautology. Its being a tautology does show, of course, that putting the
crotchet '~' in front of a proposition reverses its sense, but that is a
function of a purely conventional choice of connectives, and would
seem to show something about our *notation*.

Part of Wittgenstein's claim might be saved with the following
construal: that a certain string is a tautology shows something about
the external or truth-functional structure of certain complex *molecular* propositions.[38] Thus at 6.1201 he offers the example of '(p ⊃ q)
· (p) : ⊃ : (q)'; that this is a tautology, he writes, shows that 'q'
follows from 'p' and 'p ⊃ q'. Again this seems to show us little more
than the effects of the logical signs involved, which shows us nothing
about the formal properties of the propositions. But if we take 'p' and
'q' to be two *unanalyzed* molecular propositions, then the tautology
in question would show us something about the two propositions,
namely that 'q' was part of the content of 'p'. But then what logical
propositions show seems to be mere therapy directed towards the
misleading superficial form of ordinary language.[39] Interestingly,
these puzzles about the role of logical propositions may be rendered
moot by Wittgenstein's next claim: *we really don't need logical
propositions at all.*

---

[38] This interpretation is supported by 6.1221, where he speaks of 'p ⊃ q' as being a tautology. But
since no elementary proposition entails any other, it is clear that he must take 'p' at least to be
truth-functionally compound.

[39] The most general suggestion concerning what Wittgenstein might have in mind is that
tautologies show that propositions are bipolar and that there is always an operation which
reverses the sense of a given proposition. This might show something about the internal, ineffable
nature of any proposition by showing something about the nature of a picture. But one would think
that by this stage in the argument, the picture theory would be taken for granted.

It is perhaps significant that in the examples of tautologies given in 6.1201, the tautology in
question (enclosed in single quotes) shows something *not* about the constituent propositions but
rather about the putative facts which these propositions mirror. Thus whatever tautologies show
is not merely about our notation.

> It follows from this that we can actually do without logical propositions; for in a suitable notation we can in fact recognize the formal properties of propositions by mere inspection of the propositions themselves.[40]

This too we shall have occasion to discuss later.

Wittgenstein makes a final puzzling remark about what logical propositions show; the whole class of tautologies jointly shows or mirrors *"das Gerüst der Welt."* Pears and McGuinness translate *Gerüst* as 'scaffolding', but the equally acceptable term 'framework' might be less misleading, insofar as scaffolding is normally temporary. (When the renovations on the Statue of Liberty were finished, the scaffolding was removed, but the [strengthened] framework remains.) Wittgenstein's claim that tautologies mirror the logical framework of the world is rooted in a deep conviction on his part. On one hand, he is clear that there can be no representatives for the logic of the world and that logical propositions therefore *say* nothing. On the other hand, his realistic tenets make repugnant the conventionalists' view that logic is concerned *solely* with more or less arbitrary rules for symbol-manipulation. The result is his peculiar position that logic is not merely conventional but that its connection with the world cannot be represented.

But what exactly *is* this connection? The truth of logical propositions, we have seen, is not simply given, but "presuppose[s] that names have meaning and elementary propositions sense ..." (6.124). Thus, the truth of logical propositions *come what may* shows something about the logical framework of the world—the "substance of the world" of 2.021–2.0211. It shows that there can be no question of the being of Objects, and thus no question about the sense (although not the *truth*) of elementary propositions. This is perhaps what Wittgenstein means at 6.126.

> One can calculate whether a proposition belongs to logic, by calculating the logical propositions of a *symbol*.
>
> ... For, without bothering about sense or meaning, we can construct the logical proposition out of others using only *rules that deal with signs* ...

---

[40] 6.122. The alleged "illustrations" of this remark in 6.1221 do little to clarify the nature of such a notation. 6.122 also appears to be one of the Tractarian passages which hints that only fully analyzed propositions are pictures; this seems, however, inconsistent with the general remarks on the picture theory.

The occurrence of 'symbol' in the first remark and 'sign' in the second—the emphasis, by the way, is Wittgenstein's—implies that insofar as the sense of elementary propositions is guaranteed, we can identify tautologies through purely formal rules for manipulating signs. Thus we can construct rules which say "Do this with this widget and that with that and you'll get a proposition which is always true." Thus *that* logic can be dealt with in such purely conventional terms shows that the existence of such conventional rules presupposes something about reality. That Names have meaning, for example, presupposes not only the being of Objects but the being of the metaphysical subject. This will become increasing evident in chapters VIII through XI.

Logic and the Nature of Philosophy

In the passage which heads this chapter, Wittgenstein writes Russell that the distinction between what can be said and what can only be shown is not only central to the *Tractatus*, but is "the cardinal problem of philosophy." In a section labeled "Preliminary" which begins the 1913 *Notes on Logic*, he writes "[Philosophy] consists of logic and metaphysics, the former its basis." Earlier in the same section he flatly declares: "In philosophy there are no deductions; it is purely descriptive." These claims taken jointly indicate Wittgenstein's belief that his new view of logic, based as it was on the notion of showing, entailed a new vision of the nature of philosophy. A "new way" needs to be contrasted with some *old* way, and I think that it is safe to say that the "old way" which Wittgenstein wished to contrast with his way included what might loosely be called "scientific philosophy." (Of course it includes *more* than this; we must always keep in mind Wittgenstein's total rejection of any psychologistic element in philosophy.) This conception of philosophy, very deeply ingrained in the western tradition, was represented for Wittgenstein by Russell and perhaps Schlick and Neurath.[41] Since Russell's view represents the *general* position against which Wittgen

---

[41] The view is Cartesian, although I do not know whether Wittgenstein had read any or enough of Descartes to recognize this. There is a passing allusion to Descartes in the *Blue Book* (p. 69), but Descartes does not appear on Father Hallett's list of "Authors Wittgenstein Knew or Read"; Hallett *op. cit.*, p. 760.

stein rebels, as well as a concrete influence on his thought during the Tractarian period,[42] let us briefly review that position.

Like Descartes, Russell bemoans the apparent lack of progress in philosophy: "Philosophy, from the earliest times, has made greater claims, and achieved fewer results, than any other branch of learning." (*OKEW*, p. 14) Such stagnation contrasts starkly with science, where Russell's pre-Kuhnian picture of science led him to see substantial and more or less constant objective progress manifested. Obviously philosophers have pursued their theories with at least as much vigor as scientists, so the lack of progress in philosophy indicates that philosophy needs a new *method*. (*Ibid.*, p. 13) Thus if philosophy is to advance as science does, it needs to be more closely connected with science, not so much in results but in methods. (*M&L*, p. 98) But the analogy Russell sees between science and philosophy goes far deeper than a mere methodological recommendation. Like Descartes, Russell holds that ordinary beliefs are in some important sense dubious, and the role of philosophy is to give some support for our ordinary views, or, conversely, to reject them if we find no support. "I have been throughout anxious to discover how much we can be said to know and with what degree of certainty or doubtfulness," he wrote later of his philosophical career.[43] Thus just as a given perceptual judgment stands in need of a scientific justification— say through an optical or physiological analysis of perception— Russell held the currently unfashionable view that *every judgment stands in need of philosophical justification*. The reason is that no proposition can be true (or even meaningful) unless the entities for which its denoting expression purport to stand exist. There can be no true statements about irrational numbers, for instance, if every number can be written as a ratio between two integers, and no true statements about cats and mats if one or the other fails to exist. What is needed, then, is a wide-ranging proof that certain wide

---

[42]At least if we stick to Wittgenstein's technical sense of 'fact'. Ramsey seems to believe that Russell held there to be vague facts; in a letter to Wittgenstein dated 2.20.24 he writes "[Russell] *indignantly denied ever having said that vagueness* is a characteristic of *the physical world.*" *Letters to C. K .Ogden*, p. 84. The odd emphasis is Ramsey's. Russell's indignation probably well-grounded; a year earlier he wrote "Vagueness and precision alike are characteristics which can only belong to a representation of which language is an example." "Vagueness," *Australasian Journal of Philosophy*, vol. I (1923), p. 85. Henceforth, the work, B. Russell, *Our Knowledge of the External World* (Allen and Unwin, London, 1914), shall be referred to as *OKEW*.

[43]*My Philosophical Development*, p. 11. Compare with Descartes at *HR* I, p. 144.

classes of entities exist, and for Russell this is always a *philosophical* matter.

How will this be achieved? "Philosophy," Russell writes, "like all other studies, aims primarily at knowledge."[44] But what sort of knowledge, and how is it to be gotten?

> Philosophical knowledge ... does not differ essentially from scientific knowledge; there is no special source of wisdom which is open to philosophy but not to science, and the results obtained by philosophy are not radically different from those obtained by science. (*Ibid.*, p. 149)

This point combined with the previous one highlights one chore to which philosophy—utilizing as its tool the new mathematical logic—must address itself, namely the construction of a "philosophical zoo," a universal catalogue of the most general sorts of things that there are. Philosophy differs from pomology, for instance, only insofar as the latter is concerned with a narrower range of entities. But like pomology (and unlike Meinong's Theory of Objects and the doctrine of Terms in *PrM*) logic and philosophy do not for Russell extend beyond the bounds of the actual. The claims that result from such philosophical investigations are thus purely extensional.

> Logic, I should maintain, must no more admit of a unicorn than zoology can; for logic is concerned with the real world just as truly as zoology, although with its more general and abstract features. (*IMP*, p. 149)

In accord with Russell's extensional analysis of possibility the sign of a logical proposition is mere de facto generality.

> I do not myself admit necessity and possibility as fundamental notions; it appears to me that *fundamental truths are merely true in fact*, and that a search for "sufficient reason" is mistaken.[45]

Philosophy thus assumes the role of "queen of the sciences" through being the most general of human endeavors, but is otherwise

---

[44]B. Russel, *The Problems of Philosophy* (Oxford U. Press, Oxford, 1912) (henceforth abbreviated *PP*) p. 154. Note that Russell makes this claim, which Wittgenstein will dispute, *as if it were a truism.*

[45]"Some Explanations in Reply to Mr Bradley," *Mind*, 1910, p. 374. Bear in mind that Russell had advanced beyond this view of logical truths by the time he wrote *PM*, probably largely due to Wittgenstein's influence.

qualitatively indistinguishable from the special sciences. It seeks (or ought to seek) general but factual truths about the world.

One mark of scientific theories is their hierarchical or deductive structure, where general laws combine with boundary conditions to entail specific predictions or explanations. The parallel view holds logic, and thus philosophy, to be a deductive system, where certain primitive axioms and postulates allow deduction of the remaining logical propositions. Philosophical truths are thus to be accepted or rejected according to whether they help unify the realm of science (*PP*, p. 154), and to that extent have some inductive support (*OKEW*, p. 103). The same sorts of considerations apply to logic:

> We have . . . avoided both controversy and general philosophy, and made our statements dogmatic in form. The justification for this is that the chief reason in favor of any theory of the principles of mathematics must always be inductive . . . In mathematics the greatest degree of self-evidence is usually not to be found at the beginning, but at some later point; hence the early deductions, until they reach this point, give reasons rather for believing the premises because true consequences follow from them . . . (*PM*, p. i)

Logic and philosophy are thus continuous with science; in fact, Russell conjectures that some of the lack of progress in philosophy may be merely apparent, since as a portion of philosophy becomes more developed (he offers psychology as an example) it breaks off to form an autonomous science.[46]

Wittgenstein has very little truck with such scientific philosophy, as we shall see in the next chapter. This lack of sympathy is due to several factors, including the contrast between his notion of science and Russell's rather Eddingtonian conception, the influence of Schopenhauer's limitation of the role of science, and certain visceral feelings concerning ethics and aesthetics, visceral elements which gather support and confirmation from the development of the Tractarian views on logic and language.

We can briefly develop some of points of antipathy. Since logical propositions are *sinnlos*, they make no claims—general or otherwise—about things in the world. Logical propositions are thus assuredly *not* the most general scientific statements, since if they were, they would have senses, and thus could not be certain a priori.

---

[46]*PP*, pp. 154–55. Compare with J. L. Austin, "A Plea for Excuses," in his *Philosophical Papers* (Oxford U. Press, Oxford, 1961), pp. 169ff.

(This is slightly misleading, as we shall see in the next chapter.) Fundamentally different from scientific propositions, Wittgenstein believes that his analysis of logical propositions "assign[s] them a unique status among all propositions" (6.112). But more important perhaps for our purposes are two other corollaries which follow from the tautology theory of logical truth. The first is that logic cannot be seen on the model of axiom and theorem. At 6.127 Wittgenstein writes:

> All the propositions of logic are of equal status: it is not the case that some of them are essentially primitive and others essentially derived.
>
> Every tautology shows that it is a tautology.

and at 6.1265:

> It is always possible to construe logic in such a way that every proposition is its own proof.

The view that there are first principles in logic is based on two facts: that a given notation may appear to *assign* a more prominent role to one proposition than to another, and that certain propositions might *appear* more "self-evident" than others. But the first is conventional and the second suspect. That a certain notation assigns a special place to a given proposition may tell us something about *that notation*, but nothing more. Likewise, any appeal to "self-evidence" carries with it the taint of psychologism.[47] Thus, there is no logical "pecking order," and thus no room for postulate and theorem.

But there is a more striking and radical consequence. Logic deals with the forms of propositions, and derivatively with the possible structure of the world. But *every* proposition shows its logical form; if a tautology thus does this especially well, this can be due only to a combination of psychological conditions and misleading or opaque notation. The upshot is clear:

> ... we can actually do without logical propositions; for in a suitable notation we can in fact recognize the formal properties of propositions by the mere inspection of the propositions. (6.122)

---

[47]Wittgenstein chides Frege for allowing such psychologistic elements to creep into his philosophy of logic; cf. 6.1271, 5.1363, 5.4731. Black points out that this is rather unfair to Frege, since he takes great pains to insist that logic need borrow nothing from experience. Cf. Black *op. cit.*, p. 339.

Thus all that has traditionally been considered logic can be boiled down to two things: logical propositions—that is, tautologies—and recommendations for perspicuous notation. The role of the latter remains to be seen.

The oft-repeated claim of the *Notebooks*—"Logic must take care of itself"—ought now be clearer. We cannot frame an "illogical proposition" (2.203, 3.03); the sense, and thus the logical form of a genuine proposition, shows itself. Genuine logical inference cannot produce any "surprises" (6.1251), since it too depends on the logical forms of the propositions in question, and that logical form is, as it were, *right there* in front of us. Surprise is appropriate only where discovery is possible, and in logic there is nothing to discover.[48]

Finally, logic could not even possibly supply—even as a subsidiary task—the universal inventory which Russell envisioned. Since 'Object', 'Form', 'Proposition' and so forth are *formal* concepts, it is impossible that any proposition assert, for instance, that thirty-two different logical forms exist, or that there are twenty Objects in the world. But such pseudo-propositions are also unnecessary; what they try to say is shown by there being x different propositional forms, and y number of Names.[49]

Since the *Notebooks* tell us that philosophy consists only of logic and metaphysics, such a radical view of logic entails a parallel radical view of the nature of philosophy.[50] Wittgenstein rejects wholly the possibility of philosophy becoming a science. If philoso-

---

[48]The careful reader will detect a certain tension at this point. On one hand logic takes care of itself; we cannot construct an "illogical proposition," thus "illogical thought" is impossible too. Since ordinary language partakes of the nature of language in general, it too is in "perfect logical order" (5.5563). Yet the *Tractatus* is full of warnings about the pitfalls of misunderstanding the logical structure of our language, and even positive suggestions for improved notations. The tension is serious but in part only apparent; it arises through a tendency to conflate the psychological/pragmatic shortcomings of a notation with real logical shortcomings. In chapter XI we shall sharpen this tension by paralleling it with a similar problem concerning poetry. But the tension will also be the source of real difficulties concerning Wittgenstein's conception of the nature and role of philosophy.

[49]This shows, incidentally, a flaw in Russell's criticism of a truth-functional reduction of general propositions, and subsequently a flaw in his argument that facts, not objects, are the primary existents. Russell argues that '$(x)(Fx)$' cannot mean 'Fa · Fb · Fc ...' since we would need to add "And there are the only things that there are." For Wittgenstein, there being no more Objects, and no more elementary propositions of the form 'Fx', is shown by there being no more Names to instantiate in those propositions.

[50]The term 'philosophy' of course did not have a wholly unproblematical sense for Wittgenstein. Time and again he returns to the question: what is the relationship between what we are doing and what has traditionally been called philosophy? In some contexts we see a tracing of continuity, in others a drawing out of contrasts. Cf. for instance "Wittgenstein's Lectures of 1930–33" in Moore, *Philosophical Papers*, esp. pp. 322–24.

phy did become a science, it would cease to be philosophy, and, as we shall see, perhaps cease to be very important. Unlike Russell, the post-enlightenment liberal, Wittgenstein would not see science as a goal towards which human efforts ought to strive. Since the world is a contingent aggregate of mutually independent *Sachverhalte*, and since at 4.11 we get a preliminary characterization of science as "the totality of true propositions," the special sciences presumably address themselves to some delineated subset of those propositions. But each of these propositions, insofar as they have a sense, would lack the necessity which marks philosophical propositions. On the other hand, the only necessary propositions are tautologies and contradictions, which lack sense. Thus there can be no philosophical propositions *about* the world.

It is tempting to picture philosophy as dealing not so much with existence but with the *possibilities* of existence—Russell's Theory of Terms, Meinong's Theory of Objects—and not, like the sciences, with *actual* existence. (Cf. *PI*, #97) But this cannot be consistently developed. *Every* proposition pictures a possibility, but this possibility cannot (and need not) be said. There can be no propositions which *say* that certain possibilities exist, and no proposition could deny that a given situation is possible. *Thus there could be no set of propositions which could be considered philosophical propositions.* The place of philosophy must be, as Wittgenstein cryptically puts it, something "whose place is above or below the natural sciences, not beside them." (4.111) Where then is there room for an enterprise which might legitimately fall heir to the title of philosophy?

Certainly not, as the long post-Cartesian tradition has maintained, in the construction of a theory of knowledge.[51] Such justification could be of philosophical interest only if the relations between evidence and proposition were logical relations, and they are clearly not. Any attempt to trace the actual ways in which people come to believe what they do is steeped in psychologism, which Wittgenstein of course rejects as anathema.

---

[51]Some readers may be uncomfortable with the characterization of the British Empiricists from Locke to Russell as "Cartesians." But they stand behind Descartes in assuming (a) that ordinary beliefs stand in need of justification, (b) that knowledge is grounded in some special class of beliefs, and (c) that justification involves discovering or constructing logical connections between these foundational beliefs and ordinary ones. The empiricists differ from Descartes only in (d) their estimation of what this class of foundational beliefs is, and (e) what the nature of the logical relations between foundational and ordinary beliefs might be. One classic sustained criticism of this view of knowledge is J. L. Austin, *Sense and Sensibilia* (Oxford U. Press, Oxford, 1962).

> Psychology is no more closely related to philosophy than any other natural science. Theory of knowledge is the philosophy of psychology. (4.1121)

The actual perceptual apparatus which human beings currently possess, along with the de facto history of concepts, either personal or societal, is irrelevant to philosophical concerns, just as Kekule's dream of snakes is irrelevant to the ring structure of benzene and Archimedes' bath to the notion of specific gravity. (This Wittgenstein maintains, in a way, in his later philosophy, where the actual history of a concept is in no way superior to an *imaginary* history.) Since the actual state of our perceptual apparatus is irrelevant, so is the actual history of that development; "Darwin's theory has no more to do with philosophy than any other hypothesis in natural science." (4.1122)

Philosophy, however, is connected with the natural sciences in a somewhat more elusive manner. "Philosophy sets limits to the much disputed sphere of natural science," Wittgenstein writes at 4.113, following immediately with:

> It must set limits to what can be thought; and, in doing so, to what cannot be thought.
> It must set limits to what cannot be thought by working outwards through what can be thought. (4.114)

There are several points of interest in this passage, not the least the introduction of the notion of a *limit*, which will rapidly rise in importance in succeeding chapters. Importantly, since philosophy puts limits on the natural sciences, which exhaust the realm of the sayable, these limits themselves must be ineffable. Further, the passage seems to assign a certain regulatory role to philosophy vis-à-vis science, perhaps excluding a priori from the realm of scientific investigation certain topics. Such a regulatory role for philosophy seems to conflict with the claim of *NoL* that philosophy cannot "confirm or confute scientific investigations." (p. 93) The claim is certainly true insofar as philosophy cannot decide upon the (contingent) *truth* of any scientific proposition, but by 1918 Wittgenstein seems to have come to the view that philosophical investigation can show that certain alleged sciences could not exist. In particular, I think Wittgenstein has in mind any attempt to formulate "scientific ethics," "scientific aesthetics," or "scientific theology," all of which he held in contempt. It is probably also directed towards the psychologistic attempt to reduce logic to the "science of the mental."

4.114, with its emphasis on "what can be thought," suggests another role for philosophy. This purported role—"clarification of thoughts"—has the virtue of providing at least superficial continuity between the *Tractatus* and the positivistic works which claim it as their predecessor, but it also points again to a certain tension that I have alluded to above. The assertion that philosophy is not a natural science is followed by:

> Philosophy aims at the logical clarification of thoughts.
> Philosophy is not a body of doctrines but an activity.
> A philosophical work consists essentially of elucidations.
> Philosophy does not result in 'philosophical propositions', but rather in the clarification of propositions.
> Without philosophy, thoughts are, as it were, cloudy and indistinct; its task is to make them clear and to give them sharp boundaries. (4.112)

The intent of the passage is unmistakable: philosophical puzzles arise because we fail to understand the "logic of our language," as the Preface puts it. These confusions lead us to draw unwarranted parallels between certain forms of expression (e.g. 'Green is green'; 3.323) or perhaps more damaging, to try to say what can only be shown. Viewed this way, the *Tractatus* suggests nothing more radical than the housekeeping function which the British empiricists champion against the Platonists with respect to abstract ideas.[52] This function would thus be fulfilled by the invention and use of a perspicuous notation, such as Frege's *Begriffsschrift*, breaking down the Russellian gap between the real and apparent logical form of propositions. This notion of a perspicuous notation held great attraction for Wittgenstein, and lies behind the series of remarks from 4.002–4.0031.

Yet there are, on Wittgenstein's principles, serious difficulties with this view. How, for instance, can a thought be "cloudy and indistinct"? Thoughts are propositions with mental signs, and every proposition must have *perfect* sense. We are assured again and again that every proposition—and thus the propositions of ordinary

---

[52]Berkeley writes "abuse of language ... has occasioned innumerable errors and difficulties in all parts of Knowledge," arising from the mistaken opinion that "the mind has the power of framing *abstract ideas* or notions of things." *Principles of Human Knowledge*, section 6.

language—are in *perfect order* just as they stand. But what then could count as the "clarification of a proposition"? How is there both room for and the need for such clarification? Ramsey writes, "I think that a written sentence is 'clear' in so far as it has *visible* properties correlated with or 'showing' the internal properties of its sense." (*FoM*, p. 283) Black counters that this emphasis on the visible properties of a symbol is misguided, suggesting that a symbol is clear when "the rules for its use are followed correctly and without fumbling or hesitation." (*Op. cit*, p. 186) But certainly such rules cannot help Wittgenstein unless they are manifest in the *symbol itself*, and we return to the vexed question: where is there room for "fumbling and hesitation"?

These points represent a fundamental tension in Wittgenstein's early work. The perfection of every proposition is marred, as it were, by an overlay of psychological considerations, which leads to the confusions Wittgenstein thinks inhabit philosophy. But on one hand, such considerations (psychological, social, or historical) are of no philosophical interest; on the other hand, without concern about them philosophy seems barren. This is curiously parallel to the problems which face any rationalist: if the truth of clear and distinct ideas (to take Descartes' formulation) is immediately evident, and if such ideas are innate, how do we explain the apparent effort taken to retrieve them? Why, for instance, does the slave boy need Socrates' coaching *at all?* The typical rationalist response to such challenges involves recourse to the effects of some contingent environment on the mind—for Plato the trauma of entering the world of becoming, for Descartes the overriding influence of the senses and the imagination on the understanding. Wittgenstein's analysis of philosophy and logic cannot, I think, be fully appreciated without reference to something quite like this; exactly what that is we shall see in subsequent chapters. But before transition to the next chapter it is worthwhile to consider Ramsey's criticism of the whole project of the *Tractatus*. Natural science exhausts the realm of the sayable, but produces propositions devoid of philosophical interest as well as—not incidentally for Wittgenstein—devoid of value. But then what happens to the propositions of the *Tractatus* itself? Would they not appear not even *sinnlos* but *unsinnig?* Would not philosophy, to play on the shifting meanings of the word, become senseless? As Russell points out in the Introduction, Wittgenstein does seem to teach us, whether or not we accept Russell's contention that he manages to "say a great deal of what cannot be said." The doctrine of showing introduces a whole realm of new difficulties, and if we are serious about the doctrine and its consequences, then we ought to simply shut up. "What you can't say you can't say, and you can't whistle it either," as Ramsey puts it. Elsewhere Ramsey comments:

> Philosophy must be of some use and we must take it seriously; it must clear our thoughts and so our actions. Or else it is a disposition we have to check, and an inquiry to see that this is so; i.e., the chief proposition of philosophy is that philosophy is nonsense. And again we must take seriously that it is nonsense, and not pretend, as Wittgenstein does, that it is important nonsense.[53]

The sorts of difficulties which Ramsey indicates will bring to the forefront the metaphor of the "ladder" of 6.54, which one must climb and then discard to "see the world aright." (They also indicate the extent to which Ramsey's priorities differ from Wittgenstein's.) This metaphor and its contents will increasingly dominate the following chapters.

---

[53] "Philosophy," in *op. cit.*, p. 263.

VII

The Principles of Mechanics

*Jeans has written a book called The Mysterious Universe,
and I loathe it and call it misleading. Take the title. This
alone I would call misleading ... I might say that the title
The Mysterious Universe includes a kind of idol worship,
the idol being Science and the Scientist.*

The status of physics, particularly the principles of mechanics,
will be the central focus of this chapter, and in it we will see several
strains of our discussion begin to converge. From the logical side, the
principles of mechanics are troubling for several reasons. They seem
necessary, yet they are not tautologies, and the picture theory cannot
tolerate this. They are *general*, yet they cannot, so it would seem, be
reduced to truth-functions of non-general propositions, and the
thesis of extensionality cannot tolerate *this*. But on a deeper and
perhaps more important level, Wittgenstein wants to loosen the grip
that science has both on the world and the mind. Schopenhauer
saw the existence of etiological laws as evidence for his thesis of
universal voluntarism, as a manifestation of the will-like nature of
reality. In chapter X we shall see Wittgenstein offer a Kantian
analysis of value with emphasis on the will as the bearer of value, and
his rejection of the Schopenhauerian philosophy of science—the
subject of this chapter—will begin to drive a wedge between the
sayable—the world, the existence and non-existence of *Sachverhalte*—and anything of genuine value. Ironically, we shall see the
world as will (in the guise of "my world") return to play a central role
in Wittgenstein's theory of value.

The connection between a discussion of science and the nature
of value might not be evident to the casual reader of the *Tractatus*,
but the connections are real and very deep. At 6.371 Wittgenstein
writes:

> The whole modern conception of the world is founded on the illusion that
> the so-called laws of nature are the explanations of natural phenomena.

In the *Tractatus* this passage is followed immediately by 6.373—"the
world is independent of my will"—which we shall see effectively

eliminates the world as a possible locus of value. But perhaps more significantly, the parallel passage in the *Notebooks* (p. 74) precedes the remark "What do I know about God and the purpose of the world?", followed by a list of claims about value, the self, the will, meaning, and so forth. Science brings us, as it were, not one step closer to God.

But first we must see what Wittgenstein regarded as the fundamental wrong-headedness of Schopenhauer's philosophy of science. We shall facilitate this by examining the effects on Wittgenstein's view of science of his long-standing admiration for the dazzling neo-Kantian physicist and philosopher of science, Heinrich Hertz. Born in Hamburg in 1857, in his short lifetime (he died at age 37) Hertz made notable contributions to the axiomatization of mechanics, which, with the parallel development of non-Euclidian geometries, characterizes nineteenth-century physics, and to the relatively novel field of electric waves.[1] But beyond his rightfully acclaimed scientific work, Hertz stands as an important figure in the history of the philosophy of science, and it is this facet of his work with which we shall be largely occupied.

The depth and duration of Hertz's influence on Wittgenstein cannot be overestimated. Before settling on a quote from Nestroy, Wittgenstein considered using a passage from Hertz's *Principles of Mechanics* as the motto for the *Philosophical Investigations*.[2] Janik and Toulmin argue with some persuasiveness that Hertz's theory of dynamical models was the paradigm for the picture theory; *Principles* section 428 in particular supports this reading. (*Op. cit.*, pp. 139–41) But it is Hertz's views on the status of the Principles of Mechanics which will chiefly occupy our interest. In particular, I will argue that Hertz offers Wittgenstein solid grounds for rejecting the Schopenhauerian argument that the existence of general laws confirms the Thesis of Universal Voluntarism. Hertz's own neo-Kantian analysis, purified by Wittgenstein of any hint of psychologism (transcendental or not) points towards the Tractarian view of

---

[1] For Hertz's electrical researches, cf. H. Hertz, *Electric Waves*, trans. D. E. Jones (Dover, New York, 1900), and his *Miscellaneous Papers* (London, 1896). For the historical context of his work, see Holton and Roller, *op. cit.*, sect. VII, and, for a more general discussion, P. and E. Morrison, "Heinrich Hertz," *Scientific American*, Dec. 1957.

[2] Cf. Baker and Hacker, *op.cit.*, p. 26. The quote is this: "When these painful contradictions are removed, the question as to the nature [of force] will not have been answered, but our minds, no longer vexed, will cease to ask illegitimate questions." For the aptness of the proposed motto, see *Blue Book*, p. 26 (with its explicit reference to Hertz), and *PI*, #89–90 and *passim*.

science. The issues which we shall examine go very deep in Wittgenstein's system indeed.

Mach and Sensationalism

My manner of introduction of the issues of this chapter—a discussion of some central views of another towering figure in nineteenth-century German thought, Ernst Mach—may seem unduly roundabout at first. But Hertz's views are best seen in reaction to Mach's, and further, Mach's neo-Humean, positivistic, historicistic, psychologistic views, so sharply antithetical to Wittgenstein's, will allow us to draw together some Tractarian themes with greater clarity.[3]

The opening chapter of Mach's *An Analysis of Sensations*,[4] entitled "Introductory Remarks: Antimetaphysical," presents three theses which announce the general themes of Mach's philosophy. First, science is at bottom *anticipatory*, so that the criterion of explanatory success is accuracy and comprehensiveness of prediction. Second, laws of nature represent nothing more than generalizations of "facts." Finally, any attempt (e.g. Schopenhauer's) to provide science with a metaphysical underpinning is doomed to failure. Let us examine these three important claims.

The first claim is anticipated in *The Science of Mechanics*[5]:

> In the infinite variety of nature many ordinary events occur; while others appear uncommon, perplexing, astonishing or even contradictory to the ordinary run of things. As long as this is the case we do not possess a well-settled and unitary conception of nature. Thence is imposed the task of everywhere seeking out in natural phenomena those elements that are the same, and that amid all multiplicity are everywhere present. By this means, on one hand, the most economical and briefest description and communi-

---

[3] On an even broader scale, Mach's pervasive influence on the Viennese intellectual community directly contributed to certain theories of art which Wittgenstein found repugnant and dangerous. Janik and Toulmin offer the examples of the *Jung Wien* poet Herman Bahr, who sought a philosophical basis for impressionism in Mach's sensationalism (*op. cit.*, p. 81), and Robert Musil, whose "Holiday Language" of vol. II of *A Man without Qualities* is a Machian protocol-language. In chapter X we shall further investigate the grounds for Wittgenstein's hostility towards such psychologistic theories of art.

[4] E. Mach, *An Analysis of Sensations and the Relation of the Physical to the Mental*, trans. C. M. Williams (Open Court, Chicago, 1914). I will refer to this work, originally published in 1896, as *AS*.

[5] E. Mach, *The Science of Mechanics: A Critical and Historical Account of its Development*, trans. T. J. McCormack (Open Court, La Salle, IL, 1942). This work, which originally appeared in 1883, will hereafter be abbreviated *SM*.

cation are rendered possible; and on the other, when a person has acquired the skill of recognizing those permanent elements throughout the greatest range of phenomena, of seeing in them the same, this ability leads to a *comprehensive, compact, consistent and facile conception of the facts.* When we have reached the point where we are able to detect the *same* few simple elements, combining in the ordinary manner, then they appear to us as things that are familiar; we are no longer surprised, there is nothing new or strange in the phenomena. We feel at home with them, they no longer perplex us, they are *explained*.[6]

This passage highlights two fundamental facets of Mach's philosophy of science. The first is the familiar Galilean method of reduction and composition; when we are faced with a multitude of seemingly different phenomena, we show that they can be construed as a few elements combined in various ways.[7] This involves both specifying the simple elements (which Mach apparently takes to be relatively few in number) as well as the various modes of combination. When confronted with novel phenomena, such a method allows us to see the new as a variation on the familiar.

But on the other hand, when we have reduced a given phenomenon to its elements, and specified the rules of combination, we have done all that is "objectively" possible. The second major theme of the passage presents *familiarity* as the characteristic sign of explanation. Mach's Galilean analysis reduces the unexpected to the familiar, and a given theory will be evaluated in terms of its ability to predict future combinations. Thus the criterion for explanatory success is fundamentally *psychological;* an event is explained if we are not surprised by its occurrence.[8] The fruits of

---

[6] *Ibid.*, p. 7. This psychological analysis of explanation has, as we shall see, very crucial connections with Mach's phenomenalistic epistemology, and may well be presupposed by it; compare this passage with *AS*, ch. I.

Compare with Comte: "Comte's 'positivism', his thesis that all knowledge consists in a description of the coexistence and succession of phenomena, was already familiar to Mill ... the novelty lay in Comte's historical hypothesis that positivism is the last stage in the development of inquiry ... In the theological stage ... men explain phenomena by referring them to the arbitrary actions of spiritual beings; in the metaphysical stage, they substitute 'powers' or 'faculties' or 'essences' for spirits; only in the third, positive stage do they come to see that to 'explain' is simply to describe the relations holding between phenomena." John Passmore, *op. cit.*, p. 16.

[7] For instance, the motion of a cannonball can be seen as simple horizontal rectilinear motion combined with familiar acceleration due to gravity. The method has philosophical as well as scientific applicability; cf. Hume's *Treatise* I/i/1, and the analysis of causation in I/iii, and "Socrates' dream," *Theatetus* 201d ff.

[8] If a theory lacks predictions with respect to future novel combinations, then we have no grounds for accepting or rejecting the alleged theory, and it is for us empty. This element connects Mach with the positivist movement; one Viennese splinter group styled itself the "Ernst Mach Verein."

science are thus quite limited. We can "explain" an event only to the extent of anticipating its occurrence by combining familiar elements according to a rule, but why the event happens, the knowledge which human nature urges us towards, we cannot explain. Nothing further can be expected.[9] Mach offers a startling and fascinating observation, reminiscent of the pessimism of the preface to the *Tractatus:*

> Let it be remarked in conclusion, that the principle of virtual displacements, like every general principle, brings with it, by the insight which it furnishes, *disillusionment* as well as elucidation. It brings with it disillusionment to the extent that we recognize in it facts which were long before known and even instinctively perceived ... and elucidation allows us to see everywhere through the most complicated relations to the same simple facts.[10]

Granted that the sign of successful explanation is predictive power, how is such prediction to be facilitated? Via *general laws*, which structurally relate certain classes of phenomena to simpler ones. This claim is uncontroversial, but Mach's further characterization of such laws is debatable. Laws, he holds, are nothing but *generalizations on experience*, gained by abstracting from experiences of a certain sort those features which do not interest us. The principle of the parallelogram of forces, for instance, "clearly discloses itself as a proposition derived from experience." (*SM*, p. 50) Doubt as to whether "derived from experience" means something more complex than "generalized" are immediately put to rest: "The principle [of the parallelogram of forces] is *just as much an observation as any other.*" (*Ibid.*, my emphasis)

Being mere generalizations on experience characterizes not only such low-level laws; it is the essence of a scientific law. The role of natural law is to provide, via abstraction, a compact and portable survey of our past experiences, as concise and compressed as possible. Science as an institution thus grows in so far as it represents the constantly expanding chronicle of human experiences.[11]

---

[9] Compare with *Treatise* I/i/1.

[10] *SM*, p. 88. Compare with further remarks on "disillusionment" on pp. 40–41. "Instinctively perceive" echoes a Machian technical term, "Instinctive experience"—half-forgotten but familiar experiences sometimes mistaken for a priori knowledge.

[11] *Ibid.*, pp. 103–4. Such a view carries with it the methodological principle that rationally acceptable theories must be consistent with those currently held; cf. T. S. Kuhn, *The Structure of Scientific Revolutions* (U. of Chicago Press, Chicago, 1962), Ch. 9.

But science cannot be a mere catalogue of *personal* experience: it must chronicle the public. Thus we first abstract from our experiences all elements of idiosyncrasy. But we also ignore those elements which are of no interest *to us*, and so even mechanics is to an extent anthropocentric.[12] Mach constantly emphasizes this pragmatic element in the process of abstraction that leads to science:

> A rule, reached by the observation of facts, cannot possibly embrace the entire fact. In all its manifold wealth, in all its inexhaustible manifoldness: on the contrary, it can furnish only a rough *outline* of the fact, one-sidedly emphasizing the feature that is of importance for the technical (or scientific) aim in question.[13]

> This [conceptual formation of a law] is effected by isolating and emphasizing what is deemed of importance, by neglecting what is subsidiary, by *abstracting*, by idealizing. (*SM*, p. 161)

Since laws represent abstract generalizations of experience, the peculiar talent of the successful scientist lies in his ability to ignore certain aspects of experiences; Mach offers as examples Huygens (*SM*, p. 212) and Galileo (*SM*, pp. 17, 26–27).[14] In addition to the ability to abstract, the other laudable characteristic of the scientist is *hardheadedness*. The symptom of hardheadedness is concentration on the "actual facts," an expression with myriad emphatic occurrences in *SM*. For instance,

---

Compare: "... I am not going to tell you my name ... For one thing, it would take a very long, long time; my name is growing all the time ... my name is like a story. Real names tell you the story of the things they belong to in my language ..." Treebeard the Ent in J. R. R. Tolkien, *Lord of the Rings*, bk III, ch. 4. Note the diametrical opposition to Wittgenstein's conception of a name in Treebeard's emphasis on the history of a name, a relic of psychologism. Compare also with *PI*, #79, 87.

[12] "Even *Mathematics, Natural Philosophy and Natural Religion*, are in some sense dependent on the science of Man ..." Hume, *Treatise*, p. xv.

[13] *SM*, p. 90. Compare with Schopenhauer's parallel theory of concept-formation by abstraction, with its emphasis on the inferiority of concepts to intuitions. This inferiority plays a central role in Schopenhauer's arguments for the metaphysical ascendency of art over science. Note also that Mach's empiricism leads him to treat concepts on the model of eyesight. No concept cannot adequately represent, say, a cat, just as we cannot see the "whole cat" at any one time, but just one side or aspect of the cat.

[14] Mach's views here are to be contrasted with the quite different picture of scientific creativity offered by Arthur Koestler in *The Sleepwalkers* (Grosset and Dunlap, New York, 1963), Epilogue.

> Galileo did not supply us with a *theory* of falling bodies, but investigated and established, wholly without preformed opinions, the *actual facts* of falling.[15]

Likewise, Newton "begins with the *fact* of universal gravitation" (*ibid.* p. 233) and "... is not concerned with the causes of the phenomenon, but has simply to do with the investigation and transformation of *actual facts.*" (*Ibid.*, p. 326, contrast p. 280). These examples could be easily multiplied.

The laws of mechanics thus represent merely abstract general compilations of past experience, and their role is wholly pragmatic. Were it that human beings had greater capacity for discursive memory, laws could in principle be disposed of.[16] As generalizations on experience, they are innocent of any hint of the a priori. Mach is willing to extend this empiricist analysis even to such fundamental principles as that of the transitivity of equality of mass:

> No *logical* necessity exists whatever, that masses equal to a third mass should also be equal to each other. (*Ibid.*, p. 268)

So far we have seen a certain overlap between Mach's views and those of Schopenhauer; in particular, Schopenhauer agrees that fundamental etiological principles allow of no further *scientific* grounding. But he also holds such laws to be meaningless until buttressed by a philosophical or metaphysical analysis of their grounds, and this additional step Mach vehemently rejects. In the context of a critique of classical mechanics, he argues that whatever problems infect Newton's formulation of physics are due to a lack of "epistemological critique" on his part (*SM*, pp. 339–40). What constitutes such a critique? As a youth Mach read a copy of Kant's *Prologomena* which he had found in his father's library, and became convinced that there is no need to employ the notion of a thing-in-itself as opposed to a phenomenon.[17] The world, he became convinced, could be dealt with *en toto* in terms of its elements, which

---

[15] *SM*, p. 167. For Galileo's experiments, cf. Holton and Roller, *Foundations of Modern Physical Science* (Addison-Wesley, Reading, MA, 1958), pp. 18–25. Mach's claim about Galileo being "without preformed opinions" is dubious; cf. P. K. Feyerabend *Against Method* (Verso, London, 1975), chs. 6–13; with respect to a figure like Kepler it is ludicrous; cf. T. S. Kuhn, *The Copernican Revolution*, chs. 4–5.

[16] For an imaginative rendering of such an individual, see J. L. Borges, "Funes the Memorious," in *Ficciones*, trans. A. Kerrington (Grove Press, New York, 1962), pp. 107–16.

[17] *AS*, p. 30. For Kant's defense of the validity of the concept of a noumenon, see *CPR*, pp. 257–75.

he takes to be *sensations.*[18] Since concepts are merely abstract representations of sensations or clusters of sensations, the realm of thought is restricted wholly to sensations and constructs on sensations:

> The assertion, then, is correct that the world consists only of our sensations. In which case we have knowledge *only* of sensations …[19]

Any justified claim that we make is therefore about sensations or relations among sensations.

But it follows that the only possible goal of science—or for that matter *any* human enterprise which aims at truth—is to find the connections between elementary sensations and to represent them in the most useful and economical manner possible (cf. *AS*, p. 22). The first step is the aforementioned abstraction of uninteresting properties. The second step involves inductive projection of whatever regularities then appear, in accord with what Mach calls the "principle of continuity":

> When the inquiring intellect has formed, through adaptation, the habit of connecting two things, *A* and *B*, in thought, it tries to retain this habit as far as possible, even when the circumstances are slightly altered. Whenever *A* appears *B* is added in thought. The principle thus expressed, which has its root in an effort for economy, and is particularly noticeable in the world of the great investigators, may be termed the *"principle of continuity."*[20]

But at this point Mach makes a radical move. Once we have arrived, via the principle of continuity, at general statements which express regularities among sensations, *there is no further work left for the*

---

[18] So far as I know, Mach makes no attempt to say explicitly what he means by 'sensation'; in the context of the opening passages of *AS* it is introduced as a substantive correlate to the verb 'to sense' and its cognates. (pp. 1–2) Mach claims that "my starting point is not essentially different from Hume's …" (*AS*, p. 46), and thus we might consult Hume's introduction of the term 'perception' in *Treatise* I/i/1.

[19] Note that Mach's claim is *not* one frequently criticized in the history of philosophy, namely that from "All knowledge comes through the senses" it follows that "All I can know are my own sensations, etc." (Cf. for instance Moore, "A Refutation of Idealism," in his *Philosophical Studies*, pp. 1–30.) His claim is rather this: to know something means (at least) to have a representation which corresponds with the world. Since the world is nothing but sensation, it follows that the only possible object of knowledge is a sensation.

[20] *Ibid.*, compare with p. 168. The parallel with Hume's theory of belief is obvious, and the *Treatise* may well be the source of Mach's principle; cf. I/i/4 and I/ii/7–12. Interestingly, Mach exhibits no interest in the "unphilosophical probabilities" of I/ii/13, inferences and beliefs which, although arising from the same source, lead to undesirable results.

scientist, or, for that matter, for *any* human investigator who makes truth-claims. In particular, we must scrupulously avoid the temptation to posit a world of objects different from sensations which underlie those sensations, and thus some metaphysical underpinning for the observed regularities.[21] This constitutes the "epistemological critique" which Mach demands. The strictly limited role it leaves for science presumably leads to the "disillusionment" of which he speaks.

It is thus impossible to offer any account of the source of the regularities found among our sensations. But what, then, accounts for the nearly universal tendency, found not only in philosophers but in the common man as well, to postulate the existence of a trans-sensational realm? Nothing more than a propensity to extend modes of speech appropriate to *certain cases* into a universal mode of speech:

> It has easily become a disturbing element in unprejudiced scientific theorizing when a conception which is adopted to a particular and strictly limited purpose is promoted to be the foundation of *all* investigation. This happens, for instance, when all experiences are regarded as "effects" of an external world extending into consciousness. This conception gives us a tangle of metaphysical difficulties which it seems impossible to unravel. But the specter vanishes at once when we look at the matter as it were in a mathematical light, and make it clear to ourselves that all that is valuable to us is the discovery of *functional relations*, and that what we want to know is merely the dependence of experiences on one another. It then becomes obvious that the reference to the unknown fundamental variables which are not given (things in themselves) is purely fictitious and superfluous.[22]

Certain groups of sensations stand in relation to one another in such a way that we speak of one *causing* another. Thus, we say that fire *causes* heat. But we must remember that causation so defined is a relation *between sensations*. It is tempting to ask "What causes sensations *in general?*" but this is an illegitimate extension of the notion of cause. Note the interesting parallel with—perhaps the

---

[21] "Bodies do not *produce* sensations, but complexes of elements (complexes of sensations) make up bodies." *AS*, p. 29. Compare with *Treatise* I/iv/2 and (only for example) A. J. Ayer, *Foundations of Empirical Knowledge* (London, 1940), pp. 265 ff.

[22] *AS*, pp. 34–35. Note that Mach speaks here as if reference to things other than sensations is not impossible but irrelevant, as well as his tendency to conflate things in themselves with phenomena.

influence of—Schopenhauer's thesis that the notion of cause has only phenomenal applicability; the will, he insists, *cannot be a cause.*

We can now lay out the three central theses of Mach's philosophy of science, which together stand in stark contrast with Hertz's. Mach's *Grundgedanken* is that the elements of the world as known by us are without exception sensations or patterns of sensations. Our knowledge is thus *in principle* restricted to representation and prediction of these sensations and their patterns. From this fundamental claim two important subsidiary theses follow. First, the goal of science is the analysis of patterns of sensation into the elements of which they are formed, and the provision of an economical and pragmatically useful representation of these combinations. Second, the laws of nature represent merely abstract generalizations from experience, and their sole purpose, *as well as their sole capability*, is to support prediction by providing the aforementioned concise representations.

Mach's claims mark sharp divergence from the Schopenhauerian model of science. Schopenhauer agrees that the discovery and articulation of etiological regularities is the goal of *scientific* investigation, and he likewise agrees with Mach that such regularities, as they stand, yield little save mystification. But while Mach's empiricism makes him more willing to accept the disillusionment which follows from accepting such regularities as primitive, Schopenhauer offers for them a metaphysical grounding in the nature of the world as will. But let us leave both Mach and Schopenhauer in limbo for a while, and turn to Hertz's philosophy of science, which we shall see as an attempt to speak to both. More particularly, we shall see the grounds for both Wittgenstein's equivocal attitude towards science, and the rejection of one aspect of the world as will.

Hertz and the Principles of Mechanics

> What a Copernicus or a Darwin really achieved was not
> the discovery of a true theory but of a fertile new
> point of view.
>
> —WITTGENSTEIN, 1931

Hertz opens *PrMe* with a very general claim about one goal of science as a human intellectual enterprise:

> The most direct, and in a sense the most important, problem which our
> conscious knowledge of nature should enable us to solve is the anticipation
> of future events, so that we may arrange our present affairs in accordance
> with such anticipation. (p. l)

At first blush this seems quite in accord with Mach's position; the
goal of science is to allow us to predict. But it is important that Hertz
does not represent prediction as *the* problem of science, merely the
most "direct" and further "only in a sense" the most important. This
hints at a divergence from Mach which, as we shall see, will provide
considerable insight into Wittgenstein's treatment of the principles of
mechanics.

Hertz takes over from Kant the Cartesian starting-point which
characterizes much of classical modern philosophy; all that we are
ever aware of directly are *representations*, mental entities of some
sort.[23] However, we can deal indirectly with things other than
representations by constructing for ourselves mental images or
pictures, which we then treat as proxies for things as they exist
independently of us. "The images of which we speak," Hertz writes,
"are our conceptions of things." (*Ibid.*) But clearly what scientists
seek are not merely any arbitrary images of things, but rather images
with a claim to *truth*. In order to pick out those images most likely
to be true, we require of them satisfaction of several general
standards, the primary one being:

> ... the form which we give to [our images] is such that the necessary
> consequences of the images in thought are always the images of the
> necessary consequences of the things pictured. *(Ibid.)*

This general requirement is obviously inapplicable as it stands, since
we cannot directly compare either our *image* of a thing or the
consequences of that image with the thing itself. Hertz thus replaces
this simple and general requirement with three less general but
applicable requirements, which do not depend on direct comparison
of image and thing. These requirements jointly serve as methodological criteria governing our choice of images or models.

---

[23] Hertz never explicitly commits himself to this point, but his theory of dynamical models would
be pointless without it. Further, his neo-Kantianism would probably make it go without saying. It
is important to distinguish this claim from the Machian thesis that our experience is entirely of
sensations, since for a Kantian every experience has some non-sensory element.

First we require that our model be *logically possible*, a
requirement which is not as straightforward as it seems on first
blush. It is tempting to interpret Hertz as demanding that our images
not be literally *self-contradictory*, but the requirement thus construed becomes empty, since we cannot indicate what a self-
contradictory image might be. Hertz's own attempt at clarification
yields little elucidation: "We should at once denote as inadmissible
all our images which implicitly contradict *the laws of our thought."*
(*Ibid.*, p. 2, my emphasis) The expression "laws of our thought" is
ambiguous, meaning either the principles of pure general logic, e.g.
the law of contradiction, Kantian transcendental principles (universal and necessary conditions on consciousness), or empirical
psychological laws. For reasons I will soon set forth, I take Hertz to
mean a combination of the first and second. Images which meet this
condition are termed *permissible*.

The second demand bears a close relation to the original
general condition, demanding that the relations of the image-
elements mirror the relations of elements in actuality. We have noted
the impossibility of directly comparing the model with reality; if we
could, the model would be rendered superfluous. The mark of
correspondence will thus be efficacy in predicting future occurrences of representations. Any model which (so far) meets this
condition will be provisionally labeled *correct*, those which do not
incorrect.

However, an array of quite different models, all purporting to
represent the same reality, can be both permissible and correct. How
do we decide between acceptable competing models? Given two
competing models, equally correct and permissible, Hertz terms one
more *appropriate* if it includes, "in addition to the essential
characteristics, the smaller number of superfluous or empty relations—the simpler of the two." (*Ibid.*, p. 2) If two models "work"
equally well, Hertz urges an Ockhamistic preference for the simpler.

In summary, any models which we form to represent the world
outside our representations must be evaluated with respect to three
criteria: permissibility, correctness, and appropriateness. Put in
non-Hertzian terms, our theoretical systems must be logically
coherent, empirically satisfactory, and the simplest available. It is
difficult to quarrel with such criteria for theory-acceptance, and thus
what Hertz has offered so far is neither terribly original nor terribly
controversial. However, Hertz immediately qualifies the character-

ization of appropriateness with a remark which prefaces a discussion of central importance.

> Empty relations cannot be altogether avoided; they enter into the images because they are simply images—images produced by our mind and *necessarily affected by its mode of portrayal.* (*Ibid.*, p. 2)

This recognition of the inevitable presence of extraneous relations points towards a fourth methodological condition to be placed specifically on *scientific* images—an "additional postulate," as Hertz puts it.

> We require [that we should have] a clear conception of what properties are to be ascribed to our images for the sake of permissibility, what for correctness, and what for appropriateness. (*Ibid.*)

Thus it is incumbent upon us qua scientists to be critically aware of the status of the different components of our theories.[24]

Why this additional demand? Only if scientific models meet this fourth requirement, Hertz argues, can we allow for the possibility of changing and improving our models, that is, *progress.* Of particular interest are those aspects of our theories which we attribute to objects for the sake of appropriateness, since these elements are "contained in the notation, definitions, and abbreviations and, in short, in all that we can arbitrarily add or take away." (*Ibid.*, p. 3) Thus what is associated with satisfaction of the appropriateness condition is always to a certain extent *conventional,* as opposed to the a priori or empirical demands of the first two conditions. What is permissible is given by formal logic and by the transcendental demands of the human mind, what is correct is determined by the nature of the extramental world, but the often conventional demands of appropriateness are, paradoxically, frequently the source of considerable debate. Since scientific progress can be greatly retarded by useless debate over merely conventional elements of our

---

[24] The considerable work done in the last twenty-five years on the "theory-ladenness of perception" highlights both the extent to which Hertz anticipates contemporary problems in the philosophy of science, and the extent to which his distinctions need overhauling. Cf. Kuhn, *op. cit.*, ch. X, Feyerabend, *op. cit.*, pp. 55ff., and N. R. Hanson, *Patterns of Discovery* (Cambridge U. Press, Cambridge, 1969), ch. 1–2.

models,[25] we need some criterion for deciding whether or not a given element of our model is conventional. The criterion will be whether alteration of the property in question alters the correctness or appropriateness of the image.

There is obviously a trivial sense in which everything in a model is conventional, insofar as the signs which we choose are conventional. Nothing in the nature of the animal requires that we use the string 'dog' to refer to canines. But Hertz is interested in a deeper sort of conventionality, and for a philosophical reason. He believes that when we treat theories uncritically we tend to attribute reality to merely conventional elements of our model, and, since there will be no possible *empirical* evaluation of such elements, they will appear to us as *necessary elements of nature*.[26] Since the issues in question do turn on conventional elements of the respective models, disputes will be particularly difficult to settle. The upshot will be that theories which differ only conventionally will give us radically differing pictures of reality. This theme will be central to Wittgenstein's philosophy of mechanics, and thus we must look closely at such conventional elements in the principles of mechanics.

The Principles of Mechanics

The term 'principles of mechanics' allows of both strict and loose usage. In the looser sense, we often refer to any historically important proposition as a principle—Hertz offers the example of d'Alembert's Principle.[27] In a stricter sense, though, a principle is a member of the set of propositions which:

> satisfies the requirement that the whole of mechanics can be developed from it by purely deductive reasoning without any further appeal to experience. (*PrMe*, p. 4)

---

[25] Consider William James's famous discussion of the question of "whether the squirrel goes round the tree." *Pragmatism* (Hackett Publishing, Indianapolis, IN, 1981), p. 25.

[26] It is crucial to keep in mind that Hertz believes that in addition to such phoney "necessary elements of reality," there are *real* general elements of the world, including those provided by the neo-Kantian transcendental contributions of the mind.

[27] An interesting example for Hertz to pick, since d'Alembert maintained that the Cartesian-Leibnizian debate over whether kinetic energy or momentum was the "true measure" of force turned on a confusion in terminology. Cf. Halliday and Resnick, *Physics* (Wiley, New York, 1966), p. 22.

Philosophically and scientifically such principles are of cardinal interest, since they afford us "the simplest image which physics can produce of things in the sensible world and the processes which occur in it." *(Ibid.)* Such principles deal with the *primitives* of our knowledge of the physical world, and Hertz thus shares the interest in primitives which Russell and Moore took respectively in logic and ethics.[28] Hertz's task is to uncover and categorize these primitive principles, and in accordance with the "additional postulate," *PrMe* is comprised of two books. Book I deals with the a priori elements of mechanics, the neo-Kantian transcendental contributions of space and time, while book II deals with the contingent empirical component, in the form of the "fundamental law."

Within the formalization of any axiomatic system there is of course a certain amount of play. By choosing different sets of primitives, we can produce different primitive representations or models and ultimately different conceptions of the world, each of which can be tested for permissibility, correctness, and appropriateness. Hertz's goal is to establish which elements of the model are present to meet which standard, in particular which are present to meet the appropriateness condition. Bearing this in mind, let us examine Hertz's challenge to the permissibility of one historically important model or image of mechanics.

The "model" in question, which Hertz calls "the customary representation of mechanics," is that of Newton. The primitive elements of this model are space, time, force, and mass. Newton sets forth three fundamental principles expressing the functional relationships between these quantities. These three laws, together with the Universal Principle of Gravitation, are principles of mechanics in the strict sense, since from them all of classical mechanics can be derived. Jointly they thus yield a "general image of the world." It is arguable that I have overstated the primitives of Newtonian mechanics by including among them force, since the second law appears to define forces in terms of masses and accelerations, as time derivatives of displacement. However, Hertz argues that the concept of force cannot be so defined, since it "is introduced as the cause of motions, existing before motion and independently of it."[29] That is, if

---

[28] The interest in primitives was not confined to these two; cf. Jager, *op. cit.*, pp. 112–17.

[29] *PrMe*, p. 4. Compare: "Gravitation, *n.*. The tendency of all bodies to approach one another with a strength proportional to the quantity of matter they contain—the quantity of matter they

motions (or more accurately, changes of motions) are seen as the result of forces, then we must have a distinct idea of force, one independent of our concept of motion.

Such priority of force over motion in the "first image of the world," as Hertz calls Newtonian mechanics, is very important for his argument, since Hertz wants to challenge the permissibility of Newtonian mechanics by charging the concept of force with logical incoherence. It may seem odd to query the coherence of such a venerable system as Newton's, and Hertz concedes that it may be far-fetched for him to challenge such a deeply intrenched and highly successful model. Yet he adds that we are often tempted to attach to fundamental laws "certain considerations bred largely by our mode of expression," which are "a hindrance to clear thinking." Consider the following puzzle: I attach a long string to a stone, and swing the stone in circles above my head. I can *feel* my hand exerting a force, which constantly accelerates the stone by deflecting it from a rectilinear path into a closed orbit. Given the third law, there must be some other force, equal to the one my hand exerts, but opposite in sense, and this we postulate as a "centrifugal force." But this is curious: we have remarked that forces are the causes of motions, and yet this new force—the centrifugal force—is not the cause of a motion at all, but rather the *effect* of such a motion. But worse, we have already taken this force into account in terms of the inertia of the stone, a property we have connected with its mass. Have we now counted it twice, once as a force, and once as a mass? And if so, is the centrifugal force really a force *at all*, and if not, what becomes of the third law?[30]

These difficulties arise, Hertz continues, insofar as we use the word 'force' equivocally. It has a rather different meaning in the context of the first two laws than it does in the third, and it is through equivocation on these different senses that the puzzles of the preceding paragraph arise. Our puzzlement is, however, a sign of a deeper difficulty:

---

contain being ascertained by the strength of their tendency to approach one another." Ambrose Bierce, *The Devil's Dictionary*, (Stemmer House, Owen's Mills, PA, 1978), p. 91.

[30] I take Hertz to be arguing that the notion of force is *self-contradictory* when taken as a primitive. Compare with the alternative reading of J. J. C. Smart, "Heinrich Hertz and the Concept of Force," *Australasian Journal of Philosophy*, vol. 29 (1951) pp. 36–45, P. Foulkes, "The Concept of Force," *ibid.*, pp. 175–80, and Smart's reply in the next volume of the same journal, pp. 124–32.

[We frequently hear that] the nature of force is still a mystery, that one of the chief problems of physics is the investigation of the nature of force, and so on. . . . Now, why is it that people never in this way ask what is the nature of gold, or the nature of velocity? Is the nature of gold better known to us than that of electricity, or the nature of velocity better known than that of force . . . ? Certainly not. . . . I fancy that the difficulty must lie in this. With the terms 'velocity' and 'gold' we connect a large number of relations to other terms, and between these relations we find no contradictions which offend us. . . . But we have accumulated around the terms 'force' and 'electricity' more relations than can be reconciled amongst themselves. We have an obscure feeling of this and want to have things cleared up. (*PrMe*, p. 7)

This "obscure feeling" finds expression (quite wrongly) in questions about "the nature of force"; we are tempted to imagine that there must be obscure facts, hidden facets of the concept of force which we do not yet understand. This is not the case, however.

But the answer which we want is not really an answer to this question [viz., what is the nature of force?]. It is not by finding more and fresh relations and connections among things that it can be answered: but by removing contradictions between those already known, and thus perhaps by reducing their number. (*PrMe*, p. 8)

We are still faced with a difficulty. Hertz has argued that a contradiction lies at the very heart of Newtonian mechanics; we are driven to regard centrifugal forces both as forces and non-forces. However, the existence of this contradiction stands in stark contrast to a remarkable fact; classical mechanics has been extremely successful at predicting and explaining the phenomena of the physical world.[31] One is inclined to expect that to be correct an image must be *at least* permissible, but Newtonian mechanics, if Hertz is correct, is simultaneously impermissible and correct. We can, however, eliminate the air of paradox which surrounds this apparent contradiction by re-evaluating the nature of the concept of force. These contradictions:

cannot consist of contradictions between the essential characteristics of our image, nor, therefore, of contradictions between those relations of mechanics which correspond to the relations of things. They must rather lie in the

---

[31] Although even in Hertz's day not universally successful: cf. Kuhn, *op. cit.*, ch. VI, Hanson; *op. cit.*, pp. 100ff.; and Feyerabend, *op. cit.*, ch. V.

inessential characteristics which we have ourselves arbitrarily worked into the essential content given by nature. *(Ibid.)*

The difficulty thus arises through our failure to take seriously the additional requirement which bears upon scientific images:

> Perhaps our objections do not relate to the content of the image devised, but only to the form in which this content is represented. It is not going too far to say that this representation (i.e., Newtonian mechanics) has never attained scientific completeness; it still fails to distinguish thoroughly and sharply between the elements in the image which arise from the necessities of thought, from experience, and from arbitrary choice. *(Ibid.)*

Thus many of the problems which we encounter in thinking about mechanics—perhaps even the most serious and perplexing problems—are due *not* to mysterious and unknown relations between things in nature, but rather to our *mode of representation*, our language. We eliminate these problems—"show the fly the way out of the fly-bottle," as Wittgenstein later puts it—not by producing new theories or eliciting further facts, but by becoming clear whether the elements of our image are logico-transcendental, empirical, or conventional. After clarifying these roles, we may decide to replace our model with one which is logically and empirically equivalent, but less misleading. This is Hertz's project.

But of more immediate relevance to our upcoming discussion of Wittgenstein's philosophy of science is Hertz's comment on the correctness or the empirical adequacy of Newtonian mechanics. With respect to such correctness "we can pronounce judgment more easily [than its permissibility] and with greater certainty of common assent."[32] Within the whole range of our experience, Hertz maintains, the correctness of Newtonian mechanics has been vindicated. But this is of course mere inductive support, and what comes from experience may be annulled by experience: "as far as future experience is concerned, there will yet be occasion to return to the question of correctness." *(Ibid.)* Yet Hertz points out that many physicists would treat such caution as ludicrous; we cannot even conceive, they argue, of a future experience which would disconfirm

---

[32] *Ibid.*, p. 9. Contemporary philosophers, brought up on the theory of truth-functions, may find it boggling that a certain theory might be correct but of dubious permissibility, since a logically incoherent theory would entail *every* consequence. Of course for Hertz this is not immediately evident.

Newtonian mechanics.[33] What is the source of this "over-favorable opinion"? Hertz argues that such certainty:

> must obviously arise from the fact that the elements of experience are to a certain extent hidden in [the fundamental principles] and blended with the unalterable conditions which are necessary conditions of our thought. *(Ibid.)*

That is, we fail to distinguish, in accord with the additional requirement on scientific models, between the inductive support for the empirical elements of our model, and what for Hertz is the a priori certainty of the logico-transcendental elements.

Thus the two books of *PrMe:* book I deals with the kinematics of material systems, and of this book Hertz writes:

> The subject-matter of the first book is completely independent of experience. All the assertions are *a priori* judgments in Kant's sense. They are based upon the laws of the internal intuition of, and upon the logical forms followed by, the person who makes the assertions . . .[34]

Book I then proceeds to analyze the transcendentally necessary relations of space, time, and mass which represent conditions on any experience. The second book, however, concerns itself with the *dynamics* of material systems, and culminates in the statement and application of the "fundamental law" of section 306; "Every free system persists in its state of rest or motion on a straightest path."[35] Of this principle Hertz writes:

> Our statements [in book II] concerning the relations between times, spaces and masses must . . . not only satisfy the demands of thought, but also must be in accord with possible, and in particular, future experiences. These statements are based, therefore, not only on the laws of our intuition and thought, but in addition on experience. [They will be] comprised in a single general statement which we shall take for our fundamental law. *(Ibid.,* p. 139)

---

[33] Cf. Hanson, *op. cit.*, pp. 100ff.

[34] *PrMe*, p. 45. Compare with the further comments on the a priori in sections 295–96. Note Hertz's tendency to *psychologize* the transcendental conditions of experience, and compare with chapter III above.

[35] For a definition of 'system', cf. *PrMe*, ch. II, for 'straightest path', pp. 90–95.

Since the Fundamental Law is empirical, it contrasts sharply with the a priori principles of book I. The unbounded faith on the part of many physicists in Newtonian mechanics is thus based on a failure to clearly distinguish between the a priori condition that the material world be describable in terms of propositions whose variables take as their arguments magnitudes of space, time, and mass, and the Fundamental Law, which places empirical constraints on the functional relations between those variables. Faith that mechanics of a certain sort must be true is conflated with certainty that a particular system of mechanics is necessary.[36]

Finally, let us look at Hertz's notion of a *complete explanation:* this will help underline the connections and contrasts between Hertz, Schopenhauer, and Mach, and prepare us for a discussion of Wittgenstein's philosophy of science. All physical explanation, Hertz argues, is *mechanical* explanation,[37] which consists roughly of showing that a phenomenon of a given sort can be deduced from the Fundamental Law and the appropriate time-independent boundary conditions:

> we consider the fundamental problem of mechanics to be to deduce from the properties of material systems which are independent of time those phenomena which take place in time and the properties which depend on time. (*Ibid.*, sect. 308)

However, there is a broader sense of 'explanation' in which the provision of a mechanical explanation is only partial. We contrast a simple mechanical explanation with a *complete explanation*, which is accomplished by the completion of three tasks. (*PrMe*, sect. 314)

(a) The deduction of the events of the physical world in terms of the Fundamental Law and the requisite boundary conditions; that is, provision of a mechanical explanation.
(b) An explanation of the Fundamental Law.
(c) An explanation of the time-independent properties of objects which serve as the boundary conditions.

---

[36] This point in many ways parallels a certain mistaken criticism of Kant, which holds that Kant enthroned the mathematics and physics of his day as a priori. The Second Analogy, for instance, tells us merely that every event must be subsumable under *some* causal law. It does not (and cannot) stipulate any particular laws as a priori.

[37] In accordance with this claim, Hertz held a mechanical model of electromagnetism. Cf. *Electric Waves* and E. Meyerson, *Identity and Reality* (Dover, New York, 1962), ch. II.

Of these the physicist qua physicist can offer only the first, although nothing Hertz says rules out the provision of (and desirability of) some *non-physical* (non-scientific, non-mechanical) explanation of (b) and (c). Mechanical explanation, and thus scientific explanation in general, is inherently *incomplete*.

Recall that this is precisely Schopenhauer's position. Mere etiological ordering of our representations does nothing towards rendering them understandable; in fact, the causal laws produced in this way themselves stand in need of explanation. Only a metaphysical grounding of these laws gives them any real explanatory power. Also remember that the source of Mach's "disillusionment" was his inability to even *conceive of the possibility* of precisely this sort of explanation. Mach, unable to advance beyond sensations but also apparently unable to accept the Hempelian claim that explanation *simply is* the production of such regularities, sees man's inability to produce such explanations as a discouraging general limitation on human knowledge. Although Hertz stops short of Schopenhauer's claim that (a) above is meaningless without (b) and (c), there seems to be implied sympathy with such a claim.

In addition to this incompleteness, the second limitation on mechanical explanation considers the possibility of motions of physical bodies not subsumable under the fundamental law. Thus there is a possible "third class" of bodies (other than those which we can subsume under the law, and those which we are confident we can so subsume in the future), a class comprised of:

> those systems whose motions cannot be represented directly as necessary consequences of the law .... Amongst these are included, for instance, all systems which contain organic or living beings. (*Ibid.*, sect. 318)

With respect to those systems which *are* subsumable under the Fundamental Law, he writes:

> One can scarcely help denoting such a material system as an inanimate or lifeless one. If we were to extend the law to the whole of nature, as the most general free system, and to say—"the whole of nature pursues with uniform velocity the straightest free path"—we would offend against a feeling which is sound and natural. It is therefore prudent to limit the probable validity of the law to inanimate systems. (*Ibid.*, sect. 320)

This limitation on the Fundamental Law differs from the first limitation in being a posteriori, rendered probable only through our experiences with putatively non-mechanical systems.

We can now summarize the salient features of Hertz's philosophy of science. The models which scientists construct—and thus the principles of mechanics—contain elements of two radically different sorts. The first is a priori and contains three subclasses; the demands of pure logic, the transcendental conditions for experience in general, and certain purely conventional elements which, since they cannot be contradicted by experience, are also a priori. The second class contains the empirical elements of our picture of the world. The two classes are intricately interwoven, but it is incumbent on the scientist to recognize the contribution of each to the principles of mechanics. The scientist must of course avoid conflating the a priori with the empirical, but more importantly must clearly distinguish the conventional elements of scientific models from those which are either a priori or empirical. Although Hertz concurs with Mach that the goal of scientific explanation is the provision of accurate and pragmatically useful generalizations, he denies that laws are merely shorthand abstract generalizations on experience, and that the elements of the world can be reduced to sensations. Further opposed to Mach, he holds that investigation of the principles of mechanics can offer useful insights into the transcendental structure of the phenomenal world, and seems sympathetic towards the Schopenhauerian notion that the Fundamental Law needs further (non-scientific) support in the form of a metaphysical explanation, which would illuminate the significance of the principles of mechanics. It is against the background of these claims that we will now turn to Wittgenstein's philosophy of science.

Wittgenstein's Philosophy of Science

We can only foresee what we ourselves construct.

—*Notebooks* 15.5.16

We can stipulate only something that we ourselves do. We can only postulate the rules according to which we propose to speak We cannot postulate states of affairs.

—Wittgenstein, 1920

The thesis of extensionality, mirroring as it does the world as a contingent aggregate of facts, stands at the heart of Wittgenstein's logico-semantic theory. However, there are several ostensible counterexamples to that thesis, each of which, interestingly, constitutes a class of propositions to which Schopenhauer points as evidence for his thesis of the world as will. The first of these—propositions which appear to be about the self—we will examine in the following two chapters. But of equal importance are the principles of mechanics, the most general propositions of physics.

One salient property of such principles is their appearance of necessity. Schopenhauer took this apparent necessity to be explicable only if laws represent a phenomenal fracturing of a noumenally unified species, as multiple representations of the primordial will at some particular level of objectification. The existence of etiological regularities is a powerful argument for extending the dual nature of being as representation and will, which we immediately intuit in our own case, to the world as a whole. As a very general example—one which we shall soon see Wittgenstein's attention directed toward— the principle of induction for Schopenhauer has a very firm metaphysical ground. Since the plurality of a species is merely phenomenal, an appreciation of the underlying unity of the Platonic Idea offers sufficient grounds for generalizing from the properties of one member of a class to the rest. It therefore makes a real claim about the underlying reality of the world. *If* the principles of mechanics are significant propositions—if they say something about the world, if they have senses—then the regularities which they represent seem to stand in need of explanation, and Schopenhauer's universal voluntarism gains plausibility.

Schopenhauer's view that physical laws display or disclose a deeper and more philosophically important reality—one with a close connection to ethics —is unacceptable to Wittgenstein. Many of his reasons center on the firm and inviolable line he wishes to draw between matters of fact and values (e.g. 6.432–6.44). The connection between a discussion of science and the nature of value is by no means evident to the casual reader of the *Tractatus*, but the connections are real and run very deep.[38] At 6.371 he writes:

---

[38] But it is important to remember that for Wittgenstein ethics has a decided connection with aesthetics, both of which are interpreted realistically. Carl Schorske writes "The traditional culture of the Austrian aristocracy was far removed from the puritanical culture of both bourgeois and Jew. Profoundly catholic, it was a sensuous, plastic culture. Where traditional bourgeois

> The whole modern conception of the world is founded on the illusion that the so-called laws of nature are the explanations of natural phenomena.

Immediately following is this striking passage:

> Thus people today stop at the laws of nature, treating them as something inviolable, just as God and Fate were treated in past ages.

> And in fact both are right and wrong: though the view of the ancients is clearer in so far as they have a clear and acknowledged terminus, while the modern system tries to make it look as if *everything* were explained.[39]

This remark, with its characteristic denigration of the philosophical importance of science, is a comment on 6.37 (the only necessity is *logical* necessity). It is immediately followed by "The world is independent of my will" (6.373), reintroducing the characteristic Schopenhauerian notion of will.[40]

As we shall see in the following chapters, such independence of the world from my will is very significant for Wittgenstein. Since there are no *logical* connections between "I will that e" and "e," there can be no philosophically important sense in which my will *causes* anything to happen. Since Wittgenstein, with the German philosophical tradition, connects value with the *willing* subject, 6.373 effectively eliminates the world as a possible locus of value. Significantly, the parallel passage in the *Notebooks* precedes the remark "What do I know about God and the purpose of the world?," followed by a list of claims about value, the self, the will, meaning, and so forth. (*NB*, pp. 72–73) If scientific laws expressed real connections between things, this central thesis of the impotence of the will would be undermined. But Wittgenstein's analysis of

culture saw nature as a sphere to be mastered by imposing order under divine law, the Austrian aristocrat viewed nature as a scene of joy, a manifestation of divine grace to be glorified. Traditional Austrian culture was not, like that of the German north, moral, philosophical and scientific, but primarily aesthetic." Schorske *op. cit.*, p. 7.

[39] 6.372. Wittgenstein later characterized his thought as "100% Hebraic." He has in mind, I think, the Old Testament conception of a God who acts in inexplicable and unpredictable ways, and whose commands were correct *because he made them.* This is superior to any attempt to give morality a rational grounding. On the appropriateness of calling such an attitude 'Hebraic', cf. R. Bultmann, *Primitive Christianity* (World Publishing, New York, 1956), chs.1–3.

[40] Note the startling occurrence of the personal pronoun 'my'. At this point Wittgenstein introduces the pseudo-concept "my world" and with it the Schopenhauerian world as will in new guise. But this is another story.

science, rectifies this; since matters of value are not *in* the world (cf. 6.432), science brings us, as it were, not one step closer to God.[41]

But if Wittgenstein rejects Schopenhauer's analysis of natural laws, and with it the view that the world is through and through will, neither Mach's empiricism nor Hertz's neo-Kantianism is consistent with his needs, although it is clear that he finds the latter pregnant. Let us examine the difficulties he envisions in the analyses of Mach and Hertz, and the special problems which his own semantic theory provides.

Wittgenstein's elaborate numerical system for organizing Tractarian remarks, which he later denigrated as "funny" (humorous), in fact often give us considerable insight into connections he intended between particular Tractarian discussions. His analysis of the principles of mechanics is presented at 6.3ff. By the numbering system these remarks are comments on the thesis presented at 6, that the general form of a proposition is the same as the general form of a truth-function, and that all propositions are truth-functions of elementary propositions, and more immediately on 6.3:

> The exploration of logic means the exploration of *everything that is subject to law*. And outside logic everything is accidental.

The only necessity is *logical* necessity, and all logical propositions are tautologies. Yet it is a commonplace since Hume that causal claims are *not* tautologous: every actual causal claim, as well as the general causal principle, is synthetic.[42] Thus, there is no "logical" causal principle or, as Wittgenstein rather misleadingly puts it, "Belief in the causal nexus is superstition."[43] But if the principles of mechanics are not tautologies, there seem to be two options; they are either synthetic a priori propositions, transcendental conditions on human experience (Hertz, Schopenhauer) or condensed lists, logically contingent, of otherwise inexplicable past regularities (Mach).

Mach's view apparently never held much attraction for Wittgenstein. Mach's historical exegeses apart, such principles hardly seem

---

[41] Since all we can say concerns the existence or non-existence of states of affairs—the world (1–1.21)—it follows too that anything concerning value transcends language (6.421).

[42] Cf. *Treatise* I/iii/3. Compare with Kant, *CPR*, B14–19.

[43] 6.373. This passage is certainly misleading insofar as the pragmatic canons of rationality dictate that we make causal judgments. Compare with *Treatise* I/iii/8 ("unphilosophical probabilities") and *PI*, #466, 469.

to arise through mere tabulation of long experience (in fact, given Wittgenstein's realism, the historical grounds for a belief would be irrelevant anyway); as he points out at 6.3211:

> Indeed people even surmised that there must be *a* 'law of least action' before they knew exactly how it went. (Here, as always, what is certain *a priori* proves to be something purely logical.)

But lists lack precisely that property which makes scientific laws valuable; in discussions with Waismann and Schlick during 1929– 1930 Wittgenstein argues against the view that laws are pragmatically valuable substitutes for long lists of experiences:[44]

> A law is not another method of giving what a list gives .... People always pretend that the one is an indirect method of doing the other. I could supply a list: but as this is too complicated or beyond my powers, I will supply a law. This sounds like saying, Up until now I have been talking to you, when I am in England I shall have to write. (*Ibid.*, p. 103)

This point appears to allow, contra Mach, for something other than a merely psychological basis for predictive power of physics:

> *Physics is not history.* It prophesies. If you tried to conceive of physics merely as a report of the facts observed to date, it would be lacking its most essential element, its relation to the future.[45]

Such predictive power additionally underlines the non-tautological nature of mechanical principles; in a roughly contemporary passage Wittgenstein criticizes on the same grounds what he believes to be Poincaré's view that hypotheses are *definitions*. (*WVC*, p. 21)

On the other hand, Hertz's Neo-Kantian Transcendental Idealism held no appeal for Wittgenstein. A weak interpretation of the

---

[44] These discussions, taken from L. Wittgenstein, *Ludwig Wittgenstein and the Vienna Circle*, recorded by F. Waismann (Barnes and Noble, New York, 1979) (hereafter *WVC*), I take to be of a piece with the Tractarian views. It is, however, important to keep in mind that by 1929 Wittgenstein no longer took all inference to be tautological: cf. for instance p. 64. However, he still maintains that the nature of a proposition is to picture (p. 90), and there is no evidence that he had rejected the claim that no picture can be a priori. Thus, no necessary proposition can be significant.

[45] *Ibid.*, p. 101. Compare: "One of the most important things about an explanation in Physics is that it should work, that it would enable us to predict something. Physics is connected with engineering. The bridge must not fall down." L. Wittgenstein, *Lectures and Conversations on Aesthetics, Psychology and Religious Belief*, ed. C. Barrett (U. of California Press, Berkeley and Los Angeles, 1972), p. 25.

transcendentalists' claim that such apparently a priori laws represent principles inherent in the human mind and constitutive of human experience reduces logic to psychology, and as we saw in chapter III, for Wittgenstein any psychological intrusion into logic is anathema. Stronger interpretations of Transcendental Idealism, of the sort to which Hertz and Schopenhauer appeal, he rejects on the grounds of a complex, subtle, and extremely important set of arguments, which we shall investigate in chapter VIII. Hertz's claim that the principles of mechanics represent at least in part the result of transcendental conditions on experience thus holds little promise for Wittgenstein.[46]

Scientific laws, and the principles of mechanics as paradigm examples of such laws, thus present Wittgenstein with a dilemma. They are not mere summaries of experiences, or in fact general empirical propositions of *any* sort (Mach), yet they cannot profitably be regarded as transcendental principles either (Hertz, Schopenhauer). They certainly differ from logical propositions, since the latter are tautologies and thus say nothing about the world. And they also differ from mathematical propositions, which are analytic; Wittgenstein takes particular pains to contrast natural laws with mathematical propositions (6.342, *NB*, pp. 66–67). Thus the principles of mechanics do not fit very comfortably into any of the standard categories provided by Wittgenstein's theory of meaning.

Wittgenstein's solution to the dilemma turns on Hertz's distinction between the empirical, transcendental, and conventional contributions to mechanical models. Since Wittgenstein rejects the transcendental element, what remains is a form of conventionalism, reminiscent of Poincaré, Duhem, and the early Quine, and probably more familiar to modern readers than it was in 1922.[47] Roughly put, the principles of mechanics represent the "forms of laws," freely chosen rules which stipulate canonical form for propositions which will be considered mechanical. Since they are stipulations about the

---

[46] Carnap seems to have taken this to imply that Wittgenstein rejected the significance of laws *en toto*. "... we shall differentiate between limitedly universal sentences, analytic unlimitedly universal sentences and synthetic unlimitedly universal sentences, whereas Wittgenstein ... exclude[s] sentences of the third kind (laws of nature) from language altogether, as not being amenable to complete verification." *The Logical Syntax of Language*, trans. A. Smeaton (Littlefield, Adams and Co., Paterson, NJ, 1959), pp. 51–52. If Wittgenstein *were* to reject the significance of laws, it would certainly not be on the basis of questions of verification.

[47] Whether any of the mentioned authors influenced Wittgenstein is difficult to ascertain. Neither Poincaré nor Duhem, for instance, appear on Father Hallett's list of "authors Wittgenstein knew or read." (*op. cit.*, pp. 759–75) There is a passing reference to Poincaré in *WVC*, but its vagueness hints at secondhand knowledge of Poincaré's work.

forms of propositions, they are not themselves significant propositions, nor are they tautologies. On the other hand, that all of the
phenomena which we choose to class as physical can be represented
in propositions of a given form is by no means *guaranteed*. Thus the
principles, while conventional, are certainly not *arbitrary;* that the
world can be described in such and such a manner is due to certain
contingent features of the world, and thus the principles show, in a
manner, certain general features of reality. We must now fill out this
sketch.

As very general examples of the "forms of laws" of which he will
speak, Wittgenstein offers the "law of causality,"[48] the more general
Principle of Sufficient Reason (6.34, 6.35), "laws of continuity in
nature" (6.34), and the Principle of Least Action (6.3211), Hertz's
"Fundamental Law" being an example of the last of these. Wittgenstein suggests that all of the general principles mentioned above are
"*a priori* insights about the forms into which the propositions of
science can be cast" (6.34). The suggestion is less than wholly
transparent; let us try to unpack these claims somewhat.

Consider the very general example of the law of induction,
noting how this treatment meshes with the dual claims that (a)
outside of logic there is no necessity (6.3) and (b) logical propositions are *Sinnlos*, that is, picture no facts in the world (4.461, 4.462).
Schopenhauer, we recall, explains the existence of lawlike regularities through the unity of the Platonic Idea underlying the phenomenal plurality, and the principle of induction finds its metaphysical
ground in this noumenal unity. But at 6.31 Wittgenstein points out
that the "Law of Induction"—it is not wholly clear what he means by
that rather nebulous description—is obviously a proposition with a
sense. What he means, I think, is that any principle which canonized
inference from past regularities to general laws could clearly be
shown to be false; it is of course quite possible that the world will be
much different in the future than it is now. Thus any inductive
principle contrasts starkly with real logical laws, which, since they
say nothing about the world, cannot possibly be false.

On the surface this seems to conflict with 6.363, where
Wittgenstein writes "The procedure of induction consists in accept-

---

[48] 6.32. He does not stipulate what he means by this expression, but we might take Schopenhauer's
version: "If a new state of one or several real objects appears, another state must have preceded
it upon which the new state follows regularly ...." (*FRSR*, p. 53) Compare with Kant, *CPR*,
B232–33.

ing the *simplest* law that can be reconciled with our experiences." On that view, the inductive principle would appear to be a methodological suggestion, not amenable to truth and falsity, and thus a priori after all. But I think that the contradiction is only apparent. In 6.31 he is clearly referring to some inductive principle which is seen as having metaphysical roots. In the later passage he is explaining the *actual use* of induction in science. The two are clearly not the same.

What does this tell us about the Principle of Induction, with its projection of lawlike regularities? At the very least, it stipulates that we speak of the world in such and such a manner. Wittgenstein's most concrete treatment of this matter is directed towards the example of Newtonian Mechanics, and takes the rather unsatisfactory form of an analogy.

> Let us imagine a white surface with irregular black spots on it. We then say that whatever kind of picture these make, I can always approximate it by covering the surface with a sufficiently fine square mesh, and then saying of every square whether it is black or white.[49]

We can construct the same sort of referential apparatus by stipulating an arbitrary origin, constructing Cartesian axes and metricizing those axes. We can then refer to each square via a unique ordered pair of numbers, which would represent, say, the lower right hand corner of the square; for instance, one square might be $(3, 7)$, another $(0, -4)$. I then stipulate whether the "squares" named by these coordinates are white or black, and "propositions" in this language would have the form $(3, 7, B)$, meaning that the square $(3, 7)$ was black. Since the whole surface can be described with such "propositions," we have achieved the "unified form" of which Wittgenstein speaks.

Note several salient points concerning this analogy. That the world is the way it is—that certain parts of the plane are black and others white—is wholly independent of our choice and use of a grid system. This will be reflected in the truth or falsity of particular propositions about the world; these propositions are pictures of facts and like all pictures, cannot be decided a priori (2.225). On the other hand, the properties of the grid are purely geometric (cf. *NB*, p. 38),

---

[49] 6.341. The genesis of this example can be traced to the 1913 *Notes on Logic;* cf. *NB*, p. 95.

and thus the properties of the grid can be laid out in advance. Since the method for constructing "propositions" about the grid is recursive, we can confidently predict the form of *every* square-description. This does not mean, of course, that our grid-system and the propositions based on it will prove adequate to describe the world. But this cannot be the whole basis of the grid-method and thus the principles of mechanics, since Wittgenstein is anxious to *contrast* mechanics with mathematics. "Mathematics is a logical method. The propositions of mathematics are equations, and therefore pseudo-propositions." He writes,[50] and the crucial passage 6.342 begins, "And now we can see the relative position of logic [and thus mathematics] and mechanics." So the "inner logic," the geometry, of the grid cannot be all that is involved.

Suppose that we begin by projecting some such grid on our "world." One problem which might arise in such an attempt to completely and accurately describe the world is *undecidable squares*. The world might be such that there are many "toss-up" squares, just about half white and half black. We could conventionally decide to treat such squares as white or black, but although for certain purposes useful (just as navigators choose to treat the stars as stationary) such a method seems unduly arbitrary. It is possible that such problem squares could be eliminated by substituting a grid with a finer mesh, that is, with smaller squares. This would increase the "accuracy" of our description (although we could not guarantee that it would eliminate or even reduce undecidable squares), but it would also make a description of any part of the world—any section of the grid—consist of more "propositions." The need to mention more grid-squares in describing a given part of the plane would roughly correspond to a loss of economy in a scientific description; we would be adding, as it were, epicycles on our epicycles.

But an alternative way to deal with toss-up squares might be to substitute a grid or network with a different geometry; for instance a grid composed of triangular elements. Presumably the "grammar" of our descriptions would change were we to make this substitution. If we define the *gauge* of a grid as the area subsumed by one of its elements, it might emerge that a triangular grid of a certain gauge

---

[50] 6.2. Equations cannot be real propositions since the identity sign is not a name, not a sign for an object or a relation between objects (5.5301) and is eliminable in favor of a convention (5.53), which, given Russell's Theory of Descriptions, amounts to a metaphysical kiss of death.

would allow us to describe our "world" just as accurately—that is, with as few toss-up squares and as little arbitrariness—as a square grid with a considerably smaller mesh. The triangular grid would provide a certain advantageous conciseness. The metricization of our original grid is linear, but for certain purposes we might choose some non-linear metricization, such as the Richter scale, or the measurement of sound in decibels. But in any case, we have developed a universal method for describing the constituents of our primitive two-dimensional "world."

These alternative grid systems should be contrasted with alternative notations for a given grid system. Instead of the Cartesian method we have utilized, we might have stipulated a base line and an origin and represented each point in terms of a directed distance from the origin. In this polar system of coordinates, the general form of a proposition about reality would have the form '$(r; \varnothing)$', r being a scalar distance from the origin to the point, $\varnothing$ being the angle between that line and the base line. The formal equivalence between the two systems could be established by providing transformation rule for taking any proposition of the form '(x, y)' into one of the form '$(r; \varnothing)$'.

Which form of grid we pick, and by analogy the canonical form of a mechanical proposition, will thus arise from two factors: our more or less conventional choice of a form, and the suitability of that form for describing the way the world is. But having chosen a form, we can easily imagine confusions which would arise from a failure to properly distinguish these two elements in our system of representation. One party says, "The essence of the world is to be composed of dots, and the essence, the form of a dot, is (x, y)," while his opponent would contrawise argue for $(r; \varnothing)$. But through their confusions, each of our partisans is correct in two rather different but important ways. Each is first correct in his a priori conviction that *every* point without exception can be so described, and this belief is *not* based on induction. They take themselves to have grasped a deep and subtle regularity in nature, one that includes *all* possibilities, and herein are contained the confusions which Hertz warns against. But at a deeper level, they may well be correct even about this latter point, since (as we shall see in our discussion of 6.3431 below) that such a notation allows complete description of the world *shows* us something about the world, namely *that it can be described completely in such and such a manner.* We shall shortly see the significance of this seemingly trivial claim.

But our exploration of alternative notations above also must be contrasted with a rather different case. Suppose that instead of black and white squares, the world was composed of colored squares which emitted sounds of different pitches, and further suppose that there is no successful reduction of color or sound to the geometric patches. In this case (although we might be able to utilize the same grid system) the "propositions" of our first example, which characterized the contents of a certain grid-squares as (4, 7, B), would no longer be adequate. This case, parallel to Hertz's suggestion that the world might be such that the Fundamental Law was not wholly adequate, would show that our grid system did not possess the proper *multiplicity* to successfully model the world. More would need to be added; the grammar of our "propositions" would need to be expanded to express these added aspects of the world. This case might further be contrasted with one in which a successful reduction of position and color to pitch was discovered; in this case, our grid itself would become otiose.

These points lead to the Machian question: what is gained through a successful scientific description of the world? In order to facilitate an answer, let us consider a rather curious dichotomy in Wittgenstein's descriptions of science. At 4.1–4.11 Wittgenstein writes

> Propositions represent the existence and non-existence of states of affairs.
>
> The totality of true propositions is the whole of natural science (or the whole corpus of the natural sciences).

This passage seems to identify science with a Machian list of true propositions, and is particularly puzzling when contrasted with 6.341. Part of this puzzlement can be dispelled by examining the context; here Wittgenstein is setting forth his views on the nature of philosophy, and is anxious to contrast (contra Russell) science, which speaks of the world, with philosophy, which does not consist of propositions which assert the existence of states of affairs.[51] But

---

[51] This is in sharp contrast with Russell's program to establish a "scientific method in philosophy." "Philosophical knowledge ... does not differ essentially from scientific knowledge; there is no special source of wisdom which is open to philosophy but not to science, and the results obtained

it is troubling because scientific papers and books clearly do not consist of lists of propositions, and if they did, they would lack just the predictive and organizational ability that Wittgenstein has pointed to as crucial. But if Newtonian Mechanics, for instance, does not describe a new realm of facts, what then does it do?

The rather long passage 6.342 gives us some insight.

> And now we can see the relative position of logic and mechanics. (The net might also consist of more than one kind of mesh: e.g., we could use both triangles and hexagons.) The possibility of describing a picture like the one mentioned above [i.e., the black and white blobs] tells us *nothing* about the picture. (For that is true of all such pictures.) But what *does* characterize the picture is that it can be described *completely* by a particular net with a particular size of mesh.

> Similarly the possibility of describing the world by means of Newtonian mechanics tells us nothing about the world: but what does tell us something about it is the precise *way* in which it is possible to describe it by these means. We are also told something about the world by the fact that it can be described more simply with one system of mechanics than with another.

What does this mean? Propositions show, among other things, their senses—the facts to which they would correspond if they were to be true—their logical form, and through the Names which make them up the Objects to which they refer. That the principles of mechanics tell us "nothing" about the world at least means there are no scientific facts which correspond to them. Nor do they point, à la Schopenhauer, to a deeper reality. However, the corpus of mechanics as a whole does show us certain things about the world. That it is possible to represent the world adequately (which for Wittgenstein always means *perfectly*) with a grid of a certain sort (and here we must take the grid as a metaphor for some uniform system of representation; clearly Wittgenstein does not mean to imply that a spatial grid will always be sufficient) shows the multiplicity of the world. "The precise *way*" that it describes the world shows us, rather indirectly, that certain propositions are true and others are not, by ruling out certain forms and countenancing others. (In the same way, that the world can be described more simply in terms of one system

---

by philosophy are not radically different from those obtained by science." *The Problems of Philosophy* (Oxford U. Press, Oxford, 1912), p. 149. "Logic, I should maintain, must no more admit of a unicorn than zoology can; for logic is concerned with the real world just as truly as zoology, although with its more general and abstract features." *IMP*, p. 149.

of mechanics than another *shows* something about the world, as well as, in a manner similar to Hertz's considerations of appropriateness, something about the symbolism.) Thus "the laws of physics, with all their logical apparatus, still speak about the objects of the world."[52] This point is of primary importance. Physics is an attempt to provide a general description of the world, and this generality will be geometrical and thus a priori. But physics has a connection with the world; we build bridges that do not collapse. Keep in mind this puts mechanics in sharp contrast with both logic and mathematics, as we saw above.

On the other hand, that the world has certain features is shown just as well by listing all the true propositions, and the multiplicity of the world is likewise shown by the multiplicity of every proposition about the world. *Thus physics tells us nothing new about the world.* Although Mach is wrong in his claim that the principles of mechanics represent compressed lists of true propositions, he is correct in a sense, insofar as the description of physics at 6.3ff. collapses into that of 4.11. Physics *says* nothing about the world, and what it *shows* is already shown by any proposition. Thus science loses any aura of philosophical importance.

What is the upshot of Wittgenstein's investigation of the principles of mechanics? First, the Schopenhauerian attempt to see the universal applicability of scientific laws (if in fact actual) as a reflection of the underlying metaphysical reality of the world is misguided. No causal order underlies the world, peeking through in the laws of physics; the world of science is not a reflection of something deeper or higher. At the very most, the applicability of the principles of mechanics *shows* something, but certainly not more than what the totality of true propositions in themselves would show. (We saw a parallel point with respect to logic in chapter VI, and a further parallel point can be made concerning art.) But this does not mean that such principles are mere truth-functions of non-scientific propositions, true or not. Hertz is certainly correct when he argues that the regularities represented by the principles of mechanics are due in part to anthropocentric contributions, but his thoroughgoing realism drives Wittgenstein to treat these contributions not as

---

[52] 6.3431. Note the loose sense of 'object', as opposed to the technical sense of 2.01ff. In this loose sense my typewriter, for instance, counts as an object.

reflections of transcendental principles, but rather as due to the mode of representation which has been chosen. Thus, we might say that the principles of mechanics represent neither phenomenal manifestations of the underlying unified will (Schopenhauer), nor laundry lists of phenomenal experiences (Mach) nor transcendental contributions of the human mind (Hertz), but rather something like the fact that all messages produced by typewriters like mine have pica characters. Thus the Schopenhauerian is rather like Dorothy and her companions in the Emerald City: the dazzling green of the city is due not to architectural wizardry, but to the green glasses through which they are forced to view it.[53] But unlike the Idealists' use of the same metaphor, the glasses are of our own construction, and their effect can be factored out.

But by far the most important implication of Wittgenstein's philosophy of science *for him* concerns less the elucidation of science than the location of value. The Schopenhauerian world as will has in part been discredited, and so the principles of mechanics cannot be seen as reflections of the underlying (and value-bearing) will at all. This amounts to an abandonment of any philosophically interesting notion of causation, and this will have profound impact indeed, as we shall see in the succeeding chapter. The upshot is that only in logic is there room for real necessity, and logic is excluded from the realm of the sayable. Thus the Machian pessimism about science is well founded; as Schopenhauer emphasizes, science takes us *even farther* from what is real and valuable, tracing only the phenomenal aspects of the world. This is what Wittgenstein had in mind, I think, when he wrote:

> The whole modern conception of the world is founded on the illusion that the so-called laws of nature are explanations of natural phenomena. (6.371)

He follows this remark with the striking passage presented in part at the beginning of this chapter:

---

[53] Douglas Hofstader writes of the "G-plot," a computer-produced graphic representing energy bands for electrons in certain idealized crystals under the influence of a magnetic field. The graphic is rather striking, since it is composed wholly of an array of miniature versions of itself, and Hofstader recalls "an agnostic friend" of his describing it as "a picture of God", which Hofstader characterizes as "not blasphemous at all." Cf. *Gödel, Escher, Bach* (Basic Books, New York, 1979) pp. 138–42. This line of argumentation is represented by the computer scientist Dale Kohler in John Updike's *Roger's Version* (Knopf, New York, 1986). Compare with the quote which heads this chapter, but also perhaps reserve judgment until chapter X.

Thus people today stop at the laws of nature, treating them as something inviolable, just as God and Fate were treated in past ages.

And in fact both are right and wrong: though the view of the ancients is clearer in so far as they have a clear and acknowledged terminus, while the modern system tries to make it look as if *everything* were explained. (6.372)

This remark, a comment on 6.37 (the only necessity is *logical* necessity) is immediately followed at 6.373 by "the world is independent of my will," with its introduction of the characteristic Schopenhauerian notion of will and the startling occurrence of the personal pronoun 'my'. The unraveling of 6.373 will be one major thread of the argument of the next three chapters.[54]

---

[54] In this chapter I have obviously concentrated on Wittgenstein's Tractarian views of the nature of science, and their roots in Hertz and Schopenhauer. For discussion of his later views, see Derek Phillips, *Wittgenstein and Scientific Knowledge* (MacMillan, London, 1977).

VIII

Propositional Attitudes and the Empirical Ego

> But what then am I? A thing which thinks. What is a
> thing which thinks? It is a thing which doubts, understands,
> affirms, denies, wills, refuses, which also imagines
> and feels.
>
> —DESCARTES

Most of the central themes of this book converge in this chapter and the subsequent one; whether the reader accepts my picture of Wittgenstein's early thought will turn, to a large extent, on accepting the claims in these chapters. The actual subject matter of the chapter appears somewhat more mundane. Among the apparent counterexamples to the thesis of extensionality—that is, propositions which appear to be compound but not truth-functionally so—are those characterized by verbs such as those appearing in the above quote from Meditation II. An example of such a proposition is 'Othello believes that Desdemona loves Cassio.' Propositions of this sort are usually referred to by the term Russell coined: 'propositional attitudes.'

The verbs which Descartes lists (with the dubious exception of 'imagine' and 'feel') differ from normal transitive verbs insofar as they characteristically demand *propositional* objects. 'Othello believes that Desdemona loves Cassio' *appears* to be a molecular proposition, containing as a constituent the proposition 'Desdemona loves Cassio.'[1] However, the apparent occurrence is not a truth-functional one, as we discover when we replace 'Desdemona loves

---

[1] The rough-and-ready notion of a *constituent proposition* that I use here is too simplistic; 'Lincoln was an actor' is certainly not a constituent of 'The man who shot Lincoln was an actor.' Cf. J. A. Martin, "How Not to Define Truth-functionality," *Logique et Analyses* XIV no. 52 (1970), pp. 476–82, and I. M. Copi, *Introduction to Logic*, sixth edition (Macmillan, New York, 1982), p. 279. Since what I ultimately want is a notion of containment which is defined in terms of fully analyzed languages, where molecular propositions consist only of atomic propositions and logical connectives, I can safely bypass these difficulties.

Cassio' with some *other* false proposition.[2] Othello's mistaken opinion about Desdemona does not entail that he believes *every* false proposition. Such propositions thus appear as counterexamples to the Thesis of Extensionality, which as we saw in chapter IV represents no mere logic-chopping crotchet but rather a principle mirroring the deepest insights of an atomistic ontology.

But a further feature of propositional attitudes recommend them to our attention. The most straightforward and natural characterization of such propositions construes them as relating a person to a proposition, and thus they seem to refer in part at least to persons, subjects, agents, minds, and so forth. In fact, the non-truth-functional nature of such propositions—the "intentional inexistence" of their objects—has frequently been picked out in the history of philosophy as a *sign* of the mental.[3] David Pears writes:

> The life and movement of a proposition is the life and movement of thought. It is inside the mind of the person who thinks that something is so, although of course it may be externalized in the words which express his proposition. So the theory of judgment cannot confine itself to the studying of propositions apart from their connection with people ... the investigation of [propositional attitudes] inevitably leads back to people.[4]

Talk of the inner life of persons ought to remind us immediately of Schopenhauer's fourth class of representations for a subject, and the profound role that class plays in the development of his Universal Voluntarism. Furthermore, for the realist the study of such propositions is tantamount to a study of the self insofar as it is part of the world. Although a rather crude expression of the thesis of this chapter and the next, such a characterization will serve us for the present. In Wittgenstein's analysis of propositional attitudes we shall see the disappearance of the Schopenhauerian world-as-will as manifested from the *inside,* as it were. More significantly, we shall see its reappearance in another and perhaps more profound sense.

---

[2] Carnap points out the striking fact that this is true even if the substituted proposition is logically equivalent to the original; 'Othello believes that squares have four sides' can be true while 'Othello believes that regular quadrilaterals have four sides' is false. Cf. Carnap, *Meaning and Necessity* (U. of Chicago Press, Chicago, 1956), sect. 13.

[3] Cf. W. Sellars, "Intentionality and the Mental," R. M. Chisholm, "Sentences about Believing" and the resulting correspondence, in Feigl et al., eds., *Minnesota Studies in the Philosophy of Science,* vol. II (U. of Minnesota Press, Minneapolis, 1958), pp. 507–39.

[4] Pears, *op. cit.*, pp. 207–8.

Unfortunately, this sense falls outside the realm of the sayable, and upon this will turn, if I am not mistaken, much of the obscurity of the *Tractatus*.

I want to spend a good deal of time in this chapter examining certain views concerning the proper analysis of propositional attitudes, or in turn of the century philosophical jargon, *theories of judgment*.[5] The views I examine are largely those of Russell, whom I choose insofar as he was the major figure in British philosophical logic in the first fifty years of the century, and because he influenced and was influenced by Wittgenstein's thought. But since Wittgenstein's theory of judgment cannot be grasped without these competing theories as foils, were there no Russell I would have been forced to invent one.[6]

The Multiple Relation Theory of Judgment

Russell's early interest in the theory of judgment, a topic which seems vaguely exotic to contemporary philosophers, stems historically from his early Hegelianism and the continued skirmishes with Bradley. But apart from such philosophical warfare, Russell continually struggles to produce a theory of judgment which, while thoroughly realistic, can still account for *false beliefs*. This struggle, as we shall see, continues right up until his rejection of the existence of a substantival self in 1919. Let us examine the difficulties which attend to a realistic theory of judgment.

The realist holds that every mental act (ignoring believing that I have a toothache, etc.) must have some extramental object. Russell writes:

---

[5] "Almost all English logicians speak of the Proposition and not of the Judgment. This does not matter, so long as we are agreed about what they mean. They must mean the proposition *as understood*, and this is what we call the judgment." Bosanquet, *Essentials of Logic* (Kraus Reprint, New York, 1968), p. 82. I will point out where necessary Russell's evolving usage of the term, where it sometimes means "fact," sometimes (almost) means "sentence" and sometimes something in between.

[6] In doing so I may occasionally collapse some distinctions which Russell finds fundamental, but I do not believe myself to have misrepresented any of Russell's views. Readers interested in a closer look at Russell's views may consult, in addition to the cited works, Jager *op. cit.*, ch. 8 and Pears *op. cit.*, chs. 12–13. Also of interest are David Bell, *Frege's Theory of Judgment*, (Oxford U. Press, Oxford, 1979), Guy Stock, "Russell's Theory of Judgment in Logical Atomism," *Revista Portuguesa de Filosophia*, XCIII (1972), pp. 458–88, and the same author's rather curious "Wittgenstein on Russell's Theory of Judgment" in Vesey *op. cit.*, pp. 62–75, where he conflates epistemological with logical issues in a manner quite foreign to Wittgenstein's early thought.

In all cognitive acts, such as believing, doubting, disbelieving, apprehending, perceiving, imagining, the mind has objects other than itself to which it stands in various relations ... Judgments, also, consist of relations of the mind to objects ...[7]

But what are these extramental things towards which the mind is directed? In many cases they will be different. In the case of perception, Russell is clear that they are *sense-data*. But what is the object of judgment? It is tempting to say that judgment is directed towards a fact or situation; when I judge that the cat is on the mat, the object of that judgment is the cat being on the mat. But a little reflection shows that this will not do. If Othello judges that Desdemona loves Cassio, and Desdemona does *not* love Cassio, what is the object of Othello's judgment? Or more generally, towards what is the mind directed, when it judges *falsely?*

Traditional logic offers a superficially attractive answer. Essentially the logic of *terms*, it holds that judgment consists of an experimental putting-together of such terms.[8] As we have seen in chapter III, it is very tempting to view these terms *psychologically,* as ideas or notions. Part of that attractiveness stems from the obvious fact that when Othello judges—truly or falsely—that Desdemona loves Cassio, there are before Othello's mind *some* ideas of Desdemona, Cassio, and love. But apart from the obvious response that when I judge elephants to be larger than cats I am not making a judgment about my *ideas* of elephants and cats, Russell argues that such subjectivization is the route to scepticism:

On this view ideas become a veil between us and the outside things—we never really, in knowledge, attain to the things we are supposed to be knowing but only the ideas of them.[9]

Moore, in his 1899 paper "On the Nature of Judgment," tries to rectify this difficulty through Platonizing the entities in question (Moore calls them "concepts"), thus conferring upon them objective status.

---

[7] "On the Nature of Truth and Falsity," p. 150, in *Philosophical Essays* (Simon and Schuster, New York, 1966), pp. 147–59. This paper is hereafter designated "ONTF."

[8] E.g., "... Judgment consists in coupling together two notions or ideas ..." S. Jevons, *Elementary Lessons in Logic* (London, 1875), p. 11.

[9] "Knowledge by Acquaintance and Knowledge by Description," p. 221–22, in *M&L*.

But Moore is never able to satisfactorily develop this suggestion.[10] Russell sometimes tries to foist on Meinong's Theory of Objectives the claim that there are "false facts," like Desdemona loving Cassio, which would then serve as the objects of false judgments. But even if we are willing to swallow such ontologically unpalatable entities, we are still left with the mystery of how the non-existent or "false" Objective Desdemona-loving-Cassio can be a constituent of the *actual* fact that Othello believes Desdemona to love Cassio.

Such difficulties with the objects of false belief lead Russell to formulate the "Multiple Relation Theory of Judgment (MRTJ)," which appears in the 1910 paper "On the Nature of Truth and Falsity," the first edition of *Principia* and, as an object of criticism, in the fourth of the 1918 Lectures on Logical Atomism.[11] Belief, and thus judgment, carry for Russell particular importance insofar as belief is the fundamental bearer of truth-value:

> Broadly speaking, the things that are true or false in the sense with which we are concerned, are statements, and beliefs or judgments. The truth or falsehood of statements can be defined in terms of the truth or falsity of beliefs.[12]

Since the nature of truth is clearly a first-water philosophical concern, so must be an acceptable analysis of judgment.

To be objective, judgments must have some connection with the world, which Russell views as composed of objects having certain properties and standing in certain (external) relations one to another. Some of these objects are complexes—objects standing in

---

[10] Bradley argues that the thesis that judgment is a mere connection of ideas or concepts leads to a dilemma: either every judgment is hypothetical, or reality is *nothing but* these concepts. Bradley takes this as a *reductio* that judgment is merely connection of terms, but Moore, at least in 1899, cheerfully embraces the second option. Cf. Bradley, *PoL*, I/I/ii (pp. 44–46) and Stock, "Russell's Theory of Judgment in Logical Atomism," p. 462.

[11] The MRTJ was an object of intense debate between Russell and Wittgenstein. An early version appears in a largely unpublished manuscript entitled "Theory of Knowledge" (some of which appeared in *The Monist* from 1914 through 1915). Wittgenstein saw this manuscript and "attacked it violently"—cf. the letter from Russell to Ottoline Morrell dated 5/28/13 in R. W. Clark, *The Life of Bertrand Russell* (Weudenfeld and Nicolson, London, 1976), p. 204, and Wittgenstein's letter of 7/22/13 in *LRKM*, p. 24. David Pears discusses this version of MRTJ in his excellent "The Relation between Wittgenstein's Picture Theory of Propositions and Russell's Theories of Judgment," in *Wittgenstein: Sources and Perspectives*, ed. C.G. Luckhardt (Cornell U. Press, Ithaca, NY, 1982), pp. 190–212, esp. pp. 190–91.

[12] "ONTF," p. 148. The reducibility of statement to judgment gives rise to the rather surprising claim in *Principia* that unasserted propositions are incomplete symbols, and thus stand in need of the assertion sign. Compare with 4.442 and *NoL*, p. 96. The sentiment behind such a view is closely connected with the matters we shall look at in the following chapter.

particular relations—and some of these complexes are perceptible. With respect to perceptible complexes one can define the simplest sort of judgment, a *judgment of perception.* In a judgment of perception we simply record our awareness of such-and-such constituents standing in such-and-such relations to one another. Such judgments, often referred to as "analytic" by the Idealists, insofar as they merely analyze a current presentation, "go right to the facts" and are therefore incorrigible. The object of a perception cannot be "a nothing," as Russell puts it; if we perceive aRb, then aRb must be actual. This apparent privileged position is short-lived, however:

> This does not mean that in a judgment which appears to be one of perception, we are sure of not being in error, since we may err in thinking that our judgment has been derived merely by analysis of what was perceived. (*PM*, p. 43)

The incorrigibility claim reflects certain Russellian psychological and epistemological views which need not detain us. What we are interested in is Russell's claim that such judgments are marked by a characteristic *logical form.* What is the logical form of a judgment?

I have mentioned the temptation of seeing propositional attitudes as representing a relation between a judger and a fact. But as we have seen, this will not work in the case of false judgments, since unless we are willing to take recourse to the unintuitive notion of a false fact, there is no such fact to which the judger is related. But even if we accept false facts difficulties arise. If a false judgment is related to a false fact in the same manner that a true judgment is related to a true fact, and if false facts are awarded objective status, then it becomes wholly mysterious why truth is preferable to falsehood. Equally seriously, logical principles such as double negation and excluded middle become problematical. But Russell's realism precludes falling back on the *ideas* involved as the objects of judgment—when Othello judges that Desdemona loves Cassio, it is not primarily his *ideas* about which he is judging.

Russell attempts to avoid this dilemma by suggesting that a judgment does not have a single object—a fact, complex, or proposition—but rather several interrelated objects:

> ... judgment is not a dual relation of the mind to a single object, but a multiple relation of the mind to various other terms with which the mind is

concerned. Thus if I judge that A loves B, that is not a relation of me to A's love for B, but a relationship between me and love and A and B. ("ONTF," p. 155)

More generally, when I make a judgment, I judge that certain things have certain properties or stand in certain relations, but the objects of my judging are the things and relations, and *not* the complex which exists if my judgment is true. In the case of believing that the cat is black, the relation is triadic, relating me, the cat, and blackness, while Othello's ill-fated false belief involves a quadratic relation, relating Othello, Desdemona, Cassio, and loving.[13] Of course, Desdemona, Othello, and so forth may turn out to be complexes too, perhaps non-existent complexes; in that case, they would be analyzed away in the manner of the present King of France. In the end our judgment will concern the relations of particulars (Russell's version of Objects, we recall), which cannot fail to exist, although Russell is not clear about this point until 1918, when he has wholly assimilated Wittgenstein's influence. Note that MRTJ as I have sketched it is a *reactionary* theory, reversing the trend of logic since Frege by substituting judgment about terms for judgment about propositions.

The MRTJ, however, affords several virtues. First, it allows the realist to maintain that the perceiver stands in immediate relation to the constituents of a perceptual presentation; there is no veil of ideas between the mind and the world. Further, it offers hope (temporary, we shall see) for a correct analysis of false belief. Finally, it allows Russell to avoid ontological commitment to false facts and even to propositions, since expressions which appear to denote propositions turn out to be incomplete symbols and disappear under analysis in favor of relations among their constituents. The upshot is that the proposition 'Desdemona loves Cassio' is not, as it *appears* to be, a constituent of 'Othello believes that Desdemona loves Cassio.' MRTJ thus manifests an important continuity with Russell's treatment of 'The present King of France is bald.' When we have a puzzling context which appears to mention a certain entity, thus committing us to recognition of its existence, analysis of the troublesome

---

[13] Russell takes this to show that 'believe' is thus systematically ambiguous in the manner of 'exist'—cf. *L&K*, p. 226. Note the relationship between this solution and Russell's criticism of Leibniz, viz. that Leibniz could not deal with relations and was thus blinded to those other than the dyadic relations between subject and predicate.

proposition reveals a real logical form quite different from its superficial form. Under analysis the suspect expression disappears.

Unfortunately, for all its initial promise MRTJ is infected with serious difficulties. Let us examine in detail two of the most germane, since they relate to the key issues of the unity of a proposition and the status of Objects as universals or particulars.

In 1910 Russell presents the first problem in rather narrow focus. The judgment 'S believes that aRb' cannot merely relate S, a, b, and the general relation R. We can see this most easily by examining non-symmetrical relations, such as love. Since there is a clear (if unfortunate) difference between Desdemona loving Cassio and Cassio loving Desdemona,

> ... the relation must not be abstractly before the mind, but must be before it as proceeding from A to B rather than from B to A.[14]

Setting aside for a moment whether we can adequately distinguish the two "senses" of the relation, notice that if we cannot we are unable to represent the difference between A loving B and B loving A. But earlier Russell provides a generalized version of this objection which went beyond non-symmetrical dyadic relations. In *PrM* sections 53–55, Russell argues that all verbs stand for relations, and that relations can be taken in two rather different ways, either as the abstract relation or "a relation actually relating." (*Op. cit.*, p. 49) If we thus consider the relation *being different from*, we see that there are two ways the associated verb can be construed.

(a) Only the general notion of the verb, and thus only the general relation, appears in a relational statement. Thus, in 'A differs from B' and 'C differs from D', we have numerically the same relation of difference occurring in each.

(b) Only the specific notion of difference enters into 'A is different from B'. The relation as it occurs in 'A differs from B' is thus numerically different from that which occurs in 'C differs from D' and thus the general notion of difference is not relevant in propositions such as 'A differs from B'.

---

[14] "ONTF," p. 158. Compare with "Meinong's Theory of Complexes and Assumptions," in Lackey ed. *op. cit.*, p. 48–49.

What arguments can be supplied for each of these competing views?

On the first view numerically the same component occurs in any proposition which features a given verb. Thus, the components of 'A is different from B' are merely A, B, and the abstract relation of difference. But this will not do, as Russell rather obscurely argues:

> These constituents, thus placed side by side, do not reconstitute the proposition. The difference which occurs in the proposition actually relates A and B, whereas the difference after analysis has no connection with A and B.[15]

On this view 'A differs from B' would be true if A existed, B existed, and *any* two things were related, but that is clearly *not* what the original proposition asserts.[16] Othello's belief is not merely that Desdemona and Cassio exist and that *someone* is in love, but that *exactly these two people* are in love.[17]

In response to such criticism Russell suggests that perhaps we have omitted from our analysis those aspects of the proposition which correspond to the words 'is' and 'from'. We might therefore want to "mention the relations which a difference has to A and B", perhaps getting something like "A, referent, different, relatum, B" (*PrM*, pp. 49–50). This suggestion unfortunately leads very quickly to a dead end. There are, Russell argues, two sorts of infinite regresses into which propositions can enter. The first kind—benign if the notion of infinity is at all acceptable—is the infinite regress of implication; 'p' entails 'p v q' which entails 'p v q v r' and so forth ad infinitum. We need not grasp the whole infinite series of implications in order to understand the original proposition 'p' and so no difficulties ensue. There is, however, another sort of infinite regress, which *is* vicious. Suppose that in order to understand 'p', I have to understand 'q', and to understand that I need to understand 'r' and so forth ad infinitum. (Compare with the vicious regress of existential

---

[15] *PrM*, p. 49. Roughly contemporaneously Moore argues ". . . the fact that we express by saying that Edward the VII was the father of George VI does not consist of Edward, George *and* the relation of fatherhood." "Internal and External Relations," in *Philosophical Studies*, p. 277.

[16] Here I have taken the conservative tack that relations exist only when exemplified. A more Platonistic interpretation, when combined with this view of relations, would imply that since relations necessarily exist, the truth of any relational statement would depend only on the existence of the relata. But then 'A is different from B' and 'A is identical with B' would both be true, which is clearly intolerable.

[17] Compare with Peter Geach's discussion of this passage in his *Mental Acts* (Routledge and Kegan Paul, London, 1957), pp. 51–52.

presuppositions in chapter IV above.) Since having achieved the first step presupposes the entire infinite regress, such a regress is tantamount to a proof of the impossibility of the first step. Now suppose that in order to analyze 'A is different from B' we need to use the terms 'is' and 'from' to mediate between 'A', 'B', and 'different'. Parity of reasoning would seem to demand some *further* terms to mediate between 'A' and 'is', and so forth. But these further terms would also be relational terms and would presumably need to be taken generally or abstractly. But then our original problem reappears, apparently demanding *new* relational terms to relate these relations to their relata. On this option it is difficult to see how we could understand any proposition without being aware of the whole infinite series.[18] Such a suggestion is clearly unacceptable, as we *do* of course understand the original proposition. This infinite regress is a sign, Russell points out, that both 'A, referent, difference, relatum, B' and the original analysis are mere *lists*, whereas the proposition we are attempting to analyze is a *unity*.

That leaves view (b). On that view, what appears in 'A is different from B' is a *special* difference, a difference proceeding from A to B and thus numerically distinct from any other difference. For 'A is different from B' to be true, A and B must exist, as well as the special relation-as-relating-its-terms. But there are two serious objections to this analysis. First, if each difference-as-relating is distinct from every other such difference, why do we call them all *differences?* They must have *something* in common to justify our lumping them together. Russell suggests that the most general (and thus weakest) way in which two terms can share something in common is through a relation they each bear to a third term. But if no two pairs of terms can share the *same* relation, even this very weak sense of similarity appears hopeless. A more serious problem attends trying to make sense of what a concrete, specific relation-as-relating-its-terms might be. Consider the relation of difference-as-actually-relating-A-and-B. It is very difficult to see how this could be anything other than *the actual fact* that A is different from B. But then the concrete relation Desdemona-loving-Cassio cannot be part of the analysis of 'Othello believes that Desdemona loves Cassio,'

---

[18] The failure of this suggested analysis is part of the reason that Wittgenstein insists Objects must fit together *immediately,* "like links on a chain." (2.03) No *other* Objects could possibly serve as the "glue" to bind them.

since Othello's belief is false. Thus we either must accept *false* or *non-existent* relations-as-relating-their-terms—in essence, *false facts*—or reject this suggestion. Suggestion (b) thus founders on the problem of false beliefs.

Both (a) and (b) thus fail to offer an adequate analysis of the nature of relations in judgment; the former is too weak, the latter either wholly mysterious or infected with commitment to ontologically dubious false facts. Although puzzled by these difficulties, Russell ultimately opts for a version of (b):

> The verb, when used as a verb, embodies the unity of the proposition, and is thus distinguishable from the verb considered as a term, *although I do not know how to give a clear account of the precise nature of the distinction.* (*PrM*, p. 50, my emphasis)

The problems attendant to supplying an analysis of judgment capable of accounting for the unity of the judged proposition continued to plague Russell on up to the 1918 Lectures on Logical Atomism, where he confesses that although until recently he entertained no doubts that an analysis of belief-contexts was possible, currently that faith was wavering (*L&K*, p. 218). Rather than offering an analysis of such contexts in the lecture ostensibly given over to that task, Russell admits, "One has to be content on many points at present with pointing out difficulties rather than laying down quite clear solutions." (*Ibid.*, p. 209)

In fact, the lecture is given over to the defense of two wholly negative (though not for that reason insignificant) theses: that we cannot treat belief-facts as relations between a subject and a proposition (*ibid.*, p. 226) and that the "subordinate verb"—that is, the verb in the judged proposition—cannot be treated on the same level as the main verb in the manner that MRTJ treats it (*ibid.*). The two points are intimately connected, and will be illustrated with the same example in the following paragraph. Belief facts, he reluctantly concludes, are a primitive and hitherto unrecognized species in our "philosophical zoo." Since the 1918 position serves as a watershed for Russell, and since it highlights many points relevant to Wittgenstein's position, let us look briefly at his position in the Lectures.

Russell tells us that "spatial maps" of facts are sometimes valuable in displaying the logical form of those facts. 'Plato loves

Socrates' has the same logical form as 'Desdemona loves Cassio,' which can be seen by allowing a spatial relation to replace in each case the specific relation.[19] Thus the first fact can be represented as:

Plato ————————————————→ Socrates
(loves)

where the spatial relation of standing to the right of goes proxy for the relation of being loved. 'Desdemona loves Cassio' has the same logical form, since it, as well as 'Desdemona kicks Cassio,' can be gotten by making the appropriate word-substitutions within this framework. It is tempting to try to represent 'Othello believes that Desdemona loves Cassio' in an analogous manner:

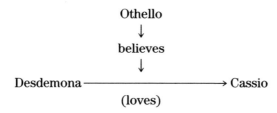

But this will not do, since we have seen that the analysis requires not the general verb 'loves' but the actual relation-as-relating-its-terms. However, as Russell puts it, "Every fact that occurs in the world must be composed entirely of constituents that there are, and not constituents that there are not." (*Ibid.*, p. 220) Othello's *actual* belief cannot have as a component the *non-actual* Desdemona-loving-Cassio. Thus no false belief can be spatially mapped, because the false belief apparently involves non-actual relations, while all the spatial relations we can draw are of course actual. But if false beliefs cannot be so mapped, certainly true ones cannot either; the logical form of belief-propositions cannot turn on something as contingent as Desdemona's affections. So we are driven to the conclusion that "You cannot get in space anything which is logically of the same form as belief." (*Ibid.*, p. 225) Russell finds himself unable to give

---

[19] There is an obvious analogy between this procedure and a primitive form of the Picture Theory. When Russell wrote the Lectures in 1918, he attributed many of the ideas which they contained to Wittgenstein (*ibid.*, p. 177), although he had not seen Wittgenstein since 1914 and writes "I do not even know whether he is alive or dead."

any adequate analysis of belief-propositions—even one which gives us some insight into their constituents—and is forced to accept them as primitive. This is for Russell a very unsatisfactory state of affairs, and one which he does not for long tolerate.

Neutral Monism and the Behavioristic Analysis

1919 marks a watershed year in Russell's career, overshadowed only by 1905. The influence of William James's neutral monism, expressed in such writings as "Does Consciousness Exist?" and absorbed during an earlier stint in the U.S., becomes increasingly attractive to him.[20] In the 1918 Lectures Russell expresses both reservations with respect to the substantival self and admiration for the ontological parsimony of the American Pragmatists. The major reason for retaining the self in philosophy, he argues, is the difficulty in otherwise dealing with egocentric words like 'this'. (*Ibid.*, p. 222) But by 1919 he is willing to accept the self too as a logical construct, and this move has profound effects on his philosophical thought, including of course his theory of judgment.[21]

The MRTJ offers a reactionary analysis of belief-contexts and similar "psychological" locutions as complexes of terms, denying that the apparent object-proposition has a real logical occurrence in the larger context. Russell ultimately admits that such an attempt fails to take into account the unity of the object-proposition. The analysis of this section attempts to construct a truth-functional analysis of such contexts by eliminating the occurrence of the term ostensibly referring to a substantival self. I shall call this the "Behavioristic Analysis," and use as stalking-horses the 1919 paper "On Propositions and How They Mean," the appendix to the second edition of *PM* and chapter XIX of the 1940 *Inquiry into Meaning and Truth.*[22]

Offering Meinong as an example, Russell observes that analytic psychologists treat presentations as being composed of three com-

---

[20] Wm. James, "Does Consciousness Exist?" in *Essays in Radical Empiricism* (Dutton, New York, 1971), pp. 3–24.

[21] Cf. *My Philosophical Development*, esp. pp. 117–19, and Jager *op. cit.*, chs. 7–8.

[22] The 1919 paper is reprinted in *L&K*, pp. 283–320 and hereafter abbreviated as "OPHM." The appendix in question occupies pages 401–8 of the abridged edition. B. Russell, *An Inquiry into Meaning and Truth* (Allen and Unwin, London, 1940), will hereafter be abbreviated *IMT*.

ponents: the mental act, the content of the act, and the object.[23] Acceptance of the act entails the existence of a subject or agent which performs the act, and prior to 1919 Russell, in accord with his general realism, accepts an act-object or subject-object model of presentation. But in that year he writes:

> I have to confess that the theory which analyses presentation into act and object no longer satisfies me. The act, or subject, is schematically convenient, but not empirically discoverable. It seems to serve the same sort of purpose as is served by points and instants, by numbers and particles and the rest of the apparatus of mathematics. All these things have to be *constructed* ... they are not of the stuff of the world ... ("OPHM," p. 305)

While the view that the self is a construct carries with it a certain ontological parsimony (and for Russell, significantly, certain epistemological advantages), it entails the consequence—unfortunate for the realist—that even in perception the constituents of a presentation cannot be identical with the constituents of what is presented. There is clearly a difference between 'aRb' and 'S believes that aRb,' which Russell in his realist stage analyzed in terms of the presence of the subject in the latter complex. But with the dissolution of the subject, such an analysis is no longer possible, and the difference must be located elsewhere. The consequence is that even perception no longer goes "right to the facts," thus calling into question in what sense we can be said to "know" the objective world at all. But this possible disadvantage is compensated for by the admission of propositions (in the linguistic rather than ontological sense) as the objects of belief. When asked, What is the object of my belief when I believe falsely?, we can now answer, I am entertaining a proposition which does not correspond with the facts.

Does this position constitute a retreat to the psychologistic view that the object of belief is a mere idea? What exactly are these propositions which are supposed to be the objects of belief? These questions both serve as a link between the 1919 paper and *PM*, and lead us to the characteristic behavioral emphasis of the new analysis. Propositions, Russell tells us, are "the content of belief" ("OPHM," p.

---

[23] "OPHM," pp. 304–5. Russell characterizes the philosophical positions of his chief contemporaries in terms of this schema: realists reject the content, idealists keep the content and the act but reject the object, and "American Realists"—that is, pragmatists—reject all but the object. *Ibid.*, p. 305.

308) or "What we believe when we believe truly or falsely."[24] Such a definition stresses the formal nature of belief while leaving open questions of ontological status. But Russell points out that propositions in their most tractable form—written or spoken—are composed of words. Thus, he adds in an oddly reactionary manner, the nature of a proposition turns on the nature of words, and likewise the question of how a proposition means can be referred back to the question of how a word means. What *are* words, and how *do* they mean?

"If we confine ourselves to spoken words in one language," Russell writes, "a word is a class of closely similar noises produced by breath combined with movements of the throat and tongue and lips." (*Ibid.*, p. 290) To view a noise as an instance of the word 'dog', then, is to say that it is a member of some class of noises more or less approximating some phonetic standard. (Let us ignore problems of homophonic words and other, more serious, difficulties with such a definition.) But granted that words are (at least) noises, so are horn honks and bird-calls, yet words differ from these insofar as they have *meanings*. What does it mean for a word to have a meaning? Russell's 1919 answer is at least formally compatible with his views as far back as *PrM:*

> It is obvious to begin with that, if we take some such word as 'Socrates' or 'dog', the meaning of the words consists in some relation to an object or set of objects. (*Ibid.*, p. 290)

But what is that relation? For Russell it is mediated by mental images which serve as bridges between words and things, and that strictly speaking the meaning of the word is the image and not the thing. The word, in the manner of the theories of Ogden, Watson, and others, conjures up the mental image through some causal relation of association, while the image stands related to the thing in question through the more intimate relation of resemblance. (*Ibid.*, pp. 300–302) These images back up words in the manner that silver backs up paper money. An analogous point can be made about propositions:

---

[24] *Ibid.*, p. 285. Russell adds "except when, if ever, the content of belief is simple" (p. 308), leaving open the possibility of non-propositional beliefs. He adds "this definition is so framed as to avoid the assumption that, whenever we believe, our belief is true or false." *(ibid.)* We shall see Wittgenstein take exception to this possibility in the following section.

> I shall distinguish a proposition expressed in words as a 'word-proposition', and one consisting of images as an 'image-proposition'. As a general rule, a word-proposition "means" an image-proposition ... (*Ibid.*, p. 308)

With the waning influence of Frege, Leibniz, and Wittgenstein on his thought, we see Russell reverting to a psychological theory of meaning, exposing the neo-Humean bedrock of his thought.[25] But note the assumption that mental images are, as it were, *self-interpreting;* this will mark the primary point of cleavage between Russell's theory of meaning and that of Wittgenstein.

The theory of judgment which Russell erects on the foundations provided by this psychological semantics comes to the fore in the *Principia* appendix and in *IMT*.[26] The proposition "A believes that p," Russell begins, involves both logical and psychological difficulties, the former connected with the nature of images and with the associative laws which govern their interaction. Many of these psychological problems can be by-passed by examining the almost equivalent proposition "A asserts that p," asserting being a sort of "believing out loud." In this case the immediate vehicle of the proposition will be the more accessible spoken words. Asserting is essentially *producing sounds:*

> To say "A exclaims 'B is hot'" is to assert a series of movements in A's speech-organs; this is a purely physical occurrence, which can be completely described without introducing any subordinate complex [i.e., the asserted proposition]. It would seem that every other state which is believing that B is hot could be similarly described. (*IMT*, p. 272)

But who or what is this subject A? If the subject is a logical construct, what is the mechanism which analyses that complex? Russell takes *awareness* as a primitive term. "The conception [of awareness] is the

---

[25] "Logicians ... have done very little towards explaining the nature of the relation called 'meaning', nor are they to blame for this, since the problem is essentially one of psychology." (*Ibid.*, p. 290) Compare with Russell's estimation of Hume's influence upon him in the preface to *IMT*, p. 7. We shall see that Wittgenstein will agree that the process of meaning is not *wholly* a matter of logic, but he would choke, as we shall see in chapter IX, on the suggestion that the residuum was "merely psychological."

[26] The 1940 theory is not *identical* with that of *Principia;* in the former, for instance, Russell distinguishes between the thesis of extensionality and the "principle of atomicity" (pp. 107–9), arguing that a superficial analysis of propositional attitudes violates both. But our purposes allow us to ignore such subtle differences. Interestingly, in 1940 Russell takes himself to be spelling out Wittgenstein's Tractarian views; cf. *IMT*, pp. 268ff.

same as when I say that my hotness is part of my experience, but your hotness is not." (*Ibid.*, p. 229) Russell then defines an "awareness-relation A," which is modeled on the R-family relation of *PM* *96:

> We may now define "the person of x" [that is, the person having awareness of x] or "the person to whom event x belongs" as "The A-family of x." We may define "persons" as "All A-families except the null class. (*Ibid.*, p. 229)

He has thus produced a formal model of the "bundle-theory" of the self which features so prominently in Hume and James.[27] As we shall see, something like this bundle-theory also appears in Wittgenstein's analysis, but there only in the negative role of separating the chaff from the grain.

We can now turn to the formal analysis of (e.g.) 'A asserts that Socrates is Greek.' In *PM* it becomes:

$$(\exists x,y,z)(x\in\alpha \cdot y\in\beta \cdot z\in\gamma \cdot x\mathrm{D}y \cdot y\mathrm{D}z) \in \mathrm{A}^{28}$$

Here 'x, y, z' are noises, 'α, β, γ' classes of similar noises, '$x\in\alpha$' means that the noise x is a member of the requisite class, and 'D' is a binary relation of close precedence, effectively insuring that the noises appear in the correct order and with the right spacing. A is the person, construed in the above manner as an A-class, and the whole says that this sequence of noises is part of that constructed A-class. Put another way, it says that there is a set of noises which is part of the A-class which constitutes a person, and these noises approximate the requisite phonetic norm for 'Socrates is Greek.'

Keep in mind that such noises function only as stand-ins for the mental images of which they are the causes; although the relation between the mental image and the referent is iconic, that between word and image is merely causal. Note also that on this analysis, there is nothing common to 'A asserts p' and 'A hopes that p' or any other propositional attitude with 'p' as its putative object. The proposition 'p' turns out to be an incomplete symbol, vanishing under analysis. Importantly, the analysans is wholly truth-functional and

---

[27] *Treatise* I/iv/7, and James, "Does Consciousness Exist?"

[28] *PM*, p. 403. For a helpful guide to the symbolism of *PM*, cf. I. Grattan-Guiness, *Dear Russell-Dear Jourdain* (Columbia U. Press, New York, 1977), pp. 210–13.

thus presents no problems for an extensional analysis of language. Finally, and of the *highest* significance, the substantival self or person A which at first glance appeared to stand in a relation to the proposition 'p' also vanishes; 'A' too is an incomplete symbol. Thus the expression "propositional attitude" is doubly infelicitous, since both the object "proposition" and the agent who is supposed to have an "attitude" toward that proposition have disappeared.

A Wittgensteinian Critique of Russell's Theories of Judgment

I am very sorry to hear that my objection to your theory of judgment paralyzes you. I think that it can only be removed by a correct theory of propositions.

—WITTGENSTEIN TO RUSSELL,
22.7.13

The purpose of this chapter is of course not merely to trace the development of Russell's theories of judgment, but to examine Wittgenstein's analysis of propositional attitudes in light of those theories. The ultimate goal is to establish the role of the self in philosophy. Note that I speak of a "Wittgensteinian critique" rather than "Wittgenstein's critique." Although Wittgenstein addresses specific complaints to the MRTJ, the bulk of this section will construct a critique, implicit in the *Tractatus*, of the behaviorist analysis. This critique will, if I am not mistaken, shed light on some murky corners of Wittgenstein's early philosophy. It will also provide the key for linking the "world of facts" examined in chapters IV–VI with the "world of values" of the closing passages of the book. Such linkage will be accomplished through a rejection of the philosophical importance of a certain sort of ego, accompanied by the emergence of another ego of great although ineffable importance. In this and the following two chapters we shall also see the re-emergence, in extremely purified form, of something like the Schopenhauerian World as Will.

It is worth mentioning that my intimate linkage of the problems of propositional attitudes with those of ethics is not wholly without explicit support in the Wittgensteinian corpus. In the *Notebooks* Wittgenstein closely connects goodness with whether there can be "functions of situations." In 1914 he writes

> When I say: It is good for p to be the case, then this must be good *in itself.*
> It now seems clear to me that there cannot be functions of situations.
> (*NB*, p. 6)

The following day we find written:

> It could be asked: How can the situation p have a property if it turns out that the situation does not hold at all.
> That is, how can "It is (would be) good that p" be true when p is *not* the case? *(Ibid.)*

The upshot is that goodness is not an ordinary property of things at all.

Criticism of the MRTJ

> Every right theory of judgment must make it impossible for
> me to judge that 'this table penholders the book.' (Russell's
> theory does not satisfy this requirement.)
>
> —WITTGENSTEIN, 1913

Wittgenstein recognizes two major difficulties with the MRTJ. The first (of little interest except in the context of Wittgenstein's Picture Theory of propositions) involves questions about the unity of a proposition and the impossibility of a "nonsensical picture." The second, much more important for our purposes, involves the presence of the ego in the world, a topic which will consume much of the following chapter.

The first objection charges that the MRTJ allows us to "judge a nonsense."[29] In 1913 Wittgenstein believed (for reasons much like those which recommend the "concrete relations" view to Russell) that propositional attitudes were compound or molecular. In "Notes on Logic" we find:

---

[29] It is worth mentioning that philosophers have not universally shared Wittgenstein's opinion that one cannot "will a contradiction." Descartes claims that the human will must be infinite, insofar as we can even will *contradictions*. Meinong holds that "the absurd" too is an object, and thus that mental acts can be directed towards it. Cf. Chisholm, ed., *op. cit.*, p. 108. Compare: ". . . the fact that an objective is either empirically or logically impossible does not prevent the agent from attempting it, provided that the agent *thinks* that success is possible. (Hobbes *attempted* to 'square the circle', and, indeed, thought that he had succeeded.)" D. M. Armstrong, *A Materialist Theory of the Mind* (Routledge and Kegan Paul, London, 1968), p. 150. Thus Black suggests that Russell might simply retort that it *is* possible to judge a nonsense. Wittgenstein's reply must wait until we construct his positive theory of propositional attitudes.

> When we say that A judges that etc..., then we have to mention the whole proposition that A judges. It will not do to mention only its constituents, or its constituents and its form but not in the proper order. This shows that the proposition itself must occur in the statement to the effect that it is judged. (*NB*, p. 96)

But with his increasing clarity about both the role of the Thesis of Extensionality and the nature of Objects, this position becomes less attractive. Since Objects "fit together" without the necessity of a framework, it is at least possible that a judgment about a proposition could be reduced to a judgment about the *elements* of that proposition. Since the terms which are the relata of Russell's N-placed relations in the MRTJ do not have this feature, it is possible then that some nonsensical pseudo-proposition could take the place of 'p' in 'S judges that p.' Thus he writes:

> The correct form of the proposition 'A makes the judgment p,' must show that it is impossible for a judgment to be a piece of nonsense. (Russell's theory does not satisfy this requirement.) (5.5422; compare *NB*, p. 96)

Why must a correct apprehension of the form of such judgments show this? Wittgenstein nowhere explicitly supports this claim, but it is plausible to assume his argument to be that no genuine proposition can have a constituent which is nonsensical. Thus if 'p' is a real constituent of 'S judges that p,' then only a genuine proposition can take the place of 'p'. This is tied up with the nature of truth-functions. In the *Notebooks* Wittgenstein connects the demand that every proposition must achieve sense *by itself* with the further claim that 'A judges that p' must entail directly 'p v ~p'. (*NB*, p. 121) Since only propositions—that is, bearers of truth-values—can be the arguments of truth-functions, only genuine propositions can stand in the place of 'p'. Wittgenstein seems to have much the same thing in mind in a letter to Russell dated June 1913:

> I can express my objection to your theory of judgment exactly: I believe it is obvious that, from the proposition "A judges that (say) *a* is in relation R to *b*," if correctly analyzed, the proposition "aRb · v · ~aRb" must follow directly without the use of any other premise. This condition is not met by your theory. (*LRKM*, p. 23)

Presumably the "other premise" mentioned would be some proposition like " 'aRb' has sense", or " 'aRb' is a genuine proposition." But
such claims are themselves pseudo-propositions.

Does Russell's theory allow us to "judge a nonsense"? If we
accept the MRTJ, then judgment is a relation between a person and
the constituents of the apparent proposition. But the relata of
Russell's judgments are such that there is no guarantee that they will
"fit together" correctly. Suppose my mind stands in a certain relation
to the terms 'table,' 'divisibility,' and 'book.' Can I therefore judge,
"This table is divisible by this book"?[30] Certainly not if we demand,
as Russell seems to, the verb-as-actually-relating-its-relata rather
than the abstract verb. That specific sense of the verb requires that
the relation at least be *capable* of relating its relata, whether it
actually does or not. But the question of whether Russell's theory
does allow us to "judge a nonsense" ought not mask the important
ground of Wittgenstein's objection. If there had to be some
restrictions placed on the sorts of symbols which could take the
place of 'p' in 'S judges that p,' then there would have to be some
science prior to and more general than logic. But then for Wittgenstein that science *would be* logic, and the problem would arise
whether restrictions had to be placed on the symbols of *that* science.
This is why "Logic must take care of itself."

The second and more important criticism of the MRTJ is that it
makes the ego part of the world. But this will emerge from our
examination of the ego in chapter IX, so I will postpone such a
discussion until that time.

A Critique of the Behavioristic Analysis

The formalists are like the watchmaker who is so absorbed
in making his watches look pretty that he has forgotten
their purpose of telling the time, and has therefore omitted
to insert any works.

—RUSSELL,

PRINCIPLES OF MATHEMATICS

---

[30] Wittgenstein offers the rather infelicitous example "This table penholders this book," which
imports the extraneous problem that 'penholders' is not a real verb at all. The resulting
pseudo-proposition is then nonsensical for two reasons, one of which has nothing to do with the
constituents not fitting together properly. Cf. *NB*, p. 96.

Wittgenstein's objections to Russell's 1919 analysis of propositional attitudes must be reconstructed, but the materials are at hand and the constructed objection is, I think, quite plausibly Wittgenstein's. It will also lead us deeper into the foundations of Wittgenstein's early thought than did the previous section.

The behavioristic analysis reduces the judgment-sentence, 'A judges that p,' to a series of propositions, truth-functionally linked with logical connectives, which describe relations between the person-complex A and a series of noises. These noises have meaning by bearing certain causal relations to mental images, which then bear iconic relations of resemblance to their purported referents. Consider this in the light of Wittgenstein's Picture Theory. Elementary propositions picture possible *Sachverhalte* by sharing with them logical form, and by being composed of Names which go proxy for the Objects which constitute the *Sachverhalt* in question. But the relation between symbol and symbolized is not *necessitated* by the nature of the symbol, *not even in the case of mental images*. In every case a method of projection is necessary. This is most obvious in the case of Names, which, standing as they do for (propertyless) Objects, can bear to those Objects *only* a relation of intention (cf. sect. 5.6 above). The projective relation then stands outside the propositional sign, as it were, and crudely put, a certain Name stands for a certain Object due to something we *do* with the Name-sign. But this entails that the behaviorist theory of judgment leaves out one crucial factor, namely what these noises *mean*. (In the following section we shall see the complications involved in any attempt to rectify this fault.) As Quine points out, if by 'killed' we were to mean what we normally mean by 'begat', then 'Brutus killed Caesar' would be false. So mere production of sounds (or for that matter mental images) will suffice to *mean* some object.

There are two reasons why Russell chooses to ignore this, both of which are crucial for Wittgenstein. First, in the tradition of the British Empiricists Russell takes the meanings of words to be *mental images*, little pictures of the referent of the word. It is tempting to see the relation between an image of a pig and the pig itself as being logically tighter, as it were, than that between the mere *word* 'pig' and the pig. Russell's growing amenability to a psychological semantics consequently makes it easier for him to assume that some signs *necessitate* their application.[31] But for Wittgenstein the linkage between symbol and symbolized is not passive but active—see for instance 3.11. Second, an intentional act of meaning requires a subject, and Russell, having rejected on Humean-Jamesian grounds any substantival *knowing* subject, is inclined to deny that there is a (primitive, non-constructed) subject in *any* sense. For Wittgenstein there is a good deal correct, but also something fatally wrong, with such a claim.

Interestingly, the behavioristic analysis shares the worst features of two different philosophical stances which Wittgenstein detests. Not only does it import a psychologism as a theory of meaning, but further represents a sort of *formalism*. The formalist becomes so fascinated with the vehicles of the symbols we use—the piles of ink, noises, mental images—that he ignores the plain fact that these signs must be used with *meanings*.

> Frege ridiculed the formalist conception of mathematics by saying that the formalists confused the unimportant thing, the sign, with the important, the meaning. Frege's idea could be expressed thus: the propositions of mathematics, if they are just a complex of dashes, would be dead and utterly uninteresting, whereas they obviously have a kind of life. And the same, of course, could be said for any other proposition: Without a sense, or without the thought, a proposition would be an utterly dead and trivial thing. And further it seems clear that no adding of inorganic signs can make the proposition live.... What must be added to the dead signs to make a live proposition must be something immaterial, with properties different from all mere signs.[32]

What this "immaterial something" was for Wittgenstein we shall see in the following chapter.

In summary, Wittgenstein rejects the MRTJ insofar as he (perhaps dubiously) believes that it allows us to "judge a nonsense"; in the following section we shall see the further problem that such an

---

[31] This Russellian theory of meaning may also be the ground for Edna O'Shaunessy's infamous claim that Names are *pictures* of Objects—cf. her "The Picture Theory of Meaning" in Copi and Beard *op. cit.*, pp. 115–32.
  Contrast with the argument in the *Blue Book* which begins "If I give someone the order 'Fetch me a red flower from the meadow,' how is he to know what sort of flower to bring me, when I have only given him a *word* ... ?" *BB*, p. 3. Compare *PI*, #84ff.

[32] *Ibid.*, p. 4. Compare with "Frege against the Formalists" in Geach and Black *op. cit.*, pp. 182–233.

analysis makes the ego a part of the world. A Wittgensteinian critique of the behaviorist analysis treats it as a blend of psychologism and formalism, a position which among other shortcomings ignores the crucial *intentional* element in propositional representation.[33] Let us now look at Wittgenstein's positive analysis of propositional attitudes, keeping in mind the goal of the next chapter, namely discovering what it is that the solipsist intends that is "quite correct."

Wittgenstein's Theory of Propositional Attitudes

Wittgenstein's remarks on propositional attitudes appear, as one would expect, as a comment on *Tractatus* 5; every proposition is a truth-function of elementary propositions. He writes:

> In the general propositional form propositions occur in other propositions as bases of truth-functions.
>
> At first sight, it looks as if it were also possible for one proposition to appear in another in a different way.
>
> Particularly, with certain forms of propositions in psychology, such as 'A believes that p is the case', 'A has the thought p', etc.
>
> For if these are considered superficially, it looks as if the proposition p stood in some kind of relation to the object [*Gegenstand*] A. . . .[34]
>
> It is clear, however, that 'A believes that p', 'A has the thought that p' and 'A says p', are all of the form " 'p' says p": and this does not involve the correlation of a fact with an object, but rather the correlations of facts by means of the correlation of their objects. (5.542)

These passages, compressed even by Tractarian standards, need a good deal of unpacking. But note that although these passages begin as a defense of the Thesis of Extensionality against putative

---

[33] I do not, incidentally, mean to imply that Russell in particular and behaviorists in general simply *ignore* the intentional. Their program of course is to construct as much of a science of psychology as can be done without recourse to intentional idioms. The victories and difficulties of that project have been well-cataloged. My point here is only that for *Wittgenstein* this represents a mistake, the seriousness of which has not yet been fully explored.

[34] 5.541 (partial). The slight awkwardness of speaking of colloquial sentences like 'Othello thinks that Desdemona loves Cassio' as "propositions of psychology" harks back to the very broad characterization of science at 4.11—as the whole corpus of true propositions—as opposed to the more sophisticated discussion of 6.32ff. Note that in contrast to the principles of mechanics discussed in the latter passages, these "propositions of psychology" are contingent.

counterexamples, they are followed immediately and interestingly by the cryptic 5.5421, which *appears* on the surface at least to support Russell's behavioristic position.

> This shows too that there is no such thing as the soul—the subject, etc.—as it is conceived in the superficial psychology of the present day.

> Indeed a composite soul would no longer be a soul.

What are we to make of these passages? The analyzability of propositional attitudes and the non-existence of a soul *of a certain sort* were bound up in Wittgenstein's thought early on. In the 1914 notes dictated to Moore, Wittgenstein claims:

> The relation of "I believe p" to "p" can be compared with the relation of " 'p' says p" to "p": It is just as impossible that *I* should be simple as that 'p' should be. (*NB*, p. 118)

Why is this? What sort of analysis of propositional attitudes is Wittgenstein suggesting, and how is such an analysis connected with his carefully restricted rejection of a certain sort of "soul"?

The physical propositional sign being easier to scrutinize than the mental correlate, let us join Russell in substituting "A asserts p" for "A believes p." What happens when a person asserts something? Russell is certainly correct that at the very least he produces a series of sounds which approximate certain phonetic norms. But we saw that these noises differ from street-sounds insofar as they have *meanings.* For Wittgenstein the meaning they have falls into two broad categories. First, the utterance must mirror some possible *Sachverhalt.* Secondly, the person uttering the proposition must *believe* it, as opposed to merely entertain or suggest it. The latter element, which Ramsey calls the "mental" as opposed to the "objective" element in belief,[35] Wittgenstein brushes aside as merely psychological and consequently irrelevant. For the same reason he rejects the assertion sign or judgment stroke as logically irrelevant

---

[35] Ramsey *FoM*, p. 137; compare with Dummett *op. cit.*, pp. 304ff., who argues that any logically adequate symbolism must include an assertion sign. Also bear in mind Hume's point that the difference between belief and disbelief (or any other attitude) cannot be a difference in the *object*, since then dispute would be impossible. Also note how Russell's constant epistemological preoccupations make it very difficult for him to distinguish the logical from the psychological components of judgment and belief; e.g. *L&K*, pp. 216ff.

(4.442), indicating only that (e.g.) Russell and Whitehead take the indicated propositions as true.

But what is the logical component of assertion? Every proposition achieves sense by duplicating the logical form of some *Sachverhalt* and by intending or "meaning" through the use of Names the Objects for which those Names go proxy. It is this dual projective relation which transforms noises into propositions. Wittgenstein later writes:

> It seems that there are *certain definite* mental processes bound up with the working of language ... I mean the processes of understanding and meaning ... We are tempted to think that the action of language consists of two parts; an organic part, the handling of signs, and an inorganic part, which we may call understanding these signs, meaning them, interpreting them, thinking. These latter mechanisms seem to take place in a queer sort of medium, the mind....[36]

Setting aside until the next chapter the nature of "mind," I think that we can use this passage as a model for an analysis of 'A asserts that p'. It will consist of two parts, one "organic", the other "inorganic." Consider the following, very crude, model:

A asserts p $=_{df}$ A makes the sounds x-y-z and these sounds mean that X-Y-Z.

Mere belief would be similar, with "mental constituents" substituted for the noises x-y-z.

The first thing to note is that the first conjunct is, in Wittgenstein's metaphor, wholly "organic," wholly explainable in terms of the natural sciences. It would thus be the job of the physiologist to tell us how it is possible for the human animal to make these sounds, and for the historian of tongues to trace how these sounds came to play the role that they do. This series of sounds will in turn be part of the philosophically uninteresting person A, who is to be construed as a psycho-physical complex. The production of a propositional sign will be such an obvious (and uninteresting) element of assertion that Wittgenstein omits mention of it from the very compressed analysis of "A asserts p" in 5.542, assuming it as given. (Cf. Black *op. cit.*, pp. 298–99) But what of the second part of the suggested analysis? We

---

[36] *BB*, p. 3. Wittgenstein is of course here *contrasting* such views with his current ones.

know that the propositional sign must have the proper multiplicity to be able to represent its sense. Thus what needs examination is the *connection* of the signs in the utterance with the elements of the sense.

How is this done? The signs themselves are "dead"; they need to be projected, meant, intended in order to become symbols. *It is crucial to note that mental as well as physical signs need such projection;* Wittgenstein flatly denies the Russellian claim that mental images mean "on their own," that they need no interpretation or projection.[37] Thus there will also be an *inorganic* element in assertion, one not amenable to investigation by the sciences. This element will be responsible for the second conjunct, " 'p' means p." But as we saw above, " 'p' means p" is a pseudo-proposition, which, like " 'A' is the name for A," " 'p' is a proposition" and so forth, attempts to *say* something which can only be *shown*. Propositional attitudes thus break into two parts: "A asserts p" becomes "A says 'p' and 'p' means p." The first conjunct is describable in truth-functional terms, is sayable and philosophically ho-hum. It states that a certain organic structure—a psycho-physical entity—is in a certain state. This psycho-physical structure, an empirical person or ego, might be called the "knowing subject" and "contains" as component parts beliefs, etc. Since it must have the complexity to mirror articulated *Sachverhalte,* the mere fact that it *is* the knowing subject entails that it must be complex. The second conjunct, however, while philosophically crucial, is ineffable; we cannot say *in* language what makes language possible.

Consider the consequences of such an analysis of proposition attitudes. First, since there are no "impossible facts," and since the propositional sign is itself a fact, it is impossible to "judge a nonsense." Thus Wittgenstein's own analysis satisfies the conditions he puts on Russell's theory. Second, and by far more important, the knowing subject, the psycho-physical ego, is simultaneously non-simple and a part of the world. The fact that it can contain as constituents articulated, complex propositions shows that it cannot be an Object, as does its describability in the manner which Russell indicates in *Principia.* On the other hand, behind the empirical ego

---

[37] Criticism of the notion that some signs are "already interpreted," and an extension of this argument to the important case of *rules*, constitutes one major thread of the opening parts of *PI*. See, for instance, #86.

must stand a metaphysical subject, a *willing subject* whose active intending turns dead signs into "living" symbols. As a necessary condition for language, it cannot be represented *in* language, and is thus ineffable. Finally, the sayable part of the analysis is wholly extensional. Like any other proposition of the natural sciences, it is truth-functional; thus the apparent counterexample to the Thesis of Extensionality has disappeared.

The empirical ego A in our analysis above, the complex which contains as a constituent the propositional sign, is both composite and part of the world. For these reasons, it lacks the necessary properties for being a bearer of ethical attributes. If it were the only sort of ego, then there would be no possibility of attributing value to any element of reality. But we have seen that it is *not* the only sort of ego; there is also the metaphysical ego, the willing subject whose intending function turns signs into symbols. Even though (or better, *because*) it has been pushed into the realm of the ineffable, the metaphysical ego is of tremendous importance for Wittgenstein. In the following chapter, we will examine the nature of this metaphysical ego and the importance of its reality. This will serve as a transition from the ineffability of metaphysics and logic to the ineffability of value which features so prominently in the closing pages of the *Tractatus*. And if I am not mistaken, it will announce the reappearance of the Schopenhauerian World as Will in new guise.

IX

Realism, Idealism, and What Solipsism Intends

Strictly from the point of view of each individual, it might
well appear that everything depended on his own personal
existence; he himself is 'all in all' and contains the whole of
reality. But ... Schopenhauer also held that what he
referred to in general as the 'knowing subject' cannot be
identified with the consciousness of any *particular*
individual, for each and every individual is simply a 'bearer
of the subject.' ... It follows that the particular self, which
considered 'subjectively' (i.e. from the standpoint of the
individual or 'microcosm') can present itself under a
gigantic aspect, so that the world as a whole—the
'macrocosm'—may seem to be a mere modification of the
individual's own nature that will perish with him at his
death ...

—Patrick Gardiner, SCHOPENHAUER

If I said "but that would mean considering intention as
something other than a phenomenon" that would make
intention reminiscent of the will as conceived by
Schopenhauer. Every phenomenon seems dead in
comparison with the living thought.

—Wittgenstein, c. 1933

Wittgenstein's disposal of propositional attitudes as putative
counterexamples to the thesis of extensionality is intimately connected with two claims, both rendered rather startling in the
contexts in which they arise. The first is that the time-honored
philosophical distinction between realism and idealism (with solipsism as a special case of the latter) is empty (5.64). The second is that
although what the solipsist tries to say is nonsense, he nevertheless aims at something which, though ineffable, is of tremendous philosophical significance. The analysis of what the solipsist
tries to say, and why he fails, will allow us to give content to the
claim of 6.52—"The world is *my* world"—the ineffable claim

which, if I am not mistaken, constitutes the major portion of the "ladder" which must be climbed and then discarded in order for us to "see the world aright."[1]

Solipsism

Solipsism (from *solus ipse*— 'the self alone') appears in western philosophy in two rather different forms. *Metaphysical solipsism* affirms the existence of a single self, the rest of the world being merely objects for that self, dependent on it in roughly the same manner in which our ideas are dependent on our minds. Solipsism in this form appears as an extreme version of idealism. *Epistemological solipsism* can perhaps best be understood in the context of the Cartesian project. Descartes argues that the immediate objects of our experience are not independent, objective things, but rather our own ideas—modes of that substance which is us. The larger part of the philosopher's chore is to argue from the existence and properties of these objects to the existence and properties of the things which we pre-philosophically take them to represent. If this project (with which Descartes thinks that he has succeeded in Meditations III and VI) fails, then we are forced to admit that all we can legitimately claim to know is ourselves and our ideas. Epistemological solipsism thus constitutes a form of scepticism, and insofar as Wittgenstein classifies all matters epistemological as merely psychological, this form of solipsism is of little interest to him.

Metaphysical solipsism, on the other hand, carried a fascination for Wittgenstein throughout his philosophical career. Some Tractarian scholars have chosen to ignore this fascination, regarding the remarks on solipsism and allied topics mere *obiter dicta*. Others argue that Wittgenstein uses the term 'solipsism' in a manner so distant from the ordinary usage as to be of little interest.[2] I want to argue that Wittgenstein uses the term in a manner quite similar to its normal philosophical usage, and further that an understanding of his contention that what the solipsist tries to say is of great importance

---

[1] Some of the material in which chapter as appeared in my paper "Pulling up the Ladder: *Tractatus* 6.54", *Idealistic Studies*, vol. XV (1985), pp. 249–70.

[2] "When [Wittgenstein] says that solipsism is correct he means his own particular interpretation of solipsism which can only be understood in the context of other doctrines of the *Tractatus*." Jaakko Hintikka, "On Wittgenstein's Solipsism," in Copi and Beard *op. cit.*, p. 158. Note that Hintikka claims that Wittgenstein baldly asserts the truth of solipsism, which he does not.

is central to becoming clear about "the whole sense" of the *Tractatus.*

Schopenhauer, we remember, likened solipsism (probably the sceptical sort) to a fortress unassailable yet impotent; although we cannot overthrow it, its defenders cannot sally forth to harm us either, and so it may be safely bypassed. But I agree with Hacker (*op. cit.*, p. 71) that Wittgenstein would regard as unsatisfactory such a "glib dismissal" of the problem, particularly bearing as it does obvious relations to the crucial fourth class of representations for a subject. (Schopenhauer's remarks bring to mind Russell's Mrs. Ladd Franklin, who proclaimed herself a solipsist and was amazed by the failure of others to share her opinions!) Wittgenstein's own ruminations on the subject occupied him throughout his career, constantly drawing him back to the problem of solipsism, his criticisms becoming refined and reformulated in ways which parallel the general development of his thought.[3] That the question of solipsism and how much truth it held was important to him is also indicated in the negative reaction Peter Geach tells us Wittgenstein had towards Frege's "The Thought"[4]: in correspondence he chides Frege for attacking idealism on its "weak side." A worthwhile attack, on the other hand, would necessarily take on idealism where it is the strongest. This "strongest side," I contend, is "The world is *my* world."

The first chore is to show why it is that realism, idealism, and solipsism as normally conceived collapse into one another. I want to do this by offering fairly straightforward, traditional definitions of 'idealism', 'realism', and 'solipsism'; later I will supplement these with "translations" into Tractarian terms.

In Chapter II I presented realism as the doctrine that, ignoring cases like realizing that I have a headache, every mental act has some extramental object. To be of philosophical interest the claim must be taken as necessary—Husserl and Frege seem to construe it thus, although some realists appear to hold that it is merely contingent.[5]

---

[3] E.g. *Blue Book*, pp. 48, 57–59, 63–64, 71; Wittgenstein, *Philosophical Remarks*, trans. Hargreaves and White (Barnes and Noble, NY, 1975), pp. 88–95; and *PI*, #401–2.

[4] See Geach's editorial preface to G. Frege, *Logical Investigations*, trans. Geach and Stoothoff (Yale U. Press, New Haven, 1977). The Frege-Wittgenstein correspondence was destroyed by bombing during the Second World War.

[5] Russell in his early days tends to conflate realism with pluralism, with the latter treated, according to Russell's desire to banish modal notions from philosophy, as contingent. For the

Idealism, on the other hand, must advance its claim as necessary; the idealist would find little comfort in a world where *as a matter of fact* people thought about nothing save their own headaches. Thus the idealist must argue roughly that the world as a whole is necessarily object-for-a-subject; it is a world of experience, and thus logically depends upon experiencers or subjects.[6] Idealism in the most extreme form becomes solipsism; all reality is an object for *one* mind, one subject. Note that each of these positions is defined in terms of the logical relations between selves or souls or minds and the objects of their experience; their precise meaning will thus fluctuate with differing conceptions of selves, objects, and the requisite logical relations.

Wittgenstein's claim is that (a) there are no philosophically important, *sayable* differences between these three positions, and yet (b) there is truth in solipsism which while ineffable is of great philosophical importance. The former position is stated straightforwardly: "Here it can be seen that solipsism, when its implications are followed out strictly, corresponds with pure realism" (5.64). The latter is represented by darker hints that the solipsist is onto something important which, unfortunately, cannot be said. Wittgenstein's arguments for these claims fall into two major classes. The first appears to deal with the non-discoverability of the self in introspection, the second with the implications of certain semantic theses.

The apparent "non-discoverability" argument is imbedded in a series of remarks formally commenting on 5.6—"*The limits of my language* mean the limits of my world." This claim—not wholly transparent itself—is followed by the long passage 5.61:

> Logic pervades the world: the limits of the world are also its limits. So we cannot say in logic, 'The world has this in it, and this, but not that.'

> For this would appear to presuppose that we were excluding certain possibilities, and this cannot be the case, since it would require that logic should go beyond the limits of the world; for only in that way could we view those limits from the other side as well.

---

former tendency, see "The Basis of Realism," *JP* vol. 8 (1911), pp. 158–61; for the latter, Russell's answer to the first question following the opening lecture on logical atomism; Marsh *op. cit.*, p. 188.

[6] Moore writes "Modern idealism, if it asserts any general conclusion about the universe at all, asserts that it is *spiritual*." "A Refutation of Idealism," p. 1, in *Philosophical Studies*. Compare with F. H. Bradley, *Appearance and Reality*, ch. 14, and Russell, *Problems of Philosophy*, ch. IV.

We cannot think what we cannot think: so what we cannot think we cannot *say* either.

This remark, apparently about logic as the "limit of the world," precedes 5.62—"This remark provides the key to the problem, how much truth there is in solipsism", followed closely by "I am my world (The microcosm)." What path leads from the first remarks to the final one? An adequate answer will, I shall contend, bring to light another limit on the world besides logic.

The opening points of 5.61 are familiar, ignoring the puzzling use of the 'world' where one would expect 'reality'. Logic dictates what possibilities there are, or better, logic embodies those possibilities. But we cannot *say* this or that is possible, insofar as this would require some *higher* court of appeal, as it were, than logic. If "logically possible" and "logically impossible" were real designations of things, then there would need to be some discipline higher than logic which dealt with them, and this discipline, one is inclined to say, would *be* logic. Thus we can only speak of what we can imagine to be different, the contingent.[7] Thus we cannot picture an "illogical world," nor can we say *how* logic permeates the world.

The connection between this point and solipsism might be illuminated by a consideration of certain conceptions of the self which were current in Wittgenstein's day. Traditional (post-Cartesian) continental philosophy saw a yawning gap between the thinking subject and material things—variations on the Cartesian notion of two different sorts of substance. But Schopenhauer's insistence, grounded on his reading of Kant, of the primacy of the willing subject, and on the voluntaristic underpinning of both mind and body, weakened the hold of the traditional mind-body dichotomy on German-speaking intellectuals. The absoluteness of the dichotomy was dealt an additional blow by the neo-Humean sensationalism of Mach. Mach's thesis that whether a given sensation was considered part of the mind or part of the external world is largely conventional exerted a powerful effect on many Viennese thinkers who influenced Wittgenstein.[8] The results of such a breakdown of

---

[7] "If I say 'I have not got stomach-ache,' then this presupposes the possibility of a state of stomach-ache. My present state and the state of stomach-ache are in the same logical space, as it were." *WVC*, p. 67.

[8] "Ordinarily the complex $\alpha\beta\gamma$ ... is contrasted as ego with the complex ABC ... At first only those elements ABC ... that more strongly alter $\alpha\beta\gamma$. ... , as a prick, a pain, are wont to be thought of

the strong walls of the ego can be detected in every aspect of Viennese life; Schorske writes of Schönberg that:

> He shared with his older contemporaries, intellectual pioneers of Vienna's elite—Hofmannsthal, Freud, Klimt and Ernst Mach—a diffuse sense that all is in flux, that the boundary between the ego and the world is permeable.[9]

We have seen a hint of such a breaking down of the importance of the distinction between the world and the ego in the analysis of propositional attitudes in the preceding chapter; we shall soon have occasion to examine it more closely. One very important result for Wittgenstein of such blending of self and world is that "mental" facts—thoughts, *Gedanken*—assume no particular significance over, say, propositions written on a blackboard.

Wittgenstein's analysis of what we might call the *empirical* ego, which begins at 5.631, echoes the sentiments of the preceding paragraph.

> There is no such thing as the subject that thinks or entertains ideas.

> If I wrote a book called *The World as I Found It*, I should have to include a report on my body, and should have to say which parts were subordinate to my will, and which were not, etc., this being a method of isolating the subject, or rather of showing that there is no subject; for that alone could *not* be mentioned in that book.

This passage is often compared (e.g. Hacker *op. cit.*, p. 59) with the celebrated passage in the *Treatise* (I/iv/7), where Hume writes:

> For my part, whenever I enter most intimately into what I call *myself*, I always stumble on some particular perception or other, of heat or cold, light or dark, love or hatred, pain or pleasure. I can never catch *myself* at any time without a perception, and can never observe anything but the perception.

---

as comprising the ego. Afterwards, however, it appears that the right to annex ABC ... nowhere ceases. In conformity with this view the ego can be so extended as ultimately to embrace the entire world. The ego is not sharply marked off, its limits are very indefinite and arbitrarily displacable. Only by failing to observe this fact . . . [are] metaphysical difficulties met with in this context. Mach, *The Analysis of Sensations*, p. 13.

[9] Schorske *op. cit.*, p. 345. But such logical blurring did little in many cases to alleviate the *existential* isolation. Consider Kokoschka's portrait of Hans Tietze and Erica Tietze-Conrat (*ibid.*, plate XV), noting the hands that reach out but fail to touch.

The thrust of Hume's argument is this: all (simple) ideas originally spring from (simple) impressions of sensation. If I have an impression of a simple self, it presumably came through introspection. But whenever I look inside myself, I find nothing which could count as a perception of a substantival self. Therefore, we have no idea of such a self (at least, no idea which comes from an impression of sensation) and by implication, there is no such subject. Is Wittgenstein's argument a Humean one?

There are good reasons to reject the tempting parallel. Consider the first premise of Hume's argument. The empiricist maxim of *Treatise* I/i/1 declares "that all our simple ideas in their first appearance are receiv'd from simple impressions, which are correspondent to them, and which they exactly resemble." (p. 4) Without this restriction on the origin of our ideas, the argument of I/iv/7, along with the parallel arguments of I/ii/6 (concerning external existence), I/iii/2 (concerning necessary connection) and so forth amount to no more than proofs of the a priori origin of such ideas. But following Frege, Wittgenstein would regard such an empiricist theory of ideas a mere prejudice, and certainly nothing of fundamental *philosophical* interest. Thus he would reject, or at least bracket, a crucial Humean premise.

Second, the *Notebooks* passage which becomes 5.631 contains a discussion of the extent to which the existence of simples—that is Objects—could be proved by *pointing to examples*. Rather, he suggests, they are known "by description," via inference, as the end-point of analysis. (This is why Wittgenstein can maintain with certainty that there are Objects even in the face of his confessed inability to give a single example.) This original context renders it quite implausible that the same argument would be used in the *Tractatus* for the purpose of showing that since no simple self is uncovered through introspection, there is no such self. The existence of a simple self, like the being of Objects, is posited on logical grounds.

Finally, and very importantly, Wittgenstein does not flatly reject the existence of a self or ego, but only a subject *that thinks or entertains ideas*. This claim ought not be wholly unexpected, since we have already seen rejected the notion that propositional attitudes represent a relation between the self and a proposition. Further, 5.631 is followed directly by the claim that the ego does not belong in the world, but rather functions as a "limit" on the world. Thus

Wittgenstein appears to be distinguishing between the empirical ego, the composite or aggregate of thoughts which featured in the previous chapter, and the metaphysical self or ego. The first is "the soul—the subject, etc.—as it is conceived in the superficial psychology of the present day" (5.5421), which Wittgenstein characterizes as lacking philosophical importance. Thus 5.631 can hardly be taken as a flat rejection of the being of a philosophically interesting self.

Although the existence of a philosophically interesting self or ego has not been refuted, the upshot of 5.631 is that nothing which could be found in the book *The World as I Found It* could qualify as such an ego. The reason is that such a soul would necessarily be *simple*. But if it could appear in the book, it would necessarily be describable and sayable, and if sayable it would be a *Sachverhalt* or composite thereof, not a simple at all. The upshot would then seem to be not that Wittgenstein rejects the existence of a simple or substantival soul in the manner of *Treatise* I/iv/7, but rather that such a soul has been excluded from the realm of the sayable.[10] Since the world and the sayable are coextensive, the preceding claim is equivalent to saying that no philosophically interesting, that is, simple, ego exists *in* the world.

How is the fruitlessness of a search for such an ego in the world connected with the claim that realism, idealism, and solipsism, when thought out, coincide? I characterized each position in terms of a relation between the ego and the rest of the world. Yet when we try to isolate the subject in the requisite manner, to examine its relations to the world, we fail. But I do not think that Wittgenstein's certainty on this matter is based solely on the Gedanken-experiment of 5.631; it has roots much deeper in his system. The very possibility of such a subject would violate some of the most basic principles of Wittgenstein's early philosophy.

The deeper argument to which I allude is connected with the "eye metaphor" of 5.633–5.6331, where Wittgenstein analogizes the relation between the metaphysical ego and the world to the relation between the eye and the visual field.[11] Following the claim that "The

---

[10] My conclusions here parallel those reached by Bernard Williams in his excellent "Wittgenstein and Idealism," in Vesey, ed. *op. cit.*, p. 77.

[11] The eye metaphor is from Schopenhauer, who introduces it in a similar context in *WWR* I, p. 491. For other occurrences and related passages, see Hacker *op. cit.*, pp. 64–65.

subject does not belong to the world: rather, it is the limit of the world" (5.632), Wittgenstein writes (5.633–5.6331)

> Where *in* the world is a metaphysical subject to be found?
>
> You will say that this is exactly like the case of the eye and the visual field. But really you do *not* see the eye.
>
> And nothing in the visual field allows you to infer that it is seen by an eye.
>
> For the form of the visual field is surely not like this

Eye—

Although much in this passage is murky, the argument seems to be that although the existence of an eye is a necessary condition for there being a visual field, the eye itself cannot be a constituent of the field.[12] If something is seen, there must be a seer, but nothing which is present in the visual field could even be a candidate for being the seer. Given the necessity of a seer for a visual field, it is less clear why Wittgenstein says that nothing in the visual field allows us to "infer" the eye: I take him to mean that *no particular object* in the visual field entails the existence of the subject (as, for instance, a dark line surrounding my visual field might entail that I am wearing glasses), but rather that the existence of the field *whatever it contains* entails the existence of the corresponding eye. Some of the puzzlement surrounding this remark will disappear when we discuss the propositional correlate.

The relation of the eye to the visual field, Wittgenstein tells us, is "connected with the fact that no part of our experience is at the same time a priori," continuing:

> Whatever can be seen could be other than it is.
>
> Whatever we describe at all could be other than it is.

---

[12] A *physical* eye? One would think not, but something rather like the "geometrical eye" of *BB*, pp. 63–64, which seems to play a role parallel to the eye of 5.6331. Note also that the sketch does not picture *two* eyes.

There is no a priori order of things.[13]

These remarks directly precede the assertion of the identity of realism, solipsism, and idealism. Let us try to unravel this skein of claims.

In order to do so, I want to translate into Tractarian terms the characteristic claims of the three theories. Let me posit a range of Objects which are egos or selves, and denote each of these as S_1, S_2, ... and denote ambiguously any arbitrary member of the set as S_x. We can now express the characteristic claims of realism, idealism, and solipsism in terms of the presence or absence of the members of this class in constituents of the world.[14]

Idealism: Every possible fact contains as a constituent some S_x, e.g. S_2, S_{13}, etc.

Realism: Some facts contain no S_x.

Solipsism: Every possible fact contains *the same* S_x, e.g. S_1.

These translations lay bare the difficulties with idealism and solipsism. Consider some elementary proposition 'ABC'. On the construals of either idealism or solipsism advanced above, it would be immediately evident, since neither contains a name of the range 'S_x', that is not even *possible*. But certainly the possibility of ascertaining *merely from inspection* that a given elementary proposition is true or not goes against the grain of the whole picture theory. No picture is true or false a priori (2.222–2.225), and no proposition fails to picture a real possibility (3.02, 2.201–2.203). Thus we cannot allow the soul or ego to enter the world either as a *Sachverhalt*, or as an aggregate of them, or as an Object which

---

[13] 5.634. 'Things' in the last sentence must be a slip for 'facts'. Objects cannot be described at all, and there is obviously an a priori order of Objects.

Hacker (*op. cit.*, ch. III) makes a great deal of the word 'experience' in this remark, but this seems misleading. Every claim made about "experience" can also be reparsed in terms of the world and its contingency. Wittgenstein's claims are certainly not *empirical.*

[14] Here it might be objected that I ignore the possibility of a mind or soul being a *Sachverhalt* of a special sort, which bears relations to others. This will not do for several reasons. First, no *Sachverhalt* has the requisite simplicity that Wittgenstein demands of a subject. Second, no *Sachverhalt* bears necessary relations to any other. Third, for reasons we have not yet unearthed, if the self were a *Sachverhalt* then it would be incapable of being either a bearer of value or the intentional/semantic agent we have seen it to be.

enters into *Sachverhalte* as a constituent.[15] What we see is that any attempt to translate into Tractarian terms the claims of realism or solipsism violates the fundamental principles of Wittgenstein's view of logic and language. Yet if we do not so translate them, there is no apparent difference between the two positions.

The self—the philosophically interesting subject, the metaphysical ego—is thus not a constituent of the world, either in the sense of being a fact or being a constituent of a fact. It lies outside the world, as a "limit." (5.632) Like the other limit—logic—it is not sayable and thus cannot appear in any description of the world. Since realism and idealism are defined in terms of propositions which assert the relation of my ego to the world, any attempt to spell out what someone means by "I am an idealist" or "I am a realist" fails. Wittgenstein makes this point at 5.64, but rather more forcefully in the *Notebooks:*

> This is the way I have traveled: Idealism singles out men from the world as unique, solipsism singles out me alone, and at last I see that I too belong with the rest of the world, and so on the one side *nothing* is left over, and on the other side, as unique, *the world*. In this way idealism leads to realism if it is strictly thought out.[16]

It is illuminating to compare these points with the similar argument of the *Blue Book* (pp. 57ff.), which leads, however, to a quite different conclusion. There, in the context of a sustained discussion of solipsism, Wittgenstein offers various notions of personal identity—various possible uses of 'I'—examining in each case the possible criteria of application. None of these seems to catch what the solipsist means when he says things like "Only *I* see things" and so forth; the upshot is that the solipsist needs some notion of personal identity which allows of no criteria of application. But by 1931 Wittgenstein seems comfortable with the quasi-positivistic conclusion that the solipsist is merely waving at an

---

[15] There seems to be one faint possibility of salvaging the view that the self is an Object. Russell thought that every proposition must include a verb, whose role was to give the proposition structure, to glue the parts together. Is it possible that the S_x play the same role? In this case, no picture could fail to contain one, and mere analysis would show the truth of idealism. Note that on this construal idealism would have no contrary, insofar as we could not even *conceive* of an alternative.

[16] By 'nothing', I take Wittgenstein to mean: nothing *sayable*, no *facts*, nothing *of the same sort as the world*. More of the content of Wittgenstein's remark will become clear when we examine what it is that the solipsist intends which is correct.

illusion. This contrasts sharply with the Tractarian position I have outlined above; there the ineffability of the ego makes it, as we shall see, a possible candidate for being the bearer of value. Although what the solipsist *says* is nonsense, the insight which drives him is quite correct, even though it cannot be said, but must make itself manifest. Having seen the negative side of the analysis—that the solipsist makes no important *sayable* claim—let us now see what it is that he means or intends that is "quite correct."

What Solipsism Intends: The Metaphysical Subject

> Don't think that I despise metaphysics. I regard some of the great philosophical writings of the past as among the noblest works of the human mind.
>
> —WITTGENSTEIN TO DRURY, c. 1929[17]

> To use the metaphorical language sometimes employed by Sartre (since literal usage tends to suggest an object rather than consciousness), consciousness is a great emptiness, a wind blowing towards objects. Its whole reality is exhausted in intending what is other.
>
> —TRANSLATOR'S INTRODUCTION TO SARTRE'S *TRANSCENDENCE*
> *OF THE EGO*

Our attempt to pin down the dispute between realism and solipsism turned up nothing in the world save the philosophically uninteresting empirical ego, the "self of psychology" of 5.631. This self, so our analysis of propositional attitudes disclosed, is a Humean bundle of *Gedanken* and other mental constituents, whose unity is external and contingent. It would be as odd to attribute a special significance to the empirical ego as it would to attribute such significance to a set of propositions on the blackboard. This is why the imaginary book *The World as I Found It* ('. . . this being a method of isolating the subject . . .') discloses nothing of philosophical interest ('. . . or rather of showing that in an important sense there is no subject . . .'). The empirical ego can play the role neither of the

---

[17] Cf. M. O'C. Drury, "Some Notes on Conversations with Wittgenstein," in R. Rhees *op. cit.*, p. 93. Contrast: "Another influential idea of Wittgenstein's was the insight that many philosophical sentences, especially in traditional metaphysics, are pseudo-sentences, devoid of cognitive content. I found Wittgenstein's view on this point close to the one I had previously developed under the influence of anti-metaphysical scientists and philosophers." Carnap's memoir of Wittgenstein from his "Autobiography," reprinted in Fann *op. cit.*, pp. 33–34.

intending agent which provides the "method of projection," nor the bearer of ethical attributes. But the rejection of a "subject that thinks or entertains thoughts" in no way precludes the being and philosophical significance of another sort of subject, the metaphysical ego. Of course it shows that the metaphysical ego cannot be the *knowing* subject, but we have handy from our study of Schopenhauer an ideal replacement, namely the *willing subject*. This section will both look back towards Schopenhauer and the analysis of propositional attitudes, and forward towards the relation of the will to the world and the possibility of value.

The passages from 5.6 through 5.641 are marked by the sudden, almost shocking intrusion of the personal pronoun 'my' — 'my world', 'my language' — but never, as Black points out (*op. cit.*, p. 307) 'my logic'. What is the source and significance of this sudden appearance of the personal in the *Tractatus*? At 5.641 Wittgenstein tells us "What brings the self into philosophy is that 'the world is my world'."[18] How is this?

First, Wittgenstein uses the words 'self', 'soul', and 'subject' in an apparently interchangeable way, indicating that he intends nothing to turn on the ordinary connotations of those terms, and that he means the semi-technical, non-composite metaphysical ego of 5.5421. (This mirrors the interchangeable use of ordinary German terms for 'Object' in 2.01.) I therefore assume that the self which "the world is my world" brings into philosophy is such a non-composite self. Further, since philosophy deals only with the *necessary* elements of the world, such unity must be necessary, in contrast with the contingent unity of the empirical ego. But what is this metaphysical ego? What is it that the solipsist *intends* which is correct?

We saw in our analysis of propositional attitudes that 'S says p' breaks rather unevenly in half, yielding 'S utters p' and " 'p' means p." The former represents the claim that the psycho-physical entity S contains, as one of the facts of which it is constituted, the phonetic sequence which represents uttering "p". But the latter claim—that these sounds have a *sense*—is dependent on two different intentional elements. The first is the projection of the logical form of the symbol-fact onto the logical form of a possible *Sachverhalt*, the

---

[18] I have slightly altered the translation; that there is no "fact" that the world is my world is the upshot of *The World as I Found It*.

second the correlation of the Names in the proposition with the Objects named, via the user of the Name meaning *just this Object.* This "user" cannot be the empirical ego, that is, the psychological component of the person S. That ego is composed of *Gedanken,* which, being propositions, *presuppose these intending acts and thus cannot be responsible for them.* Since the intending ego cannot be either a *Gedanken* or an aggregate thereof, and since knowing at least includes a relation to a propositional sign, the metaphysical ego cannot be the knowing subject, although it is presupposed by the knowing subject. Since intending is a sort of willing, it is thus tempting to say that the metaphysical subject is the *willing subject,* not a part of the world but a noumenal correlate to the phenomenal subject. This characterization is a bit too rough; in the following chapter we shall distinguish metaphysical and phenomenal senses of 'willing', and thus both a metaphysical and phenomenal "willing subject."

But in an odd way, the attempt to "isolate the subject" is wrongheaded for reasons other than that the metaphysical subject cannot be pictured and thus cannot be captured propositionally. It cannot be isolated since it manifests itself *everywhere.* Why is this?

Every thought is a proposition, that is, a logical picture of a possible *Sachverhalt.* The world is a contingent aggregate of *Sachverhalte,* and, since every elementary proposition pictures its sense with perfect clarity and precision, the world allows of being represented in speech with such clarity and precision. But behind each of these *Gedanken* must lie the intending metaphysical subject, and thus the world—everything that I can represent in language or thought—is conditioned by this intending metaphysical ego and thus is "mine."[19]

Thus the world, insofar as it can have any possible significance to me, is "my" world, the world which is conditioned, in a hitherto unexplained sense, by the presence of that intending ego which is "me." "My world" is thus bounded on the outer limit, as it were, by the most general of possible concerns—logic—and on the "inner" by the most singular—the metaphysical subject. But this cannot be said. I cannot say "This world is a logical world," because I cannot

---

[19] I use the quotes here to indicate that we are playing fast and loose with what cannot be said but only shown. I have also not yet offered any evidence for the claims that (a) this intending ego is personal in any sense or (b) that Wittgenstein thought it was.

say what could fail to be a logical world; logic permeates *every* world. Likewise, I cannot say "The world is *my* world," since any world of which I can conceive must be mine. But that each makes itself manifest everywhere, and on the side of the metaphysical subject, this is what the solipsist tries to say but fails.[20] These two claims — "the world is a logical world" and "The world is my world" — are, I think, the most general ways of representing the "ladder" of 6.54, which must be climbed and then discarded in order to see the world aright.

"The world is my world" also provides the sense of 5.6, *"The limits of my language* mean the limits of my world." Language is coextensive with the world; even wider if we take "the world" in the sense of the aggregate of *actual Sachverhalte*, since we can think and say what is *not.* But we cannot "think," cannot frame a logical picture, of the necessary conditions for the existence of language and thought. These limits are now two: logic, which provides the structure of the world, and the metaphysical self, which provides the "life," as it were, to "dead" propositional signs. But that which lies at the limit of language cannot be represented in language; we try to speak of "my language" or "my world," but the sayable force of "my" vanishes when pressed.[21] The metaphysical ego thus disappears at the inner limit in a sense precisely parallel to that in which logic disappears at the outer limit. But when we try to say this, we end up "bumping our heads against the limits of language."[22]

The attraction which the solipsist's attempted claim exerts on the human mind Wittgenstein recognized as powerful even when be himself was free of it. In a striking passage in the *Blue Book*, responding to criticism of solipsism which turns on the lack of criteria of individuation for the metaphysical ego, he writes:

---

[20] Anscombe (*op. cit.*, pp. 166–67) compares this argument with the *Blue Book* (pp. 64ff.) where Wittgenstein compares the solipsist's claims with a language in which some individual A was (by convention) used as the center, and where talk of others was put obliquely in terms of A. This analogy leads Anscombe to worry about criteria of individuation for the metaphysical subject. But there can be none, and at least in 1918 this worries Wittgenstein very little. As I have alluded to above, the quasi-positivistic atmosphere of the *Blue Book* is quite foreign to Tractarian thought.

[21] But contrary to "The world is my world," to even *try* to speak of "my logic" is pernicious nonsense. That Wittgenstein thinks that "The world is my world" attempts to say something of importance seems to me to bear heavily against "pantheistic" interpretations of the metaphysical ego and the *Tractatus* as a whole, which try to make a lot of hay out of the lack of individuating criteria for metaphysical egos.

[22] Although not in the sense of *PI*, #309. In the *Tractatus* Wittgenstein holds what might loosely be called a "realistic" view of the limits of language. In his later works such "bumpings" often turn out to be the result of confusion of the conventional with the empirical.

I can still express solipsism by saying "Only what *I* see (or: see now) is really seen." And here I am tempted to say: "Although by the word 'I' I don't mean L.W., it will do if others understand 'I' to mean L.W., if just now I am in fact L.W." I could also express my claim by saying: "I am the vessel of life": but mark, it is essential that everyone to whom I say this should be unable to understand me. (pp. 64–65)

This sentiment is present even more explicitly in the *Philosophical Remarks:* There Wittgenstein discusses an example quite similar to the *Blue Book* passage, but concludes with a rather different twist. He considers a number of egocentric languages, and argues that the one with *me* at the center is special, and that its "application"—a word now evolving from its Tractarian sense, in which it would be contingent and philosophically uninteresting, to that which Wittgenstein later attaches to it—shows this special position. But then he continues:

Only their application really differentiates languages; but if we disregard this, all languages are equivalent. All of these languages only describe a single, incomparable thing and *cannot* represent anything else. (Both of these approaches must lead to the same result: first that what is represented is not one thing among others, that it is not capable of being contrasted with anything; second, that I cannot express the advantage of *my* language.[23]

That there *is* such an advantage, a specialness, is presupposed by the passage.

"I am the vessel of life"—this is the solipsistic sentiment which lies behind many of the most striking Schopenhauerian remarks in the *Notebooks.* But by the time the *Tractatus* was composed, Wittgenstein's growing awareness of the role which the say/show distinction played in his thought brought into clearer focus the limitations and dangers of trying to say such things. Thus we get "ladders" which are discarded almost immediately, hints which result in great bewilderment. For example, we move from the remarks in 5.62, with their emphasis on the pronoun 'my', to 5.621—"The world and life are one." The transition is less puzzling (but no less striking) on the realization that it is *my* world and *my* life which are one. The *Notebooks* immediately follow the correlate of

---

[23] L. Wittgenstein, *Philosophical Remarks*, trans. Hargreaves and White (Barnes and Nobes, New York, 1975), p. 89.

5.621 with the passage "Physiological life is of course not 'Life'. And neither is psychological life. Life is the world." (p. 77)

Finally, the consideration of "The world is my world" will serve as a bridge between the logical and ethical aspects of the *Tractatus;* this will be the primary focus of the following chapter. It will also allow us to see some continuity between the apparently different senses of 'show' which appeared in chapter VI and elsewhere. A clue to this continuity can be gleaned from Wittgenstein's remark that "Things acquire 'significance' only through their relation to the will." (*NB*, p. 84). Of this passage, with its odd inclusion of 'significance' *(Bedeutung)* in scare quotes, Hacker writes:

> 'Bedeutung' is in scare quotes, I conjecture, because two distinct points are being linked. The world or life only acquires ethical meaning or sense or significance ... through its relation to my will, and equally the signs that are elements in signifying relations only acquire *Bedeutung* through their relation to my will. (*Op. cit.*, p. 47)

We must, then, using the ladder "The world is *my* world," investigate the question of the possibility of the existence of meaning and value in the sort of world which Wittgenstein has constructed in the earlier portions of the book. The project will be complicated by the ineffability of just those points which are the most central, but this difficulty will be more than compensated for by the rewards of descending to the most fundamental level of Wittgenstein's philosophical commitment.

X

The Will, Ethics, and "Das Mystische"

> Supposing that such a reader understands perfectly and
> appraises accordingly the individual aesthetic productions,
> he will nevertheless totally misunderstand me, inasmuch as
> he does not understand the religious totality of my work as
> an author.
>
> —KIERKEGAARD

In chapter I above I reproduced a portion of a celebrated letter
from Wittgenstein to Ludwig von Ficker, editor of the periodical *Der
Brenner*, which reads in part:

> The book's point is an ethical one. I once meant to include in the preface a
> sentence which is not in fact there now but which I will write out for you
> here, because it will perhaps be a key to my work for you. What I meant to
> write then, was this: My work consists of two parts; the one presented here
> plus all that I have *not* written. And it is precisely this second part which is
> the important one. My book draws limits to the sphere of the ethical from
> the inside as it were, and I am convinced that this is the *ONLY rigorous* way
> of drawing these limits. In short, I believe that where *many* others today are
> just *gassing*, I have managed in my book to put everything firmly in place by
> being silent about it . . . I would recommend you to read the *preface* and the
> *conclusion*, because they contain the most direct expression of the point of
> the book.

The Preface claims that in the book a limit is set on the "expression
of thought,"[1] and the conclusion (I take Wittgenstein to mean the last
few pages) culminates with "What we cannot speak of we must pass
over in silence." It is not immediately evident how these two claims
relate to the purported *ethical* nature of the work, and it is this
connection which we must now establish. What arises, as I have

---

[1] It is, incidentally, puzzling in light of 4 to find Wittgenstein (apparently) distinguishing between
"thought" and its "expression." I would hazard that this remark appears in the Preface only
because the doctrine which would identify the two has not yet been developed.

alluded to on several occasions, is a very purified reemergence of the "world as will." In the course of developing this theme we shall also happen upon certain fruitful parallels between the theoretical and practical aspects of art and logic, and further examine the unity of the concept of showing.

The Will and Ethics

> Only what is good is also divine. Queer as it sounds, that sums up my ethics. Only something supernatural can express the Supernatural.
> —Wittgenstein, c. 1920 (CV, p. 3)

In *Alice*, Tweedledum and Tweedledee relate to Alice the story of the Walrus and the Carpenter. The pair entice a bevy of Oysters to dance for them, and then consume them one by one amidst considerable formalities.

"I like the Walrus best," said Alice, "because he was a *little* sorry for the poor Oysters."

"He ate more than the Carpenter, though," said Tweedledee. "You see he held his handkerchief in front, so that the Carpenter couldn't count how many he took; contrariwise."

"Then he was mean!" Alice said indignantly. "Then I like the Carpenter best—if he didn't eat as many as the Walrus."

"But he ate as many as he could get," said Tweedledum.

This was a puzzler. After a pause, Alice began "Well! They were *both* very unpleasant characters ... "[2]

Lewis Carroll presents Alice with a familiar dilemma; do we evaluate the moral import of an action on the basis of its consequences, as Mill and the utilitarians urge, or on the basis of the intentions from which the action arose? Kant of course comes down squarely on the side of the latter. In the first section of the

---

[2] For this passage and a brief commentary, see Martin Gardner, ed., *The Annotated Alice* (Clarkson Potter, New York, 1960), pp. 229–44.

Foundation of the Metaphysics of Morals[3] he undertakes to analyze "common rational knowledge" of morality, in order to isolate its essential features and thus to advance from common moral knowledge to critical or philosophical knowledge of morals. In the famous opening passage he declares:

> Nothing can possibly be conceived in the world, or even out of it, which can be called good, without qualification, except a Good Will. (*Ibid.*, p. 9)

Anything other than a good will—wisdom, beauty, intelligence, wealth—cannot be good in itself, since each of these allow of bad as well as good use. Thus for Kant all moral considerations are intrinsically tied up with the will;[4] it is not through its consequences that an action gains moral import, becoming a possible object of blame or praise, but through the *intention* from which it springs. This voluntaristic analysis of ethics runs squarely up against the historical claim denying "free will," the so-called "thesis of determinism." Every event (including each of my own actions, insofar as these are events) has causal precedents which necessitate its happening, so the argument runs, and since "I could not have done other," I can be neither blamed nor praised for my actions. For Kant this difficulty is highlighted by the argument of the Second Analogy in the *Critique of Pure Reason*, where he argues for the universal objective validity with respect to appearances of the "Principle of Succession in Time, according to the Law of Causality." (*CPR*, pp. 212–32) Every event—mental as well as physical—is the necessary consequence of other actions antecedent to it, and thus each of my actions could, in theory, have been predicted. But if it can be *known* at time t that an event e will happen at $t + 1$, then clearly e must happen and cannot be the result of any "free action" on the part of the alleged "agent" who happens to be involved with it.

Kant finds the germ of the solution to this dilemma in his "Copernican Revolution," offering as it does a *via media* between the horns of the thesis and antithesis of the Third Antinomy, viz. denying either the applicability of moral concepts or the universal objective validity of the causal principle. Kant argues that they are

---

[3] Immanuel Kant, *Foundations of the Metaphysics of Morals* in Abbott, trans. *Kant's Critique of Practical Reason and Other Works on the Theory of Ethics* (Longmans, London, 1873).

[4] I ignore the extremely important distinction Kant draws between 'Wille' and 'Wilkür'; cf. Gary M. Hochberg, *Kant: Moral Legislation and the Two Senses of 'Will'.* (University Press of America, Washington, D.C., 1982), esp. ch. I.

not incompatible *if* we restrict the universal validity of the causal principle to phenomena, leaving open at least the possibility of freedom in the transphenomenal realm. Pure Speculative Reason cannot *prove* the actuality of such freedom; the first *Critique* constitutes a critical examination of the powers and limitations of that faculty, and has shown its impotence beyond the realm of phenomena. Thus Kant thinks that in that work he has "found it necessary to deny *knowledge*, in order to leave room for *faith*" (*CPR*, p. 29), although it is perhaps less misleading to replace "deny knowledge" with "present the limits of reason in its a priori application."

In chapter II above we saw that Schopenhauer accepts the universal causal determination of phenomena, while rejecting as empty what he considers Kant's relegation of morality to the merely hypothetical transphenomenal realm. Morality retains its connection with transphenomenal reality—in Schopenhauer's case with the will as thing-in-itself—but that transphenomenal reality is no longer hypothetical but available in *direct experience* through the fourth class of representations. Those events which from the phenomenal point of view we class as human actions acquire moral significance insofar as they issue not only from the confluence of internal and external causes, but from the intelligible character of the agent. Thus for him there is nothing *hypothetical* about morality; indeed, no action could ever be determined by a merely hypothetical motive. But with Kant, Schopenhauer offers a solution to the dilemma of the compatibility of morality and strict causal determinism based on the phenomena/noumena distinction.[5]

Although the framework within which Wittgenstein addresses the problem of morality is Kantian in its emphasis on intention and the willing subject,[6] the difficulties he confronts are rather different.

---

[5] From this arises a misconception, I think, that there exist what Gershon Weiler has called "two worlds"; one of actions, one of events. (*op. cit.*, pp. 439–57) Events constitute the familiar world of everyday experience, while actions are the objects of moral approbation and blame. But the difficulty is that we seemingly cannot provide a unity of these two "worlds," and if we cannot, then why does morality *matter*? We shall examine this difficulty in much more detail below. Weiler (pp. 440–47) cites Wittgenstein as an example of a philosopher beset by this difficulty, but I will argue below that this interpretation of the Tractarian position will not hold water.

[6] Wittgenstein's emphasis on intention in ethical judgment does not disappear later in his career. Rush Rhees reports that in a discussion in 1942 concerning whether Brutus's stabbing of Caesar was a noble act (Plutarch) or a very evil one (Dante), Wittgenstein declared that our ignorance of Brutus's motives rendered the point moot: "You would not know for your life what went on in his

The causal laws of the natural sciences do not, as we have seen, constitute synthetic a priori claims concerning all phenomenal events, but rather prescriptions for the form of scientific propositions, and are thus to a great extent conventional. Belief in a general causal principle is *"Aberglaube"*—superstition—and thus there are no real connections between events in the world. Even the principles of logic are *sinnlos* tautologies rather than general and necessary claims about the world. The world thus becomes (as the theory of truth-functions demands that it be) a contingent aggregate of mutually independent *Sachverhalte*, and Wittgenstein confronts not the reconciliation of morality with strict determinism but a seemingly opposite (but at bottom very similar) problem: How do we find meaning and value in a wholly contingent world? I have alluded to the kinship that exists between this problem and that of many existentialists; how, they ask, is human life possible given the "absurdity" of the world, its lack of intrinsic meaning? Various forms of recourse in the face of such absurdity have been offered: suicide, scorn, resignation, various sorts of commitment, even irony. Citing the absurdity of the world, Camus, for instance, asks how one can justify abstention from suicide.[7] He answers by asserting that "even within the limits of nihilism it is possible to find the means to precede beyond nihilism." Although Wittgenstein's problem is the same, he is no more attracted to nihilism than to scepticism in general, and the existence of value is for him never open to debate. His chore is then to show how value is compatible with the view of the world forced upon him by his semantics, and this we must now investigate in detail.

The Will and the World

At 6.37 Wittgenstein tells us:

> There is no compulsion making one thing happen because another has happened. The only necessity that exists is *logical* necessity.

This is a corollary—perhaps even the converse—of 6.3:

---

mind before he decided to kill Caesar." Cf. Rush Rhees, "Some Developments in Wittgenstein's View of Ethics," *Phil. Rev.*, vol. 74 (1965), pp. 17–26.

[7] *The Myth of Sisyphus and Other Essays*, trans. O'Brien (Vintage Books, New York, 1955); cf. p. 5. In dramatic form this question constitutes a major theme of Camus' *The Rebel*.

> The exploration of logic means the exploration of *everything that is subject to law.* And outside logic everything is accidental.

These claims turn on a rather narrow construal of "subject to law," but be that as it may, they contain the seeds of Wittgenstein's subsequent destructive analysis of scientific causality and the rejection of the "world as will" from the outside. These theses were examined in chapter VII, but now we must look closely at a further claim which Wittgenstein bases on them, namely "The world is independent of my will." (6.373).

At first blush the thesis of the independence of the world from my will seems to clash with 5.631. There Wittgenstein mentions that the book *The World as I Found It* would need to include "A report on my body," saying that he "should have to say which parts were subordinate to my will, which were not, etc. . . ." The strong implication is that there are parts of my body, and thus parts of the world, which *are* subject to my will. To eliminate this apparent contradiction, let us distinguish between the empirical or phenomenal sense of 'will' and what might be called the *metaphysical* sense.

Every person has a repertoire of what are sometimes called "basic acts" — those things which we can do *immediately,* without having to do something else to bring them about. For instance, I can raise my arms without doing something else to bring that action about. Thus we might say that in some sense my arms are under the control of my will. On the other hand, I cannot make my stomach stop producing acid; this is *not* under the control of my will. Let us call such events as the raising of arms examples of the phenomenal will. Now this phenomenal will, although it is presumably of great interest to psychologists or physiologists, is of no particular *ethical* importance, insofar as it lacks the requisite element of *necessity.* However, in addition to this phenomenal will, Wittgenstein holds that there is a metaphysical will, which *does* possess the requisite element of necessity, and is of central ethical importance. Let us trace Wittgenstein's argument.

In the *Notebooks* we find the following Schopenhauerian remark:

> What is really the situation of the human will? I will call 'will' first and foremost the bearer of good and evil. (p. 77)

But what is this "bearer of good and evil"? Wittgenstein isolates it through a *Gedanken-experiment.*

> Let us imagine a man who could use none of his limbs and hence could, in the ordinary sense, not exercise his *will.* He could, however, think and *want* and communicate his thoughts to someone else. Could therefore do good or evil through the other man. Then it is clear that ethics would have a validity for him, too, and that he in the *ethical sense* is the bearer of *will.* (*Ibid.*)

This passage was written, I think, when Wittgenstein was less clear that the empirical ego was part of the world too; it makes it seem as if merely *thinking* was willing. But a thought is merely a proposition, one with a different sort of propositional sign; the knowing subject is thus *in* the world and describable. However, later the same year (1916) Wittgenstein suggests a parallel "experiment," but with a rather more subtle conclusion.

> At any rate I can imagine carrying out the act of will for raising my arm, but that my arm does not move (E.g., a sinew is torn). True, but, it will be said, the sinew surely moves and that just shows that the act of will related to the sinew and not the arm. But let us go farther and suppose that even the sinew does not move, and so on. We should then arrive at the position that the act of will does not relate to the body at all, and so in the ordinary sense there is no such thing as the act of will.[8]

However, *something* has happened here, albeit not an act of will in the "ordinary sense."[9] Let us call this the *metaphysical will,* keeping in mind that it has so far been characterized only *negatively.*

Can we say anything positive about this will? A will, Rousseau tells us, has both *form* and *content;* put slightly differently, it has both logical properties and an end or goal. We can see the logical properties of the metaphysical will by examining 5.1362, where Wittgenstein explains the sense in which a phenomenal will can be said to be free.

---

[8] *Ibid.*, p. 86. Note that this remark is an attempt to come to grips with the "illusion" that some parts of the world are "closer to me," more intimately related to the true or philosophical subject.

[9] Compare: "Let us not forget this: when I 'raise my arm,' my arm goes up. And the problem arises: what is left when I subtract the fact that my arm goes up from the fact that I raised my arm?" *PI*, #621. Wittgenstein's answer to the problem is of course quite different by the time of the *Investigations.*

The freedom of the will consists in the impossibility of knowing actions [events?] that still lie in the future. We could know them only if causality were an *inner* connexion like that of logical inference ...

We can discern in this passage a hint about what conditions genuine, philosophically significant will would have to meet. The metaphysical will must be such that from the willing of x, it follows, with logical necessity, that x obtains. But Wittgenstein's analysis of logical implication shows that in order for 'p' to entail 'q', the latter must be contained as a constituent in the former. Thus, in order for 'I will that p' to represent a philosophically important sense of 'will', it would have to entail (and thus *contain*) 'p'. But our analysis of propositional attitudes has shown that 'p' does not appear in the analysis of such contexts.

It follows that no act of will that we can speak of—that is, represent in a proposition—could meet these conditions. The form of a genuine act of will must be such that it guarantees its own fruition,[10] and Wittgenstein's doctrine of the mutual independence of elementary propositions dictates that no describable act of will could ever do that. It is tempting to conclude that the metaphysical will is thus a chimera; some positivists offer such an esoteric reading of the closing passages of the *Tractatus*. But keep in mind the source of our discovery of the form of the metaphysical will; it represents a working out of the Kantian demand that I be blamed or praised only for those things which flow directly from the will. The contingency of the world, which has been ascertained on a purely *logical* basis, shows us that what we ordinarily call the will cannot meet these standards. This logical analysis of the structure of the world overrides even the most *consistent* pattern of happenings:

Even if all that we wished for were to happen, still this would only be a favor granted by fate, so to speak; for there is no *logical* connection between the will and the world, which would guarantee it, and the supposed physical connection is certainly not something that we could will.[11]

---

[10] Sartre's claim that "To will to love and to love are one" seems to me to be non-debatable enough to serve as an example of the *sort of thing* that would contitute a genuine act of will. Cf. J.-P. Sartre, *Being and Nothingness*, trans. Hazel Barnes (Philosophical Library, New York, 1956), p. 462.

[11] 6.3744. I take the last phrase to mean that one of our (granted) wishes could not be that there be real, that is, logical, connections between things, since there is no such possible state of affairs. Compare this remark, with its emphasis on the contrast between a priori and empirical patterns, with *PI* #107.

An immediate corollary to this claim is that ethical judgments, since they depend upon the metaphysical will if they depend upon anything at all, cannot be analysed in any naturalistic manner.[12] Thus nothing describable, nothing sayable, can have any ethical significance. At 6.4 Wittgenstein summarizes these claims by saying "All propositions are of equal value"[13]—that is, none at all—and from this concludes:

> The sense of the world must lie outside the world.
>
> In the world everything is as it is, and everything happens as it does happen; *in* it no value exists—and if it did exist, it would have no value.
>
> If there is any value that does have value, it must lie outside the whole sphere of what happens and is the case. For all that happens and is the case is accidental.
>
> It must lie outside of the world.[14]

The claim that value must be located "outside the world" entails that it must be connected either with logic, reflecting as it does the internal properties of Objects, with the Metaphysical Ego, or—a possibility I will not pursue—with some other item located outside the world of contingent facts. It also carries, as we have seen, the corollary that ethics, like logic, must be ineffable. Since what can be said is limited to the existence or non-existence of *Sachverhalte,*

---

[12] This argument against the naturalistic fallacy is rather different from Moore's, which argues that any judgment which claims that "*x* is good" means "*x* is ..." cannot possibly offer an adequate analysis of the former locution, since none will be *necessary:* it is never *self-contradictory* to say "*x* is good but not ..." Wittgenstein's point is rather that the world as envisioned in the *Tractatus* is metaphysically incapable, as it were, of sustaining the sorts of lawlike judgments necessary for ethics. Compare with Moore, *Principia Ethica,* ch. I.

It is also worth noting that ethical propositions seem to intrinsically contain an element of *generality,* some universalizable propositions, and Wittgenstein's analysis of generality makes all such propositions derivative and disposable. We shall see the effects of this rejection of generality for ethics later.

[13] 6.4 exhibits a rich ambiguity: not only can no proposition express any value-claim, but as we have seen from our examination of Wittgenstein's theory of logic, there are no "logical postulates," such as those offered by Russell or Peano, from which all other logical propositions follow. In *many* of the remarks in the closing section of the book Wittgenstein evokes rich resonances (occasionally misleading) between logic and ethics, some of which we shall examine as they arise.

[14] 6.41. Note that the phrase "lie outside the world" is difficult to reconcile with 1—"The world is all that is the case"—unless we restrict the term 'world', as I have suggested above, to contingent existence.

which are without exception contingent, there can no more be ethical propositions than there can be logical propositions.

> And so it is impossible for there to be propositions of ethics. Propositions can express nothing higher. (6.42)

> It is clear that ethics cannot be put into words. Ethics is transcendental. (6.421)

Thus ethics, like logic, must be something that "shows itself" or makes itself manifest. There is also a clear sense, as we shall see, in which ethics like logic must "take care of itself." We must now explore the general themes of this section in greater detail.

Value and Scepticism

A point of overarching importance must be stressed in any discussion of Wittgenstein's ethical views, and thus, if we take him at his word, of the *Tractatus*. One path open for Wittgenstein would be to infer from the contingency of the world that human life is devoid of value, or that what "value" exists is conventional and thus from a philosophical point of view irrelevant; to claim, with Protagoreans, Sophists, and their latter-day successors the existentialists and humanists, that the world is essentially and irreparably "absurd." *This he emphatically does not do;* it is not even clear whether he admits such a *possibility.* I have argued in chapter II above that Wittgenstein accepts as a piece the antisceptical realism of Frege. (We ought keep in mind that Schopenhauer too consistently represents himself as the arch-enemy of scepticism, even though he sees scepticism as irrefutable.) I think that it is clear that he harbors no hint of ethical scepticism either. Janik and Toulmin point to the cultural basis of this antisceptical position: in describing the difficulty of communication between Wittgenstein and his middle-class and aristocratic Cambridge students, they write of:

> The clash between a Viennese thinker whose intellectual problems and personal attitudes alike had been formed in the neo-Kantian environment of pre-1914, in which logic and ethics were essentially tied up with each other and with the critique of language, and an audience of students whose philosophical questions had been shaped by the neo-Humean (and so

pre-Kantian) empiricism of Moore, Russell and their colleagues. (*Op. cit.*, p. 22.)

I take it as given that Wittgenstein no more doubts what might loosely be called the "value aspect" of the world than he doubts the truths of logic: his problem is to reconcile the two, making (non-conventional, philosophically important) value consistent with the picture of the world which language and logic force upon us.

In this vein I want to investigate some themes from the *Notebooks*, concentrating on those which ought to be treated as *data*, albeit perhaps rough and confused, rather than as conclusions from arguments. The major entry that I have in mind is dated 11.6.16, and I will shortly quote from it at length. It appears following a series of reflections on questions of value and its relation to the will, and it is probable that they coincide with a period when Wittgenstein was rereading Schopenhauer; in any case they have a distinctive Schopenhauerian ring. Wittgenstein writes:

> What do I know about the world and the purpose of life?
> I know that this world exists.
> That I am placed in it like my eye in its visual field.
> That there is something about it which is problematical, which we call its meaning.
> That this meaning does not lie in it but outside it.
> That my will penetrates the world.
> That my will is good and evil.
> Therefore that good and evil are somehow connected with the meaning of life.
> The meaning of life, i.e., the meaning of the world, we can call God.
> And we connect this with the comparison of God to a father.
> To pray is to think about the meaning of life.
> I cannot bend the happenings of the world to my will: I am completely powerless.
> I can only make myself independent of the world—and so in some sense master it—by renouncing any influence on its happenings.[15]

---

[15] *NB*, p. 73. James Edwards, in his *Ethics without Philosophy: Wittgenstein and the Moral Life* (University of South Florida Press, Tampa, 1982), points out illuminating parallels between these theses and Tolstoy's summary of the teachings of Jesus in *The Gospel in Brief*, a book known to have influenced Wittgenstein greatly during this period. (Cf. von Wright in Malcolm *op. cit.*, pp. 9–10, or McGuinness *op. cit.*, p. 220). It seems likely that Wittgenstein was constructing his own version of Tolstoy's list. These are Tolstoy's theses:

  1. Man is the son of an infinite source: a son of that Father not by the flesh but by the spirit.
  2. Therefore man should serve that source in spirit.

At first blush these claims seem rather extravagant coming from a man who will tell us that belief in a causal nexus is "superstition" (5.1361), but more troubling is the appearance of inconsistency. How, for instance, can my will "permeate the world" when the world is also "independent of my will"? These problems will be dealt with in due course, but at this point I want to emphasize that these theses are not the *results* of an argument but the *initial data*, things that Wittgenstein claims to *know* to be true. They may (and do) turn out to be fuzzy, badly formulated, or in some cases, attempts to say what can only be shown, and thus fall into the class of nonsensical pseudo-propositions, but their *significance* is not open to doubt

This point lies behind the fruitlessness of casting Wittgenstein as a neo-Humean positivist bent on sceptical critique of purported knowledge. It can also be contrasted with the role of scepticism in Russell's philosophical career. Russell originally held the currently unfashionable Cartesian belief that *every* proposition stands in need of philosophical justification, and tells us that he originally entered philosophy in an attempt to find reasons for believing that mathematical propositions were true. Russell's project is thus from the very start quite opposite to that of Frege (and the larger portion of the whole German tradition in philosophy), where the principles of mathematics are never called into doubt. In fact, as we saw, many of Frege's arguments against Mill are reductio ad absurdum, showing that Mill's position is incompatible with the universal and necessary truth of mathematical propositions. This attitude is echoed in the Preface to the *Tractatus:*

> ... the *truth* of the thoughts here set forth seems to be unassailable and definitive. I therefore believe myself to have found, on all essential points, the final solution of the problems. (p. 5)

---

3. The life of all men has a divine origin. It alone is holy.
4. Therefore man should serve that source in the life of all men. Such is the will of the Father.
5. The service of the will of the Father of life gives life.
6. Therefore the gratification of one's will is not necessary for life.
7. Temporal life is food for the true life.
8. Therefore the true life is independent of time; it is in the present.
9. Time is an illusion of life; life in the past and in the future conceals from men the true life of the present.
10. Therefore man should strive to destroy the illusion of the temporal life of the past and future.
11. True life is in the present, common to all men and manifesting itself in love.
12. Therefore he who lives by love in the present, through the common life of all men, unites with the Father, the source and foundation of life.

This attitude is also in harmony with Wittgenstein's later philosophy; justification must come to a halt *somewhere*, and to raise doubts where none are possible is not wise or philosophical but childish (cf. 6.51). The common front against scepticism formed by Frege and Schopenhauer reinforces Wittgenstein's natural temper and sets him opposite to Russell from the start.

Bearing in mind these general antisceptical warnings, let us now turn to the primary thesis of this chapter. Consider the following puzzle. The world is independent of my will, since there is no entailment between "I will that p" and 'p', if 'p' pictures some *Sachverhalt*. But on the other hand, a little reflection shows that the will must have some connection with life, some impact on the world, or else it would be pointless and unimportant. Thus Schopenhauer argues that for the notion of the will to have content, every genuine act of the human will must be identical with some bodily action; if not, it would be mere *intention*, which is a product not of the will but of the intellect (*WWR* II, p. 248). Wittgenstein agrees: "Wishing is not acting. But willing is acting . . . . the wish precedes the event, the will accompanies it." (*NB*, p. 88)

Obviously the will must have some *object:*

> The will seems always to have to relate to a representation. We cannot imagine e.g. having carried out an act of will without having detected that we have carried it out.[16]

and

> . . . the will does have to have an object. Otherwise we should have no foothold and could not know what we willed.
>
> And could not will different things. (*NB*, pp. 87–88)

Yet given our analysis of the relation (or lack thereof) between the will and the facts which constitute the world, what form would this "foothold" take? The metaphysical will, the "bearer of good and evil," must *make* a difference to *be* a difference, but what could this difference be?

---

[16] *NB*, p. 86. Again compare this with the Schopenhauerian requirement that any act of human will must be identical with some bodily motion. A difference must *make* a difference; Frege writes "Even the timeless, if it is to be anything to us, must somehow be implicated with the temporal." ("The Thought," p. 37)

Let me sketch out very briefly the solution that I will propose to this dilemma, a sketch which I will fill out in subsequent sections. Commenting on "the correct method of philosophy" Wittgenstein writes:

> My propositions serve as elucidations in the following way: anyone who understands me eventually recognizes them as nonsensical, when he has used them—as steps—to climb up beyond them. (He must, so to speak, throw away the ladder after he has climbed up it.)
>
> He must transcend these propositions, and then he will see the world aright.[17]

There immediately follows the notorious concluding remark, "That of which we cannot speak, we must remain silent." My suggestion is that the "ladder" of 6.54 is the claim "The world is *my* world," the pseudo-proposition which attempts to express what the solipsist wants or intends to say. (Other pseudo-propositions might be substituted for this one, e.g. "There is a metaphysical ego." What they try to say is in each case the same, and each fails for the same reasons.) The solipsist necessarily fails, but in attempting to put into words the valuable insight with which the urge to solipsism presents us, our attention is directed, as it were, towards those very things which cannot be said but which make themselves manifest. Wittgenstein's relation of the will to the world is strikingly similar to Kant's resolution of the Antinomies—pairs of seemingly incompatible conclusions, each supported by a seemingly sound argument (cf. *CPR*, pp. 384–396). Kant shows that each argument is "transcendentally ambiguous": the argument for the thesis is sound only if we restrict it to the world of phenomena, that of the antithesis only if we treat is as unconditioned. Thus the apparently contradictory conclusions were opposed only in illusion. The phenomena/noumena

---

[17] 6.54. The German begins "Meine Satze erlautern . . . ." The nominalization 'Erläuterung' appears in two other contexts, both significant. 4.112 tells us that "A philosophical work consists essentially of elucidations"; the context—following 4.11—indicates that Wittgenstein means the *real* role of philosophy and thus that 4.112 is not intended as an historical characterization of what has traditionally been called philosophy. The other occurrence, however, seems to present a reductio of the suggestion that a philosophical work *could* consist of elucidations.

At 3.263 we are told that the meanings of primitive signs are given by elucidations, which are propositions containing these simple signs. Yet we cannot understand the elucidating proposition unless we understand the sign in question, since the sense of a proposition is a function of its constituents. Thus our attempt at an elucidation turns out to be empty, but we can see what we have tried to do but failed (because we attempt to say what cannot be said) turns out to be unnecessary, since what we tried to say shows itself. Thus the "contextual definitions" of Russell and the positivists are pointless, unless we take them as mere explanations of a new notation.

distinction thus allows Kant to "limit knowledge to make room for faith." Pure speculative reason can make no inroads on the realm of value. Wittgenstein's procedure, we shall see, is in an important manner parallel to this, but it is marked by a shift from what we can *know* through pure reason (remember that the theory of knowledge is for him "the philosophy of psychology") to what we can *linguistically represent*, and thus the noumenal becomes identified with the ineffable.

Action and Reward

> [In a Tatar epic] Our Lady visits Hell, and the Archangel
> Michael leads her through the torments. She sees sinners
> and their punishment. There she sees among others a set of
> sinners in a burning lake. Some of them sink to the bottom
> of the lake, so that they can't swim out, and these "God
> forgets"—an expression of extraordinary depth and force.
>
> DOSTOYEVSKY, *THE BROTHERS KARAMAZOV*

The question of the relation between the will and the world is closely connected with that of ethical reward and punishment. I want to examine this connection, and then relate the notion of reward to some of the "experiences" which Wittgenstein relates in his 1929 "Lecture on Ethics."[18]

At 6.422 we find the following:

> When an ethical law of the form "Thou shalt ..." is laid down, one's first thought is, "And what if I do not?" It is clear, however, that ethics has nothing to do with punishment and reward in the usual sense of the terms. So our question about the *consequences* of an action must be unimportant.—At least those consequences should not be events. For there must be something right about the question we posed. There must be some kind of ethical reward and punishment, but they must reside in the action itself. (And it is clear that the reward must be something pleasant, and the punishment something unpleasant.)[19]

---

[18] Published as "Wittgenstein's Lecture on Ethics," *Philos. Rev.*, vol. 74 (1965), pp. 3–12.

[19] Compare: "What does the word 'ought' mean? A child ought to do such-and-such means that if he does not do it, something unpleasant will happen. Reward and punishment. The essential thing about this is that the other person is brought to do something. 'Ought' makes sense only if there is something lending support and force to it—a power that punishes and rewards. Ought in itself is nonsensical." (*WVC*, p. 118)

Engelmann writes, "The idea of God in the sense of the Bible, the image of God as the creator of the world, hardly ever engaged Wittgenstein's attention ... but the notion of a last judgment was

Wittgenstein echoes the opening sentence of Schopenhauer's *On the Basis of Morality:*

> A commanding voice, whether coming from within or without, cannot possibly be imagined except as threatening or promising.[20]

But Schopenhauer distinguishes two quite different sorts of punishment, and analogously two distinct sorts of rewards. In section 63 of *WWR* I he distinguishes *temporal justice*, which is always future-oriented, from *eternal justice*. Temporal justice finds its seat in the State, and can be either retributive or not, but insofar as it is always in time, it is for Schopenhauer on the illusory side of the Veil of Maya. On the other hand there is eternal justice,

> which rules not the State but the world; this is not dependent on human institutions, not subject to chance and deception, not uncertain, wavering and erring, but infallible, firm, certain. (*Ibid.*, p. 231)

Schopenhauer adds:

> ... that such an eternal justice is actually to be found in the inner nature of the world will soon become perfectly clear to the reader who has grasped in its entirety the thought that we have so far developed. (*Ibid.*, p. 351)

With temporal justice comes retribution and reward in the ordinary sense, but as Schopenhauer points out, these have no real philosophical significance, partly because they are subject to error and misfire, but also because they treat of the temporal, which is merely phenomenal. The reward and punishment of eternal justice must be atemporal, and thus acausal.

On similar grounds Wittgenstein rejects "normal" reward and punishment as ethically insignificant. The fame or money (say) which rewards me for rescuing the child from the fire lack philosophical import for several reasons. First, the rescue might have come about

---

of profound concern to him." (*op. cit.*, p. 77) Von Wright reports, "The thought of God, [Wittgenstein] said, was above all for him the thought of a fearful judge." (Malcolm *op. cit.*, pp. 19–20)

[20] *OBM*, p. 55. Schopenhauer advances this claim in the context of arguing that there can be no such thing as a *categorical* imperative; every imperative is by nature hypothetical, conditioned on some threat or promise. Thus, the categorical imperative achieves quite the opposite of what Schopenhauer sees as one of Kant's great achievements, namely liberating ethics from theology. Compare with Janik and Toulmin *op. cit.*, pp. 154–55.

by accident or through some despicable motive such as greed. But more important, the act of rescuing the child is logically unconnected with either the intention to do so or the reward for having done so; thus the requisite element of *necessity* is lacking. But finally, neither money nor fame are intrinsically good, and they can therefore count as a reward only under certain circumstances.

We can therefore set out two formal criteria which an *ethical* reward must satisfy. First, the act and the reward must be such that the former *logically entails* the latter. Second, the reward must be something *intrinsically* good.

Some negative points concerning a possible ethical reward emerge through consideration of "The answer to the riddle of life" (6.4312) or "The meaning of life" (6.251): we shall see that these are nearly identical with the question of a real ethical reward. In the theses of *NB* 11.6.16 (cf. the preceding section of this chapter) Wittgenstein includes among the things that he knows about the world, "That something about it is problematical, which we call its meaning." This is immediately followed by ". . . this meaning does not lie in [the world] but outside it." But it seems to me that the second of these remarks stands on a rather different level from the first. It is not a postulate but the result of analysis, much of which we have already seen, which underlines the contingency of life and makes it difficult to see where "the riddle of life" could get a foothold in the world. From this follows something of great importance for Wittgenstein, namely that the answer to the "riddle of life" cannot be given by *science.* The natural sciences can produce only two things, depending upon whether we accept the wide characterization of 6.11 (Science is the corpus of true propositions) or the narrower one of 6.32ff. (Science stipulates a constant form for propositions about the world). The answer to the riddle of life cannot be answered by learning *more about the world* and thus immortality in the sense of living through all time would not yield the answer:

> Not only is there no guarantee of the temporal immortality of the human soul, that is to say of its eternal survival after death; but, in any case, this assumption completely fails to accomplish the purpose for which it has always been intended. Or is some riddle solved by my surviving forever? Is not this eternal life as much of a riddle as our present life? The solution to the riddle of life lies *outside* time and space.

It is certainly not the solution to any of the problems of natural science that is required.[21]

What then *is* this "riddle of life," and what is its answer? How is it connected with our search for an ethical reward? In answering these questions I want to utilize further material from Wittgenstein's 1929 Lecture on Ethics. This lecture was written over ten years after the publication of the *Tractatus*, and it is certain that Wittgenstein changed his views on some important topics during that period, including one—the logical independence of elementary propositions—which is relevant to the general topic of the will.[22] But the general feeling of the lecture (presented to a Cambridge intellectual society called "The Heretics") is of a piece with the *Tractatus*. I shall offer some evidence for this as the relevant points arise. But more generally there is reason to think that Wittgenstein's moral views changed very little throughout his lifetime. Janik and Toulmin concur:

> Clearly enough ... Wittgenstein's change of philosophical method was for him only a continuation of his earlier intellectual policies by other means; it did not lead him *in fact* to abandon his longstanding ethical individualism.[23]

Thus I propose to treat the views of the Lecture, with their emphasis on ethical "phenomena," as continuous with the Tractarian views.

Wittgenstein begins by distinguishing two senses of moral terms, which he calls 'relative' and 'absolute', announcing that he wishes to restrict the term 'ethical' to the latter senses. (Note that this distinction parallels the difference I have marked with the terms 'phenomenal' and 'philosophical' or 'metaphysical' and their cognates.) No statement about the world, he announces, could ever be or

---

[21] 6.4312. Compare with Schopenhauer—the meaning of the phenomenal world cannot be given *in* phenomena—and Kierkegaard—the existence of a historical Jesus is *not* what is at stake for the Christian.

Some philosophers might argue that Wittgenstein's characterization of the soul as simple, without parts (as implied in 5.5421) entails its immortality. See for instance Plato's *Phaedo*, 78b.

[22] Cf. Wittgenstein's "Some Remarks on Logical Form" (1929) reprinted in Copi and Beard *op. cit.*, pp. 31–37. But note the warning by Anscombe printed at the bottom of page 31.

[23] *Op. cit.*, p. 235. Compare: "The motives for Wittgenstein's silence [about art and ethics] appear to have varied very little through the years. He agreed with Kierkegaard that the most important things are best shown, not said, and that the gifted artist is the one who can show them best." Hallett *op. cit.*, p. 255.

entail an ethical judgment in this strict sense, and he illustrates this point by considering an example evocative both of the "book" *The World as I Found It* of 5.631 and our recent discussion of the philosophical irrelevance of immortality.

> Suppose one of you were an omniscient person and therefore knew all the movements of all the bodies in the world dead or alive and that he also knew all the states of mind of all the human beings that had ever lived, and suppose this man wrote all that he knew in a big book, then this book would contain the whole description of the world; and what I want to say is, that this book would contain nothing that we would call an *ethical* judgment or anything which would logically entail such a judgment.[24]

Note that Wittgenstein here emphasizes that value can no more be found in a *state of mind* than it can in the extramental world; the empirical ego is a cluster of facts of a certain sort and has no more philosophical interest than, for instance, the class of propositions beginning with the word 'of'. With respect to Hamlet's claim that "nothing is either good or bad, but thinking makes it so" Wittgenstein writes:

> What Hamlet says seems to imply is that good and bad, though not qualities of the world outside us, are attributes of our states of mind. But what I mean is that a state of mind, in so far as we mean by that a fact which we can describe, is in no ethical sense good or bad.[25]

This is equivalent to 6.4—all propositions are of equal value; no describable fact, mental or extramental, can be the bearer of value. Every phenomenal event, everything describable, will appear at the same level, be it a murder or the falling of a stone.[26] Since propositions can express the whole realm of the natural sciences—the obtaining or not obtaining of any *Sachverhalt*, the whole contents of the book written by the omniscient person—ethics and aes-

---

[24] *Ibid.*, p. 6. Note that what the book would contain would be the whole corpus of true propositions, and thus would entail the final goal of the "natural sciences" in the weaker sense of 4.11.

[25] *Ibid.* The line (Hamlet to Rosencrantz) is from *Hamlet* Act II, Scene 2. Note that this passage seems to barely leave open the option that there are "things" which are (a) construable as "states of mind" but (b) are not describable, that is, not *facts*.

[26] Likewise they will lack *aesthetic* value; "Ethics and aesthetics are one and the same" (6.421). Note that in the lecture Wittgenstein continues to hold the Tractarian thesis of the identity of ethics and aesthetics.

thetic must be "supernatural" (Lecture, p. 7) or "Transcendental" (6.421).[27]

At this point Wittgenstein offers a rather striking restatement of the criterion for ethical value, and further distinguishes absolute from relative value.

> The right road is the road which leads to an arbitrarily predetermined end and it is quite clear that there is no sense in talking about the right road apart from such a predetermined goal. Now let us see what we would possibly mean by the expression "*The* absolutely right road." I think that it would be the road which *everyone* on seeing it would, *with logical necessity*, have to go or be ashamed for not going. And similarly the *absolute good*, if it is a describable state of affairs, would be one which everybody, independent of his tastes and inclination, would *necessarily* bring about or feel guilty for not bringing about. And I want to say that such a state of affairs is a chimera. No state of affairs has in itself, what I would like to call the coercive power of an absolute judge. (*Ibid.*, p. 7)

Keep in mind that Wittgenstein is not denying the possibility of an absolute good, but only denying that some *fact* or *state of affairs* could constitute such an absolute good. Since states of affairs— *Sachverhalte*—are the only things of which we can speak, it follows that anyone who tries to *speak* of an absolute good speaks nonsense.

There are, however, circumstances under which one feels compelled (and powerfully so) to try to speak of such things, and such a temptation is *not* due to sloppy thinking or illusion, but is rather like the solipsist trying (but failing) to say something of great importance.[28] In the Lecture Wittgenstein offers examples of the

---

[27] Wittgenstein uses these two terms as synonyms, but of course in traditional philosophical usage they are not. The transcendental is that the knowledge of which is necessary for any other knowledge (Descartes' principle of clear and distinct ideas, for instance) while the supernatural is that which does not pertain to the natural order. The transcendental would normally be a priori, the supernatural not so. There is a sense in which Wittgenstein's conclusions will identify the two somewhat more closely. It is important, though, to keep in mind that "transcendental" does *not* mean anything like "not open to experience." There is no hint of "otherworldliness" in Wittgenstein's philosophy; this, I think, is one of the profound influences that Schopenhauer has had on him.

[28] The attitude that (some) metaphysical talk is *significant* or *important* nonsense runs very deep in Wittgenstein's thought. "Don't think that I despise metaphysics. I regard some of the great philosophical writings of the past as among the noblest works of the human mind," Wittgenstein told Drury in 1930. (Rhees, *op. cit.*, p. 93) This view sharply distinguishes Wittgenstein from both what Morris Engel calls the "linguistic" and the "clinical" wings of the analytic movement. The former see such tendencies as mere illusions produced by language, the latter view them as symptoms of a sort of conceptual sickness. Cf. S. Morris Engel, *Wittgenstein's Doctrine of the Tyranny of Language* (Martinus Nijhoff, The Hague, 1971), p. 11.

sorts of situations which might lead one to try to speak of things like "the absolutely right road"; these experiences, which we will examine, might be examples of "mystical" experiences in the (yet to be examined) sense of 6.45. Importantly, Wittgenstein does not view himself as unique or even special in having had such experiences. The Lecture is not Messianic, and the existence of such experiences is not in question. The examples are offered in order to bring to mind similar experiences (characterized perhaps in different ways) which the listener himself has had. All that is needed is a certain sympathy on the part of the listener.[29]

The description of the first of these experiences is of great interest insofar as constitutes a "fleshing out" of the claims of 6.432–6.44.

> 6.432   *How* things are in the world is a matter of complete indifference for what is higher. God does not reveal himself *in* the world.

> 6.4321   The facts all contribute only to the setting of the problem, not to its solution.

> 6.44   It is not *how* the world is that is mystical, but *that* it exists.[30]

In the Lecture Wittgenstein writes of a particular experience, asserting that "The best way of describing [this experience] is to say that *I have it when I wonder at the existence of the world.*"[31] He is struck not so much by the world being such-and-such, but by there being a world at all. For example,

> I am wondering at the sky being *whatever it is*. One might be tempted to say that what I am wondering at is a tautology, namely the sky being blue or not blue. But then it's just nonsense to say that one is wondering at a tautology. *(Ibid.)*

---

[29] Frege writes: "The peculiarity of function signs, which we have here called 'unsaturatedness', naturally has something answering to it in the functions themselves. They too may be called 'unsaturated', and in this way we mark them out as fundamentally different from numbers. Of course this is not a definition; but likewise none is here possible. I must confine myself to hinting at what I have in mind by means of a metaphorical expression, and here I must rely on my reader's agreeing to meet me half-way." "What is a function?" in Geach and Black *op. cit.*, p. 115.

[30] Following Black *op. cit.*, p. 375 I have slightly altered the translation of 6.44—the reference to "things" ('... *how* things are ...') is misleading in light of Wittgenstein's technical usage of that term. Also significant is the appearance in 6.4321 of the German word *Aufgabe*, with its primary sense of a schoolboy's exercise or set-problem.

[31] *Ibid.*, p. 8. Compare this with the fragment "apropos Heidegger" in *WVC*, pp. 68–69.

"How things are" in 6.432 means roughly: which *Sachverhalte* obtain and which do not. This is, Wittgenstein tells us, "a matter of complete indifference to what is higher."[32] Thus 6.432 is the ontological corollary of 6.4, where we are told that all propositions are of "equal value." To wonder at the sky being blue or green is to wonder at the existence of some *Sachverhalt*, and although from a human point of view it may be a matter of wonder that the universe contains aardvarks or black holes or Texas Republicans, from a philosophical point of view such things cannot be matters of wonder.[33] Thus to wonder at the sky being *whatever color it is* is equivalent to wondering at the being of the possibility of coloredness. But this is the being of Objects with the requisite logical form, the correct internal properties (cf. 2.0251), and this cannot be represented propositionally.

Wittgenstein refers to a second experience, which is

> ... the experience of feeling *absolutely* safe. I mean the state of mind in which one is inclined to say "I am perfectly safe, nothing can injure me whatever happens."[34]

This feeling of "perfect safety" might be best contrasted with the feeling of being controlled by an *alien will*, in the sense of there being something which is simultaneously mine and yet not under my control. (Cf. *NB*, p. 75.)

---

[32] Note the implication that any attempt at a "natural theology," arguing from the content of the world to the existence of (e.g.) a transcendent God, must fail. Wittgenstein repeatedly asserts that religion cannot be supported by argument or experiement.

[33] There is a Schopenhauerian theme parallel to this. To wonder at the existence of aardvarks or Texas Republicans, for instance, is to seek a causal or scientific explanation. But philosophy cannot be concerned with such explanations, at least not directly, and thus the sort of wonder that brings men to philosophy must be rather different. The explanation that we seek cannot be a causal one. Compare with Russell on the nature of philosophy, or the opening of Aristotle's *Metaphysics*.

[34] "Lecture," p. 8. Both Rush Rhees, in his comments on this lecture, (*op. cit.*, p. 20) and Peter Winch, in his paper "Can a Good Man be Harmed?" (reprinted in his *Ethics and Action* [Routledge and Kegan Paul, London, 1972] pp. 193–209) claim that the locution "absolutely safe" does violence to the sense of 'safe'. Winch in particular questions whether "I am absolutely safe" could ever have a place in a moral language-game.

Without examining the grounds for such a claim, I will admit that perhaps there could be no such *language-game*, but add that (a) there is obviously a place for what such a claim *tries to say* but fails in a moral form of life, and (b) that the claim tries to say what, for example, Tolstoy's "God sees the truth but waits" (in *Twenty-three Tales*) shows eloquently.

These two experiences—wondering at the existence of the world and feeling perfectly safe—Wittgenstein correlates with certain traditional religious themes.

> The first of [these experiences] is, I think, exactly what people had in mind when they said that God created the world; and the experience of absolute safety has been described by saying that we feel absolutely safe in the hands of God. (Lecture, p. 10)

and he adds that there is a third experience which is related to the two which we have described:

> A third experience of the same kind is that of feeling guilty and again this was described by the phrase that God disapproves of our conduct. *(Ibid.)*

Setting aside for a moment Wittgenstein's usage of the term 'God', note that just as the religious versions of the descriptions of these experiences are similes, so are those which Wittgenstein presents. But if they *are* similes, Wittgenstein stresses, they ought to be similes *for* something: if I say "That man is a fox" I ought to be able to say, if pressed, which characteristics he shares with foxes. But it is characteristic of the descriptions which Wittgenstein has given that when we try to go beyond them to even *rough* literal substitutes we find none. (E.g., *ibid.*, p. 10. Keep in mind that insofar as where there is sense there is perfect sense, we ought to be able to say *exactly* what we mean, although the analysis of the simile into literal components may be very complex.) Wittgenstein rejects immediately that what we need is a better logical analysis of the descriptions of these experiences:

> Now when [the necessity of a better analysis] is urged against me I at once see clearly, as it were in a flash of light, not only that no description that I can think of would do to describe what I mean by absolute value, but that I would reject every significant description that anyone could possibly suggest, *ab initio*, on the grounds of its significance. *(Ibid.* p. 11)

That is, "Ethics is transcendent." (6.421)

We now need to investigate why Wittgenstein could think that the experiences we have set forth here qualify as candidates for "value-experiences," as descriptions of "absolute value."

God, the World, and the Self

Wittgenstein's parallel between the experiences he describes and those traditionally described in religious terms is rendered less clear by the unusual, or at least non-standard, *Notebooks* usage of the word 'God'. He nowhere speaks of a personal God;[35] as we shall see, his is very much the God of the philosophers .

In the *Notebooks* (p. 79) Wittgenstein identifies God with "How things stand"; by this I take him to mean not the actual connection of Objects into *Sachverhalte*, but rather the Being of Objects and their internal relations. This is not a passing remark. At the end of the *Proto-Tractatus* appear some unnumbered remarks which Wittgenstein had apparently intended to insert into the text, and among them appears the remark "How things stand, is God. God is, how things stand."[36] Objects, as we recall from chapter IV, are the wholly unconditioned entities which dictate the realm of possibilities. This interpretation links Wittgenstein's usage of the word 'God' with the rationalist tradition, where God is identified with the Ground of Being, substance in the truest sense. On this interpretation the first experience would be what we might call roughly *awe before the unconditioned*. We need to look at the sense in which one could think of such astonishment as *ethical*. But more seriously, it leaves totally unclear the sense in which the will can be "the bearer of good and evil," since the unconditioned reality of the Objects is not reducible to the will. Finally, in a number of passages, including the theses of *Notebooks* 11.6.16, God is equated with "the meaning of life," and life is equated in several places—for instance at 5.621— with "The world." How exactly can the unconditioned being of Objects provide the meaning of life?

On the other hand, there are numerous passages in the *Notebooks* where 'God' seems to refer to something over and above the being of Objects. In a discussion of the meaning of 'God' on 8.7.16, Wittgenstein discusses some now-familiar themes, and then appears to

---

[35] In a remark made to Drury, Wittgenstein seems to link his rejection of a personal God with his antipathy towards the Roman Catholic dogma that the existence of God can be demonstrated by reason. "It is a dogma of the Roman Church that the existence of God can be proved from natural reason. Now this dogma makes it impossible for me to be a Roman Catholic. If I thought of God as another being like myself, outside myself, only infinitely more powerful, then I would regard it as my duty to defy him." Rhees *op. cit.*, p. 123. Compare: "Can you imagine St. Augustine saying that the existence of God was highly probable?" (*Ibid.*, p. 105)

[36] *Proto-Tractatus*, p. 239.

struggle with the very problem of the relation of the will to the world which we saw in the last section, writing, "There are two godheads: the world and my independent I". (*NB*, p. 74) Compare this with the following passage in the Lecture:

> Now I am tempted to say that the right expression in language for the miracle of the existence of the world, though it is not a proposition *in* language, is the existence of language itself. (Lecture, p. 11)

Recall that although language mirrors the world, the world does not in turn mirror language. Although they share the common element of logical form, the world lacks the intentional contribution, the willing, of the metaphysical subject, which provides both the "method of projection" for the propositional sign and the necessary Name-Object correlations. Put another way, language (*my* language) has an "inside," a point of view, a vanishing point at the center, while the world does not. Thus, although the existence of the world requires only the contingent coming-together of Objects, language requires in addition the being of the metaphysical subject. Thus, if it is true that I wonder at the existence of language (or of thought), then what I wonder at the existence of is not just *the* world but *my* world. This reading is reinforced by the entry of 1.8.16:

> How things stand, is God.
>
> God is, how things stand.
>
> Only from the consciousness of the *uniqueness of my life* arises religion—science—and art.

This passage seems to imply two important things: that "my life" is unique in some philosophically important sense, and that this uniqueness (or the consciousness of it) is connected with value.[37]

---

[37] It is less clear immediately why "science" appears in this passage. Grammatically it is not even clear whether it is meant as a cognate in some unspecified way of "religion," or whether it is some additional element which arises from consciousness of the uniqueness of my life. One conjecture is that the notion of science cannot arise without consciousness of the necessity of some "perspective-neutral" view of the world—the scientific view—and this requires as contrast the notion of some perspective-laden view, my view. If this conjecture is valid, it may be that Wittgenstein is here slurring over the distinction between the empirical (knowing) subject of 5.54–5.5422 or 5.631 and the willing or metaphysical subject of 5.641. No *description* of the world could reflect my point of view; this I take to be the point of 5.631. We might say that in a sense

But what are we to make of this claim concerning the "uniqueness of my life," particularly since Wittgenstein has identified "life" with "the world"? (And whence, as Black asks, comes this startling introduction of the personal pronoun?) Suppose I say, "My dog is wholly unique"; by this I mean that my dog Heimer has hair of just *this* color, these sorts of behavior-patterns and so forth. In *Principia* (*13.01) Russell defines identity in terms of Leibnizian coextensivity of properties. We have already seen Wittgenstein's dissatisfaction with this as a *philosophically significant* definition of identity: even though it may be *always false* that two objects share all their properties, it is not *self-contradictory* to say that they do. Thus this definition cannot constitute a *formal* definition of logic, since it is not a tautology. *Principia* *13.01 is significant (since it could be false) and cannot therefore be a proposition of logic. Thus the uniqueness of the self, if construed on the model of the uniqueness of my dog Heimer, cannot be philosophically significant.

What then is the sense in which the metaphysical self is wholly unique? If we cannot say how it is different from other entities, how can we be so certain that it *is* unique? In the course of a *Blue Book* discussion of solipsism, Wittgenstein tells us that the claim "Only I really see" is closely connected with "We never know what the other man sees when he looks at a thing." (*Blue Book*, p. 60) But he then queries "Always *who*?" Who is it that "always and only sees?" This precipitates an investigation of a series of suggested criteria for the identity of such an ego, each rejected as not quite catching the spirit of what the solipsist wanted to say. Whenever we looked for something unique, we found something which was at best only contingently unique. So what could the solipsist mean when he asserts the uniqueness of the metaphysical ego?

The answer, which is consistent with the *Blue Book* exploration but not with its conclusion, is that we can attach *no* sense to such a uniqueness-claim, and it is central to Wittgenstein's purposes that we cannot. If we could supply criteria for identity of the metaphysical ego (something like *13.01, for instance), then our claim would necessarily be about something in the world, and thus would fail to be a possible candidate for the bearer of value. But as I have stressed, there is no strain of Cartesian-Russellian scepticism in Wittgenstein;

science is the empirical correlate of logic; it shows what all actual "my worlds" have in common (for, of course, different *me*'s), just as logic shows what is common to *all* worlds. Neither is sayable.

that there is a willing subject which is the bearer of value is, in Father Hallett's apt expression, "bedrock." This immediate consciousness of the criterionless uniqueness of the metaphysical ego lies at the roots of Wittgenstein's admiration for Pascal and Kierkegaard, both of whom emphasize the basis of human life in criterionless choices.[38]

The claim that we have a criterionless consciousness of the uniqueness of our self is not unheard-of in the history of western philosophy. Frege, for instance, writes:

> Now everyone is presented to himself in a *particular* and *primitive* way, in which he is presented to no-one else.

The consonance of this claim with Schopenhauer's "fourth class of representations" is obvious. MacTaggart, in his essay "Personality," writes:

> The quality of personality is known to me because I have a perception—in the strict sense of the word—of one being which possesses the quality, namely, myself.[39]

Bradley holds that "souls [what we have called "empirical egos"] are in one sense logical constructions," that is, they are the sorts of things which might be constructed of the ingredients of the book *The World as I Found It.* But at the heart of every soul lies a "finite center"—a metaphysical ego—and "that experience should take place in finite centers, and should wear the form of finite 'thisness', is in the end inexplicable."[40] These finite centers and their uniqueness are known immediately through introspection.

Thus I suggest that Wittgenstein's "mysticism" involves not only

---

[38] Although Wittgenstein would find fault with Kierkegaard's Protagoreanism and his rejection of the universal demands of logic, there are deep and illuminating parallels between the two thinkers—particularly with respect to their anti-historicism—although I have yet to see a nonsuperficial discussion of these parallels. Cf. for instance M. P. Gallagher, S.J., "Wittgenstein's admiration for Kierkegaard," *The Month*, vol. 39 (1968), pp. 43–49, with its (apparently unintentional) puns on such words as 'show' and 'aesthetic'. For a discussion of the Viennese Brenner Circle and the Kierkegaard revival, see Janik and Toulmin *op. cit.*, ch. 6 *passim.*

[39] J. McT. E. McTaggart, "Personality," in his *Philosophical Essays*, ed. S. V. Keeling (London, 1934), p. 69. McTaggart continues that the sense of perception which he has in mind is Russell's "acquaintance."

[40] *A&R*, p. 200. It is significant that in chapter xxvi Bradley connects the existence of finite centers with the rather archaically phrased question, "Nature, is it beautiful and adorable?" Cf. pp. 434–39.

"awe before the unconditioned," awareness of the absolutely primitive position of Objects with their internal relations, but also the corresponding consciousness of the total uniqueness of the metaphysical subject.[41] Note that both deal with *absolutes*—the absolutely general and the absolutely particular. Through a miraculous interaction, the melding of the most general with the most particular, arises "my world," the product of the "two Godheads" of the *Notebooks*.

If I am not mistaken, the nexus of the unconditionally general and the unconditionally particular to form "my world," and its connection with value, might lie behind an otherwise cryptic remark of Wittgenstein's.

> Waismann asks: Is the existence of the world connected with what is ethical?
>
> Wittgenstein: Men have felt that here there is a connection, and they have expressed it thus: God the Father created the world, the Son of God (or the Word that comes from God) is that which is ethical.
>
> That the Godhead is thought of as divided and, again, as one being indicates that there is a connection here. (*WVC*, p. 118.)

God the Father—the unconditioned—cannot manifest the ethical except in conjunction with God the Son—the particular (and we might say, the core of what is *human*). Note that if my analysis is sound, then the metaphysical ego is particular or "personal" in some sense. Some scholars have argued that there is but one transcendental or metaphysical ego, one "world-soul," transcendental monism from the side of the subject.[42] This interpretation is supported by one passage in the *Notebooks*—"There is really only one world-soul, which I for preference call *my* soul and as which alone I conceive what I call the souls of others." (p. 49) It is possible that Wittgenstein was merely experimenting with this notion, but even if he was not we might argue that since only one soul

---

[41] A story of Russell's about Wittgenstein has been widely repeated. "[Wittgenstein] used to come to see me every evening at midnight, and pace up and down my room like a wild beast for about three hours in agitated silence. Once I said to him: "Are you thinking about logic or about your sins?" "Both," he replied . . . ." Russell, *Autobiography* I, p. 137. If the interpretation here offered is correct, it is just possible that Wittgenstein's answer was intended to be taken literally.

[42] A. Phillips Griffiths, "Wittgenstein, Schopenhauer and Ethics" in Vesey *op. cit.*, pp. 96–97.

could stand at the heart of *my* world, and since I can offer no criterion for its individuation, to call it "mine" is in some sense gratuitous. I conceive of the worlds of others as logically possible correlates of my world, which I am free to do insofar as the metaphysical ego does not imply singularity. In any case, the monistic interpretation seems to me to clash with a number of Tractarian passages—among them 6.43—along with the passages from the *Notebooks* which I have cited. But two further points concerning such a monistic approach bear mention. First, it seems of a piece with the sceptical arguments of the *Blue Book*, whose criticisms leave, I hold, the Tractarian position untouched. Second, passages like these indicate how strong the pull of solipsism must have been for Wittgenstein.

The experiences of awe before the unconditioned and the consciousness of the metaphysical ego Wittgenstein describes as "mystical," and in that term some difficulties reside. Miss Anscombe writes:

> 'Mysticism' is a rather odd name for what Wittgenstein is speaking of; in popular language it suggests extraordinary and unusual experiences, thoughts and visions peculiar to an extraordinary type .... But Wittgenstein took the term over from Russell, who used it in a special way, with reference to an entirely ordinary feeling ....[43]

I do not know whether there is a consistent *ordinary* usage of the word 'mysticism,' but I do agree with Anscombe that Wittgenstein probably adapted his usage from Russell. But Russell's sense of the word does not seem to me to deviate significantly from the standard *philosophical* usage. The Russellian usage Anscombe has in mind is probably that which occurs in *Mysticism and Logic;*[44] there Russell attributes two characteristic features to mysticism:

> There is, first, the belief in insight as against discursive knowledge. (p. 8) The second characteristic of mysticism is its belief in unity, and its refusal to admit opposition or division anywhere. (p. 10)

---

[43] Anscombe *op. cit.*, pp. 169–70. Compare: "... it nevertheless behooves us not to confuse the ordinary usage of the term 'mystical' with all its several occurrences in the *Tractatus.*" F. R. Harrison, "Notes on Wittgenstein's Use of 'Das Mystische'," *Southern Journal of Philosophy*, vol. I (1963), pp. 3–9.

[44] B. Russell, "Mysticism and Logic," reprinted in *Mysticism and Logic* (W. W. Norton, New York, 1929), pp. 1–32.

Now these features which Russell highlights seem to me compatible with views held by other representative philosophers of his day. For instance, McTaggart writes:

> It seems to me that the essential characteristics of mysticism are two in number. In the first place, it is essential to mysticism that it asserts greater unity in the universe than that which is recognized in ordinary experience ... The second essential characteristic ... is affirmation that it is possible to be conscious of this unity in some manner which brings the knower into closer and more direct relation with what is known than can be done in ordinary discursive thought ...
>
> Thus what is asserted by myticism is firstly, *a mystical unity*, and secondly, *a mystical intuition* of this unity.[45]

Now the sense which Russell and McTaggart give to the term seems roughly Wittgenstein's. If he differs from the traditional usage, then it is only insofar as he does not regard these experiences as arcane or rare; there is, I repeat, no hint of *otherwordliness* in Wittgenstein's philosophy. As he puts it, we do not want to replace the soft with the hard, but rather only to find the hard within the soft.[46]

Let us now draw together the points made in the previous section by reintroducing the questions which led to these considerations. What sense can we make of ethical reward and punishment? How is the will—the bearer of good and evil—connected with the world? Janik and Toulmin, in speaking of the connections between Wittgenstein's value-problems and those of Kierkegaard, write:

> The sphere of facts and the sphere of values, which in Kant were distinct but by no means separate, come to be separated widely in the philosophy of Schopenhauer. In the thought of Soren Kierkegaard, this separation becomes an unbridgable chasm. (*Op. cit.*, p. 157)

Perhaps the major contention of this essay is that Wittgenstein bridges this gap with the (pseudo-) concept of "my world." As I have argued in chapter VIII, the existence or being of the metaphysical ego

---

[45] J. McT. E. McTaggart, "Mysticism," in Keeling, ed. *op. cit.*, p. 47. Compare with Wm. James, *Varieties of Religious Experience* (New American Library, New York, 1958), lectures 16–17.

[46] "The characteristic of my philosophy. Things lie directly before our eyes, with no veil over them.—Here religion and art part company." Manuscript 109, quoted in Hallett *op. cit.*, p. 217.

and the correlative (ineffable) distinction between the world and *my* world allow Wittgenstein to simultaneously allow for what the solipsist intends that is correct, and to give the will a foothold in (my) world. What this foothold is we shall see presently, but first let me remark again upon what a wondrous thing my world is. A combination of the most general possible and the most particular possible, it represents a melding of the twin limits—inner and outer—of the world. It also represents what is left of the Schopenhauerian world as will after it is purged of extraneous elements by Wittgenstein's acid test of antipsychologism. It is, simultaneously, my world, life, the microcosm; the source of all meaning and value, it is nevertheless itself beyond the grasp of the sayable. Any attempt to put it into words is "gassing," yet nothing needs to be said about it. Ethics, like logic, "takes care of itself."

My world has certain properties which "the world" cannot. Like "the world" it is limited on the "outside" by logic—by the being of Objects—a property which it shares with all other possible worlds. But it also makes manifest an *inner* limit, namely the metaphysical ego, and it is this inner limit which provides the *unity* of (my) world alluded to in 6.45. (This incidentally supports my contention that the mystical cannot be *merely* awe before the unconditioned in the sense of our apprehension of the Objects.) Since the metaphysical ego is "present"—a term I coin with some apprehension, since the ego is not an element of a fact in the sense that a particular Object is an element of a *Sachverhalt*—in every aspect of my world, my world is unified *on the side of the subject*.

(Note that "subject" does not seem quite the correct term here; I would rather say that my world is unified by the inner limit. To say that it is unified through the subject hints at something like old-fashioned solipsism, and our investigation in chapter VIII has shown that will not do at all.)

The preceding shows how the will can have a foothold on the world in a formal way, but we have left the material content of that foothold undetermined. We identify the material content of the foothold only by returning to the question of ethical punishment and reward. Without reward and punishment, ethics would be empty, and we have shown that the possibility of such reward lies in its location in *my* world. It is for the purpose of explicating the material nature of such ethical reward that Wittgenstein introduces the (pseudo-) concept of Happiness.

> If the good or bad exercise of the will does not alter the world, it can alter only the limits of the world, not the facts—not what can be expressed by means of language.
>
> In short the effect must be that it becomes an altogether different world. It must, so to speak, wax and wane as a whole.
>
> The world of the happy man is a different one from that of the unhappy man.[47]

Although the notion of happiness (the German term *Glücklichkeit* also carries the connotation of "luck") occurs but once in the *Tractatus*, there are many occurrences in the *Notebooks*.[48] Let us examine the "logic" of the notion of Happiness, the happy man and his world.

As the previous paragraph implies, 'happy' as an adjective appears modifying both 'man' and 'world'—the world of the happy man is a happy world, and, to stretch grammar a bit, the man of a happy world is a happy man. We might best understand this by taking 'happy' in its primary sense to modify 'life'. Since 5.641 tells us that "The world and life are one" and 5.63 "I am my world," 'life' presumably contains reference both to my world and to the metaphysical subject. The happy man and the happy world mirror one another. How is happiness brought about? On one hand, the happy life is frequently connected, both in the *Notebooks* and in the *Tractatus*, with *living in the present*. This is partly a vestige of the Schopenhauerian treatment of time and space as the phenomenal

---

[47] 6.43. *NB*, p. 73 adds to the second paragraph "As if by accession or loss of meaning." Black writes of this passage "the expression [wax and wane] might suggest a change in the totality of facts, but this has already been excluded." (*Op. cit.*, p. 372) If the general thesis of this chapter is correct, then Black seemingly fails to distinguish my world from the world.

A. Phillips Griffiths points out a more serious problem, namely that the passage seems to imply something "very implausible; that Wittgenstein thought that the meaning of the world could have a degree, which is something quite incompatible with everything else he says concerning meaning." Cf. "Wittgenstein, Schopenhauer and Ethics," pp. 107–8, in Vesey, ed. *op. cit.* Compare with G. Hallett's "Happiness", *Heythrop Journal*, v. 17, (1971), pp. 301–3, on the issue of whether happiness allows of degree.

[48] E.g. pp. 73, 74, 76, 78, 81, 86. Not all of these passages can be rendered consistent; Wittgenstein's views on the subject are in flux throughout this period.

forms of the Principle of Sufficient Reason, partly a logical consequence of Wittgenstein's conviction that the meaning of the world
must lie "outside space and time" (6.4312), and partly due to the
impossibility of any temporal act of willing having the requisite
relation of necessity to its realization. The *Notebooks* discuss the
feeling of being controlled by an "alien will." "I cannot bend the
happenings of the world to my will," he writes, "I am completely
powerless." (*NB*, p. 73). However, one can feel "powerless" only
when there is some aspect of the world over which one believes he
ought have power but does not.[49] But a mere analysis of propositions
purporting to show causal connections will show that no proposition
of the form "I will that p" could entail "p," and so, *on purely
intellectual grounds*, I can disabuse myself of a belief in the efficacy
of this sort of willing. My world will then become "harmonious"—
one sign of the happy world (*NB*, p. 73)—insofar as it is *not
inharmonious;* there is no struggle, since I see that struggle is
impossible. But this intellectual acceptance of the futility of attempting to alter the world cannot, I should think, be sufficient for
happiness. If happiness is connected with good and evil, and these
are attributes of the *willing* subject, then they cannot be brought
about by change of *beliefs.*

Living in the present then seems to be a necessary but certainly
not sufficient condition for the happy life. The happy life, we have
seen, is "harmonious" and the happy man is "doing the will of God"
(*NB*, p. 78); one who lives out of time and thus "without hope and
fear"—Goethe's "twin enemies of mankind"—may not face an
unharmonious world, but it does not follow that his world will have
the positive quality of happiness, of "fitting together," of all "falling
into place." This positive quality is perhaps what Wittgenstein had in
mind when he once said:

> Sometimes, we go into a man's study and find his books and papers all over
> the place, and we can say without hesitation: "What a mess! We really must
> clean this room up!" Yet, at other times, we may go into a room which looks
> very much like the first; but after looking around we decide that we must

---

[49] Compare: Descartes argues that although I do not have an infinite understanding, I am not
therefore "incomplete" or "faulty," since I am not the sort of thing (a finite created substance)
which is *supposed* to have an infinite understanding. Cf. *HR* I, pp. 173–74.

leave it just as it is, recognizing that, in this case, *even the dust has its place.*[50]

Likewise it would seem that we can feel that we are not *contradicting* the will of God without thereby feeling that we are in accord with that will: I feel neither in accord with nor contradictory to the will of, say, the Chinese people.

If we recognize the extent to which my will penetrates *my* world, happiness cannot be the basis of an intellectual argument, although intellectual argument may pave the way by eliminating certain blocks which stand in the way of this realization. But further, unlike the independence of the world from my will, the dependence of my world on my will cannot be described:

> The happy life seems to be in some sense more harmonious . . . But what is that sense?

> What is the objective mark of the happy, harmonious life? Here it is again clear that there cannot be any such mark that can be *described.*

> The mark cannot be a physical one, but only a metaphysical one, a transcendental one.[51]

This is why, I think, Wittgenstein is so anxious in the Lecture to emphasize that the character of value-experiences can be grasped only from one's *own* case.[52]

Finally, happiness has the requisite status of end-in-itself:

> And in this sense Dostoyevsky is right when he says that the man who is happy is fulfilling the purpose of existence.

> Or again, we can say that the man is fulfilling the purpose of existence who no longer needs to have any purpose except to live. That is to say, who is content. (*NB*, p. 73)

---

[50] A remark made at a Cambridge at-home in 1947, quoted in Janik and Toulmin *op. cit.*, p. 207.

[51] *NB*, p. 82. Note that "physical" here is explicitly contrasted with *metaphysical*, not "mental" or "psychological".

[52] Compare: "Now this knowledge [of clear and distinct ideas] is not the work of your reasoning nor information passed on to you by your teachers; it is something your mind sees, feels and handles . . ." Descartes to Silhon in March of 1648. Cf. A. Kenny *op. cit.*, p. 230.

That this stage has actually been reached by men seems to be implicit in 6.521:

> The solution to the problem of life is seen in the vanishing of the problem.
>
> (Is this not the reason why those who have found after a long period of doubt that the sense of life became clear to them have been unable to say what constituted that sense?)[53]

Let us now briefly retrace the path which we have traveled. Wittgenstein is faced with a dilemma concerning ethics: the bearer of value must be the willing subject, yet the world is wholly independent of this willing subject. Ethics must in some manner involve reward and punishment—otherwise, it would make no difference in life. Yet where can this reward and punishment be located? Not in the world, since the world lacks the requisite necessary connection to the acts of the willing subject. These difficulties, however, can be resolved by reconsidering what it is that the solipsist intends which is correct—that the world is *my* world—and using the (nonsensical pseudo-) proposition "The world is *my* world" as a "ladder." Although *the* world—the world of facts—is independent of my will, *my* world is permeated by that will, just as it is permeated by its other necessary condition, logic. My world represents the nexus between the impersonal realm of Objects and the wholly unique and personal metaphysical ego, between the completely general and the utterly singular. My world reflects throughout its center—the metaphysical ego—and in this reflection arises the possibility of reward or punishment, namely the happiness or unhappiness of my life. None of this of course can be *said;* but attempting to say it and seeing that we must fail constitutes a considerable philosophical victory which frees us forever from pseudo-ethical rhetoric.

---

[53] Wittgenstein's claim here is open to misunderstanding in a way which certainly the early Wittgenstein and probably the later would have little sympathy. "At other times, however, we are tempted to apply this word ['meaning'] to words such as 'life'—asking ourselves , for example, such questions as 'Does life have a meaning?' Here we are confronted with a question which we do not quite know how to answer or what to make of it, and this puzzles us. What Wittgenstein, I believe, would say here is that to apply the word 'meaning' to 'life' is to misapply it and to come up with an impossible question. It may now be difficult for us to see that this *is* an illegitimate question, for having used the word in this context so long, it no longer seems strange to us." (Engel *op. cit.*, p. 29) In fairness, Engel is concerned mostly with the *Blue Book*, where such quasi-positivist elements do sometimes occur.

The notion of my world, the combination of the ego and logic, offers solutions to part of the dilemma we have examined. Wittgenstein's logic is pluralistic, yet his ethical views drive him towards a monistic picture of the world, a *connectedness*. But Wittgenstein's "Copernican Revolution" supplies the key to the solution of this problem. The world—the world of facts—is unaffected by my "finite center", my metaphysical ego, yet my world is permeated with it. But since my world is a possible world, it shares a common substance with *the* world, and my world is permeated with my ego and my will, and thus value finds a foothold in human life. The solution thus supplied is ineffable, although in order to get clear about both its ineffability and its importance we must *try* to say it. Then we see the emptiness, from the point of language, of such phrases as "my world", "my life", and so forth. We must throw away the ladder after we have climbed it.

Abbreviations

LRKM	L. Wittgenstein, *Letters to Russell, Keynes and Moore* (Cornell U. Press, Ithaca, 1974)
M&L	B. Russell, *Mysticism and Logic* (W. W. Norton, New York, 1929)
NB	L. Wittgenstein, *Notebooks 1914–16*, ed. G. E. M. Anscombe (Blackwell, Oxford, 1969)
NoL	L. Wittgenstein, "Notes on Logic," in *Notebooks 1914–16*, ed. G. E. M. Anscombe (Blackwell, Oxford, 1969)
OBM	A. Schopenhauer, *On the Basis of Morality*, trans. E. F. J. Payne (Bobbs-Merrill, Indianapolis, IN, 1965)
OKEW	B. Russell, *Our Knowledge of the External World* (Allen and Unwin, London, 1914)
"ONTF"	B. Russell, "On the Nature of Truth and Falsity," p. 150, in *Philosophical Essays* (Simon and Schuster, New York, 1966)
"OPHM"	B. Russell, "On Propositions and How They Mean," (1919; reprinted in *Logic and Knowledge*, ed. R. C. Marsh [Capricorn Books, New York, 1956])
PI	L. Wittgenstein, *Philosophical Investigations*, 3rd ed., trans. G. E. M. Anscombe (Macmillan, New York, 1958)
PM	B. Russell and A. N. Whitehead, *Principia Mathematica* (Cambridge U. Press, Cambridge, 1910)
PoL	F. H. Bradley, *Principles of Logic*, vols. I and II (Oxford U. Press, Oxford, 1883)
PP	B. Russell, *The Problems of Philosophy* (Oxford U. Press, Oxford, 1912)
PrM	B. Russell, *The Principles of Mathematics* (Norton, New York, 1903)
PrMe	H. Hertz, *Principles of Mechanics*, trans. Jones and Walley (Dover, New York, 1956)
SM	E. Mach, *The Science of Mechanics: A Critical and Historical Account of its Development*, trans. T. J. McCormack (Open Court, La Salle, IL, 1942)
SoL	J. S. Mill, *A System of Logic* (John Parker, London, 1851)
WN	A. Schopenhauer, *On the Will in Nature*, trans. K. Hillegrand (G. Bell, London, 1897)

WVC   L. Wittgenstein, *Ludwig Wittgenstein and the Vienna Circle*, recorded by F. Waismann (Barnes and Noble, New York, 1979)

WWR   A. Schopenhauer, *The World as Will and Representation*, vols. I and II, trans. E. F. J. Payne (Dover, New York, 1969)

Index